Collaborative Governance and Public Innovation in Northern Europe

Edited By

Annika Agger

Bodil Damgaard

Andreas Hagedorn Krogh

&

Eva Sørensen

Department of Society and Globalisation
Roskilde University
Denmark

CONTENTS

CHAPTERS

Author Biographies

Annika Agger is an associate professor in public administration at the Department of Society and Globalisation, Roskilde University. She has written articles and contributed to books on how to create institutional settings for public deliberations. She is currently involved in a research projects with peace and conflict scholars in Lund University in Sweden analyzing the everyday practices of public frontline workers and their ability to handle contested issues and conflict management. Among recent publications are: Agger & Sørensen (2014) Designing Collaborative Policy Innovation: Lessons from a Danish Municipality in Torfing & Ansell (eds) *Public Innovation through innovation and design,* Routledge.

Linda Lundgaard Andersen PhD and Professor, co-director of the Center for Social Entrepreneurship and director of the PhD School of Lifelong Learning and Socialpsychology of Everyday Life, Roskilde University. Her research includes theoretical, conceptual and empirical work in learning, social entrepreneurship and social innovation in welfare services, democracy, forms of governance, leadership and hybridity, life history and ethnographies of the public sector, NGO and social enterprises. Corresponding editor of *Journal of Social Work Practice, Routledge* and *Social Enterprise Journal*, editor and co-editor of several Danish and international books on social entrepreneurship, psycho-societal learning and social innovation.

Corine Balder worked several years as a project manager in the corporate world and local government. She currently works as a teacher and researcher at the *Hogeschool Leiden* where she teaches research methodology, conflict resolution and communication skills. As a researcher, she participated in projects on empowerment in welfare administration, child protection and on recovery from severe mental illness.

Arwin van Buuren is an Associate Professor Public Administration at Erasmus University Rotterdam. His research focuses on complex governance and innovation processes in the domain of water management, climate adaptation, and sustainable energy. He is a co-editor of the *International Journal of Water Governance* and is responsible for various large research projects in the field of the governance of climate adaptation and innovation in flood management.

Helle Vibeke Carstensen is an HR and innovation expert. She has extensive theoretical and practical experience of implementing innovation projects, train leaders in innovation and knowledge sharing, as well as advising public and private executives. She has for many years led frontrunner innovation departments in the public sector and has also been the CEO for INSP! Innovation I/S. Her work is based on the experiences and practices from the private sector and is used to achieve greater efficiency and better services in the public sector. As the originator of both the innovation office in SKAT and the cross-government innovation unit MindLab Helle Vibeke has solid practical experience in building and managing departments that increase the innovation capacity of organizations and companies. Helle Vibeke is now working with innovation as the head of office for Organizational Development at the Social Services Department in Copenhagen. She has written several articles about public innovation and received Knighthood for her achievements in innovating the public sector in 2008.

Bodil Damgaard is an Associate Professor at the Department of Society and Globalization, Roskilde University, Denmark. Her research focuses on the involvement of organized and individual interests in governance processes primarily at the local level. Recently, she has contributed to the *Oxford handbook of Public Accountability* (2014) with a chapter on "Accountability and Citizen Participation" written by Jenny Lewis.

John Fenwick Professor, BA (Hons), MBA, MSc, PhD is a fellow of the Higher Education Academy and an academic fellow of the Chartered Institute of Personnel and Development. John is a Professor of Leadership and Public Management at Northumbria University, Newcastle upon Tyne, UK. His main teaching interests include organizational analysis, public management and local government. Current research is on local leadership (specifically, the role of elected mayors), governance, and changing public sector management. John co-edited (with Janice McMillan) the book *Public Management in the Postmodern Era* and has most recently published in *Local Government Studies*, *Public Money and Management* and the *European Management Journal*.

Lynn Froggett is a Professor of Psychosocial Research at the University of Central Lancashire(UCLAN) and Research Professor at the University of Stavanger. She has a background in both social sciences and humanities and leads a research team with interests in communities, cultural citizenship, organisations, addictions and the socially engaged arts. She has a particular interest in the development of new research methodologies for the study of social innovation. Recent work incorporates visualisation, image and movement based methods in group contexts to investigate tacit and unconscious social processes in community settings.

Hanneke Gieske is an strategic advisor at the Delfland regional water authority and a PhD candidate at Erasmus University Rotterdam. She advises the authority's organization, management, and board on issues relating to strategic planning, cooperative governance and change, and knowledge management. Her research addresses the enabling and inhibiting factors of innovation in regional water management and the enhancement of innovative capacity therein.

Gro Sandkjær Hanssen (PhD in Political Science, University of Oslo), is a senior researcher at the Norwegian Institute for Urban and Regional Research. Her research interests are multi-level governance, local democracy and network governance, which she has studied in research projects about water governance, climate change adaptation and urban planning. The projects have been financed by Ministries, the Norwegian research Council and the EU's 5th and 6th framework programme for research, and the results have been published in national and international books and journals. At the time she is project leader for three large research projects financed by the Norwegian research Council.

Bert van Hemert is the head of the department of Psychiatry of Leiden University Medical Center. He was trained as an epidemiologist and psychiatrist. He has an active interest in bridging the gap between basic academic research and mental health care practice. His areas of research expertise include public mental health, emergency psychiatry and biological aspects of the mind. His latest work focuses on balanced care for mood and anxiety disorders.

Andreas Hagedorn Krogh is a fellow in Politics and Public Administration at the Department of Society and Globalisation, Roskilde University, Denmark. He has previously published on collaborative innovation and the role of public leadership and institutional design in promoting public innovation. He is currently completing his Ph.D dissertation on political and administrative meta-governance of collaborative crime prevention networks. This work is co-financed by the Danish Ministry of Justice, the Danish National Police, and the Danish Crime Prevention Council. He is a member of the Centre for Democratic Network Governance and sits on the Advisory Board of the Danish Community Safety Ambassadors Project.

Luise Li Langergaard is an Associate Professor at the Centre for Social Entrepreneurship at Department of Psychology and Educational Studies, Roskilde University. She has done a on public sector innovation and user-involvement in public services. Her particular research interest is in the democratic, normative, and political dimensions of public sector innovation, social innovation and citizen engagement.

Janice McMillan Dr., BA (Hons), PhD, is a Reader in Human Resource Development and Public Management at Edinburgh Napier University Business School, UK. She specializes in public management and organisational analysis, and was Chair of the Public Administration Specialist Group of the Political Studies Association of the United Kingdom from 1995-2006. She has published widely in the area of UK public service reform. With John Fenwick, she co-edited the book *Public Management in the Postmodern Era* and is currently co-writing a critical text on organisational behaviour in the public sector. Janice has most recently published in *Teaching Public Administration* and *Public Money and Management.*

Albert Meijer is a Professor of Public Innovation at the Utrecht School of Governance in the Netherlands. Meijer was originally trained as a chemist but became more interested in the governance of technology and obtained a PhD degree for a thesis on the use of technology in government (Erasmus University, 2002). He is the chair of the permanent study group on e-government of the European Group for Public Administration and on the editorial board of Information Polity and the Electronic Journal of E-Government Studies. Meijer has published frequently in journals such as Public Administration Review and Public Management Review on innovation, transparency, coproduction and e-government.

Dr. Marja-Liisa Niinikoski has been a Postdoctoral Researcher at Aalto University, School of Business, and is currently a Managing Director in Culminatum Innovation Ltd. Her research areas cover innovation policy analysis, particularly policy change and policy government, and innovation studies, focusing on public innovation. She has published her work in *Technological Forecasting and Social Change*, and *Science and Public Policy* for example.

Maija Setälä (PhD in Political Science, The London School of Economics and Political Science, UK, 1997) is a Professor in Political Science at the University of Turku, Finland. She specialises in democratic theory, political trust, direct democracy and democratic innovation and has published a number of articles and books on these topics. Setälä has also applied experimental methods in the study of citizen deliberation. Her articles have been published in, for example, *Inquiry, European Journal of Political Research*, *Political Studies* and *European Political Science Review.*

Eva Sørensen is a Professor of Public Administration and Democracy at the Department of Society and Globalization, Roskilde University in Denmark and at the University of Nordland in Norway. Her research focusses on theoretical, methodological and empirical issues related to the enhancement of effective, democratic and innovative public governance. Among her recent publications are: (2012), Interactive governance: Advancing the Paradigm published with Oxford University Press and co-authored with Jacob Torfing, B. Guy Peters and Jon Pierre; (2013) 'Conflict as driver of pluricentric coordination', Planning Theory 13(2): 152-169; and (2013), Collaborative Innovation: A viable alternative to market competition and organizational entrepreneurship', published in Public Administration Review 73(6): 821-830.

Jacob Torfing is a Professor in Politics and Institutions at Department of Society and Globalisation, Roskilde University in Denmark and at the University of Nordland in Norway. He is the Director of the Centre for Democratic Network Governance and Vice-Director of a large-scale research project on Collaborative Innovation in the Public Sector. His research interest includes public sector reforms, network governance, public innovation and institutional theory. He recently published an edited volume entitled *Public Innovation through Collaboration and Design* (Routledge, 2013) together with Chris Ansell from UC Berkeley. He is a former member of the Danish Social Science Research Council and features regularly in Danish media as an expert on public governance.

Joost Vos is a Managing Consultant at TNO Management Consultants. His thesis (2010) was on the Munchhausen Movement. His field of expertise includes projects and action research on collaboration within and beyond the sectors of care and justice. He is involved in numerous projects that outflow Dutch legal changes to enhance responsibilities of local communities for the coordination of social services.

Hendrik Wagenaar is a professor of Town and Regional Planning at the University of Sheffield. He publishes in the areas of urban governance, citizen participation, prostitution policy, practice theory and interpretive policy analysis. His publications include: *Deliberative Policy Analysis. Understanding Governance in the Network Society* (Cambridge University Press, 2003) (with Maarten Hajer), and *Meaning in Action*: *Interpretation and Dialogue in Policy Analysis*, (M.E. Sharpe, 2011). He has just completed a 3-year international comparative study of prostitution policy.

Esther van Zimmeren is a PhD in Law, University of Leuven, Belgium since 2011. She is a Research Professor with a Chair on Globalization, Multilevel Governance and Federalism at the University of Antwerp (Belgium) and a Senior Research Fellow at the Centre for Intellectual Property (IP) Rights of the University of Leuven. She is specialized in IP law, in particular in public governance and IP law. Her work has been published in a variety of international journals, such as *Nature Reviews Genetics* and the *International Review of IP and Competition Law*, and in edited books published by *Cambridge University Press* and *Oxford University Press.*

PREFACE

The chapters published in this book have grown out of the international *Sunrise Conference: Transforming Governance, Enhancing Innovation* hosted by Roskilde University, Denmark, in October 2012. Contemplating the link between governance and innovation, the Sunrise Conference brought together more than 100 researchers from all over Europe, about 100 decision-makers from all levels of government, and 70 students from different study programs. Over the course of three days, they worked together in parallel streams and in joint sessions to explore how transformations of governance can spur public innovation. Round tables and panel sessions with academic discussions took place alongside professionally facilitated debates among decision-makers on how to enhance innovation in the public sector, while students worked intensely to come up with the most innovative yet feasible solutions to some of the most acute wicked problems of our time. Throughout the conference, the three streams engaged with each other in thought-provoking and inspiring dialogues that advanced the collective endeavor of grasping how new forms of collaborative governance might enhance the capacity for public innovation. Thus this book deals with an expression of collaborative innovation. We wish to acknowledge all the participants in the conference for their valuable contributions. A special thanks goes to all participating authors who took time to engage in a sustained and enlightening collaboration around the invention of this volume. Finally, we wish to acknowledge the treasured collaboration with our assistant student, soon-to-be MSc in public administration and history, Anna Katrine Sand, who aligned an untold number of writing styles and reference standards into a coherent book.

Annika Agger

Bodil Damgaard

Andreas Hagedorn Krogh

&

Eva Sørensen

Department of Society and Globalisation
Roskilde University
Denmark

List of Contributors

Annika Agger	Department of Society and Globalisation, Roskilde University, Denmark.
Linda Lundgaard Andersen	Center for Social Entrepreneurship and director of the PhD School of Lifelong Learning and Socialpsychology of Everyday Life, Roskilde University, Denmark.
Corine Balder	Docent, Hogeschool Leiden. The Netherlands.
Arwin van Buuren	Department of Public Administration, Erasmus University Rotterdam, The Netherlands.
Helle Vibeke Carstensen	Organizational Development at the Social Services Department in Copenhagen Municipality, Denmark.
Bodil Damgaard	Department of Society and Globalization, Roskilde University, Denmark.
John Fenwick	Northumbria University, Newcastle upon Tyne, UK.
Lynn Froggett	University of Central Lancashire (UCLAN), UK and University of Stavanger, Norway.
Hanneke Gieske	Strategic advisor at the Delfland regional water authority and PhD candidate at Erasmus University Rotterdam, the Netherlands.
Gro Sandkjær Hanssen	The Norwegian Institute for Urban and Regional Research, Norway.
Bert van Hemert	Psychiatry of Leiden University Medical Center, the Netherlands.
Andreas Hagedorn Krogh	Department of Society and Globalisation, Roskilde University, Denmark.
Luise Li Langergaard	Centre for Social Entrepreneurship at Department of Psychology and Educational Studies, Roskilde University, Denmark.
Janice McMillan	Edinburgh Napier University Business School, UK.
Albert Meijer	Utrecht School of Governance, the Netherlands.
Marja-Liisa Niinikoski	Culminatum Innovation Ltd., Finland.
Maija Setälä	University of Turku, Finland.
Eva Sørensen	Department of Society and Globalization, Roskilde University, Denmark.

Jacob Torfing Department of Society and Globalisation, Roskilde University, Denmark.

Joost Vos Managing Consultant at TNO Management Consultants, the Netherlands.

Hendrik Wagenaar University of Sheffield, UK.

Esther van Zimmeren University of Antwerp and a Senior Research Fellow at the Centre for Intellectual Property (IP) Rights of the University of Leuven, Belgium.

CHAPTER 1

Introduction

Annika Agger*, Bodil Damgaard, Andreas Hagedorn Krogh and Eva Sørensen

Department of Society and Globalisation at Roskilde University, Denmark

Abstract: Governments all over Northern Europe have placed public innovation high on the political agenda. European governance researchers are seeking to map the impact of efforts to promote public innovation with a particular focus on the role of collaborative forms of governance in achieving this. This introductory chapter provides a description of this new field of research - its emergence, character and maturity - with reference to the case studies presented in the following chapters. The case studies draw on a broad range of different theoretical and methodological schools of thought that each offers a unique contribution to developing a new, multi-disciplinary theory of public innovation. The case studies are mainly based on qualitative data; however, the authors note that quantitative studies and mixed methods could potentially advance the research field even further. Nevertheless, the case studies presented in the book point to a number of important preliminary findings regarding the role of collaborative forms of governance in enhancing public innovation: 1) Collaborative public innovation transforms mindsets, role perceptions and work forms; 2) Design matters for the success and failure of collaborative innovation processes; 3) Leadership is important for promoting collaborative innovation; and 4) Collaborative public innovation is relevant at all levels of governance. On these grounds, the chapter concludes that a promising research field is emerging but is still in its infancy and further research is needed in order to map the potential of, and barriers to, collaborative forms of public innovation in Northern Europe.

Keywords: Collaborative governance, public innovation, public welfare production, public policy problems.

THE PRESSING NEED FOR PUBLIC INNOVATION IN NORTHERN EUROPE

Public innovation is rapidly rising to the top of the agenda at all levels of government in Northern Europe as well as in other parts of the Western world. Public innovation is increasingly viewed as an appropriate and intelligent answer to some of the key governance challenges of our time (OECD, 2011a). These

***Corresponding author Annika Agger:** Department of Society and Globalization at Roskilde University, Denmark; Tel: +45 4674 2793/+45 4674 2870; Fax: +45 4674 3081; E-mail: aagger@ruc.dk

Annika Agger, Bodil Damgaard, Andreas Hagedorn Krogh and Eva Sørensen (Eds.)

challenges include: how to meet growing demands by citizens for public services in times of fiscal austerity (Ansell & Torfing 2014); how to turn around the current disenchantment with representative democracy (Stoker 2006); how to address the increasing number of unsolved wicked and unruly problems (Rittel & Webber, 1973; Levin *et al.*, 2012); how to overcome policy execution problems that result from uninformed or ill designed policies (Macmillan & Cain, 2010); and how to enhance the capacity of the political system to deal with global policy issues (Osborne 2006). Governments express high hopes that public innovation will enhance the public sector's capacity to get more for less in order to meet citizens' demands even in times of fiscal crisis (Hood, 2010). Innovative forms of democratic participation are expected to contribute to a re-enchantment with liberal democracy (Smith, 2009). Public innovation is also expected to produce new services that are more effective than existing ones when it comes to solving wicked problems (Rittel & Webber, 1973; Levin *et al.*, 2012) such as child obesity, gang-related crime, long-term unemployment and adjustment to, and mitigation of, climate change. Moreover, policy innovations are expected to produce political visions, goals and strategies that are better suited to shaping the kind of world we want to live in (Agger & Sørensen, 2014). It is even hoped that public innovation will facilitate the design of new transnational political institutions that are capable of enhancing joint decision making capacity and governance in collaborative initiatives involving governments and other influential political actors on the global scene (Hale & Held, 2012).

Although the call for public innovation is not always followed by action, governments in Northern Europe have initiated many reforms that indicate a willingness to transform not only public policies and services but also the organizational forms, procedures and mind sets that characterize public governance. Nuances aside, these reforms fall within three broad and not necessarily mutually exclusive categories: New Public Management (NPM) reforms that promote competition in public service delivery (Hood, 1991); reforms of the Neo-Weberian state (NWS) that aim to strengthen the entrepreneurial leadership of public administrators (Pollitt & Bouckeart 2011); and finally New Public Governance (NPG) reforms that seek to mobilise and empower all relevant and affected public and private actors in the provision of public governance (Torfing & Triantafillou 2013). Each of these reform programs highlights a single innovation driver, namely competition, hierarchy or collaboration, respectively (Hartley, Sørensen & Torfing 2013). While NPG presents itself as a new and promising alternative to NPM and NWS, research into how collaboration can contribute to promoting public innovation is still scarce.

This edited volume presents a collection of chapters that contributes to developing a theoretical framework for studying collaborative public innovation, and helps to clarify to what extent, and how, collaborative forms of governance are promoting public innovation in Northern Europe. The theoretical and empirical contributions presented in this book thus aim to analyse and assess how, and under what conditions, collaborative public innovation unfolds in various Northern European contexts. It offers scholarly reflections, empirical testimonies and learning perspectives on some of the wider political, social and psychological consequences, potential and manifest gains of collaborative public innovation initiatives. *Public innovation* is here defined as the formulation, realization and diffusion of new public policies, services or procedures that produce a qualitative change in a specific context. We speak of *collaborative public innovation* when multiple public and/or private actors interact in a shared effort to promote public innovation in one or more phases of the innovation process. In line with this definition, the book presents studies of collaborative forms of governance that involve relevant and affected actors in deliberate attempts to develop public policies and services or the processes and organizational forms through which they are produced.

There are two reasons why the book focuses on innovation research in Northern Europe. First of all, research into collaborative innovation in the public sector is presently most widespread in this region. Secondly, the number of experiments and governance reforms aiming to promote public innovation in the region are numerous which means that there are plenty of empirical cases to study. Northern Europe is unquestionably the place to go when looking for cutting edge research on pioneering efforts to enhance public innovation. We should keep in mind, however, that the lessons learned in this book are not necessarily applicable to other contexts. As we will clarify below, Northern European governance systems create specific conditions for collaborative public innovation that are different from those found in other parts of the world.

The next section will briefly set the stage for our research on collaborative innovation in the public sector. Following that, we describe the contextual characteristics and specificities of governance systems in Northern Europe. Finally, we extract key lessons about collaborative public innovation from the case studies presented in the book, and we conclude by explaining the structure of the book and giving a short introduction to the individual chapters.

RESEARCH ON COLLABORATIVE INNOVATION IN THE PUBLIC SECTOR

The growing interest in public innovation among public authorities in Northern Europe is accompanied by the surge of a new strand of innovation research. Rather than taking a point of departure in private sector conditions for innovation (Sigurdson, 1986; Stankiewicz, 1997; Tassey, 1997; Wallstein, 2000), this new strand of research seeks to identify and theorise the specific conditions required to promote innovation in a public sector context (Eggers & Singh, 2009; Bommert, 2010; Sørensen & Torfing, 2011). The new public innovation research aims to clarify the innovativeness of the public sector itself and to understand how the latter can become more innovative either on its own or through collaboration with market and civil society stakeholders. This emerging research on public innovation aims to develop a conceptual framework for studying public innovation, to clarify the drivers of, and barriers to, public innovation, and to map the conditions and capacities for public innovation in different countries in Northern Europe as well as in different policy fields and at different levels of governance. The first generation of public innovation research, which saw the light of day in the early 1990s, was rooted in the New Public Management (NPM) paradigm that sought inspiration in private sector innovation theory in its efforts to strengthen the public sector's innovative capacity (Hood, 1991; Osborne and Gaebler, 1993). The NPM model saw strategic hierarchical leadership and competition among decentralized public service providers as key drivers of public innovation. The turn of the century ushered in a second generation of public innovation research. On the one hand, the Neo Weberian State (NWS) paradigm highlighted the important role of public administrators in enhancing public innovation (Pollitt & Pollitt, C & Bouckeart); while on the other, the New Public Governance (NPG) paradigm pointed to the important role of collaboration in promoting public innovation. Inspiration came from newer theories of private innovation (Teece, 1992; Powell, Koput & Smith-Doerr, 1996; Faems, Van Looy & Debackere, 2005) and governance research (O'Toole, 1999; Hartley, 2005; Osborne, 2006; Ansell & Gash, 2007).

The collaborative approach to public innovation is based on the assumption that collaboration between relevant and affected actors from different organizations, sectors and levels of governance can contribute to the formulation, implementation and diffusion of new, innovative public policies and services, as well as of the procedures and organizational forms through which they are brought about. The crux of the argument is that collaboration between public authorities and organisations on one hand, and private stakeholders with relevant innovation assets on the other, can advance public innovation in all phases of an innovation process (Eggers & Singh, 2009; Bommert, 2010; Sørensen & Torfing, 2011). Thus, for instance, collaboration can facilitate innovation with regard to addressing governance problems faced by public authorities; generate new policy goals, strategies, tool kits and services; and enable broad ownership among relevant actors of new innovative products, procedures and organisations that promote their implementation; and disseminate information about successful innovations to relevant audiences. Even though researchers have begun to pay attention to the growing interest in promoting public innovation among Western governments, only a modest amount of research exists on this topic and there are still more questions than answers.

While studies of public innovation testify that collaboration can function as a driver of public innovation (Roberts & Bradley, 1991; Borins, 2001; Dente, Bobbio & Spada, 2005; Bland *et al.* 2010; Bommert, 2010; Ansell & Torfing, 2014), these and other studies also reveal a number of barriers to public innovation that must be overcome if the full potential of collaborative forms of governance is to be realized. Some barriers are rooted in institutional factors such as bureaucratic rules and routines, rigid budget and accounting systems, control-oriented performance management tools, and positive feedback mechanisms that create inertia and hamper collaboration across institutional and organisational boundaries (Albury, 2005; Peters, 2011; Wynen *et al.*, 2013). Another set of barriers arises from rigid role perceptions that discourage the involved public and private actors from engaging in an open-ended and collaborative search for innovative ideas and solutions (Agger & Sørensen, 2014).

The new theories of collaborative innovation argue that these barriers can be overcome through skilful innovation management (Sørensen & Torfing, 2011; Ansell & Gash, 2012). This kind of management deviates in profound ways from traditional hierarchical forms of rule because it does not dictate certain predefined outcomes but aims to engage relevant and affected actors in developing, implementing and diffusing innovations. This strand of literature argues that new solutions arising from local needs for public innovation are indeed already transforming governance from the bottom up by overcoming barriers caused by existing governmental structures. However, if the pressing need for public innovation is to be met, a more top-down approach is required that can enhance the public sector's innovation capacity through collaborative institutional designs and wider governance reforms. Efforts to clarify how collaborative innovation can be managed have found inspiration in the concept of *metagovernance* developed by governance theorists (Kooiman, 1993, 2003; Kickert, Klijn & Koppenjan, 1997; Jessop, 1998, 2002; Meuleman, 2008; Sørensen & Torfing, 2009) as well as in the notion of *collaborative management* which has emerged from recent strands of planning theory and public management research (Gray, 1989; Healey, 1997; Agranoff & McGuire, 2003; Ansell & Gash, 2007; Booher & Innes, 2010)

Governance theories define metagovernance as the governance of self-governance, and point to the strategic need to design and steer the arenas in which stakeholders collaborate in a shared attempt to attain negotiated governance goals. This activity involves both hands-off and hands-on steering of networks, partnerships and other self-governing arenas. Hands-off metagovernance is exercised through the political, economic, legal, discursive and institutional framing and design of self-governing arenas. Managing by objectives, reflexive law, incentives steering and storytelling are examples of hands-off metagovernance. Hands-on metagovernance is exercised through the direct involvement and participation of the metagovernor in self-governing arenas, with the aim of enhancing actors' capacity to self-govern. Hands-on metagovernance includes different forms of process facilitation, conflict resolution, trust and identity building (Sørensen & Torfing, 2009). Theories of collaborative management and planning also point to hands-off as well as hands-on forms of metagovernance, but they focus particularly on the different ways in which managers and leaders can facilitate and moderate collaborative processes in ways that motivate stakeholders to collaborate and enhance their conflict resolution capacity. As evidenced in a number of the contributions to this book, both theories of metagovernance and collaborative management each provide a unique lens to analyse how innovation management is conceptualized and carried out in public innovation processes.

So which actors are capable of assuming a managerial role in collaborative innovation processes? In theory, any actor willing to encourage, influence and guide collaborative processes of self-governance can take on this role since innovation management is defined as a function rather than as a formal position (Torfing *et al.* 2012). The prospect of success, however, depends on whether an aspiring innovation manager has access to the necessary resources. Following Christopher Hood's theorising about government resources, the success of innovation managers may be said to depend on their Nodality, Authority, Treasure and Organization (NATO) resources (Hood, 1986). Innovation managers must function as nodes in relevant networks of actors in order to be able to strategically connect them and mediate their interactions. They must also possess the formal or informal authority needed to engage key stakeholders. Access to fiscal resources is also valuable because these can be used to motivate stakeholders to become involved and invest their own resources in collaborative endeavours. Finally, organizational capacity can be helpful in reducing transaction costs for those participating in collaborative innovation initiatives.

Although private actors sometimes possess one or more of these resources and can thus serve as successful innovation managers, public authorities tend to be in an especially strong position to take on this role when it comes to innovations in public policies and services. Public authorities have a systemically anchored legitimacy to define or endorse innovations as positive or negative contributions to promoting public purposes. Moreover, they tend to have the formal authority, treasure (financial resources) and organizational capacity to marginalize other potential innovation managers. These advantages are particularly evident in Northern European countries. At the same time, however, public authorities face specific challenges compared to individual or organized private actors from civil society or business. First of all, their position as managers of collaborative innovation processes may be weaker in cases where there is general distrust of government among the citizenry (Braithwaite & Levi, 1998). It should be noted that this kind of distrust is not only present in authoritarian regimes but also in some European and other Western democracies (RT, 2013). Two further factors that may reduce the capacity of public authorities to exercise innovation management are institutionally and culturally anchored risk aversion and hierarchical leadership and control tendencies among public actors (Bellante & Link, 1981; Bozeman & Kingsley, 1998). In the end, however, only empirical studies can provide answers to the questions of which actors serve as innovation managers, how they go about this, and the extent to which they are successful in promoting collaborative public innovation.

COLLABORATIVE GOVERNANCE AND PUBLIC INNOVATION IN NORTHERN EUROPE

As noted above, there are sound reasons to focus on Northern Europe when studying collaborative public innovation. The most pragmatic is that this is where most research on this topic is currently being done. This is partly due to the strong tradition of governance research in this region, including a long standing focus on the role of collaboration in public governance. In the early 1990s, governance researchers were particularly interested in how, and under what conditions, collaborative forms of governance promoted efficiency and effectiveness in public governance (Mayntz & Marin, 1991), but gradually, and particularly in recent years, public innovation has become a key topic among Northern European governance researchers (Dente, Bobbi & Spada, 2005; Hartley, 2005; Bommert, 2010; Sørensen & Torfing, 2011). As such, Northern Europe is the right place to look for cutting edge research on collaborative public innovation. Another reason to focus on Northern Europe is that there is plenty to study. Not only public innovation but also collaborative forms of governance have inspired recent efforts to develop and reform public governance. Although this focus on collaboration might be explained by the rise of the influential NPG paradigm, it is also deeply rooted in the Northern European tradition of corporatism and a strong civil society.

This specificity of this Northern European governance tradition is exactly why the knowledge and insights produced in this book do not necessarily translate to different contexts. We should keep in mind that there are specific conditions in Northern Europe which shape both the processes and outcomes of collaborative public innovation initiatives.

What, then, are the specific conditions for collaborative innovation in Northern Europe? As a starting point it should be stressed that there are large differences between individual countries. Nevertheless, we will argue that it is possible to identify a number of similarities at the macro, meso and micro levels of the public governance system that are likely to have implications for the fate of collaborative innovation initiatives.

At the macro level, Northern European countries are characterized by strong states as well as strong civil societies. Public sectors in Northern Europe are large, with strong regulatory capacities, and they engage actively in the everyday lives of their citizens (Katzenstein 1985; Trägårdh 2007). A product of this high level of state intervention is extensive social and economic equality and a well educated population compared to other parts of the world (Rothstein 2005; Heinrich & Fioramonti 2008; OECD 2011b, 2014). Moreover, the political system tends to be relatively decentralized although levels of local autonomy vary considerably. These strong states exist side by side with a strong civil society consisting of interest organizations and voluntary organizations as well as informal groupings and local communities that converge around specific activities. This has paved the way for new forms of soft governance and management that allow for autonomous self-regulation in civil society as well as in decentred parts of the public sector. At the meso level, the coexistence of a strong state and a strong civil society has resulted in the institutionalization of collaborative arenas that enable interaction between the two sectors. These institutionalizations stabilize and normalize norms, values, role perceptions, practices and relationships (Steimo, Thelen & Longstreth 1992; Pierson 2000; Peters 2001) that foster and support collaboration rather than hindering it (Lijphart & Crepaz 1991; Wiarda 1997). At the micro level, collaborative forms of governance prosper because citizens in Northern Europe display comparatively higher levels of social trust and trust in public authorities than in other parts of the world. People generally trust each other and political systems are by and large perceived as legitimate. These micro-level features are likely to support collaboration, not only among citizens but also between citizens and public authorities (Trägårdh 2007; Marcussen & Torfing 2007).

This description of the Northern European context suggests that conditions for collaborative public innovation are particularly favourable in this part of the world. Clarifying whether these favourable conditions actually leads to a higher level of innovation than in other parts of the world calls for comparative research, which goes beyond the ambition of this book. The case studies presented in this book suggest, however, that the trajectories and outcomes of collaborative innovation initiatives are heavily influenced both by the historical and existing structures of governance in the countries under scrutiny.

THE MAIN FINDINGS

The case studies presented in this book address the question of how public innovation unfolds in different Northern European contexts. As mentioned above, Northern Europe is the place to go for cutting edge research about pioneering efforts to enhance public innovation. The collection of case studies in this volume confirms that there are widespread attempts to advance public innovation in a broad variety of policy areas and at various levels of governance, and that these attempts are being documented and analysed by researchers from various theoretical and methodological schools of thought. The diversity in theoretical approaches to the study of collaborative public innovation is evident in the chapters' very diverse conceptualizations of what constitutes collaboration, *e.g.* in terms of governance networks (Klijn & Koppenjan, 2004); partnerships (O'Toole, 1999); interactive governance (Torfing *et al.* 2012); co-production (Ostrom, 1996; Marschall 2004; Bovaird 2007; Alford 2009; Pestoff, Brandsen & Vershure, 2012); and co-creation (Bason, 2010; Hillgren *et al.* 2011; Björgvinssonn *et al.*, 2012; Prahalad, C.K. & Ramaswamy, 2004). Theoretical differences are also apparent in the chapters' differing conceptualizations of leadership in relation to collaborative governance, *e.g.* as *civic enabling* (Sirianni 2009), *collaborative leadership* (Agranoff & McGuite, 2003; Ansell & Gash, 2007), and *meta-governance* (Sørensen & Torfing, 2007). Thus, these chapters testify to how public innovation is increasingly viewed as an important object of analysis within various strands of social science research.

At the same time, it is clear that Northern European research into collaborative public innovation has some way to go before reaching maturity as a coherent research field in its own right. Most of the research on collaborative governance still tends to focus on how collaboration can promote the efficiency and effectiveness of public governance rather than public innovation. As the chapters of this book clearly show, research on public innovation is still a quite fragmented field that explores public innovation from various perspectives, rather than a collective effort to build on common insights across countries in order to develop theoretical propositions. There is no doubt, however, that the collaborative public innovation research agenda has a great potential. At the moment, key questions are being posed and the tentative answers hold great promise for the future development of interdisciplinary frameworks that will allow for more systematic accumulation of knowledge on the advancement of collaborative public innovation in Northern Europe. The chapters of this book offer some initial building blocks to advance this endeavour.

Despite the considerable diversity in the theoretical approaches and empirical foci of the individual chapters, the case studies nonetheless present a number of fascinating insights into collaborative public innovation in Northern Europe. These can be summarized in the following four propositions: 1) Collaborative public innovation transforms mindsets, role perceptions and work forms; 2) Design matters for the success and failure of collaborative innovation processes; 3) Leadership is important for promoting collaborative innovation; and 4) Collaborative public innovation is relevant at all levels of governance.

First, attempts to enhance public innovation transform the way governing is carried out. As the chapters in this book show, the quest for new and innovative solutions to wicked problems is closely linked to the transformation of the mindsets, roles, processes and organizational structures that characterise the public sector. This is evident in Chapter 6 where Joost Vos, Corine Balder, Bert van Hermert and Henk Wagenaar show how the complex problem of dealing with habitual offenders leads to the establishment of a new collaborative institutional set-up, and how the role perceptions and relations among the participating actors are altered in the collaborative process; in Chapter 3, Luise Li Langergaard points out how a collaborative innovation process leads to the emergence of new ideas about what it means to be a public service user; and in Chapter 8 Gro Sandkjær Hanssen argues that collaboration can result in rhetorical innovations with long term effects on policies and services that go beyond *here and now* product innovation. This point is further supported in Chapter 12 where Linda Lundgaard Andersen shows how innovation in governance discourse affects the strategies and work forms of professionals in a public agency. These observations suggest that smaller innovations can produce domino effects that can have greater impact over a longer time span.

Second, design matters for the impact and success of collaborative governance processes. Many of the chapters describe novel ways in which public authorities design special arenas to spur collaborative innovation. In Chapter 2, Maija Setälä and Marja-Liisa Niinikoski present the results of a comparative study of mini-publics and a user-driven innovation initiative that clarifies how different institutional designs affect collaborative innovation processes. In Chapter 10 Helle Vibeke Carstensen tests and develops a *lead-user model* and discusses what kind of actors to include at what stages in the process, and to what extent the design promotes not only collaboration but also innovation. As noted, Chapter 6 by Joost Vos, Corine Balder, Bert van Hermert and Henk Wagenaar demonstrates how innovative process design can facilitate communication, dialogue and creative exchanges between actors with different experiences, logics and mind sets, which further enhances the potential for crafting innovative solutions to the wicked problem at hand.

Third, the chapters show how important leadership is for collaborative innovation. The challenge for leaders is to strike a balance between giving directions and regulating the innovation process, and shaping autonomous arenas in which public and private stakeholders can develop, test and qualify ideas in situations that are more or less beset by conflicts and differences in perspectives, world views and experiences. The leadership challenge is analysed in Chapter 4 where Albert Meijer show that leaders who initiate innovation endeavours can play a key role in mobilising bottom up innovation in networks. In Chapter 5, Andreas Hagedorn Krogh and Jacob Torfing argue that collaborative innovation calls for a specific kind of leadership that is able to spur cross-sectoral collaboration which challenges a public sector that favours in-house governance. In Chapter 11, Lynn Frogett likewise analyses the role of leadership and asks who is to take the lead in collaboration innovation processes. In line with Meijer, she acknowledges the great potential of bottom up innovation initiatives, but she finds that top down leadership performed by state actors is important for creating legitimacy as the latter can play an important role in mediating between conflicting interests.

Finally, the chapters in this book show that collaborative public innovation has a role to play at all levels of governance in Europe. Collaborative innovation is at play at the EU level as well as at national, regional and local levels of governance and collaborative innovation also occurs between levels. Chapter 8 by Hanneke Gieske and Arwin van Buuren, Chapter 9 by Esther van Zimmeren, and Chapter 13 by John Fenwick and Janice McMillan all show how the interplay among actors at different levels affects the outcome of collaborative innovation processes. Zimmeren observes that inspiration to innovate may travel from lower to higher levels of governance or *vice versa*, while in the case studied by Fenwick and McMillan innovation requirements originate at upper (transnational) levels and permit little room for local adaptation.

This summary of the research findings merely constitutes the tip of the iceberg, and the book offers a multitude of other compelling insights. Each chapter contributes new knowledge about the problems and potential of enhancing public innovation in Northern Europe through different forms of collaborative innovation, as well as ideas about suitable theoretical and analytical approaches to guide such studies.

THE STRUCTURE OF THE BOOK

The above findings are based on the analyses presented in the following chapters. A number of themes recur in several of the chapters, namely: How are citizens being included in public innovation processes? How is public innovation addressed in multi-level, multi-actor policy making settings in areas where wicked problems prevail? What are the conditions for learning in these processes?

The first two chapters address ways to engage citizens in producing public policies, and the consequences of this. Although this is a key feature of collaborative public innovation, we know little about how abstract notions of involving relevant and affected actors are actually transformed into concrete empirical initiatives, and we know even less about the consequences of choosing between different instruments of citizen involvement. Marja-Liisa Setälä and Maija Niinikoski add to our knowledge about this in Chapter 2. The authors analyse and compare the different underpinnings, procedures and outcomes in two public innovation initiatives that grant a more active role to citizens: a deliberative mini-publics initiative and a user-driven innovation project in Finland, respectively. The chapter concludes that while both initiatives were successful in bringing forth new ideas about how to improve policy-making and service delivery, neither was able to ensure the participation of a representative group of citizens. To enhance this type of public sector initiative, the authors call for more transparent selection of citizens as well as careful consideration of the relationship between expected outcomes and the decision-making process.

In line with her Finnish colleagues, Luise Li Langergaard explores how increased citizen involvement in collaborative public innovation changes perceptions of citizenship. In Chapter 3, Langergaard presents different conceptualizations of user involvement and 'users' *e.g.* as consumers, co-producers, lead users or citizens. The chapter discusses the implications of these different conceptualizations for citizenship in terms of political deliberation and rights. The author claims that the different conceptualizations of 'user' imply certain ideas about the public sector, state and society which have implications both in political terms and for our understanding of citizenship. The chapter is based on a literature review and uses an empirical case from a social service department in Denmark to examine differences in the democratic implications of different user conceptions. Langergaard concludes that we need an increased awareness of how to work with the different user conceptions in collaborative innovation practices, and argues that we may benefit from including the concept of 'welfare state citizen with rights', as none of the other user conceptions are explicit about rights.

We now turn to experiences of collaborative public innovation in policy areas characterised by wicked problems. In Chapter 4, Albert Meijer analyses how and to what extent innovations introduced and implemented in a public sector context affect the perceived legitimacy of the innovation in question. Meijer tests a hypothesis suggesting that bottom up initiated innovations aiming to promote organizational legitimacy are more likely to succeed than top down initiated innovations. However, a case study of the introduction of new social media in the Dutch police force shows that if top down innovations pave the way for bottom up networking they can be a key driver in promoting organizational legitimacy.

Chapter 5, by Andreas Hagedorn Krogh and Jacob Torfing, also concerns the field of public safety. Through a cross-case analysis of 14 innovation projects addressing the complex problem of gang violence and crime in the city of Copenhagen, the authors investigate the role of public leadership in overcoming barriers to collaborative public innovation. The empirical analysis suggests, *inter alia*, that collaborative innovation leadership is particularly needed in 'first mover' initiatives and larger innovation projects and that leadership tasks become more comprehensive and demanding as innovation processes develop. Based on their findings, the authors propound that in order to be successful in leading collaborative innovation public managers must encourage active participation, advance individual and collective self-regulation and allow public and private employees and local civil society activists to take on leadership roles. If public organizations wish to develop innovative solutions to wicked problems they are prompted to deliberately and systematically develop public leaders' ability to convene, facilitate and catalyse processes of collaborative innovation; allocate the necessary time and resources for such activities; and build institutional designs that strengthen vertical and horizontal coordination and collaboration among public and private stakeholders.

In Chapter 6, a Dutch foursome, Joost Vos, Corine Balder, Bert van Hemert and Hendrik Wagenaar, explore collaborative innovation in the field of public safety. The authors discuss the relative success of the *Veiligheidshuizen* (Safety Houses) in the Netherlands. The Safety Houses are an organizational innovation that brings together agencies from the care sector and the criminal justice sector in a collaborative framework for dealing with habitual offenders. The study shows that an important barrier to the initiative is that the two agencies have conflicting cultures, structures and domains. The new collaborative arena that is, in essence, a frontal attack on silo organisation is found to be relatively successful in fostering role innovation and process innovation, and helps to bridge the gap between the two sectors.

Chapters 7 and 8 both focus on water management - another notorious policy area in which wicked problems abound. In Chapter 7, Gro Sandkjær Hanssen presents the results of a study on the extent to which the establishment of eco-system based coordination networks in water management in Norway contribute to the promotion of public innovation. She concludes that although the coordination activities do not result in policy, process or product innovations they do lead to what the author terms 'rhetorical innovations' which in the long term may pave the way for management of practice innovations in the area of water management.

In Chapter 8, Hanneke Gieske and Arwin van Buuren explore how a collaborative governance process involving nine municipalities in a city region, the regional authority and a number of private actors, contributes to innovation in Dutch water management. The study evaluates the impact of the collaboration process using a

Kingdon inspired analytical framework, and identifies innovations on the macro, meso and micro levels of governance. The study shows that not only did the collaboration process enable the development of new innovative solutions, it also triggered a paradigmatic shift in the approach to regional policy.

In Chapter 9, Esther van Zimmeren analyses the case of European patent governance, thus departing from the preceding chapters in the sense that this case spans the supranational, EU and national levels. The case of EU patent governance also stands out because of the characteristics of the actors involved. The dominating actors in this case are well known in the international governing arena and many of them have powerful governing capacities. Applying her own framework of *dynamic governance* that aligns well with this book's understanding of collaborative public innovation, Zimmerman shows that particularly the non-static elements of these frameworks are also fertile when analysing collaboration among *heavy weight* actors. However, Zimmerman points out that there is a high risk that less resourceful actors may be squeezed out of governance arrangements as more powerful actors collaborate with one another, and she calls for institutional designs to counteract such exclusion.

The book then turns its attention to learning. Chapter 10 examines how public sector innovation can draw on lessons from the private sector. Based on her own practical professional experience, Helle Vibeke Carstensen analyses how the lead user model developed by private sector innovation theorists may be adapted to a public sector context. Carstensen describes the lead user model and presents the results of a design experiment that tests the lead user concept in the area of taxation. The design experiment shows that the lead user approach can be deployed in the public sector and that it increases the possibility for radical innovation, but also it is necessary to develop the model in a more collaborative direction so that it can live up to the complex goals of public sector tasks.

In Chapter 11, Lynn Frogett provides a framework for analysing an often overlooked aspect in debates about cross-sectoral collaborative innovation: the psychosocial dimension. More specifically, she looks at Third Sector Organisations (TSO's) in the United Kingdom as they increasingly provide alternatives to public services, manage community ownership of local assets, and offer relational models of production and exchange. Many TSO's have relatively flat structures, valorise peer relations and are seen as democratic alternatives to local state bureaucracies. However, Frogget argues that a psychosocial understanding of lateral peer relations is essential to avoid displacement anxiety and rivalry and to ensure that conflicts are used as productive feedback for organisational development. The author concludes that TSO's may still need the local state's vertically organised mediating functions if they need to carry out their roles effectively.

In Chapter 12, Linda Lundgaard Andersen argues that public innovation will be constrained if public employees are not adequately involved. Building on her on-going research in Danish welfare settings, Andersen observes that professionals are enthusiastic but are burdened by the dominant innovation discourse. Providing a psychosocial analysis, she argues that professionals and citizens are required to identify with the collaborative process both at a professional and private levels in order for it to be successful. While this requirement may prove to be a driver of welfare services, it may also produce anxiety, ambivalence and idealization and may thus prevent collaborative public innovations from reaching their full potential.

In Chapter 13, John Fenwick and Janice McMillan echo these concerns about exclusion and warn that in a world of flux, top down policy making may be unsuited to, and unwelcome in, local settings regardless of how *innovative* or *participatory* these policies are labelled. They argue that learning and ultimately creativity are the basis for all innovation though they caution that not all learning leads to innovation, nor is all innovation an improvement. In order for learning to be innovative, it must be predicated on actors' sense-making. Actors make sense of policy making and governance based on their own lived experiences and mediation between individual and organizational learning. Accepting Fenwick and McMillan's anti-foundationalist view, it becomes clear that policy makers situated in upper levels of government or other policy making institutions walk a fine line between facilitating creative public innovation and imposing unwelcome *one-size-fits-all*-solutions.

ACKNOWLEDGEMENTS

Declared none.

CONFLICT OF INTEREST

The authors confirm that this chapter contents have no conflict of interest.

REFERENCES

Agger, A. & Sørensen, E. (2014). Designing collaborative policy innovation: Lessons from a Danish municipality. In C. Ansell & J. Torfing (Eds), *Public Innovation through Collaboration and Design* (pp.188-208), New York: Routledge.

Albury, D. (2005). Fostering Innovation in Public Services. In Public Money & Management, 25:1, 51-56

Alford, J. 2009. The Multiple Facets of Co-Production: Building on the work of Elinor Ostrom. In *Public Management Review,* 16: 3, 299-316.

Ansell, C. & Gash, A. (2012). Stewards, mediators and catalysts: Towards a model for collaborative leadership. In *The Public Sector Innovation Journal,* 17:1, article 7.

Ansell, C., & Gash, A. (2007). Collaborative governance in theory and practice In *Journal of Public Administration Research and Theory*, 18, 543-571, http://www.innovation.cc/scholarly-style/christoffer_nsell_alison_editit_v17i1a7.pdf

Ansell, C. & Torfing, J. (Eds) (2014). *Public Innovation through Collaboration and Design,* New York: Routledge

Bellante, D. & Link, A.N. (1981). Are public sector workers more risk-averse than private sector workers? In *Industrial and Labour Relations Review* 34:3, 408-412.

Bland, T., Bruk, B., Kim, D., & Lee, K. T. (2010). Enhancing public sector innovation: Examining the network-innovation relationship. In *Public Sector Innovation Journal*, 15:3, 1-25.

Bommert, B. (2010). Collaborative innovation in the public sector. In *International Public Management Review*, 11, 15-33.

Booher, D. & Innes, J. (2010). *Planning with Complexity*, London: Routledge.

Bommert, B. (2010). Collaborative innovation in the public sector. In *International Public Management Review*, 11:1, 15-33.

Borins, S. (2001). Encouraging innovation in the public sector. In *Journal of Intellectual Capital*, 2:3, 310-319.

Bovaird, T. (2007). Beyond Engagement and Participation: User and Community Co-production of Services. In *Public Administration Review,* 67:5, 846-860.

Bozeman, B. & Kingsley, K. (1998). Risk culture in public and private organizations. In *Public Administration Review,* 58:2, 109-118.

Braithwaite, V, & Levi, M. (1998). *Trust in Government,* New York: Russell Sage Foundation.

Dente, B., Bobbio, L., & Spada, A. (2005). Government or governance of urban innovation?. In *DIPS*, 162, (pp. 1-22).

Eggers, B. & Singh, S. (2009), *The Public Innovator's Handbook*, Washington, D.C. Harvard Kennedy School of Government.

Faems, D., Van Looy, B. & Debackere, K. (2005), Inter-organizational Collaboration and Innovation: Toward a Portfolio Approach. In *Journal of Product Innovation Management*, 22:3, 238-250.

Hale, T. & Held, D. (2012). Gridlock and Innovation in Global Governance: The partial Transnational solution. In *Global Policy*, 3:2, 169-181.

Hartley, J., Sørensen, E & Torfing, J, (2013). Collaborative Innovation: A Viable Alternative to Market Competition and Organizational Entrepreneurship. In *Public Administration Review*, 73:6, 821-830.

Hartley, J. (2005), Innovation in governance and public service: Past and present. In *Public Money & Management,* 25:1, 27-34.

Healey, P. (1997). *Collaborative Planning*, Vancouver: UBC Press.

Heinrich, V. & Fioramonti, L. (Eds) (2008). *CIVICUS Global Survey of the State of Civil Society: Comparative perspectives,* Bloomfield: Kumarian Press.

Hood, C. (1986), *The Tools of Government*, Chatham: Chatham House Publishers.

Hood, C. (1991), A public management for all seasons. In *Public Administration,* 69:1, 3-19.

Hood, C. (2010). *Reflections on Public Service Reform in a Cold Fiscal Climate*, Paper for Commission on Public Service Trust, Launched 17th of June 2010.

Katzenstein, P. (1985). *Small States in World Markets: Industrial Policy in Europe,* Ithaca: Cornell University Press.

Kickert, W., Klijn, E.H. and Koppenjan, J. (1997). *Managing Complex Networks,* London: Sage.

Levin, K. Cashore, B., Bernstein, S. & Auld, G. (2012). Overcoming the tragedy of super wicked problems: constraining our future selves to ameliorate global climate change. In *Policy Science*, 45:2, 123-152.

Lijphart A. & Crepaz, L.L.M (1991). Corporatism and Consensus Democracy in Eighteen Countries: Conceptual and Empirical Linkage. In *British Journal of Political Science*, 21:2, 235-56.

Macmillan, P. & Cain, T. (2010). *Closing the Gap: Eliminating the Disconnect between Policy Design and Execution*, Vancouver: Deloitte.

Marschall, M.J. (2004). Citizen participation and the neighbourhood context: A New Look at the Coproduction of Local Public Goods. In *Political Research Quarterly*, 57:2, 231-244.

Marcussen, M. & Torfing J. (Eds.) (2007). *Democratic Network Governance in Europe,* Basingstroke: Palgrave Macmillan.

Mayntz, R. & Marin, B. (1991). *Policy Networks: Empirical Evidence and Theoretical Considerations,* Frankfurt am Main: Campus Verlag.

OECD (2011a). *The Call for Innovative and Open Government: An Overview of Country Initiatives*, Paris: OECD.

OECD (2011b). *Society at a Glance 2011: OECD Social Indicators*, Paris: OECD. DOI: 10.1787/soc_glance-2011-en

OECD (2014). *Society at a Glance 2014: OECD Social Indicators*, Paris: OECD. http://dx.doi.org/10.1787/soc_glance-2014-en

Osborne, D. E. & Gaebler, T. (1992). *Reinventing Government: How the Entrepreneurial Spirit is Transforming the Public Sector*, Massachusetts: Addison-Wesley.

Pestoff, V., Brandsen, T. and Verschuere, B. (Eds) (2012). *New Public Governance, the Third Sector, and Co-Production,* New York and London: Routledge.

Peters, B.G. (2001). *Institutional Theory in Political Science. The "New" Institutionalism,* London: Continuum.

Pierson, P. (2000). Increasing Returns, Path Dependence, and the Study of Politics. In *American Political Science Review*, 94:2, 251-267.

Pollitt, C. & Bouckeart, G. (2011). *Public Management Reform. A Comparative Analysis - New Public Management, Governance, and the Neo-Weberian State,* Oxford: Oxford University Press.

Powell, W.W., Koput, K.W. & Smith-Doerr, L. (1996). Inter-organizational Collaboration and the locus of innovation: Networks of learning in biotechnology. In *Administrative Science Quarterly,* 41:1, 116-145.

Prahalad, C.K. & Ramaswamy, V. (2004). Co-creation experiences: The next practice in value creation. In *Journal of Interactive Marketing*, 18:3, 5-14.

Rittel, H.W.J. & Webber, M.M. (1973), Dilemmas in a general theory of planning. In *Policy Sciences,* 4:2, 155-169.

Roberts, N.C. & Bradley, R.T. (1991). Stakeholder Collaboration and Innovation: A Study of Public Policy Initiation at the State Level. In *Journal of Applied Behavioural Science,* 27:2, 209-227.

Rothstein, B. (2005). *Social Traps and the Problem of Trust*, Cambridge: Cambridge University Press.

RT (2013). Three quarters of the Americans distrust government. In *RT News* 12. March 2013 http://rt.com/usa/government-trust-americans-poll-172/

Sigurdson, J. (1986). *Industry and State Partnership in Japan: the Very Large Scale Integrated (VLSI) Circuit Project,* Swedish Research Policy Institute, Lund: Lund University.

Sirianni, C. (2009). *Investing in Democracy: Engaging Citizens in Collaborative Governance,* Washington: Brookings Institute.

Smith, G. (2009). *Democratic Innovations,* Cambridge: Cambridge University Press.

Stoker, G. (2006). *Why Politics Matter: Making Democracy Work*, Basingstoke: Palgrave Macmillan.

Sørensen, E. & Torfing, J. (2007). *Theories of Democratic Network Governance*, Basingstoke: Palgrave Macmillan.

Sørensen, E. and Torfing, J. (2009). Enhancing effective and democratic network governance through metagovernance. In *Public Administration*, 87:2, 234-258.

Sørensen, E. & Torfing, J. (2011). Enhancing Collaborative Innovation in the public sector. In *Administration and Society,* 43:8, 842-868.

Stankiewicz, R., (1997). The development of beta blockers at Astra-Hässle and the technological system of the Swedish pharmaceutical industry. In Carlsson, B. (Ed.), *Technological Systems and Industrial Dynamics*, (pp. 93-137). Dordrecht: Kluwer Academic Publishers.

Tassey, G., (1997). *The Economics of R&D Policy*, Westport: Quorum Books.
Teece, D. J. (1992), Competition, cooperation, and innovation. In *Journal of Economic Behavior & Organization*, 18:1, 1-25.
Torfing, J., Peters, B.G., Pierre, J. and Sørensen, E. (2012). *Interactive Governance: Advancing the Paradigm,* Oxford: Oxford University Press
Torfing, J. & Triantafillou, P. (2013). What's in a name? Grasping new public governance as a political-administrative system. In *International Review of Public Administration*, 18:2, 9-25.
Trägårdh, L. (ed.), (2007). *State and Civil Society in Northern Europe, The Swedish Model Reconsidered,* New York: Berghahn.
Wallstein, S. (2000). The Effects of Government-Industry R&D Programs on Private R&D: The Case of the Small Business Innovation Research Program. In *The RAND Journal of Economics,* 31:1, 82-100.
Wiarda, H (1997). *Corporatism and Comparative Politics: The Other Great Ism,* New York: M. E. Sharpe.
Wynen, J., Verhoest, K., Onago, E. & Van Thiel, S. (2013). Innovation-oriented culture in the public sector. In *Public Management Review,* 16:1, 45-66.

CHAPTER 2

Deliberative Mini-Publics and User-Driven Innovation in the Public Sector: Comparing Underpinnings, Procedures and Outcomes

Marja-Liisa Niinikoski[*] and Maija Setälä

Aalto University, School of Business and University of Turku, Finland

Abstract: In this chapter, two different instruments of involving citizens and users in public sector are analyzed. More precisely, we focus on deliberative mini-publics and user-driven innovations. The chapter puts forward two empirical cases where these instruments have been experimented in Finland. These cases illustrate how the use of these instruments offers new roles and opportunities for citizens to influence policies and their implementation. The analysis sheds light on the underpinnings, procedures and outcomes of these instruments, and focuses on possible roles of citizens in public sector innovation. The cases analyzed in this chapter show that the impact of citizen involvement does not necessarily depend so much on the type of instrument used in involving citizens. Rather, openness and receptiveness by policy-makers appear to be more important than the intentions behind the used techniques. Furthermore, our case studies suggest that there may sometimes be trade-offs between the goals of inclusion and innovation capacity.

Keywords: Deliberative mini-publics, User-driven innovation, Citizen roles, Public sector innovation.

INTRODUCTION

In this chapter, we analyze two different instruments of involving citizens and users in public sector. Particularly, we analyze and compare deliberative mini-publics and user-driven innovations and put forward two empirical case studies where these instruments were experimented in Finland. During recent years, new forms of collaboration between citizens and public institutions have proliferated both in political strategies and in actual policy-making processes. The two cases described in this chapter represent such initiatives. Both cases involve the use of forums that offer new roles and opportunities for citizens to influence policies and

***Corresponding author Marja-Liisa Niinikoski:** Aalto University, School of Business, Finland; Tel: +358 40 538 4541; E-mail: marja-liisa.niinikoski@aalto.fi

Annika Agger, Bodil Damgaard, Andreas Hagedorn Krogh and Eva Sørensen (Eds.)

their implementation. Our aim is to shed light on the underpinnings, procedures and outcomes of different instruments of involving people in government. Especially, we are interested in the question what kinds of roles citizens can have in public sector innovations.

The techniques analyzed in this chapter are based on different views on citizens. Deliberative mini-publics can be regarded as democratic innovations, that is, participatory institutions which aim to engage citizens in political decision-making processes (*e.g.* Smith 2009; Grönlund *et al.* 2014). A variety of new forms of democracy have been developed and experimented during the recent decades. The research on democratic innovations has often been inspired by theories of democracy, and the design of democratic innovations reflects such basic democratic values as political equality and inclusion. New forms of democracy have been expected to help in the resolution of political conflicts and complex policy issues.

The concept of public innovation has focused on learning and practical problem-solving issues in the organization and production of public services. Studies on public innovation (*e.g.* Denhardt & Denhardt 2000), and recent studies on user-driven public innovations (*e.g.* Lovio & Kivisaari 2010; Jæger 2011; Jäppinen 2011; Sørensen & Torfing 2011), have emphasized citizens' role in the development and design of public services and institutions. The aim has been to develop and experiment innovative practices of citizens' co-operation and collaboration with public institutions and organizations. There has been a growing interest in user-driven innovation in the public management and governance literature as well as in policy and public management practice. Based on von Hippel's (2005a) idea, involving users directly in the development activities and processes could actually democratize development and innovation activities in the public sector. In this respect, the aim of user-driven public innovations is to increase citizens' influence on public decision-making, particularly on public services.

The goal of this chapter is to illustrate how different techniques of involving citizens in policy-making can be applied at the municipal level. Both techniques discussed in this chapter allow interactions between citizens and civil servants and, to some extent, elected representatives. However, while deliberative mini-publics emphasize inclusion and empowerment, user-driven innovation focuses more on the efficiency and the quality of service outcomes. We first distinguish normative goals and rationales of these techniques, as well as policy-makers' motivations for their use. Furthermore, we analyze the types of policy problems dealt with and the procedures applied in these innovation forums. Finally, we analyze the impacts of these instruments, in terms of policy-making, implementation and public discussion.

We put forward two empirical case studies carried out in Finnish cities 2011-2012. These cases exemplify what in Hartley's terminology can be characterized as governance and service innovations, and they help us to identify and compare value bases, expectations, practical aims and outcomes of these approaches. The two approaches to citizen engagement analyzed in this chapter are based, not only on different theoretical foundations, but also on different political backgrounds. In Finland, democratic innovations have traditionally been on the agenda of certain political activists and parties, especially the Green Party. Only in the 2010s, the idea of new forms of democracy has been more seriously taken up by the Ministry of Justice. Public discussion on user-driven innovation in Finland has become more active in the early 2010s; it has taken place in the framework of traditional innovation policy which focuses on socio-economic effects of innovations (Niinikoski & Kuhlmann 2014).

The findings based on our case study on a deliberative mini-public seem to be in line with studies (*e.g.* Parkinson 2004) suggesting that mini-publics often fall short of the high democratic expectations associated with them. Most importantly, the use and the impact of mini-publics remain contingent on ambitions and interests of civil servants and elected representatives. Our other case study on user driven innovation suggests that, in addition to providing pragmatic solutions to the development of public services, they can turn out be a catalyst of the politicization of underlying ideological issues at representative forums. Based on our analysis, we argue that although the different techniques have different goals and are based on very distinct theoretical foundations, there may be interesting overlaps when it comes to the actual practice.

DELIBERATIVE MINI-PUBLICS AS DEMOCRATIC INNOVATIONS

The literature on democratic innovations is based on broad conceptions of citizens and their roles in democratic government as agenda-setters, decision-makers and implementers of public decisions. In this respect, the role of citizens is understood in much broader terms than as mere users of public services. For this reason, the analysis of collaborative forms of public innovation can gain insights from the literature on democratic innovations and theories of democracy. According to Graham Smith (2009, 1), democratic innovations are "… *institutions that have been specifically designed to increase and deepen citizen participation in the political decision-making process*". The definition suggests that democratic innovations somehow supplement other forms of citizen participation used in representative democracies, most notably participation in elections.

In his book on democratic innovations, Smith deals with popular assemblies such as participatory budgeting, deliberative mini-publics, direct legislation and different forms of e-democracy. It is worth pointing out that some of the practices regarded as democratic innovations by Smith are established parts of certain political systems. This applies especially to practices of direct democracy which are an integral element of, for example, the Swiss political system. During the recent decades, the idea of reforming representative democracy has been promoted particularly by theorists of participatory democracy. For example, Benjamin Barber (1984) criticizes the practices of liberal, representative democracy and argues that new forms of democratic participation should be adopted in order to foster citizens' sense of responsibility and capacity of political judgment. Barber recommends the use of popular initiatives and referendums as well as the application of information and communication technologies to enhance public communication. In line with deliberative democrats, Barber (1984, 267-281) already emphasized the role of political talk and calls for the organization of neighborhood assemblies on local issues and televised town hall meetings to deal with difficult national issues.

Participatory democrats are particularly interested in promoting such forms of engagement which actually empower citizens to make collectively binding decisions. According to Arnstein's (1969) idea of the *ladder of participation*, participation means actual empowerment of citizens through citizen control, delegated power or partnership in public decision-making. This means that citizens would actually exert influence by making public decisions or by setting the political agenda. Despite their potential impact on policy-making, Arnstein names consultative forms of participation as *tokenism*. Common to these forms of interaction is their top-down character, and the fact that decision-makers are not obliged to take the opinions of citizens into consideration.

From a more liberal perspective, Robert Dahl (1989, 340) was concerned about citizens' alienation from politics, which is due to the increasing complexity of policy-making. Dahl recommended the use of so-called *mini-demos* for agenda-setting and advising policy-makers. Dahl suggested that mini-demos should be a permanent body consisting of about a thousand randomly selected citizens. Dahl's idea of mini-demos has many similarities to what is called deliberative mini-publics in more recent literature (see *e.g.* Grönlund *et al.* 2014). Deliberative mini-publics are also expected to be used to deal with pressing political problems caused by deep divisions in the society or the complexity of issues. Mini-publics seem to provide a new, constructive way of engaging citizens in policy-making, and therefore they have also been regarded as a potential cure for citizens' detachment from the traditional forms of political participation, such as voting and party membership.

There are two different interpretations of the term *deliberative mini-public*. Archon Fung (2003), who was first to introduce the term, used it broadly to refer to various kinds of citizen panels and assemblies to which participants can be recruited through a variety of methods, including open invitations and various sampling methods. According to this interpretation, also those citizens' assemblies, which are open to the public at large, *e.g.* participatory budgeting and town meetings, are regarded as deliberative mini-publics. In later studies (*e.g.* Goodin & Dryzek 2006), the term *deliberative mini-public* is usually used in narrower terms to refer only to those citizen panels where the representation of different societal viewpoints is ensured. For this reason, the organizers of mini-publics can either recruit participants by using different sampling methods, or they can *hand pick* participants so that they represent different perspectives on the issue (Brown 2006).

The earliest formats of mini-publics which date back to the 1970s, *i.e.* planning cells and citizens' juries, were motivated by the need to bridge the observed gap between citizens and their elected representatives. Consensus conferences, developed in the 1980s by the Danish Board of Technology, were more specifically designed to help policy-making on technically complex issues where public discussion gives little guidance for policy-making. Deliberative polls, invented by James Fishkin and Robert Luskin in the 1990s, were designed to address the problems of measuring public opinion through opinion polls (see Fishkin 2003). The aim was to provide a method of measuring enlightened and reflected public opinion by creating a situation where people can become informed and have a chance to deliberate on an issue. Sometimes deliberative polls have been used to enhance and to improve the quality of public debate on salient and contested issues. In these cases, large-scale and extensively publicized deliberative polls have been organized as a part of electoral or referendum campaigns. One of the most notable examples of such usage of mini-publics was the deliberative poll on the euro in Denmark, which was held before the referendum on the issue (Andersen & Hansen 2007).

Different formats of deliberative mini-publics were thus developed already in the 1970s and 1980s, but their use has become more widespread during the past two decades. Although there is some variation between the size and formats of deliberative mini-publics, they share some procedural similarities. In all deliberative mini-publics, participants are expected to engage in informed and moderated small group discussions. Information is provided through expert hearings and/or written information; moderators are used to ensure that all participants have a say in discussions. In large scale mini-publics participants are randomly divided into smaller groups; sometimes stratification is applied. There is some variation when it comes to the format of the outcome of mini-publics. Citizens' juries and consensus conferences come up with a written statement whereas in deliberative polls participants' opinions are only measured before and after deliberation.

So far, most mini-publics have usually had only a modest impact on policy-making (Parkinson 2004; Setälä 2011). It seems therefore justifiable to claim that democratic theorists' and activists' enthusiasms about mini-publics has not quite matched with the reality. There are several reasons for this. Deliberative mini-publics have usually been used on *ad hoc* basis, and there are very only few examples of even modest institutionalization. An example of a (relatively modest) institutionalization of mini-publics was the use of consensus conferences organized by the Danish Board of Technology since 1987. Consensus conferences were organized frequently in processes on technically complex issues, such as the regulation of different applications of genetic technology. Moreover, the final statements by consensus conferences were routinely distributed among parliamentarians and other policy-makers. However, the systematic use of consensus conferences in conjunction with legislative processes has come to an end in Denmark in the 2000s. At the same time, an array of other methods of citizen engagement have been developed and experimented by the Danish Board of Technology.

Another factor contributing to the weakness of deliberative mini-publics is their top-down character, which means that mini-public processes are usually initiated by policy-makers, *i.e.* representatives or bureaucrats, who also define the agenda for discussions. Indeed, it has been argued that deliberative mini-publics have often remained as kinds of focus groups where policy-makers *market test* their ideas (Goodin 2008, 25-8). Mini-publics have also been used for strategic purposes, that is, to strengthen particular policy position in decision-making process (Hendriks 2006). In the context of governance networks, especially, mini-publics can be used as a means to legitimize policy positions and processes through establishing claims of inclusion and representation. However, although mini-publics entail the inclusion of different societal perspectives, they not involve similar mechanism of accountability and responsiveness as traditional institutions of representative democracy (Hendriks, 2009).

Finally, deliberative mini-publics have been criticized for their lacking impact on actual policy-making. The role of mini-publics in decision-making is typically weakly defined. They are typically just characterized as being *consultative*. Moreover, those who actually make decisions do not usually participate in deliberations of mini-publics; and often they are not even committed to respond publicly to the recommendations of mini-publics (Parkinson, 2004). In several cases, policy recommendations by mini-publics have just been ignored or bypassed by policy-makers. Overall, it seems that in most cases the impact of deliberative mini-publics has been contingent on the will and interests of policy-makers.

There are only few examples of mini-publics which in Arnstein's terms have involved delegated power or partnership. In British Columbia, the Citizens' Assembly was given the right to put forward a proposal for a new electoral system which was then voted on in a referendum (Warren & Pearse 2008). This was an example of an innovative way of using mini-publics in policy-making as a method of setting the political agenda. There are even fewer examples where mini-publics have actually been vested with powers to make collectively binding decisions. In the township of Zeguo, China, deliberative polls have been used to decide on the use of public funds on certain infrastructure projects (Fishkin *et al.* 2010). It is notable that the practices of participatory budgeting in Latin America, especially in the city of Porto Alegre in Brasil, can be regarded as examples of participatory co-governance as they have made decisions concerning significant shares of municipal budgets (Baiocchi, 2005).

USER-DRIVEN INNOVATION AS PUBLIC INNOVATION

In the public sector, the concept of innovation is rather new (Lovio & Kivisaari, 2010). Surely innovations have been created and applied in the public sector but they have been referred to as, for example, good practices, organizational learning, intelligent regulation or reform. However, the adoption of the concept of innovation may help boosting orientation towards renewal and offer new perspectives and means for analysis and planning.

Recently, the concept of public innovation has been elaborated by Jæger (2011) in relation to the traditional, private sector focused innovation literature. She claims that the concept of innovation has to be re-defined in the public sector context, since the private and public sectors pursue different objectives and rationales. Moreover, private and public sectors entail different relationships with users as well as motivations and barriers for innovation. Jæger argues that we have to re-define the concept in a way that it reflects the conditions for the public sector. According to her, it is necessary to bear in mind that the value of the public sector should be determined by the public interest, and it should be governed by the citizens.

Other scholars have emphasized network approaches and, consequently, the role of collaborative processes between elected representatives, public managers, street-level bureaucrats, users and private sector actors when enhancing public innovations. Sørensen and Torfing (2011, 849) define public innovation as "... *an intentional and proactive process that involves the generation and practical adoption and spread of new and creative ideas, which aims to produce a qualitative change in a specific context*".

According to Hartley (2005, 2006), public innovation include a variety of categories, such as service and product innovation, process innovation, position innovation, strategic innovation, governance innovation, organizational innovation, policy innovation, and symbolic/rhetorical innovation. According to the broad interpretation by Hartley, democratic innovations could be regarded as specific category of public innovations where particular attention has been paid to inclusion. However, such interpretation would disguise the issues of political conflict and empowerment which have motivated the development of democratic innovations.

The literature on user-driven innovation in the public sector is even more recent than the literature on public innovation. Originally, the theorization of user-driven innovation has occurred in innovation studies focusing on the private sector. In the private sector context, reducing market uncertainty is particularly important in the early stages of innovation projects (Lüthje & Herstatt 2004, 553). By using customers as an information source in the *fuzzy front-end*, the project teams may receive valuable input for the generation of promising new product ideas (Kim & Wilemon 2002). Based on several empirical case studies in different branches, von Hippel concludes that "...*empirical studies of the sources of innovation in both industrial and consumer goods fields have shown that in many but not all of the fields studied, users rather than manufacturers are typically the initial developers of what later become commercially significant new products and processes*" (von Hippel 2002, 6).

Traditionally, public management literature has emphasized the entrepreneurial role of public managers and private contractors responding to competitive pressures (Sørensen & Torfing 2011, 845). Borins (2001) has indicated that approximately 50 percent of public innovations originate from middle managers or front-line workers, 25 percent from agency heads, 20 percent from politicians, 15 percent from interest groups, and 10 percent from individuals outside of the government. Contrary to the traditional public management studies, user-driven innovation highlights the role of users as a relevant source for innovation. As a contrast to democratic innovations which are based on the idea of the inclusion of different viewpoints or the whole community, user-driven approaches emphasize the role of users as representatives of specific groups with their own needs and characteristics (see *e.g.* Jäppinen 2011).

In addition to the role of users as a relevant source for innovation, the literature on user-driven public innovation has emphasized the focus of innovations, the definition and the role of users, and the means of fulfilling objectives of public services, and more generally public policies. According to Jäppinen (2011), user-driven approach in the governmental context means that the development of public services is based on the needs of citizens and that the focus is on users rather than on production. Also, according to the analysis of the Danish policy documents on user-driven innovation, a common feature is that innovation is seen to be based on user's needs, wishes and praxis (Jæger 2011). Furthermore, users are defined primarily as individual persons having his or her rights to services (Jæger 2011).

The focus of user-driven public innovation is primarily on public services, especially their provision and improvement, as well decision-making on services, including processes and organizations. The user-driven approach encourages public managers and employees to learn from or about different user groups in order to improve public services (Sørensen &Torfing 2011, 845; Jäppinen 2011). Sørensen and Torfing (2011, 849) claim that the *customers* in terms of users of public services are actively engaged in raising demands, providing critical feedback, and co-production solutions, and they do that much more actively than the customers in private markets. In policy practice, perspectives on user-driven innovation in selected Danish policy documents varied from a narrow approach focusing on products and services to a broad approach focusing on organizations and processes (Jæger 2011). In the analysis of user-driven innovation in two Finnish cities, Jäppinen (2011, 162) found that the approach has been applied both in decision-making on service provision and in actual service provision.

The role of users in the development processes can vary from a rather passive role to an active role as a participant (Jæger 2011). Jäppinen (2011) sees that user-driven approach can be implemented in two different ways in public service; the first one involves traditional forms of participation in decision-making on services through user democracy, and the other one involves more innovative forms of participation in service provision. Users are sometimes reduced to a passive role where they are expected to answer questions in user satisfaction surveys and interviews or to be observed by the researchers. Dialogue-based approaches entail *active participation* of the users (Jæger 2011) meaning, for instance, co-creation, co-development and co-production of services.

There are only few case studies where the user-driven approach has been implemented in the public sector context and where the specific conditions of the public sector have been taken into account (van Rijswijk *et al.* 2008; Jæger 2011; Jäppinen 2011). In general, there is significant literature on user-related or user-driven innovation, either emphasizing the role of majority users (see *e.g.* Pantzar 1996; Norman 2001; Shove & Pantzar 2005; Miettinen 2008) or the aspects of lead-users (see *e.g.* von Hippel 2001; Lilien *et al.* 2002; von Hippel & von Krogh 2003; von Hippel 2005b, 2005b, 2005a). Some empirical examples of user-driven innovation in the public sector context are given in the following Table **1**.

The city of Helsinki applied user-centric and service design methods in order to improve public business services. During the innovation process, a variety of user-centric and –driven methods were applied, such as surveys, user panels and forums, observations, user narratives, customer safaris, workshops, mystery shopping, prototyping, focus groups, co-creation, and service journey. The main goal of the pilot, carried out in Helsinki, was to test and implement new user-driven methods (Jäppinen 2011). As an outcome, due to the more horizontal and cross-sectoral approach to the service delivery in the city, the process of business services became more efficient from the point of users, and the application process sped up. These results coincide closely with earlier studies which have characterized user-driven innovations by means to modernize provision of public services especially by introducing new cross-sectoral processes, and to increase the competitiveness of municipalities and the private sector (Rosted 2005).

Jæger's (2011) analysis of the Danish policy documents illustrates the introduction of user-driven innovation in documents by the Danish government, more specifically by the Council for Technology and Innovation and the Strategic Research Council under the Danish Agency for Science, Technology and Innovation in the late 2000s. These documents more or less describe the directions which the governmental agencies aim to follow in the coming years. Furthermore, both councils recognize users' role as participants in policy networks. According to Jæger (2011), this reflects the transformation of the public administration and changes in the relationship between the state and citizens (Beck Jørgensen & Melander 1999). The analysis of the Danish policy documents shows that professionals, *i.e.* public sector managers, experts running programs for innovation and researchers, are key actors in user-driven innovation (Jæger 2011). None of the documents analyzed pointed at users of public services as key actors. Jäppinen (2011, 170-171) argues that the user-driven approach can ideally include interactive decision-making process and user-driven design in public services. Based on empirical case studies, Jäppinen shows, however, that citizens were more prepared for participation and changes required by the user-driven approach than officials or elected representatives.

Both of the above-mentioned studies seem therefore to suggest that even when users are expected to participate, it happens under conditions defined by officials or experts. In the user-oriented approach, users are actors in innovation processes, but their contribution is subordinate to management and decision-making by other actors, such as public managers and elected representatives. In the user-driven approach users are key players in innovation processes influencing decisively in the direction of the development and its outcomes.

From the users' perspective, actual control and delegated power would imply the transfer of tasks and responsibilities to them. This would mean that some parts of the community would act independently or that users would be given the responsibility for decision-making and the provision of services. However, the existing empirical analyses of user-driven approaches in the public sector context show that the role of users has been restricted. In this respect, the term *user-oriented* rather than term *user-driven* approach could be more appropriate.

SUMMARY OF MINI-PUBLICS AND USER-DRIVEN INNOVATION

Considering the experience of deliberative mini-publics so far, it appears that the procedures applied in them are rather well established. Moreover, there are a plenty of empirical case studies analyzing processes of deliberative mini-publics and their outcomes (see *e.g* Smith 2009, 72-110). These studies suggest that actual practices of mini-publics often fail in two crucial respects, especially if Dahl's ideas of mini-demos are taken seriously. Deliberative mini-publics are usually used on an *ad hoc* basis on issues defined by policy-makers, and therefore they are not an integral part of the democratic system. Moreover, their impact in policy-making often remains vague. Compared to deliberative mini-publics, user-driven approaches are primarily used for service improvement. There seems to be a tendency to interpret issues related to service reforms as apolitical by emphasizing the need for *better* and practical solutions from the point of view of users' needs. Furthermore, instead of *user-driven* approaches, *user-oriented* approaches where new solutions are conditioned by elected representatives, experts and officials seem to be dominant.

In the following table, the underpinnings, procedures and effects of deliberative mini-publics and user-driven innovation are distinguished. The table also allows us to conduct comparisons between these two types of forms of citizen engagement. It shows their fundamental differences when it comes to the underlying philosophical approaches and goals. When it comes to procedures applied, the biggest difference seems to pertain to the fact that deliberative mini-publics systematically aim to be inclusive, both in terms of how people are recruited to the panel and in terms of discussion procedures where particular attention is paid to equal participation. However, when it comes to the initiation and the outcomes of these procedures, fewer differences can be observed. Both deliberative mini-publics and user-driven approaches are typically initiated by policy-makers on an *ad hoc* basis. The effects of deliberative mini-publics and user-driven innovation are both equally obscure and dependent on the willingness of those in charge of the policy area.

Table 1: Deliberative mini-publics and user-driven innovation compared

		Deliberative Mini-Publics	**User-Driven Innovation**
Underpinnings	Background	Need for democratic reform	Need for service improvement
	View of citizens	Autonomous citizens capable of reasoning	Varies according to applied approach, in practice emphasis on user orientation instead of the user-driven approach
	Goal	Engaging citizens to resolve complex/politicized issues	Usually engaging citizens to improve services, service delivery and service provision
Procedures	Participants	A representative sample of citizens	Primarily user groups representing the same age group

Table 1: contd….

			or the same background, such as enterprises
	Initiation and agenda-setting	Ideally used routinely on issues defined by citizens, usually used on ad hoc basis on issues defined by policy-makers	Usually used on issues defined by government officials and experts
	Working procedures	Informed and moderated small-group discussion	Variety of procedures
Outcomes	Result of citizens' participation	Usually a policy recommendations	New models or sketch for services or their production and provision
	Uptake	Ideally pre-established procedures of how recommendations are taken into account; in practice contingent on the will of policy-makers	Ideally new services or new ways to produce or organize services; in practice citizens more prepared for changes than elected representatives and officials

Although the instruments described in this chapter have distinctive features, they share a common goal of integrating citizens or users of public services into the processing of problems and issues, which influence their lives. Both methods can also be evaluated from the point of view how weak or strong engagement they imply from citizens' point of view. The examples of citizens' actual empowerment appear to be relatively rare, and these participatory instruments are usually applied in ways which do not restrict the freedom of civil servants of elected representatives to make decisions. Applying Arnstein's admittedly strenuous terminology, both deliberative mini-publics and user-driven innovations can therefore be characterized as *token* forms of participation as both their use and impact remains contingent on the will of more institutionalized actors in government.

FINNISH CASES: MIKKELI AND ESPOO

In this section, we make some comparisons of the procedures of two cases where citizens were engaged in local policy-making by using the techniques described above. These projects were conducted in 2011 and in 2012.

Mikkeli

In the case of Mikkeli, the aim was to conduct a deliberative citizen forum on a politically contested issue, that is, on the role of neighborhood councils in the rural municipalities amalgamated to the city of Mikkeli. Like many other deliberative mini-publics, this forum was also based on a top-down initiative which means that the deliberative forum on this topic was initiated by a civil servant of the city. The forum was conducted in collaboration with researchers who designed and facilitated the process. A steering group consisting of civil servants, researchers and members of neighbourhood councils monitored the project. The experiment was motivated by the fact that one of the municipal merger agreements was set to be renewed in 2013. Moreover, there were ongoing amalgamation negotiations between Mikkeli and some of its neighbouring rural municipalities.

The project researchers were interested in applying the procedures of deliberative mini-publics, especially those used in small scale mini-publics such as citizens' juries and consensus conferences. The aim was to gather a citizen panel where participants would represent different gender, age and socio-economic groups. Most importantly, the expectation was that participants would represent different geographical areas of the city, including both urban and rural areas in amalgamated municipalities. However, the group of 16 people who volunteered to participate on the basis of newspaper and radio ads consisted predominantly of inhabitants of the rural parts of Mikkeli. Moreover, elderly people and women were over-represented among volunteers. It is notable that participants from the rural areas were also more active in participating in actual discussion processes, measured by turnout in the meetings of the forum. It appears that people living in rural areas had a strong interest in the topic of the forum; they appeared dissatisfied with local services and democracy after municipal amalgamations.

The participants of the forum gathered together for four times and the project researchers facilitated the meetings. During the first meeting, the participants re-formulated the agenda for the discussion and prepared questions to be set to experts. The second meeting was an expert hearing where different models of neighborhood democracy were introduced and discussed. The hearing was open to all residents of Mikkeli, but there were only a few participants outside the forum. The two last meetings of the forum were dedicated to the formulation of the public statement. The statement was nearly finished after the final meeting, but some changes in wordings were made after the forum based on e-mail discussion.

The public statement of the forum emphasized the importance of neighborhood democracy bodies and argued that these bodies should be empowered by providing them with certain budgetary and implementation powers. Moreover, their position should be strengthened in relation to the city council and other representative bodies and also in the strategic planning of the city. The public statement thus included very concrete suggestions on how to improve neighborhood democracy in Mikkeli. The reason why the forum succeeded in producing a document with such concrete proposals may have been the fact that the participants shared some basic views especially when it comes to the need to strengthen neighborhood democracy. In this respect, the failure to form a representative citizen panel may have been fruitful when it comes to the outcome of deliberations. Some authors have pointed out the importance of deliberation among the like-minded, or so-called enclave deliberation, for the articulation of interests among disempowered (Karpowitz *et al.* 2009). In addition to being rather like-minded, the deliberators had strong stakes on the issue which was conducive to what Fung (2003) has called 'hot' deliberation.

The public statement formulated by the forum was distributed among the key policy-makers in Mikkeli, that is, the members of city council and board, as well as civil servants. There were no pre-established procedures on how policy-makers would respond to the recommendations of the forum. In general, the forum and its statement received relatively much attention because of the ongoing negotiations on further amalgamations between Mikkeli and some neighboring rural municipalities. The forum's ideas of enhancing neighborhood democracy were positively received in these negotiations, and in the amalgamation contract between the negotiating municipalities it was agreed that two new neighborhood bodies will be established.

The forum and its public statement turned out to be an asset for the city of Mikkeli in amalgamation negotiations as it demonstrated the city's interest in the issue of neighborhood democracy. In practice, the ideas of the public statement were applied to enhance both the status of the neighborhood bodies in decision-making and its preparation, and their role in the development of rural areas. However, the tasks of the bodies remained almost the same as before. Only the right to make an initiative to various committees and to the city board was adopted. Furthermore, neighborhood councils were granted the right to execute rather small repair works in their immediate surroundings with given allowances.

Espoo

In Espoo, all the relevant administrative sectors were represented in the project team which was expected to decide on the area of innovation activities. Because of the new strategy of the municipal service network and demographic changes in the city involving growing number of elderly people, the idea of developing self-services for elderly people was decided to be the focus area. After this decision, the director of elderly people's services was invited to join the project team. The project researcher proposed the use of a specific lead-user method. According to the empirical findings in private organizations, this method appears to generate better results than traditional methods where information on new product needs is collected from a random or typical group of customers (Lilien *et al.* 2002).

For this study, lead-users were identified together with a development expert of senior services and through a citizens' event organized by the city. Two basic characteristics of lead-users were required, that is, capability and motivation (Lüthje & Herstatt 2004, 556). Capability means that lead-users face new needs of the market and do so significantly earlier than the majority of the customers in market segment. Motivation means that lead-users profit strongly from innovations that provide a solution to new needs.

Five persons fulfilling these requirements were identified. They all were over 70 years. Two of them were men, and the rest were women. They all lived in Espoo. One of the participants had, for example, initiated a sport card which allowed persons 68 years or older to use freely public physical training services in Espoo. Three of the participants had started an association among seniors in a housing company. Through this association, new forms of services and cooperation were developed for instance with public libraries, public service centres and with a vocational school.

Since the scope of the development area was quite broad by definition, the group of lead-users made the final decision of the object of innovation activities. After the identification of potential objects of innovation, a web-based tool was used by the group to prioritize the final object of innovation activities, which was the community-based self-service centre for elderly people. The development process is described in the Appendix 1. It consisted of workshops and web-based working with lead-users, a workshop with service providers, workshops and meetings with city officials and with the elderly citizens' council, as well as an open workshop for all citizens in Espoo where the outcomes of the designed service model were evaluated. The invitation to the open workshop was published in the local newspaper and it was distributed *via* email to relevant stakeholders, *e.g.* residents' associations. In addition to participants of earlier development phases, only nine new local citizens participated in the forum.

The project researcher was responsible for facilitating the process and for modeling, as well as conceptualizing the results of workshops and meetings. In the first workshop, the participants prioritized the key need areas where they wanted to see new self-service solutions. These thematic areas were *older people living* and *creating new culture of facing ageing people in society*. In the second workshop, lead-users identified potential service solutions for the identified needs. The ideas for solutions were prioritized through a web survey. Prioritization helped to select one solution area to be developed in a service model. Through the prioritization made by the group, the idea of community-based self-service centre was selected to be further elaborated. In the third workshop, the researcher used the method of service conceptualization as a structuring tool for the creation of the service model. Firstly, the lead-users identified requirements for users of the self-service centre, as well as its organizing and management principles. Secondly, based on the identified requirements and principles, they developed a service concept of a community-based self-service centre.

The researcher introduced the results of the workshops to municipal officials who discussed conditions, restrictions and threats related to the implementation of the community-based self-service model. Moreover, the fourth workshop was organized between lead-users and the expert in charge of service development for elderly people in Espoo in order to evaluate the service prototype and to discuss the further steps in the process. The fifth workshop gathered the members of the lead-user group and representatives of external and internal service providers. The existing service model was presented and further developed in four groups which 1) specified existing requirements, 2) developed the existing service model, 3) identified relevant future trends in services for elderly people, and 4) generated ideas for potential new services.

All these results were presented by the researcher to the project team, to the management group of the city's elderly people services, and to the council of elderly citizens. Moreover, the outcomes were presented, discussed and evaluated in forum open for all citizens in Espoo. Finally, the project team evaluated the whole innovation process from the point of view of the city management in January 2013. After the research-facilitated project phase, the city has continued with the modeling of self-service centres. The establishment of self-service centres together with citizens and their associations was put forward as one of the new cross-sectoral development programs of the city. Resources will be allocated for the implementation of these centres in case they are accepted as a measure in the program.

In the discussions of the council of elderly citizens, the question of the re-distribution of tasks and responsibilities of the organization and production of welfare services turned out to be a politically contentious issue. Although the council is advisory, *i.e.* it does not have any formal decision-making powers, the discussion in the council turned into an ideological debate on the roles of the public sector and civil society. Questions were raised on the acceptability of the idea of increasing self-service and the transfer of responsibility for services from the city to users themselves. At the same time, under economic and demographic pressures, the city officials promoted community-based self-service centres as measures in one of the new cross-sectoral development programs of the city. Furthermore, during the innovation process, city managers indicated that all the ideas initiated through the lead-user group were more unexpected and innovative than the city organization itself could have been able to produce. Moreover, new service ideas and models coming from citizens' side gave support for city managers in their argumentation and negotiation within the city organization.

Table **2** summarizes the crucial aspects of the cases of Mikkeli and Espoo. It helps to see the differences and similarities in goals, procedures, results and impact of the application of different techniques of involving citizens into policy-making process.

Table 2: Cases of Mikkeli and Espoo compared

	Mikkeli: deliberative mini-public	Espoo: user-driven innovation
Goal	Engaging citizens to resolve a politicized issue on how people can participate in local democracy	Engaging lead-users to innovate a new type of *self-service* for themselves
Participants	Unintentionally, participants consisted mostly of those strongly affected (rural communities)	Intentionally gathered group of people fulfilling pre-existing selection criteria
Procedures	Discussion was largely dominated by the viewpoints from rural communities	Primarily facilitated workshops amongst lead-users, and meetings of city officials, service providers, representatives of elderly people, and citizens
Result of the forum	Policy recommendation emphasizing the need for stronger neighborhood councils	A service model of a community-based self-service centre for elderly people enabling their living at own homes
Uptake	Established after the forum; some of the forum's suggestions will be implemented when re-defining the role of neighborhood councils The forum was an asset for the city in the negotiations on further municipal amalgamations.	Further modeling of the self-service centre Implementation of the service model might happen as a measure of the new cross-sectoral development program of the city

DISCUSSION AND CONCLUSION

Deliberative mini-publics as democratic innovations are based on such democratic principles as inclusion and they could, in principle, be used in the resolution of any politicized issue. Mini-publics have rather standardized procedures involving interaction with experts and stakeholders and moderated small group discussions. From the point of view of service users, user-driven innovations can be used in the public sector to overcome the complexities caused by the traditional sector specific administration. The variety of working methods in user-driven innovation is evident. Furthermore, the agenda of user-driven approaches is more restricted to specific services aimed at particular user groups. Unlike democratic innovations, which aim to be inclusive, user-driven innovations typically aim to involve a particular group of users. However, both methods open up new opportunities for citizens to participate in policy-making.

Both techniques applied in this project were conducive to the development of new ideas on how to improve practices of policy-making or service delivery. Moreover, some of the concrete suggestions gained through these techniques led to incremental changes in these practices. Based on Hartley's categorization of public innovations, the case of Mikkeli represented governance innovation as it entailed citizen engagement in the development of democratic institutions. The case of Espoo was primarily intended as service innovation because the aim was to develop new forms of service provision, and position innovation as it laid out new contexts of service delivery for elderly people.

In addition, the city of Mikkeli was able to use the deliberative citizen forum as a means to *defuse* concerns on neighborhood democracy in the negotiations on further municipal amalgamations. The experiment carried out in Espoo seems to lead to the implementation of a new service model as a part of the city's new development program. At the same time, strong engagement by users politicized the debate on public services and created conditions for political agenda setting. In this respect, this user-driven approach exceeded expectations associated with it.

In both cases, participants involved did not form a representative group of all citizens, although in Mikkeli, this was unintended. However, these non-inclusive formats proved to be quite fruitful in terms of their capacity to create new ideas. Despite the differences in the techniques used in public innovation processes, both of them offered citizens new roles and opportunities to influence policies and their implementation. Our case studies show that the impact of citizen involvement does not necessarily so much depend on the type of instrument used in involving citizens. Rather, openness and receptiveness by policy-makers appear to be more important than the intentions behind the used techniques.

The chapter concludes that both instruments of citizen involvement have their advantages and disadvantages. While user-driven techniques challenge such core values of the public sector as equality and inclusion, users' engagement can politicize debates on public services. If new instruments of citizen engagement were to be used to actually empower citizens, more attention should be paid to inclusion or, alternatively, to the interaction between non-inclusive and inclusive forms of citizen participation. Indeed, our case studies seem to suggest that there may sometimes be trade-offs between the goals of inclusion and innovation capacity.

ACKNOWLEDGEMENTS

Tekes – the Finnish Funding Agency for Innovation, The Finnish Innovation Fund Sitra, the city of Espoo and the city of Mikkeli, provided support for this research. We also would like to thank those citizens of Espoo and Mikkeli who participated in the research project on a voluntary basis.

CONFLICT OF INTEREST

The authors confirm that this chapter contents have no conflict of interest.

REFERENCES

Andersen, V. N. & Hansen, K.M. (2007). How deliberation makes better citizens: The Danish Deliberative Poll on the euro. In *European Journal of Political Research*, 46:4, 531-556.

Arnstein, S. (1969). A ladder of citizen participation. In *Journal of the American Planning Association* 45:2, 180-189.

Baiocchi, G. (2005). *Militants and Citizens. The Politics of Participatory Budgeting in Porto Alegre.* Stanford: Stanford University Press.

Barber, B. (1984). *Strong Democracy. Participatory Politics for a New Age.* Berkeley: University of California Press.

Beck Jørgensen, T. & Melander, P. (1999). *Livet i offentlige organisationer: Institutionsdrift i spændingsfeltet mellem stat, profession og marked.* København: Djøf / Jurist- og Økonomforbundet.

Borins, S. (2001). Encouraging innovation in the public sector. In *Journal of Intellectual Capital*, 2, 310-319.

Brown, M. (2006). Survey Article: Citizen panels and the concept of representation. In *The Journal of Political Philosophy,* 14:2, 203-225.

Dahl, R. S. (1989). *Democracy and its Critics.* New Haven and London: Yale University Press.

Denhardt, R. B. & Denhardt, J. V. (2000). The new public service: Serving rather than steering. In *Public Administration Review*, 60:6, 549-559.

Fishkin, J. S. (2003). Consulting the public through deliberative polling. In *Journal of Policy Analysis and Management*, 22, 128-133.

Fishkin, J. S.; He, Baogang; Luskin, R.C. & Siu, A. (2010). Deliberative democracy in an unlikely place: Deliberative polling in China. In *British Journal of Political Science* 40:1, 435–448.

Fung, A. (2003). Survey Article: Recipes for public spheres: Eight institutional design choices and their consequences. In *The Journal of Political Philosophy*, 11:3, 338-367.

Goodin, R.E. (2008). *Innovating Democracy. Democratic Theory and Practice After the Deliberative Turn.* Oxford: Oxford University Press.

Goodin, R.E. & Dryzek, J.S. (2006). Deliberative impacts: The macro-political uptake of mini-publics. In *Politics and Society*, 34, 219-244.

Grönlund, K.; Bächtiger, A. & Setälä, M. (eds.) (2014). *Deliberative Mini-Publics.* Colchester: ECPR Press, in print.

Hartley, J. (2005). Innovation in governance and public service: Past and present. In *Public Money & Management,* 25, 27-34.

Hartley, J. (2006). *Innovation and its Contribution to Improvement. A Review for Policy-makers, Policy Advisers, mangers and Researchers*. Department for Communities and Local Government, Warwick Business School, London.

Hendriks, C. (2006). When the forum meets interest politics: Strategic uses of public deliberation. In *Politics and Society*, 34:4, 571-602.

Hendriks, C. (2009). The democratic soup. Mixed meanings of political representation in governance networks. In *Governance*, 22:4, 689-715.

Jæger, B. (2011). *User-Driven Innovation in the Public Service Delivery.* Working paper No: 4/2011. CLIPS – Collaborative innovation in the Public Sector. Roskilde University.

Jäppinen, T. (2011). New User-driven Innovation Policy: The Key to Finnish Local Government Service Reform. In Anttiroiko, A.-V.; Bailey, S.J. & Valkama, P. (eds.), *Innovation and the Public Sector, Innovations in Public Governance*. Vol. 15, (pp. 158-173). Amsterdam: IOS Press BV.

Karpowitz, C.F.; Raphael, C. & Hammond, A.S. (2009). Deliberative democracy and inequality two cheers for enclave deliberation among the Disempowered. In *Politics & Society* 37, 576-615.

Kim, J. & Wilemon, D. (2002). Focusing the fuzzy front-end in new product development. In *R&D Management*, 32:4, 269–279.

Lilien, G.L.; Morrison, P.D.; Searls, K.; Sonnack, M. & von Hippel, E. (2002). Performance assessment of the lead user idea generation process for new product development. In *Management Science*, 48:8, 1042-1059.

Lovio, R. & Kivisaari, S. (2010). *Julkisen sektorin innovaatiot ja innovaatiotoiminta. Katsaus kansainväliseen kirjallisuuteen.* (Public sector innovations and innovation activies. Review of international literature). VTT Research notes 2540.

Lüthje, C. & Herstatt, C. (2004). The Lead User method: an outline of empirical findings and issues for future research. In *R&D Management* 34:5, 553-568.

Miettinen, R. (2008). *Rhetoric and practice in innovation policy*. Lessons from Finland. Unpublished manuscript 12.11.2008.

Niinikoski, M.-L. & Kuhlmann, S. (2014). In discursive negotiation: Knowledge and the formation of Finnish innovation policy. In *Science and Public Policy,* doi: 10.1093/scipol/scu003.

Pantzar, M. (1996). *Kuinka teknologia kesytetään – kulutuksen tieteestä kulutuksen taiteeseen.* (How to tame technology – from the science of consumption to the art of consumption). Helsinki: Otava.

Parkinson, J. (2004). Why Deliberate? The encounter between deliberation and new public managers. In *Public Administration* 82:2, 377-395.

Rosted, J. (2005). *User-driven innovation. Results and recommendations. The Ministry of Economics and Business Affairs' Division for Research and Analysis*. Copenhagen: FORA.

Setälä, M. (2011). The role of deliberative mini-publics in democratic systems. Lessons from the experience of referendums. In *Representation*, 47:2, 201-213.

Shove, E. & Pantzar, M. (2005). Consumers, producers and practices: understanding the invention and reinvention of Nordic Walking. In *Journal of Consumer Culture,* 5, 43-64.

Smith, G. (2009). *Democratic Innovations. Designing Institutions for Citizen Participation.* Cambridge: Cambridge University Press.

Sørensen, E. & Torfing, J. (2011). Enhancing collaborative innovation in the public sector. In *Administration & Society*, XX(X), 1–28.

van Rijswijk, M.; Kleijn, M.; Janson, M. & Menten, E. (2008). The process and experiences with creating user-driven innovation programmes in the Netherlands. In *Technology Analysis & Strategic Management* 20:3, 309–320.

von Hippel, E. (2001). Innovation by user communities: Learning from open source software. In *Sloan Management Review* (July).

von Hippel, E. (2002). *Horizontal innovation networks – by and for users.* In MIT Sloan School of Management Working Paper. No. 4366-02

von Hippel, E. (2005a). *Democratizing Innovation.* London: MIT Press.

von Hippel, E. (2005b). The best way to innovate? Let lead users do it for you. In *IncMagazine*, September.

von Hippel, E. (2005c). Open source software projects as user innovation networks - no manufacturer required. In Feller, J.; Fitzgerald, B., Hissam, S. & Lakhani, K. (eds.) *Perspectives on Free and Open Source Software.* London: MIT Press.

von Hippel, E. & von Krogh, G. (2003). Open source software and the private-collectiv innovation model: Issues for organization science. In *Organization Science*, 14:2, 208-223.

Warren, M.E. & Pearse, Hilary (2008). *Designing Deliberative Democracy. The British Columbia Citizens' Assembly.* Cambridge: Cambridge University Press

APPENDIX 1

Innovation process in the city of Espoo

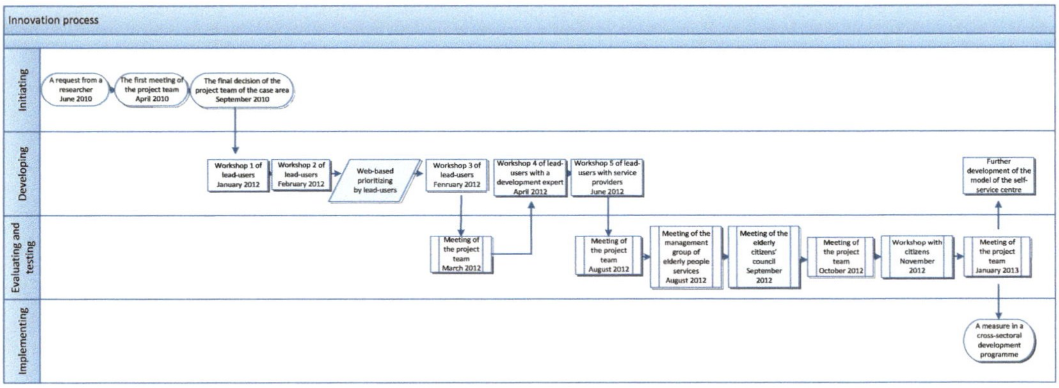

CHAPTER 3

Perspectives on User-Driven Innovation in Public Sector Services

Luise Li Langergaard*

The Department of Psychology and Educational Studies, Roskilde University, Denmark

Abstract: The chapter presents and discusses how we can conceptualize user involvement in the public sector, as well as users, in very different ways: As consumers, co-producers, lead users or citizens. One important question which is subsequently discussed, is what such different conceptualizations imply for citizenship understood in more traditional terms, *i.e.* defined by political deliberation and rights. This question is important because conceptualizations of users imply certain ideas about the public sector, state and society, which have political implications as well as implications for our understanding of citizenship. Thus, we need to be aware of what different perspectives of user involvement imply for citizenship and collaborative innovation in the public sector. The chapter is based on a literature study and uses an empirical case as an example to illustrate and discuss differences in democratic implications of different user conceptions. The chapter concludes that we need an increased awareness of how to work with the different user conceptions in collaborative innovation practices, and argues that is important to also include the concept of the welfare state citizen with rights, as none of the other user conceptions are explicit about rights.

Keywords: Citizenship, citizen-consumer, client, collaborative innovation, co-producer, democracy, lead user, participation, rights, welfare state.

INTRODUCTION

Collaborative innovation is characterized by encounters between different actors coming together and developing new ideas, solutions and practices. In these encounters, service users or citizens are important sources of ideas and solutions (Sørensen and Torfing, 2011; 11-28). Recently, users are involved not only in service design but increasingly also in policy innovation (Agger and Lund, 2011; 186). The ways 'users' of public sector services are conceptualized are, however, multiple and diverse. In recent years, we have seen an explosion in terms of denominating users of public sector services, such as customers, clients,

***Corresponding author Luise Li Langergaard:** The Department of Psychology and Educational Studies, Roskilde University, Denmark; Tel: +45 26846748; E-mail: luise@langergaard.dk

Annika Agger, Bodil Damgaard, Andreas Hagedorn Krogh and Eva Sørensen (Eds.)

stakeholders, users, co-producers and lead users, that live side by side. This chapter compares and discusses different ideas of users that can be involved in public sector innovation. One important question, which is subsequently discussed, is what such different conceptualizations imply for citizenship understood in more traditional terms, *i.e.* defined by political deliberation and rights. Four different user conceptions are systematized and discussed in connection to citizenship: The welfare state citizen, the citizen-consumer, the co-producer and the lead user. These conceptions are selected because they are the ones most frequently encountered in research and policy debates on public sector innovation.

The user conceptions rest on different normative, ontological and philosophical assumptions. Thus, it is not always clear what is exactly meant by user-driven innovation and what it implies for the status of public sector citizens when they become users. In collaborative innovation practices the user may in principle take on different roles dependent on the specific context, innovation project and the rationales about involvement that influence the process. This chapter shows how the different conceptions tend to focus on some aspects of the user while they seem to exclude others. In particular, most of the user conceptions deal poorly with citizen rights which are, however, very central to public authorities and their relationship with citizens. Thus, it is important to be aware of the differences between the user conceptions in order to make more deliberate choices with regard to involvement.

This chapter is based on a literature study of different user conceptions and their application to a case example. I shall elucidate the differences by applying an empirical example across the different user conceptions and show how the role of the citizen vary with the different perspectives. The hope is that the use of a through-going example will help elucidate the differences between the user conceptions. The focus is on the democratic implications of different user conceptions and their implications for citizen rights rather than on their implications for innovation processes and barriers. Common to three of the different user conceptions is that they represent a break with the welfare state client, who is most often seen as merely a passive recipient of public services delivered by a bureaucracy (Hartley, 2005; 29). An answer to critiques of bureaucracy has been to represent the recipients of services as *active users* (Eriksen, 1993; 141). The critique of bureaucracy and clientization seems to stand unquestioned, meaning that the traditional welfare state citizen is most often not thought of as a user at all (Agger and Lund, 2011; Hartley, 2005). However, the client is also a citizen, who is defined by rights and thus important to consider alongside other user conceptions. Welfare state critiques are often part of broader agendas for the reorganisation of the entire public sector. In this sense, the definitions of user roles are highly ideological and connect to certain ideals about public sector governance and the role of citizens and state. However, if collaborative innovation should lead to a public sector which works better as a *public sector* and deals with public needs and interests, then we need to also include citizen rights in our conception of citizens as users. Otherwise, we risk excluding the possibility of public authorities working collaboratively without undermining their core tasks and responsibilities (see Langergaard and Carstensen, 2014).

The Case – The Department of Social Services of Copenhagen

The empirical case deployed in this chapter is based on a project on user involvement carried out at the the Department of Social Services of the Municipality of Copenhagen. Based on interviews with participants of this project and a document analysis of internal documents relating to the project, I have gained insight into the user-involvement process that had the aim to identify solutions to some problems of an organization in the Municipality. The description here is based on a one hour interview with Marie-Louise Henningsen who were responsible for the innovation project. Furthermore, I have had insight into internal documents from the project and had additional information from Helle Vibeke Carstensen.

The case regards the work with user involvement in a local authority unit dealing with people with disabilities. In March 2013, a group of parents of children with disabilities went public in a Danish newspaper with a complaint to the mayor about their experiences with the authority unit dealing with their children's cases, The Handicap Center (Handicapcenter København). They complained about slow case handling procedures, errors in case handling, complicated documentation requirements and lack of proper explanations of the rulings in their cases. They argued that these conditions were a threat to their right to due process. They said that the burden of handling the contact with the authority lay on them, and that the amount of energy used to see through the system and raising questions and complaints had led to parents losing their jobs and suffering from chronic stress (politiken.dk, 29.03.2013). Based on this critique, the Department of Social Services initiated a project with the aim of finding solutions to some of the problems raised by the parents.

The Department of Social Services had run a process involving 6 parents. They were inspired by the so-called Service Journey method, using interviews to map the steps in the journey of contacts between the parents and the department. The service journey helped create a timeline of the course of events in the cases and the contacts with the handicap center, based on the stories told by the parents. The parents were encouraged to retrieve letters, emails and other correspondence to help them remember the details in their case history. The interviews covered the course of events, "moments of truths" (the moments that had most importance to the parents), the interfaces with different authorities, channels of contact (telephone, mail, personal meeting) and the moments that had emotional effects of the parents. The aim was to find out which episodes were crucial to the parents' experiences with the Handicap Center. Furthermore, the aim was to elucidate the interface with other authorities in order to clarify which other actors might be involved in order to improve services. In June 2013, a parents' committee was established by the Municipality with the purpose of involving parents together with the Handicap center in finding solutions to improve the administration through the arrangement of workshops. This had not yet been carried through at the time of my interviews with the employees in the Department of Social Services.

The case is used to show differences in the perspectives of user conceptions and shall be related to each user conception as an example. The idea is to look at the case from each user perspective, to show how they pave the way for different possibilities in the case and also to elucidate their blind spots and limitations. Thus, the case is also used to reflect upon how things could have been approached if other perspectives had been taken.

Structure of the Chapter

The chapter begins with a brief overview of the diversity in public sector user-involvement approaches. I then move on to the four different user conceptions and present them one by one. The first user-role to be presented is the idea of the welfare state citizen with rights. This is the role that has been severely criticized for leading to passivity and clientization. Second, the citizen-consumer is presented, as this conception emerged with NPM and the critique of welfare state paternalism. Third, the idea of the co-producer which is often, but not always, connected to Network Governance (NG) is presented. Fourth, the lead user is presented. The lead user does not connect to any particular model of public governance, but is a user concept which have been adopted from private sector innovation theory (von Hippel, 2005) into a public sector context. After presenting the different user conceptions, I relate them all to the case. Lastly, I discuss what the different user conceptions imply for citizen rights.

THE DIVERSITY OF USER INVOLVEMENT APPROACHES

Phenomena such as 'user involvement' and 'citizen participation' have existed prior to ideas of user-driven innovation and collaborative innovation. The history and literature on user involvement in public services are often divided into a consumerist and a democratic strand (Beresford, 2002; 96). The drive for a user mandate comes from both of these traditions (McLaughlin, 2009; 6), and they represent a break with the welfare state client. However, they express very different philosophical and ideological assumptions (Beresford, 2002; 96). The democratic approach which emphasises a clearer role in decision making perceives the public as *citizens* (Bartlett and Dibben, 2002; 45-46). It is concerned with people having a say in the agencies, institutions and organisations that have an impact on their lives (Beresford, 2002; 97). The concern of the democratic user approach is that the role of client represents an objectification of the social work relationship, where the client is someone in need of help, and the professional social worker is to identify the needs of the passive client (McLaughlin, 2009; 3). In the rest of this chapter, I shall focus on the development following from the consumerist approach, as this approach has had the major influence on idea of public sector innovation.

The consumerist approach is part of a broader development of public governance paradigms and has been very influential in relation to New Public Management (NPM) reforms which emphasise managerialism and choice in the social services provision (Bartlett and Dibben, 2002; 96). Hartley (2005) demonstrates how different ideas about public sector users are framed within broader public governance paradigms (Hartley, 2005). Following critiques of the traditional bureaucratic public administration paradigm (PA), NPM has introduced the idea of a citizen-consumer making active choices. This also represents a service oriented view on the public sector. From this perspective, the role of users and customers is mainly to contribute to service innovation in the public sector (Agger and Lund, 2011; 180). However, with the NG paradigm that challenges certain elements of NPM, we also see new user conceptions challenging the consumerist approach to citizenship (Hartley, 2005; Langergaard, 2011b). With the emergence of the co-producer users are contributing to both service innovation and policy innovation (Agger and Lund, 2011; 180). As mentioned, the conception of the citizen as a user is a break with the passive welfare state client. It is, however, also a break with the strong emphasis on equality, due process and procedural justice in the relationship between the public sector and citizens. Public administration has been criticized for being inefficient, economically complacent, obsessed with due process, and indifferent to client needs (Peters and Pierre, 1998; 228-9). Both NPM and NG pose 'post-bureaucratic' alternatives to the organisational structures and values of bureaucracy (Langergaard, 2011a).

Collaborative innovation is not necessarily connected to just one specific idea of the user or to the rationales of a particular public governance paradigm, even though we often see it linked to NG (*e.g.* Vigoda, 2002). Inter-organizational partnerships in public, private and voluntary sectors, as well as across them, is part of both NPM (Pollitt, 2000; 184) and NG. Thus, we may become more aware of the democratic implications of different user conceptions in collaborative innovation processes by elucidating the differences between these conceptions and by clarifying how each of them connect to citizenship in different ways.

Citizenship and Users

Often, citizenship theory is divided into two different political philosophical strands: a republican and a liberal strand. Each of these emphasize different aspects of the citizen and her relationship to the state or public sector. While the liberal tradition emphasises citizen *rights* (*e.g.* Marshall, 2003), the republican tradition emphasises political citizenship defined in terms of *political participation*. Republican ideas emphasise *positive liberties of citizens* and the practices of self-determination on the part of enfranchised citizens who are oriented toward the common good and understand themselves as free and equal members of a cooperative, self-governing community. In variance with the liberal tradition, it does not emphasise rights or negative liberties to secure the individual from interference from the state (Habermas, 1996; 268). Pettit formulates an idea of republican freedom in terms of non-domination from arbitrary interference from others (Pettit, 1998; 84). Central is the ethical life context of a polis in which the virtue of active participation in public affairs can develop and stabilise. According to republicans, it is through this civic practice that human beings are able to realise the *telos* of their species (Habermas, 1996; 268), and thus political activity has a prominent status. The citizen can also be defined in terms of duties or virtue. Rights are not merely entitlements to take part in political decision-making, but are also connected to duties to be oriented toward the common good (see also Langergaard, 2011a). In newer liberal notions of citizenship, we also find this notion of citizen virtues and of public reasonableness and deliberation (Forst, 2001; Kymlicka and Norman, 1994; 366). Yet, the idea of active citizenship beyond mere passive entitlements is gaining ground in the liberal tradition as well. The idea of public reasonableness and willingness to engage in public discussion with public reasons beyond self-interest and preferences is thus central to citizenship (Kymlicka, 2002; 289).

In the following, I shall analyze how different user conceptions relate to different dimensions of citizenship. Lastly, I shall use the case example to illustrate how the different perspectives each open specific possibilities for involvement and innovation.

WELFARE STATE CITIZEN

Until the 1980s, the role of the citizen in public administration theory was close to the conception on the citizen of the liberal democracy strand, where citizens express their political views through voting and participation in public debate (Agger and Lund, 2011; 182). Thus, from this perspective, the democratic influence of the citizen on the public sector goes through traditional parliamentary channels of liberal democracy. Administration is based on a legal-bureaucratic model, where precise and uniform rules regulate the way the administration deals with citizens. The rules are considered legitimate because citizens, on account of their knowledge of the rules, are able to predict the outcome of their dealing with the state (Rothstein, 1998; 108). Furthermore, public interest, as expressed through parliamentary representative democracy, is to ensure the legitimacy and accountability of decisions about public sector services. From this perspective, direct user involvement potentially poses a democratic problem because particular and private interests risk overruling political decision making processes.

The conception of a citizen with rights, as mentioned, means that equal treatment and due process are central values. The services offered by the public sector are to support equal opportunities among citizens in line with the welfare paradigm, which introduced a new category of basic social rights constituting the basis of claims to a more just distribution of social wealth (Habermas, 1996). We can specify this citizen role with T.H. Marshall's definition of citizenship based on three sets of citizen rights, that are to ensure that citizens become able to participate as full members of society: civil, political and social rights (Kymlicka and Norman, 1994; 354). Civil rights are those necessary for individual freedom, *i.e.* personal freedom, freedom of speech, opinion and religion, the right to property, to make contracts, and the right to fair trial. Political rights are rights to political influence, either as member of an agency with political authority or by electing members of such an agency. Social rights are considered to constitute the core of the welfare state (Esping-Andersen, 1990, p. 21; Cox, 1998, p.4), and are thus constitutive for the relationship between the public sector and citizens. They give the individual the right to a decent economic welfare and security and to live a civilised life in correspondence with the standards of a given society (Marshall, 2003; 53-54). Especially social rights may be understood in a compensatory sense, as they are meant to ensure a more equal distribution of *actual freedom,* not merely of negative rights (Habermas, 1996, p. 402-3). However, we may also view social and economic rights from a more universal perspective of justice and as basic human rights that all people are entitled to (Sen, 2004) and thus as a more fundamental normative obligation of states.

Thus, user-driven innovation, or just innovation, is usually not linked to bureaucracy, which is most often seen as antithetic to innovation (*e.g.* Osborne and Gaebler, 1993; Aucoin, 2008; 293; Burns and Stalker, 1994; Thompson, 1965; 1) with its rule bound and hierarchic decision making structure. But if we take a broader (more open) look at innovation, changes occur also in the bureaucratic public sector, rarely, however, with direct involvement of citizens as users. Changes within the bureaucratic paradigm are initiated at the policy level and rely on the idea of representative democracy which connects political decisions to citizens' political will. If we think of innovation as improvements, such changes could lead to better, in the sense of more procedurally just, practices or to services that strengthen the social and civil rights of citizens in certain ways. Thus, procedural and service innovation may be possible in a bureaucratic system.

CITIZEN-CONSUMER

Much has been written about the citizen-customer or citizen-consumer. The conception is linked to NPM, which is a neo-liberal and market based governance paradigm. However, It is important to mention that NPM is not just one uniform set of ideas, and that the reforms that have been carried out inspired by the ideas of NMP have been very diverse (see for example Pollitt and Bouckeart, 2004; 62). Theoretically, NPM conceptualises the public sector as a service provider that should accommodate personal preferences and needs of an individualised and rational population. NPM focuses explicitly on the efficient and effective operation of the organisation and correspondingly less on the political level or on the political character of the tasks of government agencies. Public organisations should meet the imperatives of customer service orientation and efficiency (Christensen and Lægreid, 2002; Pollitt, 2000).

This has also implications for the view on citizenship and democracy connected to NPM. In short, citizens are seen as a collection of customers with a commercial rather than a political relationship to the government and the public administration (Olsen, 2002). In this 'customer-driven approach the public interest is defined by a series of "bottom-up" processes that permit each agency and its clients to determine the content of public policy' (Christensen and Lægreid, 2002; 280). The democratic implications of this neo-liberal market based model is that it challenges the sovereign state model of governance where processes of representative democracy determine public interest, as well as the institutional state model with its emphasis on the rule of law and legal principles. Popular sovereignty is redefined from a collective, citizenship focus to an individual, consumer focus (Christensen and Lægreid, 2002) and collective consumption of public services becomes invisible (cf. Clarke, 2004; 39).

User-centred approaches from this perspective emphasise *choice* and link to attempts to *personalise services*. When citizens are conceptualised as customers they are given a chance to 'vote with their feet' by changing providers if they are not satisfied. Customer needs are thought to be personal or private, as something that 'exists out there', rather than as something negotiated or contextual (Brand, 2005). This means that the needs and preferences that the public sector faces are conceived of as pre-political. This is in contrast to republican models of democracy where public interest is a result of deliberation of citizens in the political public sphere.

Within this framework, innovation takes place mainly at the organisational level, where the citizen is involved as a customer. This may be *via* market research methods, such as surveys. Such methods lead to a representation of aggregated preferences of individual citizens. However, citizens may, in principle, also be invited to express their views and preferences with regard to public service provision in other ways. The aims of innovation are often said to be: efficiency, effectiveness and responsiveness (*e.g.* Albury, 2005; Damanpour and Schneider, 2008; King and Martinelli 2005; Moore, 2005; Mulgan and Albury, 2003). Thus, this perspective seems to deal mostly with service innovation and process innovation.

CO-PRODUCERS

The conception of co-producer is currently prominent in both public and private sector innovation research. The idea of co-production in service research emphasises genuine cooperation and the inseparability of service production and consumption and the co-production with the customer (Gustafsson & Johnson, 2003; 4-5; Howells, 2007). According to service researchers, the production of services demands a direct contact between the supplier and the consumer (Sundbo, 1998; 8-10).

In a public sector context, the term co-production goes back to Elinor Ostrom who in the 1970s argued that the production of services was difficult without the active participation of the people receiving the services (Pestoff, 2012; 16). Today, co-production is often linked with NG and the notion of innovation taking place in networks and collaborations between public, private and voluntary sector actors (Hartley, 2005; Agger and Lund, 2011). Rather than providing services, it is seen as a prime responsibility for governments and public administration to define strategic goals that can enhance partnerships and the empowerment of citizens (Vigoda, 2002). In relation to co-production, several partners, such as individual citizens, groups of citizens, communities and public service agents, may take part in innovation processes (Pestoff, 2012; 15). The co-producer is not necessarily an individual citizen or a particular public service provider. Service users and other members of the community may make significant resource contributions. There is often an emphasis on long term partnerships rather than time limited interactions and ad hoc encounters. Furthermore, co-production is not delimited to the main beneficiaries themselves, but may also include participation of family members, partners and loved ones if circumstances warrant it (Pestoff, 2012; 16-22).

The changed role of government and public administration also has implications for democracy. Some claim that NG does not support the idea of a pre-political universal common good (cf. Sørensen, 2002; 710). Decision making and political action are understood in relation to particular fields of politics, taking place between formal and informal organisations and within a given locality. The idea of a sovereign will of the people, carried by political parties, is replaced by a network based negotiation politics. Kristensen (1999) mentions the risk of democracy becoming parted between a 'little democracy', concerned with local problem solution, and a 'large democracy', concerned with the general political and economic frameworks for concrete problem-solving procedures (Kristensen, 1999; 4; Langergaard, 2011a). However, some authors also stress that active engagement of citizens in co-production is said to imply an orientation toward a common good beyond the individual and independent selves of citizens (King and Martinelli, 2005; 2). This idea of the user as a co-producer is very different from the co-producer of service marketing, who is basically a consumer who has become a producer. Preferences are not given but are created in the dialogue and interaction between citizens. According to Agger and Lund, the idea of the co-producer is rooted in republican democracy theories stressing belonging to a community and active contribution to the realisation of the good community as an important aspect of being a citizen. The citizen is collectively oriented and socialized into democratic participation (Agger and Lund, 2011; 185).

Innovation processes do not necessarily have their locus in the single public organisation. With the diversity of actors being potential co-producers, the scope of possible innovations coming from co-production is also wide: spanning from service innovation, over policy innovation, to governance innovation in terms of new involvement models. With the decreasing focus on the organisation as the locus of innovation, there is correspondingly less focus on process innovation.

LEAD USERS

The concept of the lead user was originally developed in relation to commercial innovation practices and has later been adopted into the vocabulary of public sector innovation. The lead user concept is particularly known from Eric von Hippel's work, where lead users develop products or services on their own initiative and are on the leading edge of important trends in the marketplace (Von Hippel, 2005; 22). Private companies can benefit from harnessing the ideas and products developed by lead users and commercialising them. The introduction of the concept into the public sector thus reflects an adoption of an originally commercial idea of innovation.

We find only few descriptions or research literature on lead-user innovation in the public sector, and we cannot connect the lead user to any particular idea of public governance, like we can with for example the citizen-consumer. A direct adoption of the term into a public sector context may pose certain challenges, as the public sector is a political and not a commercial context and, as a starting point, the lead user is a non-political concept. However, the more precise implications of working with a concept of a lead user in concrete public sector innovation practices depend entirely on how the concept is interpreted within the specific context.

In relation to the public sector, the lead user appears for example in a discussion paper on political administration developed in Denmark in 2012, where lead users are described as citizens with strong resources who can contribute to a development of welfare service that can benefit all citizens (forvaltningspolitik.dk; 21). Other approaches focus on the role of lead users in development of assistive technology to improve the independence and life quality of people with disabilities (Voxted and Christensen, 2012; 111-3). Here, people with disabilities or their relatives are invited to participate as active idea generators in the processes, which are, however, initiated by the organisation working to develop solutions for people with disabilities. The users are said to be lead users because their knowledge and needs form the basis for innovations, rather than because they actually *lead* the process (Voxted and Christensen, 2012; 111-3). The close cooperation between the public and private organisations in the case makes the example difficult to distinguish from co-production. This is also the case when lead users are seen not as individuals but as whole user communities, as in De Cindio *et al.,* study of community networks in development of online public services (De Cindio *et al.*, 2007).

If lead users are 'real' lead users, in the sense that they develop solutions to their own needs independently of the public or private sector's service offers, the challenge for the public sector is to identify the solution that should be adopted. Then the role of the public sector becomes to identify and implement solutions developed outside of the public sector. The solutions that should be adopted should meet needs that many citizen have and thus there is an issue of generalising the solutions. Furthermore, the challenge is to implement the solutions in ways that correspond with the laws and rules of the respective service area. The lead user in the public sector context seems to differ conceptually from the lead user of private sector innovation theory. Within the commercial framework, the lead user is a consumer, but with different traits than the 'traditional' consumer role. The lead user differs from the traditional concept of the consumer, which implicitly suggests that users are not active in product development (von Hippel, 2005; 18). Lead users are on the leading edge with regards to finding solutions, and the solutions are thought to also be relevant to other users. If we translate this from a market context into the public sector, the lead user may still be characterised by creativity, idea generation and development of solutions. In the public sector, the challenge is to find the ideas and solutions that will actually be helpful to other users or citizens (this is of course also important to a private company that wants to put a product or service into production). Thus, the problem of representativeness is relevant here. Whereas the democratic user involvement approach emphasises participation and voice rather than representativeness, the lead user concept is not imbued with such democratic underpinnings.

In principle, lead users develop services or products for themselves in order to fulfill needs that are not currently fulfilled by the products or services available. In this sense, lead user innovation is first and foremost service or product innovation. They may also be new IT-solutions or new ways of using devices. When adopted by public organizations or authorities, these user-developed solutions may also lead to other types of innovation, such as process innovation, if the new service leads to new procedures. Lead user innovation may also be seen as a type of governance innovation, which involves user in new ways.

CASE DISCUSSION

On the basis of the presentations of the different user conceptions I shall now apply them to the case in order to elucidate the practical implications of the differences of the perspectives.

If we are to illustrate the role of the welfare state citizen by the use of the case example, the citizen is the child with the disability. This child has certain rights to social services that have the aim of giving the child equal opportunities with other children as far as possible. The mayor responsible for social services in Copenhagen has argued that it is important to follow the laws in the area, and that bureaucratic procedures cannot be abandoned (politiken.dk, 29.03.2013). The bureaucratic procedures have the aim of supporting due process and protection of citizen rights – in this case the social rights of the child with disabilities. Thus, improving these procedures to actually make rulings in accordance with the law could be considered an improvement and an administrative or service innovation.

The initiative of the Department of Social Services aims to improve the services and in particular the parents' experience of the Handicap Center. In this sense, the parents appear as proxy for the child. The parents are the ones who encounter the authority and receive the service that they bring on to the child. The interviews with the parents revealed that on the one hand, the parents felt they were being treated as a mere case, with no regard for their feelings, and on the other hand that they wondered about the criteria of assessment and the role of the individual case worker. They knew of other parents of children with the same diagnosis as their child who have been granted types of support that they have been refused. This shows that the experience of good service relies on a fine balance between being seen as a specific case and at the same time receiving the same services as others in similar situations. Due to this emphasis on equal treatment it seems that upholding, but at the same time improving, bureaucratic procedures is crucial to improving the service experience, but, more importantly, to ensure due process. In this sense, process innovation, we may call it administrative or bureaucracy innovation, is closely interconnected with service innovation.

If instead, we see the case from the perspective of the citizen-consumer, we may consider the child with disabilities as a consumer. But, even if the children themselves may be consumers of the services, they are not customers in the sense that they make the choices about which services to buy – and they are not the ones who encounter the Handicap Center to exchange the services. In this sense it is the parents, rather than the child, that are customers. From the perspective of the authorities, service orientation and efficiency are important, and the approaches to involving the parents are inspired by generic service development methods such as the Service Journey. The aim of involving the parents is for the organisation to measure customer experiences of services and ask about customer feelings in order to improve services. This method approaches the user/citizen as an individual with subjective and particular feelings that authorities can learn about in order to better fulfil the preferences of the users. The citizen-consumer is also seen as an individual with subjective feelings and preferences. Thus, if we take on a consumer perspective, the users are expected to be concerned with how the services correspond to their preferences and how they match the funding from taxes allocated to the public authority, rather than with the fulfilment of basic rights of citizens as in the welfare state citizen perspective.

From a co-production perspective, the involved parties are, in contrast to the citizen-consumer, expected to aim for solutions oriented towards a greater common good – such as better conditions and life quality for people with disabilities or more equality for all citizens. As co-producers, parties involved in service innovation could be parents, the children or the public authorities. Family members, and not only the main beneficiaries, can be seen as users. The aim of mapping the interfaces with other authorities indicates that the Department of Social Services thinks in terms of partnerships with several actors, rather than the relation between the families and the Handicap Center as a bi-directional relation. The focus is on the interface and interplay between the different authorities involved in the relation between the families and Department of Social Services. The parents' committee opens up a space for the parents to participate collectively and not only individually. This may be one way to ensure more equal power relations in the interaction with the Handicap Center. The parents expressed that they had felt severe distress, had felt their right to due process violated, and had felt disempowered and distressed. By participating collectively as a group they may feel that they stand stronger in their relation with the authority. The parents that were part of the committee expressed a strong interest in finding solutions that were also beneficial to other families with the same circumstances as themselves, rather than only to themselves. Thus, they were not only taking their own subjective perspective in the work but instead took on a more general perspective. This shows an orientation towards the greater good, rather than a merely individualist, or self-interested perspective. As the employees will also be involved as co-producers, the chances of finding solutions may be improved as those working with the cases on an everyday basis have unique knowledge about the case procedures just like the parents. In this sense, this perspective seems to rely on a democratic principle of equality in both involvement process and outcome.

Lead users in the case example could be children or parents with disabilities who have developed solutions to problems with the case handling burden. Many parents had complained that it was difficult to sustain an overview of their cases and that they wished that the Handicap Center could be better at reminding them about dates for sending in applications, documentation and so on. There seemed to lack an administrative tool that could provide such an overview of the different elements of the children's cases and contact with different authorities. One of the parents had, on his own initiative, developed an Excel sheet to help organize the administration of his child's case. The parent had expert knowledge about the laws and rules in the area and could apply this knowledge to his solution. This may be considered a 'real' lead user example, as the development has been user-driven, carried through by the user himself, on his own initiative and outside of the formal public authority system. Such innovation could be adopted and further developed by the department as a tool that could help other parents as well, or as a tool that the case workers could use for a better overview of the cases. This could lead to both service and process innovation. The example is a rather practical one with a hands-on pragmatic purpose. Still, it may support better case handling procedures and the right to due process if the implementation of the tool leads to better standards and more equal results in case handling. The challenge could be to adjust the tool to the IT and administrative systems of the Department of Social Services and to make sure that it backs the rules and laws regulation in the area and fulfill requirements of the personal data protection act. Below in Table **1** the different perspectives of user are summarized.

Table 1: Overview of different perspectives of the user

User Concept	Public Sector	Characteristics	Innovation	Democracy	Role in Example
Welfare State Citizen	Democratically governed, hierarchical, authorities and social service providers, fulfilling social rights in just ways	Individual political, civil and social rights and political participation	Policy innovation, service innovation, process innovation	Liberal democracy, constitutional and welfare state	Knowing rights and actualizing them

Table 1: contd...

Customer	Service provider, separation between policy and administrative/service providing level	Individual preferences and individual needs – self-interested rationality	Service innovation, process innovation	Commercial, consumerist, service providing state, aggregative democracy	Knowing preferences and service offers, choosing the options that suit personal preferences best (voting with their feet)
Co-producer	Public sector as part of partnership and networks with third and private sector partners. Has a facilitating role.	Individual or community. Engaged, oriented towards the common good – or several common goods.	Service innovation, policy innovation	Deliberative democracy or Network Governance	Developing solutions together with Department of Social Services and employees of the Handicap Center
Lead user	Adopter of innovations created outside the sector – evaluating and choosing the right innovations is the challenge	Individual or community. Know own needs and are proactive in developing solutions, creative	Service or production innovation, governance innovation	Apolitical, technical, solution oriented, pragmatic	Developing an Excel sheet as a tool for administration of case documents and deadlines

DISCUSSION: USER CONCEPTIONS AND POLITICAL CITIZENSHIP

The presentation of the four different user conceptions elucidates differences with regard to involvement, the perception of rights, and the underlying models of democracy. Collaborative innovation may in principle involve any of these user conceptions dependent on the specific innovations and search for solutions that drive the collaboration.

The case elucidates that if collaborative innovation is to be relevant to public authorities there is a need to be aware of the rights that constitute the relationship between citizens and the public sector. Only the concept of the welfare state citizen implies a clear conception of social and civil rights. However, the welfare state citizen is typically categorized as a passive client role and thus as irrelevant to innovation. If the idea about social rights, which constitute social services of the public sector, is to improve equal opportunities of citizens, then it makes sense to consider these rights as not merely formal rights, but as rights that are to be actualised – in the sense that they actually enable citizens to do things they could not otherwise do. This moves the citizen with social rights beyond the role of a client that passively receives service to an active part in the encounter with the authority. If rights are to be effective, the citizen must somehow be empowered and this is the constitutive purpose of services grounded on social rights. This is a view on services that goes beyond the generic and a-political view found in relation to the citizen-consumer, as it explicitly stresses the political character of public services. Thus, there are good reasons to also include the rights of the welfare state citizen in the design and development of services.

The perspective of the welfare state citizen is, however, a very individualist perspective that does not seem to take into consideration that the child is part of a family, which as a whole social unit is affected by the situation. This individual perspective is also represented with the citizen-consumer conception. But, in contrast to the welfare state citizen, the citizen-consumer emphasises input from below – directly at the service providing level – rather than mainly through political channels. However, if we wish to ensure that public services really enable citizens to realise their rights, we also need to include them more directly – which is the main argument for user involvement in the first place. All the other user conceptions accept that representative democracy may be supplemented by, or is also constituted by, other input than those reached through the voting process or direct political channels. Some of the conceptions, however, risk to depoliticise the public services and the relationship between the public sector and the citizens. This is particularly the case with the citizen-consumer, which is also the conception that in many ways pose the greatest challenges when applied to the case of the parents of children with disabilities. The citizen-consumer is conceptualised as rational, self-interested and informed, but this seems as a rather awkward conception in relation to the case. The relationship between the Handicap Center and the families is not merely one of service exchange – it is a relationship between an authority and citizens, as are many public service encounters. The role of the authority is crucial to the personal lives, feelings and well-functioning of these families, and when rights are violated it is a matter of injustice and not merely a bad service experience. Thus, the citizen-consumer seems to take a rather reductionist perspective on the relation. Besides, the consumer approach does not necessarily imply qualitative input to service innovation, as the input may be either quantitative, *via* customer satisfaction surveys (which are also used in the public sector), or simply by users shifting to other providers. In these cases, the conception of citizen-consumer – even if emphasising input from below – does not ensure input to service innovation.

Lead users may in some cases also be individuals, but not necessarily. The lead user approach opens up the possibility of working with input from others than the direct beneficiaries. Lead users and co-producers work with users or citizens that are not merely individual. Lead users and co-producers may both be communities, rather than individuals. When adopting lead user innovations in the public sector, it may sometimes be necessary to modify the innovation to the specific context. In other cases, such as the case example in the chapter, the lead user was also an expert in the disability area. If solutions developed by lead users are ICT solutions to public services, they have a clear technical dimension and may thus be approached from a pragmatic perspective. However, they also carry a dimension of citizenship in the sense that competences, empowerment and service access, that may be enabled by the right IT solutions, have an influence on the capability to actualize citizen rights.

Co-production may be aimed at both service and policy innovation and does not involve only citizens but also actors from private or third sector, or, as in the case, the employees of a local authority. With regards to service innovation and the development of solutions that support citizen rights and abide by the laws of a certain authority area, it may be crucial to involve the case workers with expert knowledge in the field. This may also be a good idea from an implementation perspective, as these are the employees who are to make the new solution work in practice. The perspectives differ in relation to their understanding of needs and political claims as something prior and pre-political, as opposed to something politically justified or negotiated. This analysis demonstrates that we may be better able to choose the right approaches to innovation if we know about these differences, and that such knowledge will enable considerations about the democratic implications of certain ways of involving citizens. However, one could perhaps experiment across the different approaches and apply for example deliberative methods in relation to service innovation – which may be seen already in some ideas of co-production.

CONCLUSION

The chapter shows that an awareness of the different perspectives of user-driven innovation may raise the level of reflection on choosing between different ways of collaborating with users. It further shows that if public authorities working in highly law regulated areas of the public sector are to engage in collaborative innovation, we need to understand the role of citizen rights and include them in considerations about innovation processes. Only the traditional welfare state citizen perspective entails a strong and explicit concern for citizen rights. The other three concepts on the other hand all rely on stronger conceptions of participation.

The main theoretical finding is that the user conceptions rest on very different theoretical underpinnings and that they also support different democratic philosophies. Some of the conceptions such as the citizen-consumer and the lead-user may depoliticise the role of the citizen if they are not reinterpreted to fit into the specific democratic, political context. The welfare state citizen contains the strongest elements of traditional citizenship traits, but is not thought as providing input at the more specific service level. This does not rule out that such conceptions could provide the basis for involvement in service development processes with focus on how to strengthen citizen rights. Using a through-going example as a case on all four perspectives shows that specific user involvement projects can be interpreted from and may represent elements from more than one of these user conceptions. It further shows that each user conception emphasises certain elements of inclusion and citizenship, while being more or less blind to others.

The analysis furthermore shows that different user conceptions favour certain types of innovation, dependent on the understanding of the role of the public sector and its relationship with citizens. The analysis has focused on the democratic implications of different citizenship conceptions in relation to rights and participation. In that sense, the analysis rests on the normative assumption that public sector innovation must take such citizenship implications into account. Thus, even if focus has not been on one particular kind of innovation, the assumption has been that all public sector innovation should create value for citizens as *citizens* and not merely as users, and that it should support the public sector in improving its functions as a political and public institution. In a European perspective, the chapter could form a basis for empirical comparisons of how the different user conceptions appear in innovation processes in different countries. Collaborative innovation may take different forms, but the example taken from a Danish context may nevertheless show more general traits of collaborative innovation. The chapter elucidates the close connection between political and democratic systems and specific conceptions and foci of user involvement. Thus, these different user conceptions may have different relevance and may be interpreted differently across the different state and welfare systems in Europe.

ACKNOWLEDGEMENTS

I wish to thank Helle Vibeke Carstensen and Marie-Louise Henningsen from the Department of Social Services of the Municipality of Copenhagen for interviews and insight into the case.

CONFLICT OF INTEREST

The author confirms that this chapter contents have no conflict of interest.

REFERENCES

Agger, A. & Lund, D.H. (2011). Borgerne og brugerne i samarbejdsdrevne innovationsprocesser. In E. Sørensen & J. Torfing (eds.): *Samarbejdsdrevet innovation i den offentlige sektor*. (pp.177-196). København: Jurist- og Økonomiforbundets Forlag.

Albury, D. (2005). Fostering Innovation in Public Services. In *Public Money & Management,* January 2005, (pp. 51-56).

Aucoin, P. (2008). The design of public organizations for the 21st century: why bureaucracy will survive in public management. In *Canadian Public Administration/Administration Publique du Canada,* 40:2, 290-306.

Bartlett, D. & Dibben P. (2002). Public Sector Innovation and Entrepreneurship: Case Studies from Local Government. In *Local Government Studies*, 28:4, 107-121.

Beresford, P. (2002). User involvement in Research and Evaluation: Liberation or Regulation?. In *Social Policy and Society,* 1:2, 95-105.

Brand, R. (2005). The citizen-innovator. In *The Innovation Journal: The Public Sector Innovation Journal*, 10:1.

Burns, T. & Stalker, G.M. (1994). *The Management of Innovation*. Oxford: Oxford University Press.

Christensen, T. & Lægreid, P. (2002). New Public Management: Puzzles of Democracy and the Influence of Citizens. Symposium on Accountability, Publicity and Transparency, In *The Journal of Political Philosophy*, 10:3, 267-295.

Cindio, F. de; Ripamonti, L.A. & Peraboni, C. (2007). Community Networks as lead users in online public services design. In *The Journal of Community Informatics*, 3:1.

Clarke, J. (2004). Dissolving the public realm?: The logics and limits of neo-liberalism. In *Journal of Social Policy*, 33:1, 27-48.

Cox, R.H. (1998). The Consequences of Welfare Reform: How Conceptions of Social Rights are Changing. In *Journal of Social Policy*, 27:1, 1-16.

Eriksen, E.O. (1993). *Den offentlige dimensjon: verdier og styring i offentlig sektor*. Bergen: Tano.

Esping-Andersen, G. (1990). *The Three Worlds of Welfare Capitalism*. Cambridge: Polity Press.

Forst, R. (2001). The rule of reasons. Three models of deliberative democracy. In *Ratio Juris*, 14:4, 345-78.

Gustafsson, A. & Johnson, M.D. (2003*). Competing in a Service Economy*. San Francisco:Jossey-Bass.

Habermas, J. (1996). *Between Facts and Norms – Contributions to a Discourse Theory of Law and Democracy*. Oxford:Polity Press.

Hartley, J. (2005). Innovation in Governance and Public Services: Past and Present. In *Public Money & Management,* 25:1, 27-34.

Howells, J. (2007). Services and Innovation: conceptual and theoretical perspectives. In P. Daniels & J. Bryson (eds): *The Handbook of Service Industries*. (pp. 34-44). Northamton:Edward Elgar.

King, C.S. & Martinelly, A.S. (2005). Introduction – Innovations in Citizen Engagement and Empowerment: Beyond Boundaries. In *The Innovation Journal: The Public Sector Innovation Journal*, 10:1, Introduction, 1-8.

Kymlicka, W. (2002). Citizenship Theory: The virtues and practices of democratic citizen – find reference. In W. Kylicka, *Contemporary Political Philosohy – An introduction*. Second edition. Oxford: Oxford University Press.

Kymlicka, W. & Norman, W. (1994). Return of the Citizen: A Survey of Recent Work on Citizenship Theory. In *Ethics,* 104:2, 352-381.

Langergaard, L.L & Carstensen, H.V. (2014). Democracy innovation in public authorities. Learning from the Danish Ministry of Taxation. In *The Innovation Journal – Public Sector Innovation Journal*, 19:1, A Special Issue on Democracy. (Forthcoming)

Langergaard, L.L. (2011a). *Innovating the publicness of the public sector – a critical philosophical discussion of public sector innovation*. Ph.D. thesis.

Langergaard, L.L. (2011b). Understandings of 'users' and 'innovation' in a public sector context. In Sundbo, J. & Toivonen, M. (eds.): *User-based Innovation in Services.* (pp. 203-226). Cheltenham UK and Northhampton, MA, USA: Edward Elgar.

Marshall, T.H. (2003). *Medborgerskab og social klasse.* København: Hans Reitzels Forlag.

McLaughlin, H. (2009). What is a Name: 'Client', 'Patient', 'Customer', 'Consumer', 'Expert by Experience', 'Service User' – What's Next?. In *The British Journal of Social Work,* 39, 1101-1117.

Moore, M.H. (2005). Break-Through Innovations and Continuous Improvement: Two Different Models of Innovative Processes in the Public Sector. In *Public Money & Management*, 25:1, 43-49.

Mulgan, G. & Albury, D. (2003). *Innovation in the Public Sector*. Strategy Unit.

Olsen, J.P. (2005). *Maybe it is time to rediscover bureaucracy*? Working Paper, No. 10, March 2005. Arena, Center for European Studies, University of Oslo. (pp. 1-42).

Osborne, D. & Gaebler, T. (1993). *Reinventing Government – How the Entrepreneurial Spirit is Transforming the Public Sector.* London: Addison-Wesley Publishing Company, Inc.

Pestoff, V. (2012). Co-production and thirds sector social services in Europe: Some crucial conceptual issues. In V. Pestoff, T. Brandsen & B. Verschuere (eds.), *New Public Governance, the Third Sector and CoProduction.* (pp. 13-34). New York, London: Routledge Francis and Taylor Group.

Peters, G.B. & Pierre, J. (1998). Governance without government? Rethinking public administration. In *Journal of Public Administration Research and Theory*, 8:2, 223-243.

Pettit, P. (1998). Reworking Sandel's Republicanism. In *The Journal of Philosophy*, 95:2, 72-96.

Pollitt, C. (2000). Is the Emperor in his Underwear? An Analysis of the Impacts of Public Management Reform. In *Public Management*, 2:2, 181-199.

Pollitt, C. & Bouckaert, G. (2004). *Public Management Reform – A Comparative Analysis.* Oxford: Oxford University Press.

Sen, A. (2004). Elements of a Theory of Human Rights. In *Philosophy and Public Affairs*, 32:4, 315-356.

Sundbo, J. (1998). *The Organisation of Innovation in Services.* København: Roskilde University Press.

Sørensen, E. & Torfing, J. (2011). Samarbejdsdreven innovation I den offentlige sector. In Sørensen, E. & Torfing, J. (eds.) *Samarbejdsdrevet innovation - i den offentlige sektor.* (pp. 19-37). København: Jurist- og økonomiforbundets forlag.

Thompson, V.A. (1965). Bureaucracy and Innovation. In *Administrative Science Quarterly*, 10:1, 1-20.

Vigoda, E. (2002). From Responsiveness to Collaboration Governance, Citizens, and the Next Generation of Public Administration. In *Public Administration Review,* 62:5, 527-540.

von Hippel, E. (2005). *Democratizing innovation.* Cambridge, MIT Press.

Voxsted, S. & Christensen, C.J. (2009). *Innovation: Medarbejder og Bruger.* København: Hans Reitzels Forlag.

WEBPAGES

www.ebst.dk

http://www.forvaltningspolitik.dk/files/manager/documents/debatoplã¦g%20lang%20v ersion.pdf

Politiken: http://politiken.dk/indland/ECE1933135/handikapfamilier-goer-oproer-mod-koebenhavn

CHAPTER 4

Public Innovation and Organizational Legitimacy: An Empirical Analysis of Social Media in the Dutch Police

Albert Meijer*

Utrecht School of Governance, The Netherlands

Abstract: This chapter aims to enhance our understanding of the relation between public innovation and organizational legitimacy. On the basis of the literature, we formulate the expectation that top-down innovation results in strengthening of a bureaucratic logic to producing legitimacy whereas bottom-up innovation results in more emphasis on a network logic. To investigate this expectation empirically, the chapter analyses the introduction and use of social media by the Dutch police. The outcomes challenge the expected relation: top-down innovation resulted in a more networked arrangement for legitimacy. We explain this finding by pointing out that the innovation process was infrastructural and empty in content: the content was provided through bottom-up innovation. We conclude that combinations of top-down and bottom-up practices can form a conceptual lens for studying the involvement of different organizational actors in processes of public innovation.

Keywords: Public innovation, organizational legitimacy, police, social media.

INTRODUCTION

Technological innovation in the public sector enables new forms of coordination and execution of work processes. The introduction of information and communication technologies in the public sector has been studied since the 1980s and this had resulted in an understanding of the transformative effects of these technological innovations (for example: Van de Donk & Snellen, 1998; Fountain, 2001; Bekkers & Homburg, 2007). Previous research highlights that large-scale technological systems are generally implemented from a system's perspective on organizations with the objective of rationalizing coordination and optimizing management control. A fascinating feature of our current times is that the new technologies, social media, contain a different *script* and put an emphasis on

***Corresponding author Albert Meijer:** Utrecht School of Governance, The Netherlands;
E-mail: a.j.meijer@uu.nl

Annika Agger, Bodil Damgaard, Andreas Hagedorn Krogh and Eva Sørensen (Eds.)

individual persons - public professionals, civil servants, police officers, *etc.* - working within these organizational systems. To enhance our understanding of this new wave of technological and organizational innovation, this chapter studies the introduction of social media by the Dutch police.

We need to open the *black box* of social media innovation to understand the resulting positioning of social media communications in public organizations (Bekkers *et al.*, 2011a; Meijer, 2013). This chapter investigates how organizational contexts shape the use of new technologies, and how new technologies in turn transform the organizations in which they are introduced. The underlying assumption is that the direction of the innovation process is of key importance for the outcome of the innovation processes. New technologies have certain characteristics but how these characteristics are connected to organizational practices depends on the process of innovation (Orlikowski, 1992). Organizational actors frame the new technological innovation in the organization and determine how this innovation is to be embedded in the organization. The dynamics of innovation are studied to understand how the proliferation of social media use in public organizations brings about institutional change.

This chapter focuses on innovation processes in the police. The police have continuously been at the forefront of adopting new technologies to strengthen the quality of their work. Formal information systems play a key role in police reporting but also in providing them with instruction and formal work planning. Stol (1996) has emphasized that these systems are used to strengthen organizational control over the work of police officers. These systems are also used for communication with professional peers but this type of communication has been structured according to a bureaucratic logic. Information systems for contacts with citizens were lacking but recently community police officers - like many other public officials (Mergel, 2013) - have started to use social media for communication with citizens. Social media as an infrastructural innovation forms the focal point for this study.

External communication plays a key role in the production of legitimacy and that is why government organizations have professionalized this function to embed it in a centralized system of control. The central research question in this paper is: *how does the introduction of social media as an organizational innovation transform police-citizen relations and thus alter the production of police legitimacy?* This paper conceptualizes the production of legitimacy as a combination of two logics: a bureaucratic logic and a network logic. These logics are continuously being renegotiated and the introduction of new media influences these negotiation processes. The paper proposes that the way new media are introduced in the organization - through top-down or bottom-up innovation processes - influences the balance between these logics. The empirical material demonstrates how processes of innovation can be emergent rather than planned and controlled and how, rather than being distinct forms, top-down and bottom-up innovation are combined. The case confirms that the evolving patterns of social media usage are not determined by technological characteristics but contingent upon the specific nature of the innovation processes that occur when new communication technology is introduced into public organizations.

This research contributes to our academic understanding of the relation between innovation processes and organizational arrangements for legitimacy. Much research focuses on the contribution of innovation to the effectiveness of organizations and, while it has been acknowledged that innovation is also a means to strengthen organizational legitimacy (Verhoest, *et al.,* 2007), the relation between the form of the innovation process - top-down *versus* bottom-up innovation - and the resulting organizational arrangement for legitimacy has not yet been analyzed. The chapter highlights that qualitative empirical studies that trace and map the innovation processes are crucial for understanding how social media use in public organizations transform the way in which public legitimacy is produced.

This chapter first presents a theoretical framework that builds upon the literature on public innovation (paragraph 2) and on organizational arrangements for legitimacy (paragraph 3) to develop a model for the relation between innovation and organizational legitimacy (paragraph 4). Second, it will present the methods that have been used to investigate this relation in the specific case of social media innovation by the Dutch police (paragraph 5). Third, the findings of this empirical research are presented and analyzed to see what we can learn from this case about the relation between innovation and organizational arrangements for legitimacy (paragraph 6). The chapter ends with conclusions and suggestions for further research (paragraph 7).

PROCESSES OF PUBLIC INNOVATION: BOTTOM-UP & TOP-DOWN

Public innovation had attracted more attention from both scholars and practitioners since the 1990s (Altshuler & Behn 1997; Walker 2006 Bekkers *et al.* 2011a; Sørensen & Torfing 2011). The basic idea behind public innovation is that processes of change in the public sector do not only take place through electoral renewal but also through processes of organizational learning and adaptation (Bernier & Hafsi, 2007). Public organizations came to develop organizational structures and positions for public innovations and resources were increasingly made available. Technological innovation in the public sector has existed for many years but has evolved from a practice in selected organizations (tax departments, military organizations, the police, engineering departments) to become prominent with the introduction of personal computers in eventually all organization the public sector (Van de Donk & Snellen, 1998).

Most research on public sector innovations focuses on the innovation of public policies, products, services, organizational structures and processes (Osborne & Brown, 2005; Hartley, 2005). Social media innovation should be regarded as an *infrastructural innovation* (Lyytinen & Rose, 2003) in the sense that it provides new opportunities to develop new services, products, processes, *etc*. One can compare this to an infrastructure such as a railroad system: the railroad provides opportunities for passenger transport and freight transport but these service innovations can only be developed if a railroad system has been built. Social media can be used to create more government transparency, to stimulate citizens' participation and to facilitate network collaboration, opening up opportunities for further policy, strategic or governance innovation (Hartley, 2005).

Innovation is conceptualized here as planned change (Osborne & Brown, 2005). The basic idea is that public organizations can plan required change in response to or anticipation of changes in the environment or new opportunities. These changes can be either incremental or transformational and especially the latter type of change has triggered much interested both in the academic community and among practitioners (Osborne & Brown, 2005). This chapter follows Bekkers *et al*. (2011b, 197) who define innovation as "*a learning process in which governments attempt to meet specific societal challenges*". The aspiration is that innovative change can help to adapt government organizations to changing environments.

Innovations are both developed in organizations and adopted from other organizations. Most often, innovations in organizations are adaptations of innovations that have been developed elsewhere. Processes of adaptation and innovation are often described in the form of phase models (Damanpour 1991; Oliver, 2000; Meijer, 2013). We can make a distinction between idea generation, idea testing, idea scaling-up and idea diffusion. Certain actors introduce the idea of using new technologies to strengthen organizational processes (idea generation) and, after small-scale experiments with use of the new technologies (idea testing), the technology is rolled out in the organization (idea scaling-up and idea diffusion). Different actors are involved in these stages and the different barriers need to be tackled to bring the innovation process to a successful end.

The process of technological innovation entails more than simply using a new piece of technology. The New Medium Studies (Deibert, 1997; Hutchby, 2001, 2003) highlights that new media have certain characteristics that do not determine but enable certain communication patterns. Sellen & Harper (2002, 17, 18) define an affordance as follows: "*An affordance refers to the fact that the physical properties of an object make possible different functions for the person perceiving or using that object*". The affordances of new technologies are to a certain degree determined by processes of technological construction that take place outside of the organization (Orlikowski, 1992). This means that, in a study of the impacts of social media on the role of community police officers, we need to analyze which functions are being attributed to social media by police organizations in innovation processes. The dynamics of the innovations - the cognitive, normative and strategic interactions between various actors- determine how the technology is constructed and used in organizational practices.

To understand the affordance that is attributed to a new technology, we need to study the process of innovation within an organization. The introduction of social media and the attribution of function to these media can occur through top-down or bottom-up processes of innovation (Hesselbein, Goldsmith & Sommerville, 2001; Borins, 2002). Top-down innovation refers to innovation processes that start at the central - management or staff - level. The work floor is asked - persuaded, stimulated, forced - to use the innovation and managing innovation is to a large extent about managing this change process. Bottom-up innovation originates from frontline staff and is based upon their efforts to improve practices and their knowledge about the work situation. Success depends on the extent to which management picks up these forms of innovation and stimulates their diffusion in the rest of the organization. The crucial difference is that top-down innovation takes place from the perspective of the organization as a system and translates system-level analyses into individual actions while the bottom-up perspective takes individual actions as a starting point and views the organizational interest as an aggregation of individual actions (see Table **1**).

Table 1: Two types of innovation processes

	Top-down Innovation	**Bottom-up Innovation**
Origin	Central level	Work floor
Focus	Improving the organization	Improving work floor practices
Key to success	Support on work floor	Attention from management

The literature on innovation in the police concerns new methods for police investigations such as data analysis and DNA techniques but also the use of technology for organizational steering (Mullen, 1996; Schneider *et al*., 2008). The large scale information systems that were introduced in the police - and other government organizations - from the 1990s on were mainly introduced from a top-down perspective (Stol, 1996). Bottom-up innovation played a much bigger role in the introduction of e-mail in public organizations and individual employees played an important role in the assignment of function to this new technology (Meijer, 2008). The direction of the innovation process matters since it means that different affordances can be assigned to the technology in the process of innovation and these affordances matter, among other things, for the organizational production of legitimacy.

BUREAUCRATIC OR NETWORKED PRODUCTION OF LEGITIMACY

Organizational legitimacy is crucial to the continued existence of the organization and, therefore, the production of legitimacy has received much attention both by academics and practitioners. It is also a much debated concept that has been conceptualized in many different ways. This papers follows the much-cited definition of legitimacy by Suchman (1995, 574): "*Legitimacy is a generalized perception or assumption that the actions of an entity are desirable, proper, or appropriate within some socially constructed system of norms, values, beliefs, and definitions*". Police legitimacy can arise from perceptions of the procedures of the police but also from the outcome of their work (cf. Tyler, 2004). Perceptions of police work are formed through personal experiences and personal contacts with the police but also through stories from others and stories in the media. In both cases the organization of and communication over police work play a crucial role in forming the perceptions and, hence, they are important instruments for the production of police legitimacy (Elsbach, 1994).

Power (2003) highlights that public organizations have various systems to produce legitimacy. These consist both of internal arrangements such as accounting and recordkeeping and external arrangements such as transparency and accountability. Overall, two dominant logics have been identified in the organizational production of police legitimacy: a bureaucratic and a networked logic (cf. Powell, 1990; Meijer, 2008).[1] The bureaucratic logic builds upon the idea that vertical control of the police organization and embedding it in a system of democratic and representative government are crucial to police legitimacy while the networked logic highlights that direct interactions between (community) police officers and societal actors - actual encounters - produce organizational legitimacy. The bureaucratic argument basically states that individual police officers are legitimate since the organization is legitimate while the network logic highlights that it is the other way around: the police organization derives its legitimacy from the legitimacy of the individual police officers.

The bureaucratic logic is based upon Weberian ideas about government organizations. The organizational logic is about the contributions of individual employees to the attainment of organizational objectives. Employees are *wheels in a machine* and these wheels should be adjusted to the machine's overall desired outputs. A central problem of organization is how to deal with *centrifugal tendencies*, *i.e.* mechanisms that undermine the unity of organization (Kaufman, 1960). Organizations develop objectives but need these to be enacted by employees to be realized (cf. Kaufman, 1960). Employees may have various reasons to act in a different manner and therefore organizations develop a range of mechanisms to ensure that employees act in accordance with organizational objectives. The objectives and policies are developed in response to political and public demands that result in priority settings and choices in the allocations of scarce resources. Garland (2001,18) emphasizes that the new managerialism in policing has narrowed professional discretion and tightly regulated working practice.

In some organizations, the organizational logic may leave little leeway for situational reasoning but in so-called street-level bureaucracies the acting bureaucrats have a certain degree of autonomy (Lipsky, 1980). For practical reasons, the behavior of community officer cannot be determined fully by organizational rules and procedures. This results in instructions for street-level police officers that are based on an organizational logic but that creates a certain room for applying this in a specific situation. This means that the realization of organizational objectives does not only depend on structures and procedures but also on the way street-level bureaucrats act in a specific (underdetermined)

[1] Other logics may be important in other sectors. A professional logic is, for example, of crucial importance to producing legitimacy in healthcare and a market logic may be of crucial importance in a sector such as public housing.

situation. Lipsky (1980) emphasizes that street-level bureaucrats such as police officers play a key role in actually realizing the policy.

That leaves us with the question how street-level bureaucrats can produce police legitimacy if they make decisions not prescribed by the hierarchy. Based on Lipsky (1980) their production of legitimacy can be conceptualized as more personal and situated. The horizontal logic of networked contacts with societal actors forms a complementary mechanism to the vertical logic of the bureaucracy. Several mechanisms play a role here such as which societal actors manage to establish contacts with the community police officers, how clearly they express their demands and how sensitive the police officer is to these demands. The nature of community networks plays a key role in the demand articulation of customers of community police officers (Trojanowicz & Bucqueroux, 1990).

This discussion of the literature shows that two complementary and sometimes competing logics play a role in the production of police legitimacy.[2] These logics rely on different modes of communication (cf. Meijer, 2008). The bureaucratic logic is based upon the idea of centralized external communication and a focus on issues that are of relevance to the whole organization in the external communications. The networked logic, in contrast, focuses on fragmented, individualized external communication and a focus on issues that are of specific importance to police officers and the setting in which they work. These two logics are summarized in Table **2**.

Table 2: Logics for the production of police legitimacy

	Bureaucratic Logic	**Network Logic**
Focus of legitimacy	Legitimacy of police organization	Legitimacy of individual police officer
Key argument	Police officer is legitimate since he is a member of a legitimate organization	Police organization is legitimate since its members are legitimate
Dimension 1. **Control over external communication**	Communications department determine external communications.	Individual police officers have leeway for external communications.
Dimension 2. **Content of external communication**	Global issues of relevance to all citizens within the police department.	Local issues of relevance to the citizens in a specific neighbourhood.

[2] The introduction of community police officers is, by itself, a means to strengthen the network logic in the production of police legitimacy and complement the bureaucratic logic. The basic idea is that police legitimacy is strengthened by creating short, direct connections between individual police officers and citizens. In a way, this transforms the police organization from an inaccessible bureaucratic organization to a more accessible network of police professionals.

This brief summary of debates about the production of government legitimacy provides some building blocks for our analysis of the impact of social media. The two logics complement each other but may also result in tensions. Temporary balances in these logics are socially constructed and reconstructed in what is regarded as the correct way to produce police legitimacy. This temporary balance may be challenged by the introduction of social media as an organizational innovation in the police.

EXPECTED RELATIONS BETWEEN INNOVATION & LEGITIMACY

On the basis of this exploration of theories of media affordances and innovation, this chapter proposes that the nature of the innovation process will determine the resulting effect of social media use on the organizational production of legitimacy (cf. Orlikowski, 1992). Social media create opportunities to strengthen external communication with citizens but these opportunities may be used and embedded in the organization in different ways. Social media can either be used to strengthen a bureaucratic logic or a network logic to producing legitimacy. Previous research into the introduction of new technologies in government organizations has identified the mechanism that those that control the innovation process will use it to strengthen their own position (Danziger *et al.*, 1982; Kraemer & King, 2006). This would mean that centrally controlled innovation would result in a strengthening of a bureaucratic logic to producing legitimacy whereas control over the innovation process at the work floor - bottom-up innovation - would result in a strengthening of the network logic.

Previous research highlights that technologies such as databases and workflow systems were mainly introduced through top-down innovation and this resulted in a stronger bureaucratic logic in the production of legitimacy (Zuurmond, 1994; Stol, 1996; Jorna, 2009). These systems were used to strengthen the bureaucratic organization and exert more control over street-level bureaucrats. These studies did not explicitly address the question how these systems change the organizational arrangement for legitimacy but the case descriptions of these studies into social benefit agencies (Zuurmond, 1994), the police (Stol, 1996) and government subsidies (Jorna, 2009) clearly highlight that these systems strengthen the bureaucratic logic of producing legitimacy.

Previous studies almost exclusively focused on large scale technological systems. A key feature of these systems is that they are expensive and need to be designed and developed to fit organizational processes (Zuurmond, 1994; Jorna, 2009). Social media have different features since they are readily available and can be used without much training or support. No heavy technological infrastructure is needed to make these technologies work. Basically, this technology has been developed for the consumer market and not for use within organizations. These features make social media rather different from the database and workflow systems that have been studied before and this new wave of technological innovations in the public sector demands attention since little is known about the way as these technologies are introduced within organization.

One previous study focused on social media strategies of police organizations and also touched upon the way social media were introduced within the organization (Meijer & Thaens, 2013). This study of three North American police departments - Toronto, Boston and Washington DC - showed variation. While social media innovation started at the work floor in Toronto, the police departments in Boston and Washington DC introduced social media through a process of top-down innovation. Meijer and Thaens (2013) describe how the police departments in Boston and Washington DC opted for a centralization of external communications while Toronto developed a decentralized system with community police officers as external communicators. That study did not focus on the organizational arrangement for legitimacy but it does highlight that police department follow different innovation trajectories in their implementation of social media and these trajectories seem to result in different organizational arrangements for external communications.

To enhance our knowledge of the relation between social media and the production of legitimacy, the relation between the innovation process and the resulting arrangement for organizational legitimacy is explored through empirical research in the Netherlands. The research aims to find out what types of innovation take place in police organizations, what the resulting effects are on the production of police legitimacy and whether the assumed theoretical relations are confirmed in these findings.

RESEARCH DESIGN AND METHODS

Public innovation is studied as the process by which social media are being incorporated and used in the police for supporting specific tasks and functions. Top-down innovation is concluded to take place when the attribution of function is steered by formal policy guidelines for the use of social media and the diffusion of social media in the organization depends on central decisions about resources for social media (*i.e.* smart phones for police officers). Bottom-up innovation is observed when the use of social media is initiated by community police officers and its use spreads through the organization by example (*i.e.* horizontal diffusion).

The role of social media in the organizational production of police legitimacy is operationalized as follows:

The *bureaucratic logic* is reflected in the use of social media for centralized communications. Social media are predominantly used at the central level for external communications. The messages communicated to the audience mainly contain content of general interest to all citizens in the police department.

The *networked logic* is reflected in the use of social media for decentralized communications. Community police officers use social media to create individual communication channels with society. The messages communicated to the audience mainly contain content of specific interest to citizens in a neighborhood or small town.

The research focuses on the use of Twitter by the Dutch police. Twitter is a freely available social networking and microblogging tool that can be used to post messages in 140 characters. Tweets are publicly visible by default and followers see these messages in their *timeline*. In contrast with Facebook, relations on Twitter are asymmetrical: one can follow another person without being followed by that person. Twitter is the most popular social medium for professional communication and its use has spread rapidly within the Dutch police since 2009 (Meijer *et al.*, 2013).

The use of Twitter and its effects were investigated in four police departments in the Netherlands. We will refer to them here by the main cities in these departments: The Hague, Utrecht, Apeldoorn and Eindhoven.[3] These departments were selected on the basis of their level of social media use (all relatively high users) and differences in more urban and more rural environments. In view of the similarities between these departments in terms of formal structure and organizational culture, this is a most similar case design. The cases will be used to obtain an in-depth understanding of innovation dynamics in similar organizations.

In these departments, we used a combination of (mostly qualitative) methods to investigate the innovation process and the resulting organizational arrangement

---

[3] The official names for the police departments are Haaglanden, Utrecht, Gelderland-Noord-Oost en Brabant-Zuid-Oost.

for legitimacy: interviews with one communication officer in each department, interviews with 20 community police officers, a quantitative analysis of the tweets of all community police officers in each department and a qualitative analysis of the tweets of all community police officers in each department. The results were used to analyze the process of innovation first and then analyze the impact of social media on the organizational production of police legitimacy.

FINDINGS

Patterns of Innovation

Twitter has been introduced in the Dutch police fairly recently. The introduction started around 2009 with a few individuals using Twitter without any policy guidelines or formal mandate to communicate about their police work. These individuals were being noticed by other departments and they told enthusiastic stories about the value of Twitter for supporting police communications. These enthusiastic stories raised interest in social media for police communications all around the country (Meijer *et al.,* 2013).

The use of Twitter started at the communication departments of the four police departments in 2009 and 2010. These communication professionals informed police chiefs but did not ask for permission (and this was not needed because they did not require funding). The reasons for wanting to use Twitter differed to some extent. The Utrecht Police Department saw social media as a means to draw attention to a website that had been developed for informing citizens about crime in their neighborhood and asking for information about thefts and misdemeanors. Social media was seen as a pointer to more exhaustive information and that could help to draw the attention of citizens to this initiative. The Eindhoven Police Department started using Twitter to communicate press releases to a broader audience than just journalists. The The Hague Police Department started using Twitter for crowd control and used Twitter during the world cup football in 2010. Subsequently, they raised broader citizen interest by Twittering a selection of news releases. The Apeldoorn Police Department started with a central account with press releases and then split these up in press releases for local groups. In sum, all four police departments started with centralized information provision through Twitter and then came to realize that local information provided by community police officers could be of additional interest to citizens.

Subsequent innovation dynamics were highly similar in all four police departments. The initiatives were seen as successful and the communications departments decided to broaden up the use of social media to community police officers, often at the request of technology-savvy police officers. The communication professionals felt that citizens would be most interested in local information and therefore they developed the idea that community police officers should use Twitter for presenting information to citizens. The realization of this idea took some time because money had to be made available for financing PDAs for community police officers. When this money had been made available, community officers were asked whether they were willing to start using Twitter for communication with citizens. These requests were open in nature and the police officers had much autonomy in its use of Twitter in whatever way they deemed fit. A community police officer stated:

> *"There was a bottom line but above that the message was primarily: do your own thing, experiment with the new medium and use your professional knowledge and common sense to identify what can and what cannot be done".*

Many community police officers were interested and the use of Twitter grew rapidly. Community police officers became interested because their colleagues were telling them enthusiastic stories about the new medium and the resulting interactions with citizens. Communications departments monitored the Twitter use of police officers and, if necessary, provided feedback to ensure that there would be no transgressions. In parallel, the communications department developed (brief and relatively open) guidelines for the use of Twitter. One police officer said the following:

> *"At a certain stage we ran into some situations that did not seem suitable for tweeting, sometimes in view of media coverage and sometimes because of not wanting to interfere with police investigations. Then we started to limit certain uses. This resulted in guidelines for police officers".*

The development of formal policies meant that police officers that started to use Twitter later had more guidelines to regulate their usage of the new medium. But all communication departments except for the one in The Hague emphasized that the police officers could still use a *personal touch* in their Twitter communications.

The innovation processes in these four departments shows that, at the start, the driving force was the Communications Department. All police departments started with central accounts and only at a later stage were community police officers asked to provide local information. At that time, the community police officers obtained few instructions regarding the content of the information to be communicated through Twitter. They could use the medium as they saw fit. Guidelines for use by community police officers evolved later. One cannot conclude that the process of innovation evolved in a bottom-up manner since communication departments drove the introduction of social media in the four police departments. Nevertheless, community police officers had much leeway in exploring the possible uses of the new medium and in developing patterns of use that they regarded as appropriate. The top-down innovation was rather *empty* in content: an infrastructure was provided but individual users further developed the use of that infrastructure. The communication departments only came to provide some guidelines at a later stage. Social media innovation in the Dutch police can be characterized as an interactive relation between top-down and bottom-up innovation.

Social Media and the Two Logics of Producing Legitimacy

The two dimensions of the production of legitimacy - control over external communications and content of communication - will now be used to structure our empirical findings and explore how social media usage affects the organizational production of police legitimacy.

A first difference between the bureaucratic and the network logic is the organization of external communication. If the use of Twitter in these police departments would take the form of the bureaucratic logic, Twitter would be used for communications controlled by the communications department: they would use the new medium to develop an additional channel of communication with citizens. Leeway for external communication for the individual police officers would reflect the network logic since the communications department would be able to regulate but not control these communications. Which logic did we find?

The numbers of central Twitter accounts - run by the communications department - and Twitter accounts of community police officers are presented in Table **3**.

Table 3: Central and individual Twitter accounts in the four police departments

	Number of central Twitter accounts	**Number of followers central Twitter account**	**Number of individual Twitter accounts**	**Total number of followers of the individual Twitter accounts**
Eindhoven	4	7,629	31	22,348
The Hague	1	20,350	87	41,541
Apeldoorn	2	6,604	72	38,257
Utrecht	3	21,540	28	24,660

The table shows that there are many more Twitter accounts at the community police officer level than at the central level. In total there are more than 20 accounts of community police officers for each central Twitter account. These central Twitter accounts tend to have more followers - even over 20,000 for the central account of the The Hague Police Department - but added together the accounts of community police officers have more followers in all four police departments.

These findings highlight that the communications department have control over the most followed Twitter accounts but community police officers have considerable leeway to use Twitter and they have been able to attract a high number of followers. This indicates that the bureaucratic logic is reproduced in the control over the organizational and most followed Twitter accounts. However, the network logic seems to make more use of the opportunities of the new medium to communicate with citizens by using it to generate a fragmented but overall larger audience for social media communications. No differences between the four police departments were found.

A second difference concerns the content of the communication. The bureaucratic logic emphasizes the use for issues that are of interest to all citizens in the area of the police department while the network logic emphasizes content that is of relevance for the local neighborhood.

The central account is mostly - about one third of the messages - used for asking citizen for information related to crimes or to missing persons. In addition, the police frequently tweets successes (about one quarter of the tweets). They inform citizen about criminals that have been apprehended. A third major group is messages related to prevention or general citizen information. The following tweets are examples of communications at the central account level:

> *"Arrested: man suspected of hitting and kicking a girl in [the town of] #lopik. Arrested on May 2nd".* (Utrecht, 3 May 2012)

> *"Dutch coffee shops will be private clubs only accessible for Dutch citizens' http://www.new-rules.eu/newrulesnl"* (Eindhoven, 4 May 2012)

We have also asked the community police officers to highlight the functions of Twitter. Three functions were mentioned consistently by the community police officers: show what community police officers do, obtain information from citizens and strengthening community networks. The following Tweets present some examples:

> "About to have a meeting with the city about our approach of youth groups in [the neighborhood of] #hoograven! Any ideas? #dtv Henkg" (Utrecht, 19 April 2012).
>
> *"Report of beer theft at [local supermarket] in goylaan. Nice footage! Now we need to find the perpetrators. [the neighborhood of] #hoograven best robv"* (Utrecht, 18 April 2012).

We found some distinction between the centralized accounts and the tweets of community police officers but the difference was not as was expected. Centralized accounts also focus on local issues but they tend to only tweet issues that are of major importance (violent crimes) while the community police officers also tweet about crimes with less impact (beer theft from supermarket) and even local meetings. The difference, however, should not be exaggerated. Central accounts and Twitter accounts of community police officers also regularly retweet each other's tweets. The findings still illustrate that the local network logic results in more *minor news* for citizens related to their own neighborhood. It also results in a different perspective on policing since not only high-impact issues are communicated but also normal police work.

The findings show that social media are primarily used for strengthening the networked logic of community police officers. Most Twitter accounts are run by community police officers and these accounts have more followers than central accounts. The content of central and community officer accounts has similarities but central accounts tend to focus more on *larger issues* whereas trivialities are also presented in community police officers accounts. Overall this shows that the use of Twitter strengthens the networked production of legitimacy more than the hierarchical production.

Process of Innovation and Resulting Organization Arrangement for Legitimacy

Combining the analysis of the innovation process and the changes in the production of legitimacy, we found that there is a facilitated process going on, whereas the top does not dictate what should be done at the bottom, but rather initiates the process and provides the infrastructure needed for the innovation process to develop. Community police officers were - and are - encouraged to use social media to communicate with citizens. The push was open in nature and gave them much autonomy to develop their own patterns of usage albeit that they are to some extent being monitored by communication professionals and guidelines are provided to indicate what they can and cannot do with Twitter.

The resulting organizational arrangement for legitimacy is mostly in line with the networked logic. All police departments have more individual than central Twitter accounts and, even though these central accounts have on average many more followers, the number of followers of the central accounts is higher. The central accounts do sometimes communicate local issues but they tend to focus on *larger issues* whereas more trivial issues are only communicated through the accounts of community police officers. This highlights that the communication of more trivial local issues increases through the use of Twitter. The number of accounts and the content of the communications highlight that Twitter is mostly used to strengthen the networked production of legitimacy.

An analysis of the relation between innovation and the organizational arrangement for legitimacy challenges our expectations. The innovation process started top-down and the central communications department was in the lead and initially the new medium was primarily used to strengthen the bureaucratic logic. Subsequently, the communications department provided opportunities to community officers to frame the new medium according to their own needs and wants for communication with citizens. The top-down innovation became rather empty in the sense that the responsibility for the content was shifted to the community police officers. Still, the channel for strengthening the networked logic for legitimacy was provided by the central level. This indicates that the *empty* top-down innovation process resulted in a more networked production of legitimacy.

CONCLUSION

The empirical findings present interesting insights in the public innovation. A first insight was that *infrastructural innovations* generate new opportunities for communication but do not stipulate how these opportunities are to be used. Twitter is provided as a medium of communication to community police officers but few clear objectives and guidelines are presented to them. While previous information and communication technologies were developed to strengthen operational, service or control processes, there is no direct link between the introduction of the new innovation and its purposeful use within the organization. Uses of the infrastructure are developed in organizational practices rather than in explicit strategies.

A second, related, insight is that public organizations may come to provide a new channel of communications - a new infrastructure - without an explicit strategy: the process of innovation is emergent. This *emergent innovation* shows many similarities to the diffusion of e-mails in public organizations (Meijer, 2008): police departments feel a public pressure to use new media and employees within the organization ask for the media (which they often already use privately). In response, the department creates the facilities for using social media but no objectives or guidelines are formulated. Individual employees are to put Twitter to their own use and, as a consequence, new practices are being constructed by community police officers in close connection with communication departments.

Thirdly, this study has provided important insights in the relation between *top-down and bottom-up innovation* in the public sector. The study shows that these two types of innovation can be combined rather than they are different forms. The study showed two ways of combining top-down and bottom-up innovation. The first one is a temporal combination: the innovation process had more of a top-down nature in the beginning when the communication department started to experiment with central Twitter accounts, gave ample room for bottom-up innovation at a later stage when community police officers could experiment with the new medium and, again, had some characteristics of a top-down process when the communication departments drafted guidelines for the use of Twitter. The second way of combining top-down and bottom-up innovation is a substantial one. The cases showed how an empty top-down innovation - the opportunity to use Twitter - was filled with content in a bottom-up process when community police officers started to develop communication practices. These combinations of top-down and bottom-up practices can form a conceptual lens for studying the involvement of different organizational actors in processes of public innovation.

Fourthly, the study highlighted that the evolving patterns of social media usage are *not determined by technological characteristics*. Even though the pattern of innovation was highly similar in all four Dutch police departments, these findings are different from what has previously been found in the Boston and Metropolitan (Washington DC) Police Departments (Meijer & Thaens, 2013). The use of Twitter in those police departments resulted in a strengthening of bureaucratic patterns while the Dutch police departments used Twitter to strengthen their networked logic. Further comparative work is needed to understand these differences and to explore to what extent they result from cultural, institutional or process features of the innovation process.

This exploratory study has identified the relation between innovation and legitimacy as an important research topic. While many studies pay attention to the legitimacy of innovations as a requirement for a successful innovation process (Hekkert *et al.*, 2007), few studies evaluate how innovations change organizational arrangements for legitimacy. Legitimacy is a key value in public administration that plays an important role in the structure of public sector organizations. More research into this relation is crucial to advance our understanding of innovation in the public sector.

ACKNOWLEDGEMENTS

Declared none.

CONFLICT OF INTEREST

The author confirms that this chapter contents have no conflict of interest.

REFERENCES

Altshuler, A.A., & Behn, R.D. (Eds.) (1997). *Innovation in American Government.* Washington, DC: Brookings Institution.

Bekkers, V., Edelenbos, J., & Steijn, B. (Eds) (2011a). *Innovation in the Public Sector. Linking Capacity and Leadership.* Houndmills: Palgrave MacMillan.

Bekkers, V., Edelenbos, J., & Steijn, B. (Eds.) (2011b). An innovative public sector? Embarking in the innovation journey. In: Bekkers, V., Edelenbos, J. & Steijn, B. (Eds). *Innovation in the Public Sector. Linking Capacity and Leadership.* (pp. 197-221). Houndmills: Palgrave MacMillan.

Bekkers, V., & Homburg, V. (2007). The myths of e-government: Looking beyond the assumptions of a new and better government. In *The Information Society*, 23:5, 373-382.

Bernier, L., & Hafsi, T. (2007). The changing nature of public entrepreneurship. In *Public Administration Review,* 67:3, 488-503.

Borins, S. (2002). Leadership and innovation in the public sector. In *Leadership & Organization,* 23:8, 467-476.

Damanpour, F. (1991). Organizational innovation: A meta-analysis of effect of determinants and moderators. In *Academy of Management Journal,* 34:3, 555-90.

Danziger, J.N., Dutton, W.H., Kling, R., & Kraemer, K.L. (1982). *Computers and Politics.* New York: Columbia University Press.

Deibert, R.D. (1997). *Parchment, Printing and Hypermedia.* New York: Columbia University Press.

Elsbach, K.D. (1994). Managing organizational legitimacy in the California cattle industry: The construction and effectiveness of verbal accounts. In *Administrative Science Quarterly*, 39:1, 57-88.

Fountain, J.E. (2001). *Building the virtual state: Information technology and institutional change.* Washington: Brookings Institution Press.

Garland, D. (2001). *The Culture of Control. Crime and Social Order in Contemporary Societies.* Chicago: The University of Chicago Press.

Hartley, J. (2005). Innovation in governance and public services: past and present. In *Public Money & Management*, 25:1, 27-34.

Hekkert, M.P., Suurs, R.A.A., Negro, S.O., Smits, R.E.H.M., & Kuhlmann, S. (2007). Functions of Innovation Systems: A new approach for analyzing technological change. In *Technological Forecasting and Social Change,* 74, 413-432.

Hesselbein, F., Goldsmith, M., & Somerville, I. (2001). *Leading for Innovation*. San Francisco, CA: Jossey-Bass.

Hutchby, I. (2001). *Conversation and technology. From the telephone to the Internet.* Cambridge (UK): Polity.

Hutchby, I. (2003). Affordances and the analysis of technologically mediated interaction: A response to Brian Rappert. In *Sociology*, 37, 581–589.

Jorna, F. (2009). *De autobureaucratie. Informatisering en leren van uitvoering*. Delft: Eburon.

Kaufman, H. (1960). *The Forest Ranger: A Study in Administrative Behavior*. Baltimore, MD: Johns Hopkins Press.

Kraemer, K.L., & King, J.L (2006). Information technology and administrative reform: Will E-government be different? In *International Journal of Electronic Government Research*, 2:1, 1-20.

Lipsky, M. (1980). *Street-level Bureaucracy; Dilemmas of the Individual in Public Services*. New York: Russell Sage Foundation.

Lyytinen, K., & Rose, G. (2003). Disruptive information system innovation: the case of internet computing. In *Information Systems Journal,* 13:4, 301-330.

Meijer, A.J. (2008). E-mail in government: Not post-bureaucratic but late-bureaucratic organizations. In *Government Information Quarterly*, 25:3, 429-447.

Meijer, A. (2012). Co-Production in an Information Age. In Pestoff, V., Brandsen T., & Verschuere, B. (Eds.), New Public Governance, the Third Sector and Co-Production. New York/London: Routledge.

Meijer, A. (2013). New media and the coproduction of safety: An empirical analysis of dutch practices. In American Review of Public Administration. doi: 10.1177/0275074012455843.

Meijer, A., Grimmelikhuijsen, S.G., Fictorie, D., Thaens, M., & Siep, P. (2013). *Politie en sociale media: Van Hype naar onderbouwde keuzen*. Amsterdam: Reed Business.

Meijer, Albert J. & Marcel Thaens, (2013). Social media strategies: Understanding the differences between North American police departments. In *Government Information Quarterly*. 30:4, 343-350.

Mergel, I. (2013). Social media adoption and resulting tactics in the U.S. federal government. In *Government Information Quarterly*, 30:4, 123-130.

Mullen, K. (1996). *The Computerization of Law Enforcement: a diffusion of innovation study*. Doctoral Thesis. Albany: State University of New York.

Oliver, W.M. (2000). The third generation of community policing: moving through innovation, diffusion, and institutionalization. In *Police Quarterly,* 3:4, 367-88.

Orlikowski, W.J. (1992). The duality of technology: Rethinking the concept of technology in organizations. In *Organization Science*, 3:3, 398–427.

Osborne, S.P., & Brown, L. (2005). *Managing Change and Innovation in Public Service Organizations*. Milton Park: Routledge.

Power, M. (2003). Auditing and the production of legitimacy. In *Accounting, Organizations and Society,* 28:4, 379-394.

Powell, W.W. (1990). Neither market nor hierarchy: Network forms of organization. In *Research in Organizational Behavior,* 12, 295–336.

Schneider, M.C., Chapman, R., & Schapiro, A. (2008). Towards the unification of policing innovations under community policing. Policing. *In International Journal of Police Strategies and Management*, 32:4, 694-718.

Sellen, A.J., & Harper, R.H.R. (2002). *The myth of the paperless office*. Cambridge: MIT Press.

Sørensen, E., & Torfing, J. (2011). Enhancing collaborative innovation in the public sector. In *Administration and Society,* 43:8, 842-68.

Stol, W.Ph. (1996). *Politie-optreden en informatietechnologie. Over sociale controle van politiemensen.* Lelystad: Koninklijke Vermande.

Suchman, M.C. (1995). Managing legitimacy: Strategic and institutional approaches. In *Academy of Management Review*, 20, 571-610.

Trojanowicz, R.T., & Bucqueroux, B. (1990). *Community Policing: A Contemporary Perspective*. Cincinnati: Anderson Publishing Company.

Tyler, T.R. (2004). Enhancing police legitimacy. In *The Annals of the American Academy of Political and Social Science*, 593, 84-99.

Van de Donk, W.B., & Snellen, I.T.M. (1998). Towards a theory of public administration in an information age?. In *Public Administration in an Information Age, A Handbook*, 3-19.

Verhoest, K., Verschuere, B., & Bouckaert, G. (2007). Pressure, legitimacy, and innovative behavior by public organizations. In *Governance,* 20:3, 469-497.

Walker, R.M. (2006). Innovation type and diffusion: An empirical analysis of local government. In *Public Administration*, 84:2, 311-35.

Zuurmond, A. (1994). De Infocratie, Een theoretische en empirische heroriëntatie op Weber's ideaaltype in het informatietijdperk [The infocracy. A theoretical and empirical re-orientation on Weber's idealtype in the Information Age]. Delft: Eburon.

CHAPTER 5

Leading Collaborative Innovation: Developing Innovative Solutions to Wicked Gang Problems

Andreas Hagedorn Krogh* **and Jacob Torfing**

Department of Society and Globalisation, Roskilde University, Denmark

Abstract: Collaborative innovation presents itself as a promising method for crafting innovative solutions to wicked problems. While the barriers and drivers of collaborative innovation have been studied extensively in the expanding collaborative innovation literature, there is still a need for more empirical studies of the role of public leadership in overcoming the barriers and strengthening the drivers of collaborative innovation. In order to contribute to this endeavour, this chapter conducts a cross-case analysis of 14 cases of collaborative innovation aimed at curbing gang violence in the city of Copenhagen. The chapter provides empirically informed answers to the questions of when and where leadership is particularly needed, what public leaders should be aware of when leading collaborative innovation processes and how they should go about developing innovative solutions to wicked problems such as the current Danish gang problem.

Keywords: Collaborative innovation, gangs, leadership, public safety, wicked problems.

INTRODUCTION

Recent public policy and administration research suggests that networks and collaboration between public and private actors have great potential when it comes to generating innovative solutions to complex problems (Roberts and King, 1996; Van de Ven *et al.*, 2007; Eggers and Singh, 2009; Sørensen and Torfing, 2011). The growing body of literature on collaborative innovation in the public sector has prompted scholars to ponder the specific type of leadership needed when public and private stakeholders come together to produce public innovation (Crosby & Bryson, 2010; Morse, 2010; Page, 2010; Ansell & Gash, 2012; Sørensen & Torfing, 2012). While the theoretical argument for collaborative innovation leadership is well developed, there is still a lack of empirical research investigating when and where leadership is particularly needed, what public

***Corresponding author Andreas Hagedorn Krogh:** Department of Society and Globalisation, Roskilde University, Denmark; Tel: ++ 31 253 8101; E-mail: ahkrogh@ruc.dk

Annika Agger, Bodil Damgaard, Andreas Hagedorn Krogh and Eva Sørensen (Eds.)

leaders should be aware of when leading collaborative innovation processes, and how they should go about developing innovative solutions to complex problems. In this chapter, we conduct a cross-case analysis of 14 innovation projects addressing the problem of gang-related violence and crime in order to provide empirically informed answers to these questions.[1]

The chapter is organized in the following way. First, we demonstrate how the acuteness and wickedness of the current Danish gang problem spur an urgent need for public innovation. We then review the latest theories of collaborative innovation leadership in order to present key concepts and concerns. Next, we explain how the 14 empirical cases were selected and how the data was collected and analysed, before presenting key findings from the cross-case analysis. Finally, we conclude the chapter by proposing some tentative answers to the question of how public leadership can enhance public sector capacity for collaborative innovation.

THE WICKED DANISH GANG PROBLEM

In recent years, the Danish gang problem has grown considerably in scope and complexity. Today, it constitutes a *wicked problem* since it is not only hard to solve, but also difficult to define (Rittel & Webber, 1973). Historically, the Danish gang scene has been dominated by outlaw motorcycle gangs, as in other Scandinavian countries. The two dominant biker gangs, *Hells Angels* and *Bandidos*, expanded from the U.S. to Scandinavia in the 1980s and 1990s. In *The Great Nordic Biker War* from 1994 to 1997, extensive confrontations between these two rival gangs resulted in 11 killings and 74 attempted murders before they reached a peace agreement to cease fire and cancel all plans to set up new chapters in any of the Nordic countries (Høyer, 1999).

A seven year period of relative stability was interrupted in the mid-2000s. In 2004, the government decided to shut down *Pusher Street* in *Christiania* – an area of Copenhagen known for its open cannabis trade. The well-established gang turfs were disrupted and gang-related drug trafficking spread throughout the city of Copenhagen. The old biker gangs were increasingly challenged by ethnic minority youth gangs that had emerged in deprived neighbourhoods since the mid 1990's (Danish National Police, 1998, 1999, 2005).

---

[1] This chapter builds on research presented and discussed at greater length in the book *Samarbejdsdrevet innovation i bandeindsatsen* (Torfing & Krogh, 2013).

The ethnic minority youth gangs are less formalized than the well-established biker gangs and it has proven difficult for the authorities to keep up with their constantly shifting factions and alliances. Typically, recruitment takes place among friends, local acquaintances and younger siblings. Threats of fines and detention are often overshadowed by the benefits of belonging to the gangs. The incentives to join a gang are not only material but also include protection and security, social integration, a resistance identity and excitement in an otherwise dull and depressing environment (cf. Jankowski, 1991).

The rise of the ethnic minority youth gangs has significantly compounded both the complexity of the gang formation processes and the overall gang situation in Denmark. In this situation, standard solutions fall short, creating an urgent need for public innovation through cross-sector collaboration. In the summer of 2012, the Minister of Justice, Morten Bødskov, summarized the strategy to curb gang-related violence and crime as follows:

> *"We are intensifying our efforts in marginalized neighbourhoods where bikers and immigrant gangs recruit. (.) But it's an illusion to think that the police can do this alone. If we are to stop the gang recruitment of rootless youths, we need to involve the local community and the schools. These young people need to get an education and to enter the labour market as this will dramatically lower their risk of being recruited to gangs. But we also need the parents of the young immigrant boys to tell their sons: 'Stay away from these environments, even though they're your peers'" (Politiken, 10.06.2012, translated by the authors).*

Following this line of reasoning, Gang Councils were established in strategically selected municipalities in 2009. Here, the local authorities meet regularly with a diverse group of local community representatives to discuss the current gang situation and how to intervene. While public officials on all levels of government are prepared to engage with non-public actors to find new and innovative solutions to the complex gang problems, there is a lack of practical knowledge about how to lead such collaborative innovation processes. New theories of collaborative innovation leadership seek to capture the specificities of this type of leadership.

THEORIES OF COLLABORATIVE INNOVATION LEADERSHIP

In recent years, we have witnessed a growing interest in collaborative innovation in the public sector (Roberts & King, 1996; Van de Ven *et al.*, 2007; Eggers & Singh, 2009; Sørensen & Torfing, 2011). With its emphasis on multi-actor interaction in networks and partnerships, collaborative innovation offers a new approach to public innovation that builds on microeconomic theories of *social innovation* (Phills, Deiglmeier & Miller, 2008), *open innovation* (Chesbrough, 2003) and *co-creation* (Prahalad & Ramaswamy, 2004). These theories all stress the need to involve external stakeholders, *e.g.* customers, users, experts, *etc.*, in corporate innovation processes.

While innovation is here defined as the development and implementation of new ideas that produce a qualitative change in a given context (Roberts & King, 1996), we define collaboration as the constructive management of differences in order to find joint solutions to shared problems (Gray, 1989). Emergent problems, persistent challenges or new opportunities kick off open-ended search process for new and creative ideas that are assessed, selected, implemented and sometimes scaled up and spread to other contexts and organizations (cf. Eggers and Singh, 2009). As argued in the introduction to this edited volume, theories of collaborative innovation claim that all phases of the innovation process can be strengthened through collaboration between various public and/or private actors (Sørensen & Torfing, 2011). The definition of problems and challenges will be more accurate when actors with different types of knowledge and expertise on the subject are involved. Creativity increases as multi-actor collaboration disturbs the actors' perceptions and taken-for-granted assumptions and new ideas emerge and develop through mutual learning processes. The cost/benefit analyses and risk assessments of new, alternative solutions become more nuanced, enabling the selection of the most creative and promising solutions. Implementation of the selected solutions is also strengthened since multi-actor collaboration facilitates the mobilization of resources, stimulates inter-organizational coordination, and builds joint ownership of bold new initiatives. Finally, the participating stakeholders act as *innovation ambassadors* who help diffuse the innovative solutions to other parts of their organization or to other organizations in their respective networks. Collaborative innovation thus presents itself as a very promising method for public innovation.

In practice, however, the great potential of collaborative innovation is not always fulfilled. Getting relevant, interested and resourceful actors together to collaborate and produce public innovation is no easy task due to various commonplace barriers. First, barriers to stakeholder participation may be present. These barriers include the absence of a tradition of participation in a given field; bad experiences from previous participatory processes; and uncertainty among the stakeholders about the level of engagement of the other actors, the benefits of participation, as well as the requirements and costs of participation (Ansell & Gash, 2007; Gray,

1989). Second, barriers may exist that prevent constructive collaboration between different actors, *e.g.* organizational and mental silos, lack of mutual trust between the parties as well as deeper conflicts of interest (Straus, 2002). Finally, there may be barriers which impede both the formulation and implementation of innovative solutions. These barriers include the emergence of a tunnel vision among actors who frequently work together and know each other well (Skilton & Dooley, 2010); risk aversion on the part of actors who avoid trying something new due to the risk of failure (Mulgan, 2007); and low degrees of institutionalization in collaborative arenas, leading to unclear divisions of responsibility and a lack of administrative routines and thereby to a failure to implement new and creative solutions (O'Toole, 1997).

In order to overcome these and similar barriers, a specific type of leadership is needed (Ansell & Gash, 2012; Sørensen & Torfing, 2012). Recent research on collaborative innovation leadership draws on theories of distributive, collaborative and integrative leadership in order to identify distinct collaborative innovation leadership roles that respond to the challenges of engaging relevant stakeholders in constructive collaboration that will result in innovation (Crosby & Bryson, 2010; Morse, 2010; Page, 2010; Ansell & Gash, 2012). These roles we will label the *convener*, the *facilitator* and the *catalyst* (Torfing, 2012; Torfing & Krogh, 2013; Kankaala & Krogh, 2014).

The primary task of the *convener* is to initiate collaboration and set up the collaborative arena. The convener identifies relevant stakeholders, assembles the team and brings the parties together by creating institutional frameworks, processes and incentives that promote collaborative action, *e.g.* by constituting a *burning platform* and stressing the actors' interdependence. The convener can also pre-empt future conflicts by helping the parties to align their expectations and clarify their respective roles and responsibilities from the outset. Being clear about who will do what in which parts of the innovation process reduces uncertainties for the actors involved, increases commitment to the process, and lowers the risk of disappointment with other actors.

When the relevant stakeholders have agreed to collaborate, the *facilitator* enters the stage. The role of the facilitator is to help parties with different interests and perspectives to work together. The facilitator's primary task is to continuously support the collaboration process by promoting collaborative relationships and mutual trust among participants, *e.g.* by helping them to formulate common rules, establish a shared knowledge base and develop a common language. The facilitator organizes meetings that enable the active participation of relevant stakeholders and drives the process forward by following up on the steps and actions agreed upon by the participants. In cases of persistent disagreements about the distribution of costs and benefits of innovative solutions, it is the task of the facilitator to mediate negotiations among the involved actors. It is important to note that the facilitator's task is not simply to avoid conflicts by building consensus. It is precisely the differences between the actors in terms of their worldviews, forms of knowledge, ideas and points of view that make their collaboration potentially innovative. The facilitator should be aware that disputes, disagreements and conflicts are not only very likely to arise when diverse actors are brought together in sustained interaction, but can in fact be an important source of innovation. Thus, the facilitator's role is to help the participants to make these clashes and conflicts productive rather than destructive.

When collaboration has been established and trust has been built between the collaborators, the need for the *catalyst* arises. The task of the catalyst is to inspire participants to *think outside the box* by challenging any basic assumptions, perceptions and understandings that restrict the way in which the problem is conceived and the problem-solving options available to them. Thus, while the facilitator's role is to support and enhance collaboration, the role of the catalyst is to disturb the collaborators' cognitive processes. Disturbances can be introduced by bringing new actors onto the arena, by supplying the participants with new knowledge about the problem, and by pointing to the limited reach and/or direct negative consequences of both the established and the alternative solutions being discussed. Like the other leadership roles, the catalyst's role is not limited to *hands-on leadership* through direct participation but can also take the form of *hands-off leadership*. *Hands-off* innovation leadership involves making strategic changes in the institutional design in question with a view to challenging social conventions and interaction patterns among the participants. This can be done by changing the site and form of the meetings and the way in which information is distributed between meetings.

Since collaborative innovation unfold in complex processes characterised by jumps, feedback loops and iterations (Van de Ven *et al.*, 2007), the three types of innovation leadership must often be exercised simultaneously and in varying sequences depending on the needs that arise along the way. Also, it is important to note that the three leadership roles can be performed by one or more individuals, *e.g.* politicians, public administrators or participants involved in a collaborative innovation process, as well as organizations inside or outside the collaboration such as government agencies, administrative units and secretariats; and/or metagoverning networks, assemblies and other collaborative bodies.

After considering how the cases were selected and how the data was collected, we will compare the 14 innovation projects across four key analytical dimensions: the problems addressed; the type of innovation developed; the scope of collaboration; and the role of leadership and management. We examine the challenges to, and needs for, leadership as experienced by the participants in order to advance our understanding of when and where collaborative innovation leadership is particularly needed, what public leaders should be aware of when leading processes of collaborative innovation and how they should go about it.

CASE SELECTION AND DATA COLLECTION

Studying collaborative innovation through case studies involves a choice between carrying out in depth analysis of one or two cases, or looking for similarities and differences in comparative studies of a larger number of cases. We have chosen the latter option because we want to explore variation in collaborative innovation processes and because we do not yet have sufficient knowledge to select a typical or extreme case that will permit hypothesis testing.

The cases were identified through reputational sampling. We used mass media and websites to identify a number of key actors engaged in efforts to curb gangs in Nørrebro, allegedly the most gang-ridden borough of Copenhagen. These key actors were asked to point out local projects that were trying out something new and that involved different local actors in the design and/or implementation phase. Individuals involved in the identified projects were then asked the same questions. When we reached a point where we rarely heard about new projects and initiatives, we suspended the search for new projects. Through this process, 14 projects aiming at reducing gang-related violence and crime were identified, all of which we deemed relevant as examples of collaborative innovation.

The projects involve the establishment of *parent networks* that take collective responsibility for the children in the neighbourhood and promote positive norms and codes of conduct; *local police officers* who walk or cycle through the local area on a daily basis to show presence, allay conflicts and build trust; *street outreach teams* that build relationships with young people and help calm things down when trouble is brewing; *open school events* where social workers and other community resources are present at the local school after regular opening hours in order to help families with their social problems and concerns; the provision of *after-school jobs* that provide young people with an alternative income to that obtained from the gangs while fostering a sense of ownership over neighbourhood maintenance; *resource centres* that keep young people off the streets, create positive social communities and provide opportunities for meaningful leisure activities arranged by volunteers; and an *outdoor music festival* that encourages the local community to reclaim the streets.

The reputational sampling method proved valuable in identifying a relatively large number of relevant cases within the same policy area in a relatively short period of time. However, the method also introduces some bias into our sample. First, the vast majority of our cases (13 out of 14) involve public funding and/or participation, which might at least partly be explained by the fact that most of the key actors initially contacted were civil servants. Second, the identified innovation projects are all relatively successful, which might be caused by reluctance on the part of actors in the field to report on failed projects. Finally, we cannot determine whether our sample is representative of the general population of collaborative innovation projects addressing gang violence in Nørrebro since we do not know the total number of projects. However, we consider this a secondary concern since our aim is first and foremost to identify and describe examples of collaborative innovation within the same policy area in order to better understand the role of leadership. The data collected mainly consists of semi-structured interviews with a total of 30 interviewees in key positions with respect to our cases. Some of the interviewees were involved in more than one innovation project, enabling them to shed light on several of our cases. In some cases we carried out follow-up phone interviews or asked for clarification *via* e-mail. Furthermore, a substantial amount of written material was collected and analysed. Apart from the material publicly available on websites, all interviewees were asked to provide written material on the innovation project at hand. The documents obtained include pamphlets, newspaper articles, meeting minutes and policy reports. Finally, we enriched our empirical data collection by organizing a theatre workshop where key actors were invited to take part in a discussion about collaborative innovation. The workshop was videotaped and used as data material alongside the qualitative interviews. For each case the data was coded according to the key analytical dimensions of i) the problem addressed; ii) the solution to the problem; iii) the scope of collaboration; iv) leadership and management; and v) drivers and barriers in the process. In the following section, we compare the 14 innovation projects across the first four dimensions before examining the challenges to, and needs for, leadership as expressed by the participants in the collaborative innovation processes.

COMPARING THE 14 INNOVATION CASES

In Table **1**, the 14 innovation cases are compared across four key analytical dimensions. As the comparison reveals, it is primarily the lack of services and the failure to meet the social needs of youth at risk and their families and neighbourhoods that spur the search for new and innovative solutions. While there are some examples of innovative projects that target existing gang members ('The Exit Strategy' and 'Mankind'), the predominant focus is to prevent youth at risk from being recruited to gangs. Some of the projects aim to serve a broader social purpose and include parents and families in their target groups ('The Holistic Community Strategy' and 'The Open School Project'). Finally, more general problems such as real or perceived insecurity in the neighbourhood have also given rise to innovation ('Your Police Officer' and 'Songs from the Borough').

Most of the innovative projects take the form of *service innovations* that offer new and alternative ways of catering to the needs of specific citizens and population groups (cf. Hartley, 2005). Interestingly, many of the specific service innovations involve *process innovation, i.e.* innovative processes for the production and delivery of public services. Several examples show how these initiatives push the limits of the public sector, *e.g.* by involving volunteers in the provision of services and thereby bringing about *governance innovation.*

Regarding the scope of collaboration, multi-actor collaboration is mostly limited to smaller and more manageable innovation projects requiring less coordination and support (such as 'First Floor', 'The Uncle Network', and 'Mankind) and to initiatives that adopt innovative solutions developed in other local contexts ('The Night Owls'). Furthermore, the data reveals deeper and wider collaboration in the implementation phase than during the project formulation phase, suggesting that difficulties may arise from the involvement of many different people and organizations in the phase where new and innovative ideas are being developed. Conversely, collaboration, coordination and support are clearly important during the implementation phase. Finally, only four of the 14 projects exclusively involve public actors ('The Exit Strategy', 'Your Police Officer', 'First Floor', and 'The Street Team'), and only one project involves only private partners ('Mankind'). Collaborating across the public-private divide seems to be appealing – especially in the implementation phase – perhaps because of the significant benefits that can be obtained by leveraging complementary public and private resources.

In several cases, we observe a shift in leadership during the collaborative innovation process whereby individual innovation leadership only plays a role in the first phases, while a more traditional form of operational management takes over during the implementation phase. One example of this is 'Resource Centre Outer Nørrebro'. At the beginning, one or more passionate proponents would

Table 1: Comparison of the 14 cases across four analytical dimensions

Case	Problem	Innovative solution	Collaboration	Leadership
'The Exit Strategy'	Gang members have a hard time leaving the gangs	Timely, holistic and customized services for gang members (service and process innovation)	Collaboration between four municipal administrations	A shared secretariat provides administrative support and facilitates collaboration
'Your Police Officer'	Police cars with wailing sirens erode feelings of safety among residents and complicate police investigation	Local police officers walk or bike through the local area to defuse conflicts and build trust (service and process innovation)	Collaboration between local police department, local politicians and civil servants in local government	Politicians initiate the innovation and the local police conducts operational management
'The Holistic Community Strategy'	Residential area with high concentration of social problems and marginalized ethnic minority youth serves as a breeding ground for gangs	Residents are involved in solving social problems, improving conditions for children and youth and enhancing public safety (service and process innovation)	Collaboration between municipal administrations, tenant association, housing association, and local community organizations; considerable number of external conflicts.	A steering committee leads the collaboration and conducts operational management
'Resource Centre Outer Nørrebro'	Lack of spare time activities in marginalized residential areas increases risk of gang formation and recruitment	Provision of local leisure activities in close collaboration with citizens and local community organizations (governance innovation)	Collaboration between local politicians, municipal administrations, local QUANGO, associations and residents	Politicians initiate the innovation and day-to-day manager conducts project management with executive committee, advisory board, and youth council
'First Floor'	Youth hang out on the streets and lack various kinds of support	Drop-in Centre offering spare time activities, doing outreach work and developing positive role models (service and process innovation)	Collaboration between director and employees of the Centre, local schools, local police and municipal administrations	The director of the Centre initiates innovation and facilitates support from authorities and employees
'Club 36'	Public cutbacks have created a need for services for children and youth in a marginalized residential area	Tutoring, homework café, sports activities and organized day trips seeking to involve girls and their mothers (service and process innovation)	Collaboration between a local community organization, the municipality, Danish Refugee Council and local volunteers	A local community organization initiates and manages the innovation

Table 1: contd…

'The Portable Cabins Project'	Youth hanging out and hassling passers-by at a town square	Temporary, custom-made initiative offering cabins as a place for youth to hang out (service innovation)	Collaboration between SSP (Schools, Social services, and Police), municipal administration, local community organization, local police, 'First Floor', 'The Street Team' and local gym; conflicts with tenants association.	The SSP initiates the innovation and a local community organization conducts operational management and maintains contact with collaborators
'The After-School Job Project'	Youth at risk engage in criminal activity instead of getting an education and seeking employment	Introducing youth to the labour market and procurement of after-school jobs in the public and private sector through the Jobindex website (service innovation)	Collaboration between local politicians, municipal Job Centre, Jobindex, immigrant association, municipal administration, local youth network and local community associations	The mayor initiates the innovation, a project manager in the Job Centre establishes a steering committee, and the committee conducts operational management and maintains contact with collaborators
'The Street Team'	At-risk youth in a deprived residential area need support to avoid a criminal career	The Street Team walks the neighbourhood and provides on-the-spot counselling in the community (service innovation)	Public employee-driven innovation without collaboration in the initial phases, however broad network of various service providers later on	An employee at the local Service Centre initiates the innovation and a project coordinator manages external contacts
'The Uncle Network'	Ethnic minority youth lack support, recognition and advice from adults with the same ethnic background as themselves	A group of fathers and other grown men act as 'uncles' to children and youth in a conflict-ridden neighbourhood to promote dialogue and a peaceful code of conduct (service and governance innovation)	Collaboration between an informal parent group and employees in a local community organization	A local community organization initiates contact to a parent group and manages the network
'The Night Owls'	Youth feel unsafe at night due to occasional acts of violence and the presence of police	Local teams of adult volunteers are present at particular hot-spots at night to make youth feel safe and calm things down if conflicts arise (service and governance innovation)	Collaboration between volunteers, local police and residents	The national association of Night Owls provides project management tools to local volunteers conducting operational management

Table 1: contd...

'The Open School Project'	A local school receives a large amount of inquiries from ethnic minority parents who need help addressing social and family problems	Every other week, a diverse team of public employees offers on-site support and case management at the local school (organizational and service innovation)	Collaboration between the principal, consultancy company, public employees from various municipal administrations, unpaid association guides, pupils and parents	The principal initiates the collaboration and brings together the relevant stakeholders to find a solution to the problem
'Mankind'	Public authorities and projects have a hard time reaching gang members and influencing their norms, values and identities	A community association advocates positive male roles in order to limit the use of violence and threats that make life unsafe for families of gang members (governance innovation)	Collaboration between private citizens and local community associations.	A passionate local resident with previous experience from social work and crime prevention leads the innovation
'Songs from the Borough'	Tensions between police and local residents and an increase in gang-related shootings	Private initiative sets up a residents' church choir, arranges an outdoor music festival where the choir sings alongside the police choir, and urges residents to reclaim the streets (governance innovation)	Collaboration between citizens, the local church, police, municipality, local associations and local businesses	A passionate local resident initiates and leads the innovation process

often act as conveners, facilitators and catalysts for collaborative innovation initiatives. Later on, more formalized steering groups and committees have tended to take over primary responsibility for leading and monitoring the projects. For instance, in 'The After-School Job Project' the mayor and a project manager from the Job Centre set the agenda and created an alliance between key stakeholders before handing over operational management of the project to a steering committee. However, there are still examples of individual innovation leadership enduring beyond the first phase (*e.g.* 'First Floor', 'The Street Team', 'The Open School Project', and 'Mankind'). Second, the data shows that collaborative innovation is initiated both from below by actors on the ground and from above by central decision makers. Most of the projects were initiated by public and private employees applying for public and private funding and other kinds of resources from higher up in the system. A few of the projects were initiated by incumbent politicians ('Your Police Officer', 'Resource Centre Outer Nørrebro', and 'The After-School Job Project'); others by local civil society activists who had managed to establish collaborative relations with private and public partners ('Mankind' and 'Songs from the Borough'). Finally, the data also shows that not only public leaders exercise collaborative innovation leadership: local community organizations, private associations and citizens also take on responsibility for convening, facilitating and catalysing collaborative innovation processes.

Barriers to Collaborative Innovation

Having broadly compared the 14 collaborative innovation cases, we will now discuss the challenges experienced in the innovation processes and the leadership needed to address them.

The cases show that innovation leaders are faced with a number of barriers to innovation which they try to tackle. As pointed out by the theories of collaborative innovation leadership presented above, a first challenge is to get relevant and resourceful actors engaged in collaboration. Several of our interviewees point to the lack of incentives for otherwise relevant actors as a particularly important barrier in this regard. If relevant associations and organizations cannot discern any clear benefits from spending time and resources on collaboration with other actors, collaborative innovation processes are likely to be hampered. For example, it is obviously relevant for street outreach workers, the police and others to collaborate with local sports clubs to set up new, alternative activities for youth who would otherwise be hanging out in the streets increasing the risk of recruitment by gangs. However, public employees report that sports clubs show little interest in such collaboration. As one public leader says:

> *"Local sports clubs have no impetus or motivation to collaborate around anything other than what they already do. If they have sufficient members and training hours and otherwise function fairly well why should they get involved in social work in marginalized neighbourhoods? Why would they want to enrol all the troublemakers into their club and do something for them?"* (Interview, translated by the authors)

A second challenge arises when relevant stakeholders do come together to find a new and innovative solution to a common problem, but fail to collaborate productively. While minor conflicts may be fruitful in the sense that they force the actors to sharpen their ideas and arguments and revise their proposed solutions, serious conflicts may destroy collaboration and create insurmountable deadlocks that prevent innovation. Destructive conflicts are triggered by various factors. Some stem from the divergent interests of different project managers and organizations that all want to cater to the same group of users. There are, for example, competing after-school projects launched by the municipal Job Centre, the Steering Committee of 'The Holistic Community Strategy' and a resourceful local block association, respectively, causing tension among these otherwise obvious collaborators. Conflicts also arise because stakeholders have different professional approaches and all take pride in their own particular endeavours and ways of thinking. As a seasoned project manager explains:

> *"Although there are many enthusiasts who all have good intentions, that doesn't mean that they are open to other people's ideas. There are a lot of people who want to appear to have done the best job. So to be honest, there is a lot of infighting"* (Interview, translated by the authors).

Several other interviewees confirm that there is often a "*battle to take credit for new ideas and projects, which can obstruct the projects themselves*". Since no single actor is responsible for the final results of these complex collaborative innovation processes, the participating organizations engage in disruptive battles for credit and glory, hampering both current and future collaborative innovation processes.

Finally, barriers exist that are attributable neither to lack of interest in collaboration nor to collaboration difficulties, but rather have to do with the stakeholders' ability to produce innovative solutions to the problems at hand. In some cases, key stakeholders experience the collaborative processes as being 'locked', and feel that they have little or no opportunity to move beyond what has already been thought of. As a prominent member of the local trade association puts it:

> *"When you enter the public bureaucracy, it's often difficult to push things forward and bring about change. Very often, the collaboration is organised around something that has been decided upon in advance, and which they simply want us to legitimize. It has already been decided on and now they want us to say that it's a good idea in order to ensure support and encouragement to do this or that. But people's inclination to participate evaporates if they have no influence"* (Interview, translated by the authors).

Such experiences do not only indicate constraints on the public sector's immediate capacity for collaborative innovation; they are also remembered by the involved actors for years to come and thus constitute a barrier to collaborative innovation in the future.

Collaborative Innovation Leadership

In order to succeed in fostering collaborative innovation and enhancing the capacity for collaborative innovation in the public sector, the barriers mentioned above must be overcome, mitigated or at least addressed through innovation leadership. This places new demands on public leaders. Interviewees employed in local government and the police generally agree that the pool of talented and ambitious public leaders is larger than ever before. This is perhaps most notable within the police. As one police commissioner says:

> *"I think we are better educated today than the leaders before me. They were perhaps more conservative and rigid. Today police leaders are handpicked to a much larger extent than just 10-15 years ago. We also have an HR department, which we certainly didn't have before"* (Interview, translated by the authors).

New, more open and competent public leaders are certainly conducive to collaborative innovation. But even for skilled leaders, the leadership tasks in question are not straightforward. A local project manager reflects on the needs and challenges of collaborative innovation leadership:

> *"You can't put one of the participating organizations in charge of the collaboration as the others get jealous. There has to be some kind of 'Mother Earth' that governs them all; a central body that governs all participants and activities in the collaboration. They may well accept that, especially if they trust the governing body"* (Interview, translated by the authors).

The point is not only that there is a need for collaborative leadership, but also that this kind of leadership should come from the outside or at least from a well-connected actor who is trusted by the other actors. If leadership is exercised by a participating organization in the collaboration rather than, for example, by a professional facilitator or a secretariat, it can be a challenging task to exercise impartial leadership for the benefit of the whole network while acting in the role of an interested party (cf. Provan og Kenis, 2007).

It appears essential that leadership of multi-actor collaboration does not revert to traditional forms of hierarchical leadership involving the exercise of authority through orders, control and sanctions. Management must provide space for the participants to act and encourage active participation as well as individual and collective self-management. An experienced public leader confirms the need for this type of leadership when dealing with collaborative innovation processes:

> *"When it comes to leadership, it is important for the municipality to give employees the freedom to work with what they are most passionate about and to assure them that what they are doing is okay and that*

> *collaborating with others is alright. Because this is often how new ideas come to life and flourish. If problems arise and they come back to me and tell me that things are not working out the way they should, then it is my job to facilitate the process"* (Interview, translated by the authors).

From this perspective, collaborative innovation leadership should primarily be conducted *hands-off*, while *hands-on* leadership should be conducted only if problems arise. When it comes to the exercise of *hands-on* innovation leadership, the empirical data confirms the importance of the convener role in assembling the right team by hand-picking actors with relevant innovation assets. As one public leader says:

> *"When you want to start up a new project, the municipality calls in the relevant actors that have the necessary competences and who know something about what it takes to succeed. I myself think that we are good at picking out the important and relevant people, but you cannot force people to collaborate..But it definitely means a lot if you are able to gather the right people to solve the right problem"* (Interview, translated by the authors).

When the team is assembled, there is also a need for facilitative leadership. As mentioned, collaboration is complicated by the fact that both public and private firebrands tend to focus on their own achievements. It is a demanding leadership task to facilitate collaboration in this kind of environment. As one public leader says:

> *"The project managers of the individual projects are often very proud of their projects and they basically think that they are the best and the brightest. Of course it's a good thing that they are proud of what they do, but it's our job to get them to loosen up and collaborate with each other. Get them to sit down together and discuss the pros and cons of different solutions. Take their respective strengths and convey them to the others. That's a huge task"* (Interview, translated by the authors).

As may be apparent at this point, there is no evidence of a single, ground-breaking innovation in efforts to reduce gang-related violence and crime; rather, we see a large number of incremental innovations. Several interviewees point to the need for better coordination of, and between, the various projects. Although coordination differs from collaboration in the sense that it does not involve any attempt to work upon and transform a common 'boundary object', coordination appears to be an important element in the attempt to establish good and productive relations between relevant stakeholders and to optimize the overall performance of the ecology of innovation projects. Thus, coordination can help defuse and prevent destructive conflicts between project managers that constitute a barrier to future collaborative innovation processes.

CONCLUSION

The empirical findings presented in this chapter add to the growing literature on collaborative innovation leadership by answering key questions about when and where leadership is particularly needed, what public leaders should be aware of when leading processes of collaborative innovation, and how they can contribute to the development of innovative solutions to wicked problems such as the current Danish gang problem.

The need for collaborative innovation leadership seems particularly pertinent in 'first mover' initiatives that are not simply adopted from other contexts and in larger innovation projects where multi-actor collaboration is both extensive and complex. Furthermore, when projects move from the project formulation phase to the implementation phase, collaboration tends to deepen and widen, indicating that the need for collaborative leadership increases as processes of innovation unfold. By the same token, leadership tends to shift from individual innovation leadership to project management undertaken by formalized steering groups, committees and administrations, suggesting that leadership tasks become more comprehensive and demanding as innovation processes develop.

Since collaborative innovation is not only initiated from above but also from below, political leaders and public managers should continuously scan the field for new and promising initiatives and be ready to step in to provide the necessary support. Such a search for new and promising initiatives should exceed the boundaries of the public sector since collaborative innovation is not only initiated by public leaders and employees but also by private and third sector parties. When public organizations do step in, they should be careful not to stifle innovation by taking over full responsibility for the projects and preventing joint ownership over the processes since stakeholders become disinclined to participate if they feel they have no say. For this reason, public managers should encourage active participation as well as individual and collective self-regulation, allowing public and private employees and local civil society activists to take on leadership roles.

When exercising collaborative innovation leadership, the data suggests that public leaders should be particularly aware of the importance of constituting 'burning platforms' and stressing the interdependence of relevant actors since the lack of incentives proves to be a particularly important barrier preventing relevant and resourceful actors from engaging in collaboration. Also, they should be aware of the challenges of exercising impartial unbiased leadership for the benefit of the entire network while acting in the role of an interested party. In order to avoid destructive conflicts and disruptive battles for credit and glory, *hands-off* leadership must be exercised by common or neutral secretariats and steering committees and *hands-on* leadership by professional facilitators or, if this is not feasible, by well-connected and trusted actors. Finally, public managers should be aware of the importance of coordination for establishing good and productive relations between relevant stakeholders and optimizing the overall performance of the ecology of innovation projects unfolding in various local contexts.

Even when talented public leaders and managers are aware of the specific type of leadership needed to drive collaborative innovation processes forward, it is still a demanding task to lead complex processes of collaboration among multiple actors, each with their own resources, interests and professional approaches. If public organizations wish to develop innovative solutions to wicked problems they must train, encourage and support public leaders by deliberately and systematically developing their ability to convene, facilitate and catalyse processes of collaborative innovation; enable and urge public managers to exercise *hands-on* and *hands-off* innovation leadership by allocating the necessary time and resources for such activities; and ease the leadership tasks by building institutional designs that strengthen vertical and horizontal coordination and collaboration among public and private stakeholders.

ACKNOWLEDGEMENTS

Declared none.

CONFLICT OF INTEREST

The authors confirm that this chapter contents have no conflict of interest.

REFERENCES

Aagaard, P., Sørensen, E., & Torfing, J. (eds) (2014). *Samarbejdsdrevet innovation i praksis*. Copenhagen: DJØF Publishing.

Ansell, C. & Gash, A. (2007). Collaborative governance in theory and practice. In *Journal of Public Administration Research and Theory*, 18:4, 543-571.

Ansell, C. & Gash, A. (2012). Stewards, mediators and catalysts: Toward a model of collaborative leadership. In *The Innovation Journal*, 17:1, 1-21.

Chesbrough, H. (2003). *Open Innovation*, Boston: Harvard Business School Press.

Crosby, B. C. & Bryson, J. M. (2010). Integrative Leadership and the Creation and Maintenance of Cross-sector Collaboration. In *Leadership Quarterly*, 21:2, 211-230.

Danish National Police (1998). *Gadebander i Danmark 1998*, Copenhagen: Rigspolitiets styregruppe vedrørende bandekriminalitet.

Danish National Police (1999). *Gadebander i Danmark 1999*, Copenhagen: Rigspolitiets styregruppe vedrørende bandekriminalitet.

Danish National Police (2005). *Strategi for en forstærket indsats mod de kriminelle grupper og netværk, der begår alvorlig kriminalitet*, available at http://www.politi.dk.

Eggers, W. D. & Singh, S. (2009). *The Public Innovators Playbook*. Washington: Harvard Kennedy School of Government.

Gray, B. (1989). *Collaborating: Finding Common Ground for Multiparty Problems*. San Francisco: Jossey-Bass.

Hartley, J. (2005). Innovation in Governance and Public Services: Past and Present. In *Public Money & Management*, 25:1, 27-34.

Høyer, Thorkild (1999). *Den store nordiske rockerkrig*. København: Gyldendal.

Jankowski, M. S. (1991). *Islands in the Street: Gangs and American Urban Society*. Berkeley: University of California Press.

Kankaala, E. & Krogh, A.H. (2014). Ledelse af samarbejdsdrevet innovation i den kriminalpræventive indsats. In P. Aagaard, E. Sørensen & J. Torfing (eds), *Samarbejdsdrevet innovation i praksis*. Copenhagen: Jurist- og Økonomforbundets Forlag, (pp. 309-327).

Morse, R. (2010). Integrative public leadership: Catalyzing collaboration to create public value. In *The Leadership Quarterly*, 21:2, 231-245.

Mulgan, G. (2007). Ready or not? Taking innovation in the public sector seriously. In *Provocation*, 3, London: NESTA.

O'Toole, L. J. (1997). Implementing Public Innovations in Network Settings. In *Administration and Society*, 29:2, 115-138.

Page, S. (2010). Integrative Leadership for Collaborative Governance: Civic Engagement in Seattle. In *Leadership Quarterly*, 21:2, 246-263.

Phills, J. A. J., Deiglmeier, K. & Miller, D. T. (2008). Rediscovering Social Innovation. In *Stanford Social Innovation Review*, 6:4, 34-43.

Politiken (2012). *Straf er en del af resocialiseringen*, June 10th, PS, (p. 8).

Prahalad, C. & Ramasway, V. (2004). *The Future of Competition: Co-creating Unique Value with Customers*. Boston: Harvard Business School Press.

Provan, G. P. & Kenus, P (2007), Modes of Network Governance: Structure, Management, and Effectiveness. In *Journal of Public Administration Research and Theory*, 18, 229-252.

Rittel, H. J. & Webber, M. M. (1973). Dilemmas in a general theory of planning. In *Policy Sciences*, 4, 155-169.

Roberts, N. C. & King, P.J. (1996). *Transforming Public Policy*. San Francisco: Jossey-Bass.

Skilton, P. F. & Dooley, K. (2010). The effects of repeat collaboration on creative abrasion. In *The* Academy of Management Review, 35:1, 118-134.

Straus, D. (2002). *How to Make Collaboration Work*. San Francisco: Berrett Koehler Publishers.

Sørensen, E. & Torfing, J. (2011), Enhancing Collaborative Innovation in the Public Sector. In *Administration and Society*, 43:8, 842–868.

Sørensen, E. & Torfing, J. (2012). Introduction: Collaborative Innovation in the Public Sector. In *The Innovation Journal*, 17:1, article 1.

Torfing, J. (2011). Teorier om offentlig organisation og styring: Fra stillestående bureaukrati til samarbejdsdrevet innovation. In E. Sørensen & J. Torfing (eds), *Samarbejdsdrevet innovation i den offentlige sektor*, Copenhagen: DJØF Publishing, 117-138.

Torfing, J. (2012). Samarbejdsdrevet innovation i den offentlige sektor: Drivkræfter, barrierer og behovet for innovationsledelse. In *Scandinavian Journal of Public Administration,* 16:1, 27-47.

Torfing, J. & Krogh, A.H. (2013), *Samarbejdsdrevet innovation i bandeindsatsen*, Copenhagen: DJØF Publishing.

Van de Ven, A., Polley, D., Garud, R. & Venkataraman, S. (2007), *The Innovation Journey*. Oxford: Oxford University Press.

Wenger, E. (1998), *Communities of Practices*, Cambridge: Cambridge University Press

CHAPTER 6

Overcoming Conflicting Logics of Care and Justice: Collaborative Innovation in Dealing with Habitual Offenders in the Netherlands

Hendrik Wagenaar*, Joost Vos, Corine Balder and Bert van Hemert

The Department of Town and Regional planning at University of Sheffield, UK; TNO Management Consultants; Hogeschool Leiden; The Department of Psychiatry of Leiden University Medical Center, The Netherlands

Abstract: Dutch cities suffer from the behaviour of a small group of treatment-resistant serious habitual offenders. This situation challenges service coordination between municipal authorities, and representatives from care and criminal justice systems. In the last decade Dutch government introduced the *Veiligheidshuis* (Safety House) as a platform for managing the above safety issues; a network environment for coordinating social care and criminal justice interventions in the realm of crime and security. This study aims to analyse the nature of the problem of persistent lack of service coordination and the value of the introduction of the Veiligheidshuis. The collaboration with in the Veiligheidshuis in two cities was studied and the service career of six of the most persistent habitual offenders was followed and discussed with the concerned professionals and teams. In this action research grounded theory was used to analyse data from interviews and observations. This study demonstrates how the practical work of dealing with habitual offenders is afflicted by conflicting logics of care and criminal justice. Conflicting cultures, diametrically opposed organizational structures and poorly connecting professional domains result in fragmented and often ineffective interventions towards habitual offenders. This study also demonstrates that cross-sector collaboration in a dense network of agencies to help bridge the gap between divergent professional sectors is possible. The innovation of the Veiligheidshuis leads to the development of a collaborative framework for action and the creation of various coordination mechanisms. These in turn stimulated the timely sharing of information, and the development of mutual trust and support. As a practical result from this study case management meetings were redesigned in a recursive way. Thus the effectiveness of these meetings as a management tool was greatly enhanced.

Keywords: Conflicting logics, organisational innovation, coordination, collaboration, habitual offenders, criminal justice sector, care sector, Veiligheidshuizen.

***Corresponding author Hendrik Wagenaar:** University of Sheffield, UK; Tel: +441142226924; E-mail: h.wagenaar@sheffield.ac.uk

Annika Agger, Bodil Damgaard, Andreas Hagedorn Krogh and Eva Sørensen (Eds.)

INTRODUCTION

High expectations about the benefits of government inevitably lead to a gap between ambition and outcome and thus to a powerful call to action (Sørensen & Torfing, 2013, 847; Vos & Wagenaar, 2012). As it is in the nature of public services to fall short of their own elevated moral aspirations, innovation is a continuous desire. In today's service landscape the call for innovation is couched in the language of markets and collaboration (Hartley, 2005). This is particularly the case in innovation of service delivery across sectors.

This chapter focuses on process innovation and organizational innovation, prompted by the need of service innovation in a cross-sector collaborative setting. We build on our earlier work on the so-called Münchhausen Movement in Rotterdam, where we demonstrate that a social movement could improve collaboration by articulating norms and values in a cross sector collaborative setting (Vos & Wagenaar, 2012). We showed how a large number of organisations in the city of Rotterdam significantly enhanced collaboration by organising practice-oriented meetings between representatives of the organisations. We described how social movements in the context of social services as a collective venture were based on opposition and protest against failing practices and forged a collective orientation towards a new, morally grounded, order. Participants in social movements share ideas, identities, ideals and emotions in search for a system of care (and justice) that is better attuned both to the needs of the most vulnerable citizens and their own service ethos. They create a relatively durable community that is action oriented and that is in sustained interaction with opponents. However, although it managed to establish a genuine collaborative attitude amongst partners, the Münchhausen Movement failed to create mechanisms for coordination of recurring cases.

The subject of our study is the network of agencies that deal with habitual offenders. The extreme service resistance of a small group of habitual offenders seriously challenges the Dutch social service and criminal justice system. The Dutch government has diagnosed the problem as one of failing service coordination of agencies and organisations that deal with crime and public nuisance, in particular the bridging of activities between the care and the criminal justice sector. As an answer to this problem the government has created, in the last decade, a particular innovation, the *Veiligheidshuis* (literally, Safety House). We will show how this innovation helps to bridge the gap between the care sector and the criminal justice sector and creates new practices and new ways of organizing and managing the collaboration and coordination between agencies.

In this chapter we will analyse the nature of the problem of persistent lack of service coordination in the case of habitual offenders, introduce the *Veiligheidshuis* and show the challenges it faces by introducing the case of Mirella. We then briefly describe our research methods. We, next, demonstrate how the practical work of dealing with habitual offenders is afflicted by conflicting logics. These consist of conflicting cultures, diametrically opposed structures and poorly connecting domains. We show that the innovation of the *Veiligheidshuizen* leads to the development of a collaborative framework for action and the creation of various coordination mechanisms. In our discussion we reflect on our findings and demonstrate the value and limits of this innovation in dealing with cross sector collaboration.

THE CALL FOR INNOVATIVE SOCIAL SERVICE PROVISION

It is easy to understand how lack of coordination has become a dominant problem in social service delivery in the Netherlands. Since the early 1980s, neoliberal public administration ideology has resulted in an effective overhaul of the financial regime of social service delivery. Most service agencies now operate under new rules of financial accountability, in which they have to demonstrate the effectiveness of their interventions for the continuation of financial resources. One of the unintended consequences has been an exacerbation of fragmentation. Public agencies now operate with more autonomy, at *arms-length* from state bureaucracies. Many services are contracted out to the non- or for-profit sector. In addition the remuneration system is structured in such a way that agencies no longer have time for *non-service* activities such as consulting with colleagues, making telephone calls or attending meetings that are not remunerated under the agreed payment schedule. Yet, effective service delivery in a fragmented and discontinuous service landscape requires collaboration between multiple agencies each with their own values, practices, professional socialization and organizational loyalties.

Habitual offenders impose serious costs on society; dealing with their problems requires intensive interventions of both the criminal justice sector and the care sector. According to the definition of the Dutch Ministry of Safety and Justice habitual offenders are persons who have been convicted of a crime or misdemeanour more than ten times in their life, one time of which in the past year. Very active habitual offenders are habitual offenders with more than ten convictions in the last five years, one of which in the past year. Habitual offenders thus are a significant source of individual and family trouble and of public nuisance. The social costs of their crimes, including emotional costs and costs of the use of the criminal system are calculated to be over € 15.000 per month per person, twice the monthly costs of incapacitation and treatment within the framework of the habitual offenders law (Vollaard, 2010). Society benefits socially and economically from an effective approach to the problem of habitual offenders.

Habitual offenders are disadvantaged people with service needs that transcend professional disciplines and with an often poignant life history. Many of them are addicted to drugs or alcohol (70%), have considerable psychological problems and/or problems with work, housing and relationships (WODC, 2010). Ganpat *et al.* (2009) show that 50% of the habitual offenders have mild intellectual disability (MID). Their IQ score is in the 70 - 75 range. Several studies show that people that suffer from MID as well as people that suffer from psychiatric disorders may easily perceive situations as stressful. They show aggressive behaviour that results from an inability to grasp their own motives and behaviour. They have a restricted capacity for impulse control and social adjustment. Although they often try to create a friendly impression, under pressure an unfriendly and nasty attitude arises, caused by feelings of inferiority and fear (Kaal *et al.* 2011; Ganpat, 2009: 27-29).

The Veiligheidshuis is aimed at counteracting the fragmentation of social services. Persistent failure of multi-agency collaboration has led to numerous suggested solutions. In the archipelago of quasi-autonomous agencies that is the contemporary Dutch social service system, hierarchical control while effective as an intra-agency coordinating mechanism is seen as ineffective, if not counter-productive, in organizing multiple-agency service sectors. More corporate management techniques and marketization are not an option either, as these have contributed to the problem of fragmentation. This made collaboration the only possibility for overcoming the persistent lack of coordination.

Solutions such as the *Veiligheidshuis* and other such alliances have in common that they try to change the social service landscape by binding agencies into formal relationships. However, the incentive structure of a non-cooperative agency is not altered by *architectural* models, as Martin Rein already observed (Rein, 1983). The effectiveness of such solutions can further be questioned since changing the architecture of the service landscape will inevitably create new organizational structures that also need to be coordinated with the existing structure (Juul, 2008). These observations support Selsky and Parker's finding that architectural solutions alone hardly serve as a remedy for the ambiguity that is caused by the complex mixture of collaborative, organisational and personal interests of the actors involved (2005).

To elaborate the particular value of the *Veiligheidshuis* as a collaborative solution that is oriented to creating new means of coordination, it is useful to further elaborate the conceptual distinction between collaboration and coordination. Collaboration refers to the *process* of finding common ground for multi-party problems. Through this process, "parties who see different aspects of a problem can constructively explore their differences and search for solutions that go beyond their own limited vision of what is possible" (Gray, 1989, 5). Coordination refers to the *means* through which collaboration takes place in practice. It encompasses both the formal structure and the performative process of working together productively. It also refers to the desired outcome of collaboration/cooperation. Stein (1982), says for example: "*Coordination is self-enforcing and can be reached through the use of conventions*".

The argument we develop in this paper is that collaboration across sectors is hampered by conflicting logics and that coordination in such a fragmented, complex and dynamic environment not only calls for proper organizational routines but also for a setting that facilitates face-to-face collaborative process. This is what the *Veiligheidshuis* is all about.

THE *VEILIGHEIDSHUIS* AND THE CASE OF MIRELLA

On its national website the *Veiligheidshuis* depicts itself as a collaborative innovation: a network of *key partners*: police, municipality, district attorney, youth services, social psychiatry, and criminal justice. Occasional partners such as housing corporations or social work may join them. The network approach allows the partners to address multi-problem issues, such as youth crime, domestic violence, multi-problem families and habitual offenders; problems that combine elements of mental health, social pathology (addiction and child rearing) and criminal justice. However, in its design and aims the *Veiligheidshuis* clearly seeks to facilitate coordination. It is a space where: "*criminal justice, care and government come together to address complex problems*". (translated by authors). The partners are expected to join up in a "*person-oriented approach*" to reduce crime in and increase the safety of Dutch cities. (http://www.veiligheidshuizen.nl.). The core of the innovation is the collaboration of the social service and the criminal justice system through every day mechanisms for coordination. But, in practice, this also turns out to be its Achilles heel. When professionals from the domains of care and justice collaborate they have to bridge two distinct professional worlds. The term care is used here to address the broad field of social services and health care. This is about services for accommodation, personal finance, occupation therapy, work and psychosocial health. The term criminal justice refers to the chain of investigation and enforcement such as the work of the police, the criminal justice sector and prison sector. Probation agencies occupy an intermediate position. Their work combines elements of judicial supervision and socialisation.

Mirella is a typical habitual offender who has a history of homelessness and self-neglect. She is drug user who lives in the street and who creates nuisance by public drunkenness. She disturbs people by accosting passers-by in an aggressive tone, although she is never physically aggressive. She has a long list of offences, among which shoplifting and public drunkenness are the most frequent. She also has a long history of treatment in centers for substance abuse and psychiatric clinics. She has been imprisoned frequently. Some years ago, as an *ultimum remedium*, she did time in a specialized long stay facility for habitual offenders who are resistant to any type of treatment or punishment. That stabilized her life, but after she was discharged her condition deteriorated quickly again. She consistently evades probation.

The case team of the *Veiligheidshuis* has often discussed her situation. All participants are familiar with the history of the case. The escalation of the current situation makes clear that something needs to be done. The district attorney, an experienced, driven professional, brings up Mirella's case in the multi-disciplinary case management meeting. These meetings form a central element in the coordination process in the Veiligheidshuis. Several options pass review: admission to a clinic based on a judicial authorization; readmission to the long stay facility; withdrawal of the probation and thus putting her back in a regular prison; or just acceptance of the fact that she lives on the street and supporting her with more intensive outreach care. The team exchanges arguments for and against each option but is unable to agree. Some team members argue that admission to a psychiatric institution would be best suited, but the psychiatrist of the probation service is not willing to advise admission. He argues that her condition does not fit the legal requirements for the judicial authorization of involuntary psychiatric commitment. None of the options seems to be feasible and/or acceptable. Participants become irritable and tensions flare. The discussion goes in circles; the same options and arguments are repeated over and over again. Representatives of the two organizational domains of Care and Criminal Justice attempt to frame the problem as the other domain's issue and thus shift responsibility away from themselves. At the end of the meeting the chair cuts the knot and decides that Mirella should stand trial and be put back in prison. But that option is hardly satisfying for the team members. Many participants consider the position of the psychiatrist as rigid and are annoyed with him. They don't consider him a team player. But in the one instance in which the psychiatrist, in a similar case, let himself be persuaded to issue a judicial authorization for clinical admission, the judge denied the claim, thus affirming the psychiatrist in his original assessment of the situation. The rules of the judicial care system constrain the moral ambitions of the group. The case team meeting continues and one of the options gets discussed for the third time. Why is it so difficult to connect these organizational routines? How can we break the spell and design meaningful action? How can collaboration between the domains of care and justice be made more effective?

METHODS

The *Veiligheidshuizen* of two municipalities formed the site of our study; reducing the chronic recidivism of habitual offenders was its subject. The objective is to unravel obstacles and opportunities that emerged in implementing this innovation and making it work. In this study, we focus on a small number of multi-problem habitual offenders who put an inordinate amount of pressure on the social service system, health care, housing as well as the criminal justice system.

In our study we have followed a strategy of action research to obtain an understanding of the daily practices of the professionals, process coordinators and managers in the *Veiligheidshuis*. We selected two cities. City A, a large urban area, is a leader in public innovation and was the first in the Netherlands to develop and introduce a results-oriented approach for the collaborative action towards habitual offenders. City B is a medium size city with relatively low level of public safety issues. It was one of the last in the country to open its *Veiligheidshuis*. By selecting these cities we intended to unravel patterns of fragmentation and cooperation that are independent of the size of the city and the severity of the problems.

Data collection consisted of a 2-year longitudinal study of the intervention trajectory of six of the most persistent habitual offenders. In addition, we interviewed over 30 professionals, process coordinators and superiors about their interactions in these 6 cases and more generally about their experiences with coordination of services for this class of clients. We also observed numerous meetings of the case management teams and of the boards of the *Veiligheidshuis*.

We recorded the initial set of interviews and we documented the events and the stories that were exchanged in the meetings and informal contacts. We used grounded theory (Glaser & Strauss, 1967, Stauss & Corbin, 1997; Charmaz, 2006) to code the data of our initial observations and interviews and to develop explanatory concepts. We communicated our observations and our emerging concepts (Charmaz, 2006) to the participants in workshops. We allowed them to reflect on our findings and collaboratively learn about the meaning a case has for the service providers and the values that are at stake. In this way, we created checks on the rightness and workability of the developing insights by directly feeding them back to the field and test whether they contributed to solving practical challenges (Greenwood & Levin, 1998, 75). We created cycles of presupposition - action - effect that Greenwood and Levin (1998, 65) consider the epistemological and strategic heart of action research. Grounded theory supports the search for explanatory concepts and action research allows testing the value of our insights for practice and for deepening insight and creating credibility. Findings that where accepted by the respondents as workable were elaborated in more detail. Findings that were challenged were further investigated and reframed. Findings were considered valid when they were internally consistent and when they proved to deliver valuable insights for the practitioners. The combined use of these methods serves to construe a systematic empirical analysis of credible significance that is embedded in a relevant body of knowledge, and that contributes to develop professional practice (Wagenaar, 2011).

The study confirmed our opinion that concepts that emerged in the course of our work were helpful for understanding collaboration in the *Veiligheidshuis*, and that narratives were helpful to illustrate the functioning of these concepts *in practice*.

CONFLICTING LOGICS

As Mirella's story illustrates, characteristically the habitual offender's life is in a chronic state of turbulence and disorder. The habitual offenders in our study lived from one crisis to another. The most that service providers could do was to attenuate the situation, and even that usually required the sustained efforts of a number of different agencies from the social care and criminal justice sector. Although professionals from both domains were available in the *Veiligheidshuis*, in many cases effective interventions were not easily arrived at. Instead, as we often observed, despite the fact that collaboration structures were in place, complex cases frequently led to tensions among the participating professionals. What explains these difficulties in working together effectively?

To answer this question we focus on the conflicting service logics of the sectors of social care and criminal justice. A sector consists of a coherent set of social services or interventions that is delivered by clusters of institutions and organisations that together create a certain societal value. "These sectors are multiply embedded within the others. Their boundaries cannot be clearly drawn, as they are intertwined with one another" (O'Riain, 2000, 191). Following Glynos and Howarth we can say that a sector consists of:

> *"a particular set of subject positions* [*e.g.* psychiatrist, district attorney], *objects* [*e.g.* the client's problems; agency budgets] *and a system of relations and meanings connecting subjects and objects [e.g. professional values, institutional hierarchies], as well as certain sorts of institutional parameters* [*e.g.* laws, work routines]" (adapted from Glynos and Howarth, 2007, 136).

The practical coherence and interpretive integrity of sectors thus form formidable barriers to the kind of cooperation that is required to make collaborative innovation work. In the language of Glynos and Howarth, we define a logic as comprising:

"the rules or grammar of a practice as well as the conditions which make the practice both possible and vulnerable" (2007, 136). *Transposed to the work of public services "a logic is a set of assumptions, about the scope, method, and purpose of a particular service domain, which determines its questions, its practices, the nature of its evidence, and its principles of interpretation"* (ibid.).

We distinguish three elements in particular that stand in the way of the cooperative process: conflicting cultures, diametrically opposed structures and poorly interlocking domains (Fig. **1**). In the next sections we will further elaborate these elements. In each section we demonstrate the different characteristics of the sectors and then discuss the effects of these differences.

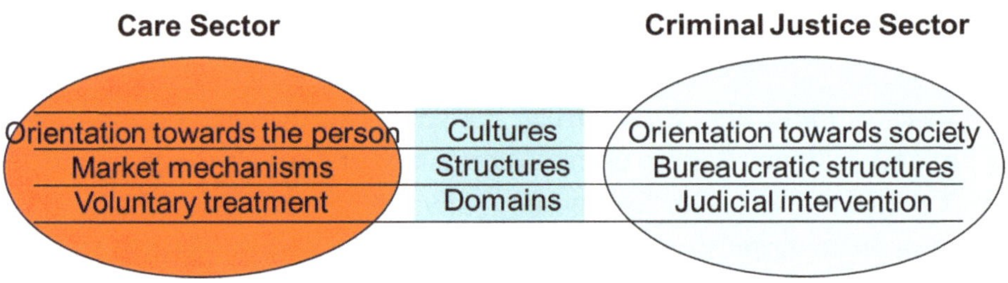

Figure 1: conflicting logic's between the sectors of care and criminal justice.

Conflicting Cultures

The concept of culture is a notoriously slippery. Hofstede (1991) describes culture broadly as a set of values and practices. Concrete manifestations of organizational cultures are symbols, heroes, narratives of origin, and rituals. Schein (1999) adds to this that culture is grounded in shared implicit presumptions that drive values, norms and practices. In this article we build on Schein's work by typifying sector cultures by their implicit presumptions and showing how these presumptions work out in practice.

The Care Sector: Orientation towards the Person

The core, guiding value of the care sector is commitment to the client. The care logic is about collaboration with the client, facilitating the client's motivation for change, and creating and sustaining continuity in the care relationship. In the care logic the professional is the client's advocate. The professional is not seen, and does not see herself, as someone who just earns a living or, ultimately, acts as an extension of the law but as someone who can make a difference for the client.

Building trust is central to this orientation. A social worker from a care institution told us how he dealt with one of his clients. During a social skills training the client engaged in behaviour that was destructive to himself and his environment. The social worker tried to contain this behaviour and from there built up a treatment relationship. His account has a mild, accepting tone. Despite his robust interventions, his language reveals that he is involved in his client's development:

> *"He came into the group being rude to everyone, using street language, so then I said 'Get out of here, I can't deal with you in the group, I'll come and see you again in two or three weeks'. ... I went to see him again after two or three weeks. ...In the meantime, he has come to see me as a leader and that is what he needs... It's about limits, this is the world we live in and each time I try to give it some structure for him... and also about valuing him, giving compliments, that's how he grows".*

Within the care logic the boundaries between the formal professional care relationship and ordinary human compassion is continuous. It is not uncommon in the case of some morally worthy clients (Maynard-Moody and Musheno, 2003) for professionals to commit themselves beyond their formal role and powers. Another social worker about one of his clients:

> *"At a certain point in time I was no longer allowed to supervise him, his process was finished. However I prolonged my supervision with three more months. Why did I do it? Er... [silence] er... because the fact that the boy was motivated and... er... was kind of appealing for help and then I tried to do something. I freewheeled a little and luckily after six months, with very good arguments, I was able to get some hours compensated in retrospect".*

The Criminal Justice Sector: Orientation Towards a Just Society

For criminal care professionals the challenge is to maintain a requisite distance between themselves and the client, rather than a client orientation and personal trust. When we observe a habitual offender hearing, distance is immediately visible. The formal manner of address during the greeting ritual, the distance in the courtroom between the suspect and the judge, the official robes, the language of the lawyers all contribute towards a distant and ceremonial stance. The implicit message is that a larger social ritual is enacted in which all participants play their carefully prescribed role. However, just as in the care logic, the boundaries between professional attitude and ordinary commitment are permeable. We observed how at certain moments the judge chooses a tone of involvement when handling a habitual offender case. He seeks to get closer towards both the victim and the suspect. He shows a human face. He inquires whether those involved understand what is going on, shows compassion for the victim and asks the suspect open questions about his motivation for proposed treatment. The case then continues in the same formal tone. Justice has to be done and this requires an unflinching commitment to the demands of the law.

The prevailing tone of the criminal justice sector is characterised by an orientation towards maintaining a safe and fair society and the integrity of the criminal justice system. Upholding the law requires an impersonal approach. The norms and values of the criminal justice sector serve a quest for an objective and equitable application of the law. Justice is not blindfolded without reason. This means that it may be expected of professionals in the criminal justice domain that they weigh the personal circumstances of the client against the rule of law.

Conflicting Structures

The structure of organisations consists of the way organisations divide the tasks and the way in which the performance of these tasks is coordinated (Mintzberg, 1983). Coordination requires mechanisms for exchange of information and dealing with transaction cost. Two typical coordination structures are markets and hierarchies. Hierarchies structure coordination through bureaucratic mechanisms for task deployment and financial control. Markets structure coordination through direct mediation of economic transactions (Ouchi, 1980). The criminal justice sector is typically coordinated through hierarchy. The care sector is structured as a (quasi-) market. Our observations show that the differences in shortcomings of the two systems create a lack of understanding between professionals who have learned to navigate their own system and who project expectations that are reasonable in their own field to professionals that function within the constraints of a differently structured domain. Beyond that, both market and hierarchy have their shortcomings in allocating attention towards difficult, undesirable clients such as habitual offenders.

Quasi-Markets as the Basic Structure of Care

The contemporary care sector system is organised as a quasi-market. Care organisations have to break even or create a financial surplus; they carry responsibility for the organization's financial viability. They have to tender for contracts with state agencies. In return, they are (somewhat) autonomous in wage setting and in how they organize their care operations. However, contrary to a real market, the care sector is strongly regulated by hierarchical controls that emanate from the Ministry of Social Policy. Social care is not coordinated through the price mechanism (Dericks, 2006). On the contrary, the increased fragmentation that is the result of the greater autonomy of the individual organizations has exacerbated the coordination problem. How does this work?

In a general context of budgetary constraints, there is a reduced supply of care and this supply follows the money. In order to enhance their effectiveness, care institutions aim at 'easy' clients; clients who are expected to benefit from the treatment and who do not disrupt the treatment routines of the agency. Habitual offenders are generally regarded as difficult clients, so in practice, we see for example that they are sequestered to a place in a sheltered accommodation project because they are drug users, and on the other hand, they are not considered for a drug rehabilitation programme because they don't have a stable housing situation. The example points towards a wider system of mutual deferral of responsibility. The economic logic of individual care agencies has perverse consequences in the aggregate.

Hierarchy as the Basic Structure of Justice

The judicial chain is organised as a bureaucracy. In a bureaucratic system, higher management distributes the work and the resources amongst institutions and units.

For coordination of the work they create systems and procedures. Information from lower units flows back to the command structures to allow them to assess performance and spending. The combined vertical control and horizontal structuring are supposed to allow for tight control on effectiveness and efficiency. However, as it is well known, between units it also evokes a diffuse battle about priorities and a strong inclination to value procedures higher than practical solutions. (Ouchi, 1980). Units filter the information that they allow to flow upwards in the hierarchy. Agencies jostle to obtain the most favourable position in the perennial conflicts over influence in the zero-sum bureaucratic environment (Allison & Zelikow, 1999). Hierarchy invites defensive behaviour and symbolic policy. Our study indeed illustrates the battle of priorities and the formal orientation with partners that are in the criminal justice system. Illustrative for the classical inertia of poorly functioning bureaucratic structures is the case of a member of the *Veiligheidshuis* who contacted the nearest police station. When she called she was referred to another station. At that station, she was told that she could only make an appointment in the afternoon. When she returned to the station that afternoon the official in question was off for the rest of that day. Upon discussing this case with representatives of the *Veiligheidshuis*, we concluded that the inward-looking perspective of the criminal justice bureaucracy acts as a disincentive for client-orientation.

Conflicting Domains

The sectors of social care and justice both deliver a set of interventions, but operate according to different operating procedures. These interventions and organizational routines reflect the mission and goals of the organizational domain. As the preceding characterizations make clear, these are in many instances at loggerheads with each other. As this group of clients is not motivated for voluntary treatment and often do not engage in the types of crimes that warrant long sentences, many standard interventions do not apply and desired interventions are not legal or appropriate. The clients fall between the cracks in the system. Nevertheless they, may pose threats to the safety of individuals, impose high societal costs, and create moral unease with professionals. The net effect is that they are impervious to interventions by the criminal law and care sector. A psychiatrist from our research project summarised it as follows.

> *"We have instruments for people who cross the line. We have instruments for people who have a treatable disorder but for people with a bad character who are seriously threatening society we are left powerless".* (van Hemert, personal communication).

Improving Personal Health as the Operationalization of the Care Mission

The care system is oriented towards diagnosing and treating those who are afflicted with illness or disorder. We illustrate the limitations of care for habitual offenders with the case of *Frank*, a man who is diagnosed with an antisocial personality disorder. He is hardly capable of recognising his own feelings, he is easily annoyed, he has a fear of intimacy and he defends himself by expressing negative feelings. He projects blame onto others and has an insufficiently developed moral sense. He is intellectually challenged with an IQ of around 70. He has a history of cocaine and alcohol abuse and experiences little pressure of suffering. He expresses himself verbally and physically in a seriously threatening manner. A psychiatrist who saw him as part of a behavioural expert's assessment was of the opinion that if the client continued to use cocaine and remained in contact with other drug abusers, there was a high chance that this would lead to escalation. Other workers in the field considered the client a "*walking time bomb*". Frank has shown over the years that he is not motivated for treatment. He does not collaborate with psychiatric investigation and he leaves each of the programs that were offered to him. A compulsory admission to a psychiatric hospital ended in an early release since there was no progress during his treatment. The case shows that the interventions for diagnosis and treatment in the care sector fall short in the case of habitual offenders, due to their limited inclination to collaborate.

Creating Safety and Justice as the Operationalization of Criminal Justice Mission

The criminal justice system is designed as the *ultimum remedium* for dealing with unlawful behaviour. Only if it has been found that no other intervention is suitable, the application of criminal law is warranted (Crijns, J. 2012). In the application of criminal law, the measure should be proportional to the offence; people cannot be punished for their intention to commit a crime. For the situation of habitual offenders, a specific intervention was introduced in Dutch law in 2004. This so called ISD intervention is a combination of confinement and treatment. By the terms of this intervention anyone with a series of convictions for small misdemeanours and crimes who reoffends can be incarcerated for two years without additional sentencing. It is used as an ultimate measure when all other options have been tried. The IDS intervention calls for a gradual transfer from inpatient to outpatient treatment during the two-year term. In the case of Frank the use of the ISD measure turned out to be unsuccessful. He was frequently aggressive (with repeated placement in isolation) and barely cooperated with treatment. The outpatient stage that constitutes the final stage of the measure was terminated due to threats of aggression. After the measure had ended and Frank was released, violent threats occurred almost immediately. He was once more put in prison. Although Frank threatened to seriously hurt his ex-partner, the judicial system could not do more than react to the offences that were actually committed by Frank. The case shows that the interventions for prevention, investigation and punishment of crime of the criminal justice sector fall short in the case of habitual offenders, due to the small size of the offences and the repetitive character. Dealing with habitual offenders requires for the combined use of interventions of care and justice.

A COLLABORATIVE APPROACH TO THE TREATMENT OF HABITUAL OFFENDERS

In this section, we discuss the positive effect of the Veiligheidshuizen as an organizational innovation, in terms of bridging the two domains of criminal justice and care. Than we highlight the different remaining barriers to collaboration that practitioners experience during their work in the Veiligheidshuizen. Finally we describe how recognition of these barriers in the setting of the Veiligheidshuizen, that created growing mutual trust, could lead to further process innovation.

Our study shows that the chances for successful treatment of habitual offenders from the separate perspectives of care and justice are limited. Over and over again our observations made it painfully visible that the social service and criminal justice domain do not connect well in the care for habitual offenders. Collaboration between these two sectors is a logical and promising perspective. Logical since habitual offenders are frequent lawbreakers and, almost without exception, suffer from personality disorders and drug or alcohol addiction. Promising since the early signs are that collaboration between care and justice can lead to a reduction of recidivism (WODC, 2012). Collaboration thus needs to be strengthened in a way that makes it possible to accommodate the different logics that define the two sectors. Formal mechanisms for collaboration are inadequate, as they tend to displace the collaborative challenge (Juul, 2008). An innovative solution is collaborative governance (Ansell & Gash, 2007). Asymmetries in information, knowledge and resources in a situation of mutually recognized interdependence, offer a promising starting point for a design that puts face-to-face collaborative process at the centre (ibid.). The *Veiligheidshuizen* are such an innovation. These collaborative designs offer the professionals a chance to jointly work on shared problems, experience their mutual dependency, build trust, and come up with creative ways of collaboration. The question is how and to what extent the new collaborative setting is able to overcome the interactive negative effects of conflicting domain logics and the specific needs and characteristics of the habitual offender.

Our interviews with professionals in the *Veiligheidshuis* confirmed the importance of direct interaction in fostering more effective collaboration. It is almost as if face-to-face contact allows a range of insights and experiences to flourish that each by them self are not that impressive but that, taken together, create a rich environment of learning possibilities. This succession of small successes boosted confidence and opened up new spaces for creative solutions, often by stretching discretionary capacity. Participants also learned that the process could be improved by relatively simple design innovations.

For example, all participants to the *Veiligheidshuis* said that working with other professionals made it clear to them that in these complex cases almost every professional suffers from an information deficiency. Working together made it possible to transcend partial knowledge and, often for the first time, obtain a more complete overview of the client and the various interventions that have been attempted in the past, This not only prevented duplication of unsuccessful interventions but also made it possible to see patterns in the development of the case that were hidden until now. For example, habitual offenders suffer from the alteration of stable and unstable periods. Instead of engaging in heroic interventions when the situation escalated once again, professionals began to focus on helping the client through the troubled phase to help him regain confidence and control over his life. Some experienced practitioners became skilled in noticing when situations threatened to escalate and intervene in timely and adequate way. For example, one of the participating police officers uses outstanding fines to arrest habitual offenders who were observed to drink in public to prevent an escalation into unmanageable behaviour. By his preventive action the police officer avoids that he would have to engage in a much more difficult intervention later when the client is drunk and unmanageable and has created a serious public disturbance.

Professionals also experience that their interdependence offers them an opportunity to learn to see the other's perspective on the case. As one professional said: "*We are much more aware of the fact that we need each other*".

We see that professionals who meet each other in the safety centres actually learn to understand one another and to respect each other's position with all its constraints and affordances. The conflicting domain logics have not disappeared of course, but working alongside each other in the *Veiligheidshuis* the professionals see their situation in a new light. They now regard their own situation as a collaborative venture in which the professional doesn't have to go it alone and can ask for support from her colleagues. The trust this generates creates space for more creative interventions, for considering a wider range of options that mix voluntary participation, coercion and punishment, often exercising administrative discretion, as the situation demands. A good example is the police officer who has tried many times to bring a deteriorating habitual offender to the attention of a judge. The judge shows himself insensitive to the argument and persists in penalizing each offense separately. Then the police officer decides to collect camera images of the violations. He shows them in court to present a compelling illustration of the street habitat of the client. With this unusual intervention the police officer manages to convince the judge to consider other interventions for this client. The case coordinators in the *Veiligheidshuis* tell us that the results ultimately come from professionals who go the extra mile. An experienced and respected professional tells us that his work sometimes feels like "*unpaid labour*". He said that it frequently happens that you have a difficult case that can only be resolved if you get together with a small group of people, outside of all structures, put your heads together and make a ground breaking plan. He outlines how solutions arise if you attempt to grasp the whole situation with each other, carefully weigh the options and then make conscious choices about which interventions to use and which not to use. In both cities we observed teams that created arrangements to confront the habitual offender with various scenarios to induce him to cooperate with treatment in order to prevent a formal legal process. A cop is sent to the habitual offender, for example, to subtly inform him of the discussed scenarios and advise him to keep a low profile.

In this study we confirm the findings of Ansell & Gash (2007, 550) showing that collaborative practices allow for shared problem definitions and the identification of common values. As a result practitioners manage to come up with small but important design innovations that help to bridge the gap between sectors. A simple example is the discretionary budget. It is a small amount of money that is allocated to the group to pay for activities that are not formally indicated but that are considered useful for achieving treatment goals. For example, the money has been used to replace a lost identity card that is necessary to be eligible for housing. Or it is used to bridge a short period in which a client is waiting for his welfare cheque and the risk is assessed that this will lead to a relapse into undesirable behaviour.

The *active ingredient* in this and similar innovations is their discretionary and recursive quality. The discretionary budget can be spent upon the judgement of the group. Similarly extra professional autonomy is granted in the hierarchical institutions. The professionals of these organisations can get additional time allocated for actions that are considered urgent by the team of the *Veiligheidshuis* and that might not necessarily fit the priorities of their own organisation. In formal terms recursiveness refers to "*a continuous and interlocking cycle of perspectives*" (Ansell, 2011, 104). In organizational terms it refers to an inversion of hierarchy. As Ansell puts it:

> *"When a level of organization shifts back and forth between being superordinate ... and subordinate ..., you have the possibility of a powerful form of recursiveness that possibly overcomes the tension between top-down and bottom-up organization".* (Ansell, 2011,107).

The discretionary budget in the *Veiligheidshuizen* is a good example of such recursiveness. Control over the agency's budget - albeit a small part of it - is handed over to practitioners who allocate it according to need.

Recursiveness also governs the organization of the case meetings. One of our first observations was that the case management platform in both cities did not function well. In one city we observed that that an average of 15 to 20 clients was discussed in a two hour meeting. Obviously there was little time for each case. We also observed that a lot of information was missing at the meeting and that many participants were unfamiliar with the case files. Often the discussion of the case had to be adjourned to obtain better and more complete information. There was no time for follow-up, so that decisions on cases were not checked off at the next meeting. No one was responsible for monitoring progress.

In our feedback sessions we addressed our concerns about the functioning of the case management platform. Case management is a costly and time-consuming form of coordination. Often more than ten representatives of different agencies attend and each one has to prepare for the meeting. Yet in situations of dynamic complexity this form of reciprocal coordination that allows for continuous and direct mutual adjustment is the only one that works (Thompson, 1967; Mintzberg, 1983; Snook, 2000, 153). Once the issue was addressed, discussions followed between the management of the Veiligheidshuis, practitioners and the research team. We agreed on a solution in which we differentiated between the functions of process and case manager. The process manager acts as the chair of the case management platform. Her task was to ensure the process of multi-disciplinary collaboration. She is responsible for the progress of the case through the chain and to solve problems of cooperation. The case manager is responsible for individual cases. She prepares and oversees individual cases and monitors their progress. Differentiation of these roles gave the process manager more freedom to develop her function as a gate keeper. She reduced the caseload in the case meetings by better distinguishing between complex cases, which were to be discussed in the case management platform and the simpler cases which could be solved in direct collaboration between two or three partners. Pressure on the case management platform was further reduced through the fact that the case manager could effectively inform the attending practitioners on the status and urgent questions of a case. The effect of this division in tasks was the reduction of the number of cases to be discussed in the case management platform and an increase of the efficiency of the meetings.

The example shows *recursiveness in action*. The process manager, usually one of the street-level practitioners, had the power to issue instructions to all the members of the case management platform. There are no clear, a priori characteristics of what counts as a complex case; moreover most cases evolve all the time and move in and out of the category of *complex* or *difficult*. Only very experienced street-level professionals were able to make this kind of assessment. By appointing one of them as gate keeper for the case meeting, effectively reduced the number of cases to be discussed. By doing so, more time was created to thoroughly prepare and discuss the cases. Various assessments show that the approach takes effect. A more systematic way of working emerged and a stricter discipline to act collaboratively upon the individual cases is a result.

CONCLUSION

In this chapter, we showed that the specific characteristics of a particular, extremely treatment-resistant group of habitual offenders led to a breakdown in the coordination of services in the Netherlands. The reaction of Dutch authorities was to create a platform in each major city for collaborative governance called the *Veiligheidshuis*. The overall picture is one of stubborn problems and hopeful signs. The literature shows that such collaboration is full of ambiguity. Our specific contribution is that we add to general knowledge about collaborative governance and collaborative innovation by identifying some issues that arise when collaboration between partners from the domains of care and criminal justice are at stake. The vital mechanism seems to be that the *Veiligheidshuis* creates a platform for collaborative process. This process was not created by the simple act of putting the different parties together in one space. It was due to the creation of teams with collaborative goals, norms and values. In working together *in practice* and reflecting on experiences, an atmosphere was created where experiences could be transformed into opportunities and where on-going learning could take place in the interaction between management and practitioners of the different fields.

Once participants are willing to engage in collaborative process a succession of small innovative steps was taken that allowed them to work across boundaries. Participants began to share information so that, often for the first time, everyone had a complete overview of the case. Mutual trust and support began to develop which allowed participants t*o think outside of the box*. Perhaps most important through the process of recursiveness, street-level knowledge and experience superseded hierarchy and formal procedure to inform everyday case management. None of these solutions represent a silver bullet to overcoming the coordination problem in social services. They are also fragile and can easily be reversed by changes in funding or leadership. But our research shows that over time a culture of collaboration emerged in the *Veiligheidshuizen* that resulted in continuous improvement of collaborative practices, and thus in improved wellbeing of this treatment-resistant category of clients and increased safety on the streets of our cities.

ACKNOWLEDGEMENT

We are grateful to the editors of this volume for their detailed and constructive commentary on earlier drafts of this chapter. We thank our partners for their wholehearted cooperation in this study. This especially applies to Esther Jongeneel, veiligheidshuis Rotterdam, Janneke van der Zalm, Veiligheidshuis Leiden and Lydia Sterrenberg, Platform 31.

CONFLICT OF INTEREST

The authors confirm that this chapter contents have no conflict of interest.

REFERENCES

Ansell, C.K. (2011). Pragmatist Democracy. Evolutionary Learning as Public Philosophy, Oxford: Oxford University Press.

Ansell, C. & Gash, A., (2007), Collaborative governance in theory and practice. In Journal of Public Administration Research and Theory, 18, 543-571.

Charmaz, K. (2006). Constructing Grounded Theory, A Practical Guide Through Qualitative Analysis. Thousand Oaks, CA: Sage Publications

Crijns, J. (2012). Strafrecht als ultimum remedium. In Ars Aequi, 11-18.

Dericks, C.L. (2006). Sturingsdilemma's in de zorg, Elsevier Gezondheidszorg, Maarssen.

Ganpat *et al.* (2009). Problematiek en zorgbehoefte van gedetineerden met een ISD maatregel in Vught. IVO, reeks 62 & Novedic Kentron. Netwerk voor verslavingszorg.

Glaser, B.G. & Strauss, A. (1967). Discovery of Grounded Theory, Chicago: Aldine.

Glynos, J. & D. Howarth (2007). Logics of Critical Explanation in Social and Political Theory. Milton Park: Routledge.

Gray, B. (1989). Collaborating, Finding Common Ground for Multiparty Problems, San Francisco, London: Jossey-Bass Publishers

Greenwood, D.J., Levin, M. (1998). Introduction to action research: Social research for social change. Thousand Oaks, CA: Sage Publications.

Hartley, J., (2005). Innovation in governance and public services: Past and present In Public Money & Management, 25, 27-34

Hofstede, G. (1991). Cultures and Organisations, New York, NY: McGraw-Hill Publishing Company.

Juul, A. (2008). Performing Coordinated Care: In Footprints of Joint Health Plans, Department of Organization, Copenhagen Business School, Draft, June.

Kaal, H.L., Negenman, A.M., Roeleveld, Embregts, P.J.C.M. (2011). De problematiek van gedetineerden met een lichte verstandelijke beperking in het gevangeniswezen. Tilburg University (UvT). Onderzoek uitgevoerd door Tranzo Wetenschappelijk centrum voor zorg en welzijn, Dichterbij Kennisn@ en Hogeschool Leiden in opdracht van het WODC, ministerie van Veiligheid en Justitie.

Maynard-Moody, S, & Musheno, M. (2003). Cops, Teachers, Councellors, Stories from the Front Lines of Public Service, Ann Arbor, MI: The University of Michigan Press.

Mintzberg, H. (1983). Structure in Fives: Designing Effective Organizations, Englewood Cliffsn NJ: Prentice Hall.

Ouchi, W.G. (1980). Markets, Bureaucracies and Clans. In Administrative Science Quarterly, 25, 129-141.

Rein, M. (1983). Coordination of Social Services. Social Policy. Issues of Choice and Change. Armonk, NY: M.E.Sharpe, Inc. (pp. 47-70).

Snook, S.C., (2000). Friendly Fire. The Accidental Shootdown of of U.S. Blackhawks Over Northern Iraq. Princeton, NJ: Princeton University Press.

Schein, E.H. (1999). The Corporate Culture Survival Guide. San Francisco, CA: Jossey-Bass.

Selsky, J.W. & Parker, B. (2005). Cross-sector partnerships to address social issues: Challenges to theory and practice. In Journal of Management, 31, pp. 849-873.

Sørensen, E. & Torfing, J. (2013). Enhancing collaborative innovation in the public sector. In Administration & Society, 43:8, 842-886.

Strauss, A., Corbin, J. (1997). Grounded Theory in Practice. Thousand Oaks, CA: Sage Publications.

Thompson, J.D. (1967). Organizations in Action. New York, NY: McGraw-Hill

Vollaard, B. (2010) The Crime-Reducing Effect of Sentence Enhancement for Repeated Offenders, www.roa.unimaas.nl/seminars/pdf2010/Vollaard.pdf.

Vos, J.J., Wagenaar, H.C. (2014). The Münchhausen movement: Improving the coordination of public services through the creation of a social movement. In American Review of Administration, 44:4, 409-439

WODC (2010). Monitor Habitual Offenders.

CHAPTER 7

Multi-Level Networks: Strengths and Weaknesses in Promoting Coordinated and Innovative Water Governance

Gro Sandkjær Hanssen*

Norwegian Institute for Urban and Regional Research (NIBR), Norway

Abstract: The chapter discusses how multi-level networks can stimulate public sector innovation. The case studied is the new water governance system in Norway. In accordance with the ecosystem principle in the EU Water Framework Directive, new multilevel networks are established in catchment areas, cutting across municipal, regional and national borders. The chapter first examines, on the basis of national surveys and empirical case-studies, whether the new networks stimulate cross-sector, multi-level coordination. Then, it discusses if and how coordination influences collaborative innovation. The study finds that the networks stimulate coordination, first and foremost understood as information- and knowledge sharing, and the coordination of world views. This type of coordination seems to spur public-sector innovation, by establishing common platforms of understanding, where the friction and conflicting interests can play out in constructive ways. Our informants report about rhetorical innovation and strategic innovation, as well as governance innovation. However, the full potentials are far from realized. Obstacles include lack of national harmonization of policy goals and sector legislation, and the lack of regional and local political will to engage actively and recognize the innovative potential in the new collaborative arenas.

Keywords: Multi-level coordination, public sector innovation, county municipalities, EU Water Framework Directive (WFD), water governance.

INTRODUCTION - ECOSYSTEM BASED GOVERNANCE NETWORKS

In recent decades, new public management reforms of specialization (*silos*) and delegation have yielded rather fragmented models that have increasingly been seen as obstructing the solution to malign cross-sectoral, wicked problems (Rittel & Webber 1973; Christensen & Lægreid 2011). The need for vertical and horizontal coordination is widespread. Moreover, this fragmentation hinders public-sector innovation, as it results in a lack of communication and knowledge

***Corresponding author Gro Sandkjær Hanssen:** Norwegian Institute for Urban and Regional Research, Norway; Tel: +47 97537362; Fax: +47 22 60 77 74; E-mail: gro.hanssen@nibr.no

Annika Agger, Bodil Damgaard, Andreas Hagedorn Krogh and Eva Sørensen (Eds.)

exchange among actors with different kinds of knowledge and experience. Governance network theory and theories on collaborative innovation suggest that multi-level and cross-institutional governance collaboration in networks and partnerships can help to solve these problems (Bekkers *et al.* 2011; Sørensen & Torfing 2014). This chapter presents a study of whether specific governance networks established to implement the EU Water Framework Directive (WFD) in Norway (formally from 2009) do so in practice. The networks follow the *ecosystem-based principle* of catchment areas: all public authorities relevant for the quality (and quantity) of water in one catchment area participate in the same governance network, in order to coordinate their efforts. Catchment areas - the area drained by a river or body of water - cut across political-administrative borders. Do the new ecosystem-based governance networks stimulate cross-sector and multi-level coordination - and if so: what form of coordination?

Further, bringing together actors from various public sectors, levels and professional knowledge (not only the *usual suspects)*, is often held to spur innovation, by improving the mutual understanding of problems and bringing forth new ideas and practices (Sørensen & Torfing 2014; Higdem & Hanssen 2013). This chapter asks: do governance networks stimulate innovation? Can public-sector innovation be observed? And how might any coordination achieved influence the capacity for innovation?

The research questions will be answered by analysing a comprehensive empirical material, with case-studies from three river basin districts and surveys of participants in all eleven River Basin District Boards in Norway. Thus, the chapter will bring some insights into how the new and innovative ecosystem-based network structure works in Norway, which has one the most fragmented and sectorized water governance systems in Europe.

The chapter starts with the theoretical framework for the analysis, and then turns to Norway's implementation of the Water Framework Directive as a background, with the new governance networks. Further, it presents the research design and data material, before analysing if and how the governance networks contribute to cross-sector and multi-level coordination. Finally, the chapter discusses how coordination influences the innovation potential of the networks.

THEORETICAL FRAMEWORK

The chapter focuses on the newly established *governance networks* that are responsible for implementing the EU WDF directive. Here, *governance network* is understood as a relatively stable, horizontal articulation of interdependent but operationally autonomous actors, interacting through negotiations within a regulative and normative framework that is self-regulating within limits set by external agencies, and that contributes to public purpose (Sørensen & Torfing 2007, 9). The aim is to coordinate efforts to reduce pressures on water[1] so as to achieve the ambitious aim of the WFD: ecologically good status for all water. Thus, *coordination* of the policies of various sectors is a prerequisite for reaching the ultimate goal (Moss *et al.* 2009; Nielsen *et al.* 2013) - a concept often defined as "*the instruments and mechanisms that aim to enhance the voluntary or forced alignment of tasks and effort of organizations within the public sector*" (Bouckaert *et al.* 2010, 16). Coordination mechanisms create greater coherence and help to reduce redundancy, lacunae and contradictions within and between policies, implementation or management (ibid).

While stimulating innovation is not an explicitly stated aim of the governance networks studied here, it is a major focus of the analysis, as we are interested in the relation between coordination and innovation. Thus, we first examine whether and how coordination is achieved, and then ask whether coordination affects the innovation capacity of the network.

In order to see whether the new eco-system based networks stimulate coordination, we differentiate between different *types* of coordination in a *ladder of coordination* (drawing on Arnstein 1969; Keast *et al.* 2007), which we use as an analytical tool for assessing the coordination achieved by the networks.

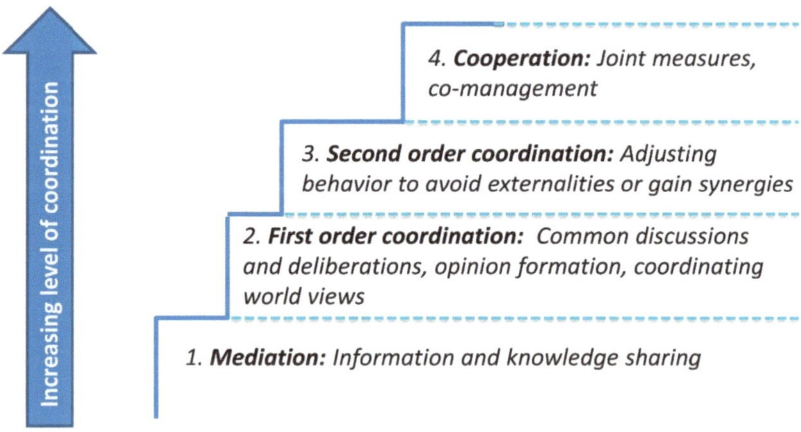

Figure 1: Ladder of coordination (Hanssen *et al.* 2013).

[1] http://www.vannportalen.no/hovedEnkel.aspx?m=31147, See for example ".the requirements of Directive for the achievement of the environmental objectives established under Article 4, and in particular all programmes of measures are coordinated for the whole of the river basin district" (WFD, Article 3.4).

As shown in Fig. **1**, with each rung of this ladder the level of coordination and mutual dependence between actors increases. The lowest level, or rung, of coordination is mediation as mutual *exchange of information and knowledge*, which Keast *et al.* (2007) refer to as *cooperation*. The second type, or rung, is *first-order coordination in the form of shared discussions and deliberations, leading to coordinated worldviews and shared understandings of challenges and solutions*. Here, bridging different (professional) discourses and the emergence of a shared language will be of special interest in our case. The bridging of discourses or change in worldviews does not necessarily call for negotiated agreements: it may also come as the gradual emergence of a shared language. Deliberative theories emphasize this type of coordination (Habermas 1996).

It is not until the third rung that the actors actually *adjust their action* to create synergies and avoid externalities and overlapping (for example, that action or measures act to undermine each other) (Pedersen *et al.* 2011). This is referred to as second-order coordination, or *coordination* in Keast *et al.* (2007), and *institutional interplay* in other strands of the literature. It describes how the effectiveness of specific institutions is affected by other potentially intersecting institutional arrangements (Nielsen *et al.* 2013, 438; Moss 2004). These adjustments can be a result of negotiated agreements, or a result of deliberation. The fourth rung of the ladder is *joint action and joint measures and shared goals*. We call it *cooperation* (*collaboration* in Keast *et al.* 2007), implying mutual commitment to work together. A topical form is partnerships that involve joint decision-making and production of services between autonomous actors (Sullivan & Skelcher 2002). When handling malign problems in a situation of institutional fragmentation, we believe there is a need for institutional solutions that are able to achieve *high levels* of coordination. Thus, the question of outcome as perceived *level* of coordination is relevant.

According to the recent literature on public-sector innovation, governance networks are needed not only to ensure coordinated effort, but also to spur *public-sector innovation* (Sørensen & Torfing 2012; 2014). Important connections and connective capacities between government and other actors are essential for creating innovative capacity and change (see Bekkers *et al.* 2011). Collaboration between public and private actors with relevant innovation assets often helps to define the problem or challenge in a new way; it can spur the generation of new ideas through mutual learning, create joint ownership to new and bold solutions, mobilize and coordinate resources in the implementation phase, and disseminate knowledge of innovative solutions and their effects (Eggers & Singh 2009; Sørensen & Torfing 2012). Thus, collaboration and network arenas, linking ideas, actors and resources, can often lead to the identification of new and more effective policy solutions.

Conflicts, dissent and grievances tend to drive innovation, making it essential to bring together actors with different worldviews and different kinds of knowledge. This can be professional knowledge, lay knowledge, political knowledge, *etc.* (Sørensen & Torfing 2014). New constellations of actors can introduce the necessary friction and constructive tension between different life-worlds and discourses, unsettling the tacit knowledge of actors and spurring new thoughts, ideas and mutual learning. That also means that too much *step-two coordination*, understood as coordination of worldviews on the network arena, might be counterproductive for innovation processes. Consensus about the lowest common denominator often favours adjustment rather than innovative change (ibid.). Still, a process that leads to a certain degree of coordination of language and worldviews may be necessary in order to establish a common platform of understanding - so that new ideas can be transformed into innovative new practices.

Compared to innovations in the private sector, public-sector innovation often has a less material, more interactive character (Osborne 2010). Hartley (2005; 2006) distinguishes between *policy innovation,* implying new policy visions and goals; *strategic innovation,* denoting new goals or purposes of the organization; *process innovations,* understood as new ways in which organizational processes are designed; *governance innovation* - new forms of citizen engagement and democratic institutions; *rhetorical innovation* - new language and new concepts; and *service innovation* - new ways of providing services to users.

This chapter enquires into the extent to which the new network arenas stimulate innovation, and if they do, what types of public sector innovation are spurred. It also combines the theory frameworks of coordination and public sector innovation, and asks what form of coordination is achieved in the networks and how it influences their innovative capacity. In this way, the chapter seeks to contribute to new understandings of how network governance in Europe can promote collaboration and innovation.

BACKGROUND: WFD - AND THE NORWEGIAN IMPLEMENTATION

The WFD addresses the fragmentation problems related to *water management,* as the quality and quantity of water are affected by actors from various sectors, from hydro-power, industry, fish-farming, agriculture, roads, waste-water and sewage, to urban and rural planning. To ensure coordinated effort, the WDF has set in motion a process of reconfiguring the scalar organization of water management. It requires comprehensive water management[2] to be conducted on the level of river basins (the ecosystem principle of catchment areas), rather than following the existing political-administrative map (Hammer *et al.* 2011, Moss 2012), in order to achieve a *good ecological status* for all water (Nielsen *et al.* 2013). Although Norway sees itself as having the cleanest water in the world, it faces important challenges, as one third of its water bodies do *not* have a good ecological status. The WFD also stipulates that the measures selected for improving water quality (quantity) do so *in the most cost-efficient way* for society (European Parliament, Council 2000). This means that decisions about measures must be taken across sectors - not only within sectors (Nielsen *et al.* 2013). This requires high-level coordination of various sector policies, and of public actors at different governmental levels (Nielsen *et al.* 2013) - a real challenge in Norway, which has one of the most fragmented water management systems in Europe.

For implementing the WDF, Norway has established 11 river basin districts, with one governance network in each, the River Basin District Boards. All relevant public authorities *within* a river basin are to coordinate their action in this governance network. Hence, the governance networks bring together all affected authorities at local, regional and national level.[3] A sub-level has also been established, with 104 sub-districts and their respective governance networks (Sub-District Boards).

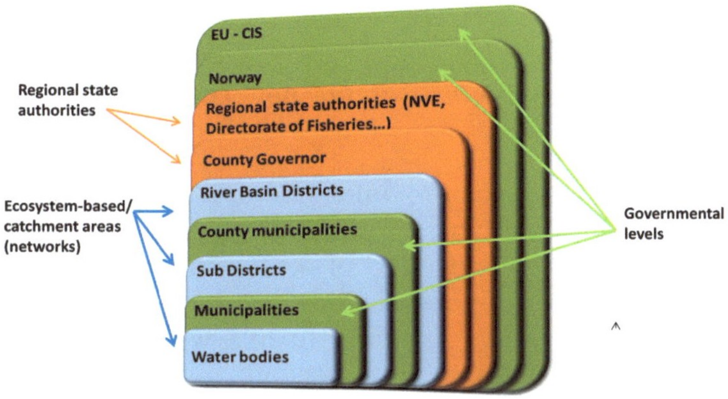

Figure 2: The new ecosystem-based water management system, located in-between existing governmental levels[4].

[2] Member States shall identify the individual river basins lying within their national territory and, for the purposes of this Directive, shall assign them to individual River Basin Districts' (Directive 2000/60/EC, art. 4).

[3] River Basin Districts (RBD, Vannregion), River Basin District Boards (RBDB, Vannregionutvalg), Sub-Districts (Vannområder), Sub-District Boards (Vannområdeutvalg).

[4] Areas for network coordination at the national level have also been established, to coordinate and clarify contradictory aims and regulations: the ministry group, consisting of representatives.

As Fig. **2** shows, the new governance networks are located in-between the existing three governmental levels, cutting across existing municipal (429), county (19) and regional state administrative borders.

The formal organizational structure of the governance networks is shown in Fig. **3**.

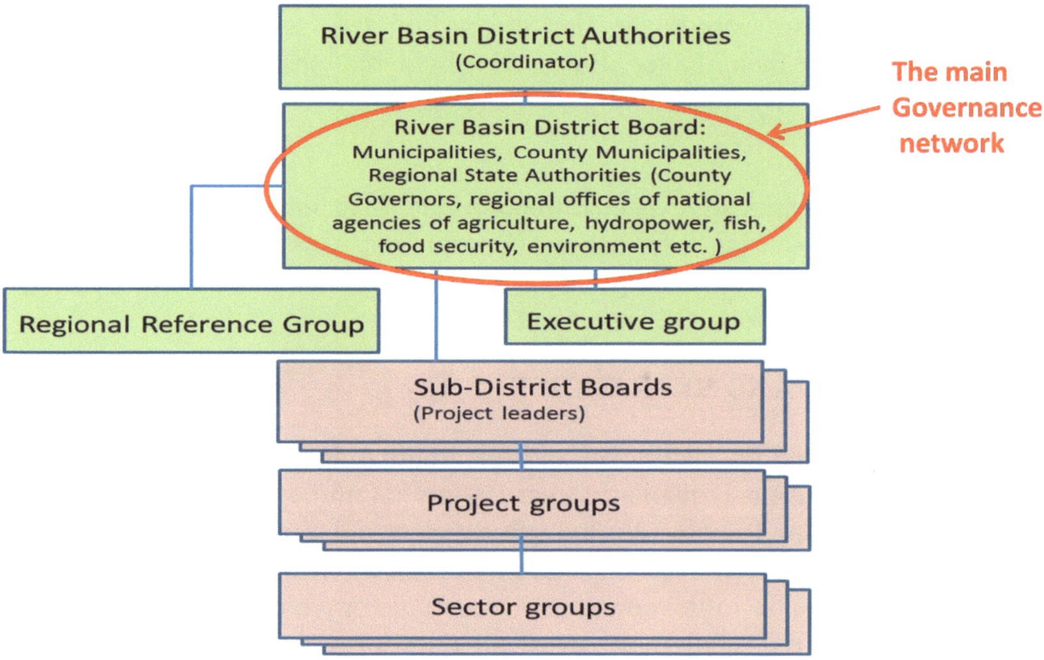

Figure 3: Organizational structure of River Basin Districts.

The governance networks (River Basin District Boards) can encompass as much as over 270 actors representing authorities from various sectors and various governmental levels. Private-actor interests are included by the establishment of broad *reference groups* with an advisory role. Eleven of the 19 counties *(fylker)* have been assigned the important role[5] of being the responsible River Basin District Authority for their areas, responsible for facilitating and coordinating the governance networks.

The role can also be interpreted as an effort to *decentralize the dilemmas* (Vike 2004) from the national to the regional level - as the counties must now handle new dilemmas of balancing conflicting sector-based interests and resolving

[5] The coordination role of the Counties has just been assigned them[5], having been the responsibility of the County Governor (regional state authority) earlier.

malign problems related to water. The counties are to coordinate regional-level state agencies over which they have no binding authority - like the county governor, the Directorate of Fisheries, the Norwegian Water Resources and Energy Directorate, the Norwegian Food Security Authority and the Norwegian Public Roads Administration. Moreover, many of these regional-level bodies cover in regions with different geographical size than the counties. The counties are also expected to coordinate the efforts of the several municipalities *[kommuner]* within their River Basin District, but these enjoy extensive autonomy, with authority traditionally comparable to or even stronger than that of the counties.

The governance networks are expected to contribute to achieve all the steps of the coordination ladder, sharing information, coordinating worldviews, adjusting the actors' behaviour, and coordinating their actions and initiating joint measures by formulating mandatory Water Management Plans.

DATA MATERIAL AND RESEARCH DESIGN

The analyses are based on qualitative and quantitative data. Firstly, the analyses are based on data from a qualitative case study of three RBDs (Vest-Viken, Hordaland and Nordland), with selected sub-districts and municipalities. The data has been gathered through semi-structured interviews with county politicians, administrative leadership in the counties, the administrative coordinators of RBD Boards and SB Boards, representatives of all relevant regional state authorities, and municipal representatives (as mayors, municipal coordinators and civil servants). We have also carried out participatory observation of meetings in the networks, as well as document studies. In addition, a survey of all members of the governance networks (the Boards) in the 11 River Basin Districts has been conducted (digital survey, April 2013). The actors represented here are municipalities and county municipalities as well as a range of national-sector authorities (their regional offices) representing the interests of agriculture, businesses, environmental authorities, road and traffic authorities *etc.* These Boards vary in size - from about 270 members to 12. Out the total number of responses in the survey was 301 (of 733), giving a response rate of 41. Of the respondents who answered the questionnaire, 64 per cent represented municipalities; of the municipal representatives 41 per cent were politicians, while 58 per cent represented administration/public services. Of the total number of respondents who answered, 24 per cent represented national sector authorities (regional offices), 8 per cent represented county municipalities, and 2 per cent represented other actors.[6] Combining survey-data with in-depth studies (interviews, observations, document studies), this study is well-suited for shedding light on the effects of the new governance networks.

DO ECOSYSTEM-BASED NETWORKS ENHANCE COORDINATION?

What kinds of coordination do the participating actors report as having been achieved through the ecosystem-based governance networks? Fig. **4** presents the results: the first column shows the percentages that report achieved coordination through the governance networks (River Basin District Boards); the second shows the percentages that mention effects of WDF work in general.

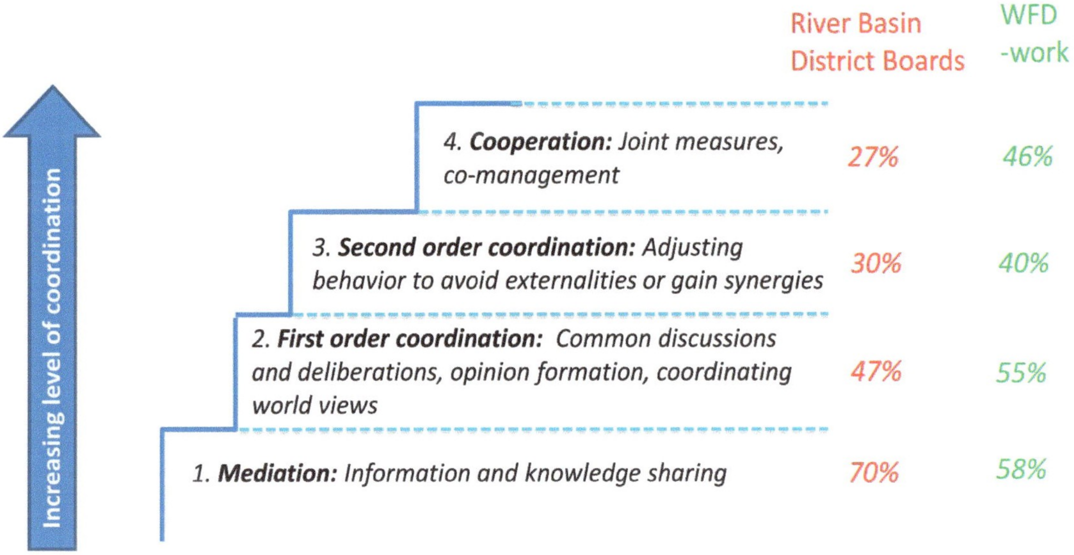

Figure 4: Coordination achieved (N=301, participants in River Basin District Boards reporting that they agree).

We see a clear tendency: respondents report that the ecosystem-based governance networks (River Basin District Boards) have achieved coordination primarily in the form of *information and knowledge sharing* and *common discussions and deliberation, coordinating worldviews* (the two lowest rungs). However, about one third also report coordination achievements as per the third rung of the ladder *adjusting behaviour to avoid externalities or gain synergies* and one fourth

[6] The study is part of the projects 'Water pollution abatement in a system of multi-level governance: A study of Norway's implementation of the EU Water Framework Directive (Wapabat)' and 'From service provider to network node: Does the counties' coordination role contribute to goal attainment and public sector innovation? (Countynode)', financed by the Norwegian Research Council (MILJØ 2015 and DEMOSREG II, respectively).

mention the coordination effects of creating *joint goals, measures, co-management*. Respondents give higher scores to these highest rungs when asked about the coordination effect of all WFD work.

Coordination as Information and Knowledge Sharing

First and foremost, the new governance networks (River Basin District Boards) have resulted in coordination in the form of *information- and knowledge sharing,* as shown by Fig. **4**. As many as 70 per cent of survey participants report this. Interestingly, we find little variation between the main groups of actors: municipalities, county municipalities and regional state authorities. The boards differ greatly in size among the 11 districts - from 12 to 270 members - and case-studies show that the boards with the highest institutional complexity function more like conferences than network meetings. These boards function primarily as vehicles for diffusion of information and ideas across policy areas, as well as awareness-raising; but also in the smaller boards, information sharing seems to be the most-reported achievement. As one county governor put it:

> *"It is very useful to be part of an arena where we meet other sector authorities, like waste-water, hydropower, fish farming, and transport. The information that is shared in these processes contributes to a higher level of mutual understanding between the sectors and of the challenges of the various sectors"* (County governor, regional state authority).

This quote shows that the network arenas are fruitful for rung 1 and rung 2 coordination, and also illustrate how these types of coordination are interlinked. Similar observations have been made in other countries (Nielsen 2013, 443).

Coordination of Worldviews

Do we find that the new governance networks help to bridge different discourses, coordinating worldviews? As indicated in the quote above, the networks seem to function as arenas where cross-sector discussions and deliberation contribute to developing shared worldviews, as is reported by 47 percent of our respondents (Fig. **4**). This is in line with earlier network governance research, which has found that deliberation, interpretation and learning require direct communication between all relevant actors. Hence, network arenas are suitable (Sørensen & Torfing 2007; 2012). However, respondents note that this type of coordination is not always easy to achieve, as some of the toughest battles between conflicting sector interests manifest themselves as conflicting problem-definitions. Such conflicts often concern which type of professional knowledge should be given most weight, especially in relation to *fish farming* (also from observations of network meetings). Here, the problem-definitions of the county governor (authority responsible for environment concerns) and the National Directorate of Fisheries are conflicting, as manifested in deep disagreement as to what scientific research institutes and publications the joint assessments are to be based on. Also in agriculture there have been similar battles over problem definitions. In Sweden, farmers in various RBDs have declared that they do not regard eutrophication to be a problem, even if the environmental authorities do (Hammer *et al.* 2011). Farmers in Norway have in the media expressed their doubts as to the knowledge basis of decisions taken as results of agreements in the networks - trusting agronomic professional knowledge more than other types of professional knowledge (for example limnology).[7] Also in our empirical study, informants representing municipalities mention farmers who do not see their water pollution as a problem for water quality.

On the other hand, our informants report that one of the consequences of the new governance networks is greater awareness and openness about these differing worldviews, understandings and professional discourses. Any disagreements within the network must now be explicitly and detailed described.[8] As one respondent remarked:

> *"with the water regulation (WFD) it is now possible for everyone to participate and have an opinion about sectors they are not responsible for"* (Interview 21.05.2012).

Thus, dominant discourses within sectors are being challenged by from other actors.

The county municipalities, as the main coordinators and RBD authorities, often find it hard to handle the conflicts between professional cultures and knowledge, they lack authority within the hierarchy and often find that network coordination have *too little muscle*. However, many municipal informants find that the governance networks actually contribute to bridging different professional discourses, by forcing them to develop a common language. As one of them pointed out:

---

[7] Aftenposten 20.09.2012

[8] http://www.vannportalen.no/ferdigakt.aspx?m=42793&amid=3605020
Forskrift om produksjonstilskudd i jordbruket

> *"the best thing about the WFD is that an overall system for water has been established, and that we have to develop a joint system of concepts across professional borders"* (Intermunicipal Agricultural Authority).

Others emphasize how the new network-organized system contributes to shared understandings of pollution problems that cut across political/administrative borders. Also the literature on Europe emphasizes the bridging of discourses as a major task in WFD implementation (Moss *et al.* 2009), as higher *rungs* of coordination are dependent on this (Nielsen 2013).

Hence, in our data material we find a clear tendency for the new governance networks to contribute to the coordination of worldviews and the development of common understandings among public authorities that represent conflicting interests.

Coordination as Taking Others' Actions into Consideration and Adjusting Behaviour

An important part of work in the River Basin District Boards is to overcome conflicts between sector interests related to the use and pollution of water (Andersson *et al.* 2012). In order to achieve the ambitious goal, coordination understood as the third rung - *taking others' actions into consideration and adjusting behaviour to achieve synergies or avoid negative externalities* - is necessary, for example to ensure that various actions or measures do not undermine each other (Pedersen *et al.* 2011). Have the new networks contributed to this kind of coordination? As Fig. **4** showed, only 30 per cent of the respondents reported this, only 30 percent. The case-studies also show that *only to a little extent* do public actors from various sectors take the actions of others into consideration and adjust behaviour in order to achieve synergies or avoid negative externalities. Sector conflicts are seen as an important obstacle to solving complex and malign problems in Norway (Christensen & Lægreid 2011), and the role of the RBDBs has been interpreted as an attempt at *decentralization of dilemmas* (Vike 2004). Our study shows that the dilemmas are not necessarily solved at this regional level, as many disagreements are expressed explicitly in the management plans and many dilemmas have been pushed up to the national level again. Examples include issues related to biological pressures from the aquaculture industry (sea lice and escaped salmon), where there is great tension between the Directorate of Fisheries and the Directorate for Nature Management (Stokke & Indset 2012), and questions related to environmental requirements for heavily modified water bodies (HMWB). Thus, the ecosystem-based governance networks, with the consensual principle as their core decision-making instrument, do not seem to have enough *muscle* to enforce the prioritizing between sector-interests in conflict at the regional level.

The networks' formulation of the management plans and programmes of measures primarily follows the *sandwich-principle*, where one measure is put on top of others on a list, without viewing them as a whole. Thus, various actors fail to take the measures of others into consideration, or adjusting their own behaviour; and cross-sectoral prioritizing is rarely conducted (Norsk Vann 2009). The WFD explicitly integrates economics into water management: Article 11 and Annex III of the Directive require cost-effectiveness analyses of alternative mitigation measures in formulating Programmes of Measures (PoMs) to achieve *good ecological status*. There is little cross-sectoral prioritizing (Norsk Vann 2011; Magnussen & Holen 2011a, 2011b). Thus, the WFD's requirement of selecting measures that improve water quality (quantity) *in the most cost-efficient way* for society can hardly been said to be ensured. In turn, most measures are concentrated around waste-water and sewage, which is a local responsibility and where municipalities have well-established legal instruments/authority at hand. The agricultural sector, which is a major contributor to various kinds of water pollution (Balana *et al.* 2011, Magnussen & Holen 2011a, 2011b; Norsk Vann 2009), is largely spared having to reduce pollution or implement measures. One of our respondents describes the agricultural measures as not ambiguous, but *actually do-able* measures. As a result, in one sub-district, municipal investments in waste-water and sewage for the purpose of reducing pollution amounted five times more than agricultural measures, even though the two sectors were considered to contribute equally to water pollution (Norsk Vann 2011, 47-48). This serves to reduce the trust and legitimacy of the ability of the new governance networks to stimulate coordination, understood as the alignment or adjustment of the action of participating public actors (Magnussen & Holen 2011a, 38-39). As a professional organisation comment:

> *"Of course the waste-water and sewage-sector has to take action, but the main challenges remain within the agricultural sector. The contemporary practices in agriculture cannot be reconciled with the goals in the water regulation, regardless of how much is invested in the waste-water and sewage-sector"* (Norsk Vann/Norwegian water 2011, 47).

As indicated by this quote, the networks seem to have an obvious weakness: they are based upon consensual agreements that need to be 'ratified' in each institution. Our empirical studies show that the traditional decision-making processes in the respective public authorities are little influenced by the actions of governance networks (RBD Boards). The low degree of *spatial fit* (Moss *et al.* 2009) between the jurisdictions of authorities responsible for agricultural measures and the catchment-areas as the basis of the governance networks can explain the tendencies observed. On the other hand, there are also some examples of up-stream municipalities having taken the concerns of other municipalities into consideration, and adjusted their behaviour to avoid negative externalities. In one of the pilot sub-districts, where the catchment area included mountain areas with hydropower actors, and fisheries interests in coastal municipalities, hydropower actors have agreed to implement *environmental flows* in the rivers to enable fish to migrate.

Coordination as Shared Goals, Measures and Co-Management

The fourth rung of the ladder is a *joint action as joint measures and shared goals.* To what extent this kind of coordination has taken place? From Fig. **4** we can see that only 27 percent of survey participants report that the new network arenas contribute to this. The joint Water Management Plans that must be formulated every six years do represent the fourth step of coordination, as they entail *formulating joint goals* for all relevant public actors related to the geographically demarcated River Basin District (catchment area). However, this has been a more symbolic than a real formulation of shared goals, as the goals are often broad and vague and do not necessarily bind the actors to take individual or joint action. Further, the Programmes of Measures related to the plans are mostly entered according to the *sandwich-principle*, with measures for one sector on top of the measures of other sectors, without viewing them in connection. Formally, the mandatory Water Management Plan is an example of coordination as per the fourth rung of the ladder, but this is seldom the case in practice.

Summing up - and Explaining the Tendencies

As shown above, the governance networks seem primarily to stimulate the coordination of information (rung 1), knowledge and worldviews (rung 2). How can the lack of *higher-level* coordination be explained? One obvious explanation is that the networks are new, most of them still being in their first planning cycle, and that all types (or rungs) of coordination take time. Secondly, the literature on coordination for solving other malign problems (climate- change mitigation and adaptation, sustainable development *etc.*) offers insights into some of the challenges encountered by governance networks. Experiences from the policy field of climate-change adaptation show that network coordination is suitable for mutual learning and raising awareness, but has little *muscle* for resolving difficult sector conflicts (Hanssen *et al.*, 2013). Our respondents say that coordination and decision-making in the new governance networks happen through deliberation and consensus, which might explain why difficult decisions about forcing sectors to take necessary measures are simply not made. As one informant representing the county governor stated:

> *"Everyone knows that it is impossible to get things done in such* [network] *arenas... there is so much hard work to be done in implementing the WFD that it does not work with committees - people sitting and chatting two hours every three months"* (Interview 21.05.2012).

Nevertheless, the main obstacle to achieving *high levels* of coordination seems to be *lack of legal harmonization of goals and legislation* between the WDF/Norwegian Water regulation and other Norwegian sector laws. Almost all our informants, irrespective of institutional belonging, single this out as the main challenge. They cited many instances where different national goals and regulations have not been harmonized and even contradict each other. For example, municipal respondents note that they have to relate to three bodies of juridical regulations, each with differing requirements as to how large the area of uncultivated land between cultivated land and water bodies must be; whether the area has to have vegetation, and if so, what kind of vegetation *etc*. However, we can also find attempts at harmonizing regulations in the agricultural sector with the WDF: the fertilization regulation is under revision, and more restrictions on fertilization distribution and storage might be introduced (Jærbladet 2011).

Thus, in water issues with intersecting sectors like agriculture and renewable energy/hydropower, and fisheries (wild/fish farms), higher forms of coordination have not been achieved due to lack of national legislation. The River Basin Management Plan has an uncertain status, as it is not clear how the objectives here rank in relation to other sector objectives. Similar findings have been reported from other European countries: studies show that in Lithuania, Latvia and Finland there have been outright conflicts between river basin planning and land-use planning (Nielsen *et al.* 2013, 443). In the case of fish farming and hydropower, coordination and conflict resolution but has required coordination at the national levels of government. Also Sweden and Finland have experienced conflicts between hydropower and river basin management; these are rooted in conflicting EU policies, as the EU Directive on Renewal Energy (2009/28) requires national targets for the use of energy from renewal sources (Nielsen *et al.* 2013, 443-34), which is not necessarily coherent with the objectives of the WFD.

All in all, these findings shed light on the limitations - and potentials - of the network mode of coordination in a *multi-level setting.* The public authorities in our networks hold various positions in the hierarchical state-regional-local government system - and the hierarchical *command-and-control* mechanisms often obstruct coordination (see Hovik & Hanssen 2014, forthcoming). The multi-level component of such networks seems to require the harmonization of legislation regulating sector authorities; further, that the actors participating see each other as equal parties, and that the delegated room for manoeuvre for all participants in the networks has been defined in advance. When these conditions are met, the governance networks seem to be fruitful arenas for the sharing of information and knowledge, professional discourses and worldviews that are often required to achieve coordination understood as adjusted action and mutual commitment to work together.

DO THE NETWORKS, AND ACHIEVED COORDINATION, SPUR INNOVATION?

Coordination does not necessarily stimulate innovation: indeed, according to Sørensen and Torfing (2014), innovation requires friction and constructive tension between different life-worlds and discourses, so as to disturb the tacit knowledge of actors and spur new thoughts, ideas and mutual learning. In particular, coordination as the second step of the ladder, as coordinating worldviews, might hinder innovation. Our case has a huge innovative potential, as the newly established networks bring together actors representing many different interests, resources, knowledge, worldviews and transformative capacities - actors that have not had to relate to each other previously. Much of the literature on public sector innovation and new public governance considers this to be crucial for innovation (see Osborne 2010; Sørensen & Torfing 2012), proclaiming that the processes where innovative policies and problem-solution take place are precisely cross-cutting multi-actor collaborations. In addition, the chapter has shown high tension and conflict levels in the networks studied, obstructing coordination understood as adjusting behaviour and developing common goals and measures. So, tensions are well represented - but do they spur innovation? Can we observe examples of collaborative innovation - and if so, what kinds of innovations?

The Hartley's (2005) distinction between various dimensions of public sector innovation will be used to discuss these questions, - distinguishing between governance innovation, strategic innovation, policy innovation, process innovations, service innovation and rhetorical innovation. It is first and foremost the latter that is most noticeable: *rhetoric innovation*, *i.e.* the creation of new concepts and a common language. In the course of only a few years, Norway's new network-based water governance has changed the way of speaking about water, adopting the rhetoric of the WFD, with *ecological good status, water bodies etc*. Even more importantly, it has creating a new way of thinking about water. Norway, which has seen itself as the country with cleanest water in the world, has in the course of a few years become far more aware of the pressures on water. Our findings show that the new networks, and the planning process required by the WFD, help public (sector) authorities at different levels to create a mutual language and a common platform for understanding each other. This also enables them to enter discussions that were not necessary previously. This type of coordination, developing common concepts and common ways of *describing* the problems, also represents rhetoric innovation. Thus, by coordinating their different worldviews, participating actors have managed to co-create a new story-line - or worldview - about the pressures on water today.

Another central finding is that the new construction, in very few years, has developed what can be called a *policy innovation:* establishing *comprehensive water governance* as a policy field. The mandatory Water Management Plans, categorized as *step four* coordination, have contributed to this. Nobody used to speak of this as a policy field in Norway, with its highly fragmented system of water governance and responsibility. The agriculture sector had certain instruments for reducing eutrophication, the hydropower sector was regulated in another way, and so on. No public authority had unique responsibility for water - and that is still the case. What is new is the establishment of a wide range of coordination mechanisms aimed at overcoming the fragmentation, and the appointment of a coordinating authority (the county municipalities). In our survey, members of the River Basin District Boards were asked if the new ecosystem-based networks result in more a comprehensive form of water governance. Fig. **5** shows the results.

We see that a large majority of all respondents report that using the ecosystem-based principle of catchment areas has in fact led to a more comprehensive perspective on water. Especially interesting is the scant variation in terms of institutional affiliation: regional state authorities report this just as much as municipalities and county municipalities, even though many of the regional state authorities have traditionally been very sector-oriented, and not particularly interested in water. This impression is strengthened by the interviews, which give many examples of a more comprehensive water policy now preparing the actors for more coordinated effort- even if tough inter-sector is still evident.

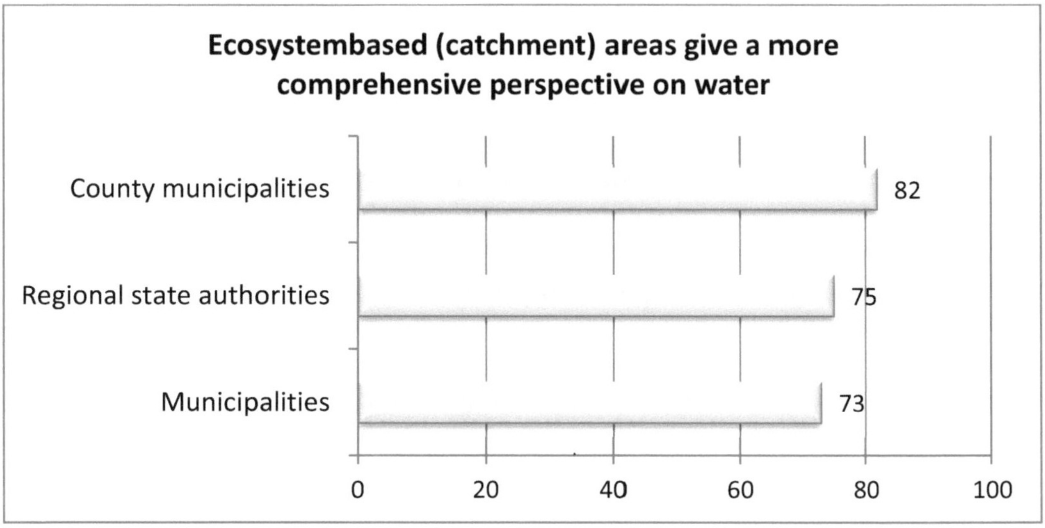

Figure 5: Percentage of RBDB members who agree that ecosystem-based/catchment areas give a more comprehensive perspective on water, by institutional affiliation (N=301).

Participants also report several examples of *process innovation.* A contributing factor is the mandatory 6-year planning cycle of the WFD - forcing the participants and coordinators (county municipalities) to establish new routines. Part of this cycle involves characterizing and classifying all 28,000 bodies of water in Norway. As a consequence, new ways of obtaining local (lay) knowledge have emerged, adding to the existing expert knowledge. Only a minority of these bodies of water have been studied by natural science experts, and the coordinators often invite NGOs like hunting and wildlife associations and local environmental organizations, and private firms, to contribute their local knowledge (have the fish disappeared? Where along the river are the eutrophication problems severe in autumn storms? *etc.*). These knowledge-obtaining routines are a clear example of process innovation that contribute to a broader range of (local) knowledge being mobilized and channelled into public planning processes.

Another example is the new established routines for involving local actors and stakeholders through reference groups - an important *governance innovation.* The WFD requires that regional reference groups be established in each River Basin District. Asked how the groups work, almost 40 percent of the members of these reference groups reported that they function as arenas where public authorities can obtain knowledge from user groups and stakeholders. However, only one-third of the participants experience that their contributions in these arenas are taken into consideration.

Other respondents say that the requirements related to the co-formulation of the Joint Water Management Plan (step four coordination) have spurred various kinds of *governance innovation* internally in municipalities and other organizations. One municipality established an internal water management group/network in order to coordinate WDF work internally. In this group, they reported interactive forms of collaborative innovation, as totally different sectors were represented. According to one informant from the waste-water sector,

> *"It is smart to involve others, to hear their comments and contributions. And every now and then they come up with ideas I'd never thought about - which I really appreciate".*

Thus, new ways of internal organization in municipalities tend to spur new ideas and solutions for how municipalities can work to ensure good ecological status for all their water.

Although we found few cases of step three coordination, understood as adjusting the behaviour of the organization in order to create synergies and avoid externalities with other actors, there were some examples of this leading to *strategic innovation* (new goals or purposes for the organization). For example, after some years of participating in these networks, national and regional agricultural authorities have gradually adjusted their goals, increasingly highlighting the goals of the Water Framework Directive in their official documents. However, this also increases the tension between the various levels of government - as the dual (and often contradictory) goals give increased room for interpretation of the sub-ordinated levels of government. An illustrative example is a negotiation of a package solution in one of the governance networks. Here, every sector authority had gone as far as they could - and agreed on tough measures. Then, the Ministry of Food and Agriculture stopped the agreement, as they found that the regional-level agricultural authorities had given greater weight to environmental goals (reduce pressure on water) than to the traditional goals of the agricultural sector (increased food production). The incident revealed the latent goal-conflict in this public sector authority.

One of the coordinating measures established is a database for various measures being developed and implemented in the River Basin Districts (called the *measure-library*). Here, all participants (municipalities, counties, county governors, other regional state authorities) are to describe the measures they are taking for reducing the pressure on water. This is an example of step one coordination: effective sharing of information and knowledge about how they work on reducing the pressures on water. The library can be categorized as a *service innovation,* which also enables effective diffusion of innovative measures - often created locally. Moreover, in cases where the sector authorities are pushed (or push themselves) to reduce their pressure on water, some are developing new and innovative approaches.

CONCLUSION

The chapter has discussed how new ecosystem-based governance networks stimulate cross-sector and multi-level coordination, and how the coordination that is achieved influenced the innovation capacity of the networks. Our findings are summed up in Fig. **6**.

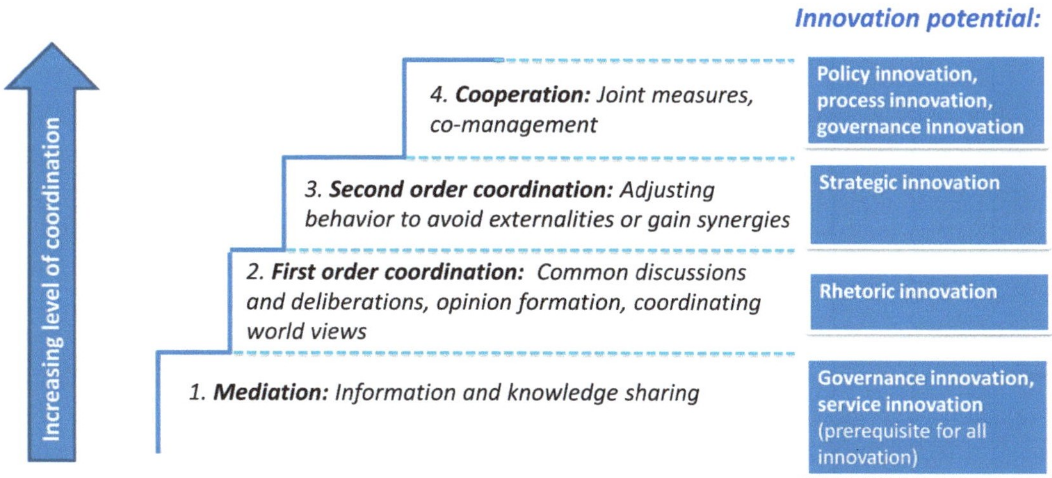

Figure 6: Coordination in networks - and implications for their innovation potential.

As this chapter has shown, the new ecosystem-based governance networks have a huge potential to spur coordination and collaborative innovation, by bringing together actors with different interests, resources, knowledge, worldviews and transformative capacities. We have seen that the networks contribute to coordination as well as collaborative innovation, in varying degrees, even though these aims are often held to require diametrical different processes. While *coordination* requires some sort of alignment of actions, *innovation* does not need to be aligned - conflict is often assumed to create fruitful friction. The new governance networks have helped to promote coordination between sector authorities, mostly in the form of extensive information and knowledge sharing (rung 1), and awareness-arising and the development of common problem-understandings (rung 2). These are reported as major achievements that can lead to adjusted action on the part of various actors in the future, even if we do not see so many examples today.

The coordination of worldviews seems to spur public-sector innovation, as it establish a common platform of understanding, where the friction and conflicting interests can play out in constructive ways. Even if the frictions are intense, our informants note rhetorical innovation. They report of emerging recognition that water management must be more comprehensive, taking many sectors into consideration. As a consequence, we can find certain traces of behavioural adjustment in the sectors (rung three coordination), in turn resulting in strategic innovation - as the formulation of new goals for the sectors. The mandatory Joint Water Management Plans, formally representing rung four of coordination, seem to spur policy innovation in establishing a new policy field, as well as process and governance innovation. The strong position of the Norwegian local authorities seems to be well-suited for adapting to the local context, and for opening up for new knowledge, ideas and understandings.

However, the full potentials are far from realized. Obstacles include lack of national harmonization of policy goals and sector legislation, leading to reluctance among some major sector authorities (representing important pressure on water). Another obstacle is the lack of political will, regional and local, to engage actively in the networks and recognize the innovative potential in the new constellations and the new collaborative arenas and procedures. More active local and regional political leadership, either participating or meta-governing these networks, can facilitate coordination and make clear the need for new solutions. A more active political leadership can also contribute to a stronger focus on an even broader inclusion, which may bring in a broader range of ideas, actors and resources - contributing to innovative processes.

ACKNOWLEDGEMENTS

This chapter is based upon the research conducted in the research projects "Countynode: From service provider to network node: Does the Counties' coordination role contribute to goal attainment and public sector innovation"?" and "WAPABAT: Water Pollution Abatement in a system of Multi-level Governance: A study of Norway's implementation of EUs Water Framework Directive". Both are financed by the Norwegian Research Council.

CONFLICT OF INTEREST

The author confirms that this chapter contents have no conflict of interest.

REFERENCES

Aftenposten (2012). Renere vann gir dårligere brød. *Aftenposten* (Norwegian daily), morning edition, 20 September. 2012, 14.

Andersson, I., Petersson, M. & Jarsjö, J. (2012). Impact of the European Water Framework Directive on local-level water management: Case study Oxunda Catchment, Sweden. *Land Use Policy,* 29, 73–82.

Balana, B.B., Vinten, A. & Slee, B. (2011). A review on cost-effectiveness analysis of agri-environmental measures related to the EU WFD: Key issues, methods, and applications. *Ecological Economics*, 70, 1021-1031.

Bekkers, V., Edelenbos, J. & Steijn, B. (eds) (2011). *Innovation in the public sector: Linking capacity and leadership*. Basingstoke: Palgrave Macmillan.

Bouckaert, G., Peters, G. & Verhoest, K. (2010). *The Coordination of Public Sector Organizations: Shifting Patterns of Public Management*. Basingstoke: Palgrave Macmillan.

Christensen, T. & Lægreid, P. (2011). Complexity and hybrid public administration: theoretical and empirical challenges. *Public Organizational Review*, 11, 407-423.

EU WFD (2000). *Directive* 2000/60/EC. Water Framework Directive.

Habermas, J. (1996). *Between facts and norms: contributions to a discourse theory of law and democracy,* translation W. Rehg. Cambridge, MA: MIT Press.

Hammer, M.B., Balfors, U., Mörtberg, M. & Quin, A. (2011). Governance of water resources in the phase of change: A case study of the implementation of the EU Water Framework Directive in Sweden. *AMBIO,* 40, 210–220.

Hanssen, G.S., Mydske, P.K. & Dahle, E. (2013). Multi-level coordination of climate change adaptation: By national hierarchical steering or by regional network governance? *Local Environment,* 18:8, 869–887.

Hanssen, G.S. & Hovik, S. (2013). EUs vanndirektiv og medvirkning – erfaringer fra Norge. *Kart og plan,* 73:5, 319–332.

Hartley, J. (2005). Innovation in governance and public service: past and present. *Public Money & Management,* 25:1, 27–34.

Higdem, U. & Hanssen, G.S. (2013). Handling the two conflicting discourses of partnerships and participation in regional planning. *European Planning Studies,* online publication 25 April 2013. http://www.tandfonline.com/doi/abs/10.1080/09654313.2013.791966#.U6c4CWeKBdg

Hovik, S. & Hanssen, G.S. (2014). The impact of network management on multi-level coordination. *Public Administration,* Online publication December *2014*. doi: 10.1111/padm.12135.

Jærbladet (2011). *Gjødselkrav kan gi kutt for jærbønder*. 15 August 2011.

Keast, R., Brown, K. & Mandell, M. (2007). Getting the right mix: unpacking integration meanings and strategies. *International Public Management Journal,* 10:1, 9-33.

Magnussen, K. & Holen, S. (2011a). *Vannprising og miljømålene etter EUs vanndirektiv: Anbefalinger om bruk av økonomiske virkemidler i norsk vannforvaltning*. Sweco report 144971-01. Oslo: Sweco/NIVA.

Magnussen, K. & S. Holen (2011b). *Økonomiske aspekter ved vanndirektivet – Erfaringer fra EU og forslag til økonomiske analyser i norsk vannforvaltning.* Sweco report 144811-1.Oslo: Sweco/NIVA.

Moss, T. (2004). The governance of land use in river basins: prospects for overcoming problems of institutional interplay with the EU Water Framework Directive. *Land Use Policy*, 21, 85-94.

Moss, T., Medd, W., Guy, S. & Marvin, S. (2009). Organizing water: The hidden role of intermediary work. *Water Alternatives,* 2:1, 16-33.

Moss, T. (2012). Spatial fit, from panacea to practice: Implementing the EU Water Framework Directive. In *Ecology and Sociology*, 17:3, 2. http://www.ecologyandsociety.org/vol17/iss3/art2/

Nielsen, H.Ø., Fredriksen, P., Saarikoski, H., Rytkönen, A.-M. & Pedersen, A.B. (2013). How different institutional arrangements promote integrated river basin management: Evidence from the Baltic Sea region. *Land Use Policy,* 30, 437-445.

Norsk Vann (2009). *Jordbruk og vannkvalitet*. Feature article in Nationen by Einar Melheim, director, & Toril Hofshagen, assistant diector. Hamar: Norsk Vann.

Norsk Vann (2010). *Innspill til melding om landbruks- og matpolitikken*. Hamar: Norsk Vann.

Norsk Vann (2011) *Vannforskriftens økonomiske konsekvenser for kommunesektoren og avløpsanleggene*. Hamar: Norsk Vann.

Osborne, S.P. (Ed.) (2010). *The new public governance? Emerging perspectives on the theory and practice of public governance*. London: Routledge.

Osborne, S.P. (2010). Delivering public services: Time for a new theory? *Public Management Review*, 12:1, 1-10.

Pedersen, A.R., Sehested, K. & Sørensen, E. (2011). Emerging theoretical understandings of pluricentric coordination in public governance. *American Review of Public Administration*, 41:4, 375-394.

Stokke, K.B. & Indset, M. (2012). Møtet mellom EUs vanndirektiv og statlig sektoransvar. Helhetlig vannforvaltning gjennom konsensusbygging og nettverk? *Kart og Plan*, 4, 278-288.

Sørensen, E. & Torfing J. (Eds) (2007). *Theories of democratic network governance*. Basingstoke: Palgrave Macmillan

Sørensen, E. & Torfing, J. (2012). Introduction: Collaborative innovation in the public sector. *The Innovation Journal: The Public Sector Innovation Journal*, 17:1.

Sørensen, E. & Torfing, J. (2014). Enhancing social innovation by rethinking collaboration, leadership and public governance. *Social Frontiers. The next edge of social innovation research*. Paper presented at NESTA Social Frontiers, London, 14–15 November 2013 http://rudar.ruc.dk/bitstream/1800/13187/1/191799289 Enhancing_Social_Innovation_by_Rethinking_Collaboration_Leadership_and_Public_Governance.pdf

CHAPTER 8

Collaborative Innovation Processes in Dutch Regional Water Governance - The Role of Niches and Policy Entrepreneurs in Fostering (Strategic) Policy Innovation

Hanneke Gieske* **and Arwin van Buuren**

Erasmus University Rotterdam, The Netherlands

Abstract: In this chapter, we investigate how collaborative governance contributes to spurring innovation in regional water management. We analyze a collaborative innovation effort in regional water management in The Netherlands. In a unique endeavour, nine municipalities united in a city region and a regional water authority, together with private parties, crafted a joint innovation program aimed at developing new knowledge and innovative solutions for persistent inundation problems in the area. In addition to innovative solutions in selected experimental areas, the collaborative effort gave rise to a paradigm shift in regional inundation protection policy – from a norm-oriented approach to a more modern, adaptive, effect-oriented approach. We apply a multilevel perspective to analyze the (co-evolving) developments at three levels: the macro level of the national (policy) landscape, the meso level of the regional water management regime, and the micro level of experimental areas or niches. Our analysis reveals that learning processes on these three levels are important to trigger policy innovation, but that these processes have to become connected by the deliberate interventions of policy entrepreneurs to really result in a paradigm shift.

Keywords: Water management, paradigmatic innovation, policy innovation, policy entrepreneurs, interaction between levels.

INTRODUCTION

Over the last two decades, we have witnessed an increasing demand for innovation in the public sector. Higher demands on public service delivery, increasing complexity of policy issues, and shrinking public budgets are important factors that push governments to search for innovative approaches in order to become more effective and efficient. However, as Sørensen and Torfing (2011, 844) state: "*Despite the growing interest in spurring innovation in the public*

***Corresponding author Hanneke Gieske:** Strategic advisor at the Delfland regional water authority and PhD candidate at Erasmus University Rotterdam, The Netherlands; Tel: 00 31 6 51 280 613; E-mail: hgieske@xs4all.nl

Annika Agger, Bodil Damgaard, Andreas Hagedorn Krogh and Eva Sørensen (Eds.)

sector, the current understanding of the sources of public innovation is inadequate". This is especially true in relation to public policy innovation. As Duijn (2009) notes: public policy innovation presupposes a shift in policy paradigm, and thus not only in existing practices but also in the underlying rules and routines, value propositions, and assumptions. Such a paradigm shift thus alters the existing policy regime and is a complex, multifaceted phenomenon.

From the literature on socio-technical transitions, we know that experimenting in relatively protected innovation spaces (Beckers *et al.* 2011) or niches (Schot and Geels, 2008) is often deemed of crucial importance to bring about enduring change on the meso level of institutional regimes. Transitions or regime shifts come out as the result of tensions that build up from micro-level niche developments and pressure from the landscape level, the macro level (Geels, 2002, Rotmans *et al.*, 2001).

However, there seems to be a long, unpredictable, and non-linear way from experimenting in pilot projects to policy paradigm shifts, and to date, we do not know much about how these two are related. Pilots are frequently used as the starting point for innovation processes in the public domain to test innovative ideas before full-scale application (Vreugdenhil *et al.* 2010; Van Buuren & Loorbach, 2009). However, several hurdles such as limited representativeness and learning, lack of institutionalization, and poor timing limit the diffusion of new practice-based knowledge from pilots into standardized policy (Vreugdenhil *et al.*, 2010).

In this chapter, we analyze the relationship between collaborative innovation at project level (in pilots or niches) and policy innovation at regime level, from a multilevel perspective. We thus try to understand how learning and change processes at several levels (niches, regime, landscape) are interrelated and how policy entrepreneurs link developments at different levels in order to realize cross-level breakthroughs. Recent literature (Huitema & Meijerink, 2010; Brouwer, 2013) emphasizes the importance of policy entrepreneurs for realizing change, but the question of how entrepreneurship, innovation, and learning are interlinked is still unanswered. For this analysis, we selected an in-depth case study of a policy paradigm shift in regional inundation protection policy at the Dutch regional water authority, Delfland, which happened in the slipstream of a pilot-based regional innovation program.

We give special attention to the organizational routines, procedures, and strategies in the implementation phase of the new policy, because the implementation phase in particular is the most important phase of the innovation cycle – as the proof of the pudding is in the eating.

The Hague Region is a cooperative entity made up of nine municipalities, administered by representatives of the nine town councils. It is a densely populated area mainly below sea level, with major cities like The Hague and important greenhouse and agricultural areas within the district of the Delfland regional water authority (see Fig. **1**). Regional water authorities are task-oriented regional government bodies with regulative authority, have an elected board, and levy taxes. Delfland is responsible for protecting the area from sea and river by dunes and dikes, for water management in the district, and for the management of water quality and sewage treatment.

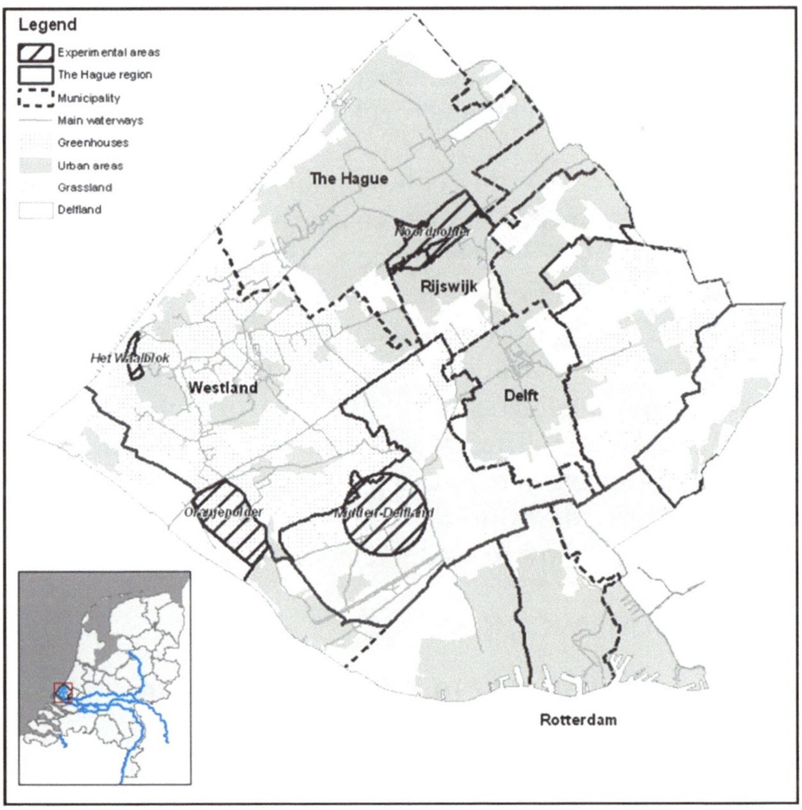

Figure 1: Delfland regional water authority, The Hague Region, and the experimental areas discussed in this chapter.

In 1998 and 2001, extreme rainfall led to flooding in The Hague Region, causing significant damage to crops in the greenhouse area and to households and firms.

Delfland therefore started to work out a water policy to prevent flooding in the future, anticipating national protection levels, which it translated into an easy-to-handle water storage norm expressed in cubic meters per hectare. It soon ran into severe implementation problems, resulting in tensions between the municipalities and the regional water authority. Responding to these tensions, the governmental actors in the region drew up a regional covenant – The Water Framework The Hague Region – to find solutions together to prevent inundation in the region, including a program aimed at finding innovative combinations of water management and other spatial functions. Additional developments – such as the availability of new hydrological models that allowed a better understanding of the physical system, and especially severe financial pressures within the regional water authority – opened up a major policy window in 2009 in which these new insights could become accepted and resulted in an intriguing policy innovation. The incumbent water policy based on water storage norms was suspended and a new effect-oriented approach was embraced and finally integrated into the regional water management policies and regulations.

In this chapter, we analyze how this policy innovation evolved in the interplay between landscape developments, regime change, and niche dynamics, and the role that entrepreneurs played in this process. In section two, we present our theoretical framework. In section three, we describe how we conducted our empirical research. In the next three sections, we describe the co-evolving developments that led to a transition from a norm-driven to an effect-driven policy paradigm, its implementation, and the role of policy entrepreneurs in coupling developments on the different levels. In section seven, we analyze this development by reconstructing the co-evolution between landscape, regime, and niche dynamics. We conclude by formulating a couple of implications that are important for the question of how to facilitate policy innovation.

THEORETICAL FRAMEWORK

Innovation, Learning, and the Role of Policy Entrepreneurs

We define innovation in the public sector as the implementation, by people in an institutional context, of a new (technical, organizational, policy, and so forth) concept that substantially improves the functioning and outcomes of the public sector (Moore, 2005; Hartley, 2005; Van de Ven *et al.* 1999). The innovation process is only completed when the innovation has resulted in the implementation of the new concept, has been integrated into the activities of the regime, and has become part of the rules, routines, and practices of the regime by institutionalization, and is therefore no longer visible or experienced as an innovation.

In order to analyze more precisely the non-linear pathway and nested character of a policy innovation at the level of the strongly institutionalized regional water management regime, influenced by tensions and interactions between the overarching national policy environment and the role of more localized pilots and experiments, we apply the notions and language of the multilevel perspective on socio-technical transitions as developed by Rip and Kemp (1998), Geels (2002), Geels and Kemp (2007). This framework seems to be useful for the study of public policy innovations as it enables a multilevel analysis of co-evolving developments on the landscape level (the wider policy and institutional environment), on the regime level of interrelated actors in a policy field, and on the level of niches or concrete projects in which the building blocks of a new paradigm are developed. In this section, we elaborate briefly on this theoretical framework and extend it with insights from literature on policy learning and the role of policy entrepreneurs.

As stated in the previous section, the multilevel perspective organizes the analysis of socio-technical systems on three levels of structuring processes: the micro level of niches (which can be seen as breeding places for new, innovative ideas and practices), the meso level of the highly institutionalized regimes currently fulfilling societal functions, and the landscape level, the macro-level context of social and physical factors. The multilevel perspective proposes that innovations at regime level come about through the interplay between processes at these three levels in different phases: niche innovations build up internal momentum, changes at the landscape level create pressure on the regime, and destabilization of the regime creates windows of opportunity for niche innovations. Transitions can follow different paths (Geels & Schot, 2007), *e.g.* more top-down reconstellation paths, bottom-up empowerment paths, and internally induced adaptation paths (De Haan & Rotmans, 2011).

Regimes consist of groups of actors, *e.g.* policymakers, scientists, public and private organizations, and societal groups, linked together in semi-coherent sets of rules, strongly embedded in institutions and infrastructures. Regime constellations are dominated by strong internal relations and relatively weak external relations (Geels & Kemp, 2007). Innovation processes can be facilitated by the creation of niches (Schot & Geels, 2008). Niches are (partly) protected institutional spaces (innovation milieus: Bekkers *et al.* 2011; Castells, 1996) in which actors have (some) freedom to think about, and experiment with, innovative ways of doing, concepts, technologies, and instruments, in specific arrangements – including pilot projects, experiments, experimental areas, and so forth – that aim at protected experimentation to find new solutions to persistent problems. Learning processes are crucial to develop better knowledge and shared meanings, and attention should be given to socio-cognitive dynamics (Schot & Geels, 2008). We assume that niche experiments become especially successful when they become connected to learning processes already happening within the regime. Niches provide innovative solutions, ideas, and concepts that can provide the answer to questions raised in the regime because of failing paradigms or ineffective policy instruments. As these learning processes generate several tensions, new ideas or concepts can help to overcome them. This theoretical framework allows for an inclusive analysis of collaborative innovation.

We thus assume that learning processes at regime level play an important role in innovation pathways, and that it is necessary to analyze the way in which learning processes at niche and regime level become interconnected and mutually strengthening. That learning is a crucial precondition for policy innovation is extensively argued by authors like Sabatier (1987), Bennett and Howlett (1992), and Hall (1993). Heclo (1974,307) defines policy-oriented learning as "*relatively enduring alterations of thought or behavioral intentions that result from experience and that are concerned with the attainment or revisions of policy objectives*". Learning may concern incremental changes within the same policy paradigm. Policy paradigms can be described as the framework of ideas and standards that specifies not only the goals of policy and the kind of instruments that can be used to attain them, but also the very nature of the problems they are meant to be addressing (Hall, 1993). Learning may also concern fundamental changes in the framework of policy ideas. These changes come from inconsistencies within the existing policy paradigm that arise when that paradigm does not result in the goals as set, and when the assumptions behind the paradigm are proven to be wrong. Until new ways of doing are fully developed and accepted, these learning processes are dominated by growing tensions between existing routines, beliefs, and values, and the growing recognition that other ways of doing are necessary to remain legitimate and effective.

Connecting niche results to learning processes within the regime presupposes the presence of entrepreneurs who are able to respond to policy windows that are open only for a short period. Such a policy window occurs when three conditions are met: there are some useful niche results that can be pushed forward, there is a quest for new answers because of tensions arising at regime level, and the surrounding landscape is receptive to a more structural reform of existing policy paradigms. From the literature we know that policy entrepreneurs (Kingdon, 1995), boundary spanners (Leifer & Delbecq, 1978, Williams, 2002), or innovation champions play an important role in advancing innovative ideas and solutions in connecting within and between the different levels. Policy entrepreneurs often operate in (deliberately constructed) niche-type arrangements, like experimental areas, pilot projects, shadow networks, and the like (Lovell, 2009). These groups are either part of the regime or build up pressure from outside the regime, but somehow have to connect their results to regular policies and activities. Strategies of these policy entrepreneurs described in policy change literature include generating and selling new ideas, building coalitions, using windows of opportunity, exploiting or manipulating venues, and managing networks (Huitema & Meijerink, 2010). From an analysis of the role and actions of policy entrepreneurs in Dutch water management, Brouwer and Biermann (2011, see also Brouwer, 2013) report attention- and support-seeking strategies, linking strategies, relational management strategies, and arena strategies.

In summary, to understand policy innovation, we look not only at the multilevel dynamics between niches, regime, and landscape, but also at the more endogenous dynamics and policy learning at regime level. We now try to uncover both the vertical dynamics (between niche developments and landscape changes) and the horizontal dynamics of learning processes at regime level, and the role of entrepreneurial, advocating, and brokering individuals therein.

METHODS

Although (socio-technical) transition theory has been developed for longitudinal analysis (and management) of transitions at the scale of societal systems, it can also serve as a framework to analyze smaller scale innovations in regional water management, which displays the characteristics of a (socio-technical) regime: its highly institutionalized character, its dependence on existing physical infrastructure, and strong entwinement between professional values, technical provisions, and legal prescriptions (see also Van Buuren *et al.* 2014).

In this chapter, we focus on the evolution of the paradigm shift within the Delfland regional water authority, which is the major regulative and executive authority for regional water management. This transition in essence has to do with the replacement of a traditional focus on applying and realizing strict quantitative norms in regional water management with a more adaptive approach focusing upon realizing effect-oriented measures as the outcome of a collaborative innovation program.

In our empirical study, we reconstructed what happened on the three levels of analysis in the period between 2001 and 2011: the landscape, the regime, and the various niches, and the role of learning processes within the niches and in the regional water authority. We further analyzed the way in which the evolvement on the various levels can be explained by either vertical dynamics (linkages between niche, regime, and landscape dynamics) or horizontal dynamics (learning processes at regime level) and whether policy entrepreneurs were important in the process by which the various levels co-evolved towards a policy innovation in terms of a paradigm shift and its implementation.

We analyzed the evolution of the regime by interviewing water experts of the Delfland regional water authority to ascertain which learning processes evolved during implementation of the former policy paradigm and how the implementation of the new policy paradigm took shape. On the basis of these interviews and of an earlier evaluation of the collaborative innovation program (van Buuren & Bressers, 2011), we analyzed the development within several niches and their main outcomes. Subsequently, we analyzed the dynamics on the landscape level (mainly national policy changes with regard to climate adaptation and water management). Then we made a time line of when landscape changes, niche changes, and regime changes occurred, and analyzed how developments on the various levels impacted one another and resulted in the observed paradigm shift. In addition, we tried to discover which actors could be characterized as policy entrepreneurs because of their activities in connecting developments at the level of landscape, regime, and niches.

TOWARDS A POLICY PARADIGM SHIFT

Developments at Various Levels

In this section, we describe the developments at the various levels (landscape, regime, and niches) that preceded and culminated in Delfland's paradigm shift. By coupling niche developments and tensions that arose at regime level, policy entrepreneurs were able to realize a breakthrough with regard to a policy paradigm that gradually became ineffective.

Landscape Developments

In the Netherlands, awareness of the effects of climate change and need for adaptation arose in the late nineties of the last century. A new national strategic water policy in 2000, Water Policy for the 21st Century, aiming to adapt to climate change, stated that water should be a guiding principle in land use planning, and excess rainwater should be first retained, then stored, and finally drained. Room for Water was the label of this new guiding principle. This is a part of larger transition from a sectoral and technocratic water management approach to a more integrated and interactive approach (van der Brugge, 2009). Municipalities, provinces, regional water authorities, and the national government agreed in 2003 to implement the new water policy. The National Water Covenant specified levels of protection from inundation due to excessive rainfall to be reached before 2015. Regional water authorities and municipalities started to work out water plans to comply with these inundation protection levels.

Regime Developments

In the framework of our study, we consider the public and private parties involved in regional water management, as well as the water-related knowledge and technologies, water-related policies, rules, and regulations as part of the regime. We focus in our description on the regional water authority as the main water-related regulative authority and the municipalities within The Hague Region, especially Westland, the largest greenhouse area in The Netherlands.

In the aftermath of flooding caused by extreme rainfall around the millennium, the Delfland regional water authority drew up a plan in 2001 to prevent flooding in the future, anticipating the national inundation protection levels. Drawing on extensive hydrological analyses, Delfland stated that a surface water storage capacity of 325 m^3/ha in its main drainage system and its 70 polders was needed, and this became a cornerstone of its inundation protection policy and regulations. In all municipalities, water storage basins were to be constructed, and regulations were put in place that obliged all private spatial construction developers to comply with this inundation protection norm in their spatial projects. The regional water authority's elected council approved initial investments of 60 million euro and an increase in water taxes. The regional water authority started ambitious, doubling pumping capacity and broadening major runoff channels, but ran into problems when it wanted to realize the agreed extra storage capacity for excess rainwater. It confronted the municipal authorities with the outcome of its calculations, which amounted to extensive claims for space, *e.g.* 600,000 ha in the agro-industrial greenhouse area and 225,000 ha in the city of The Hague, stating at the same time that it would not purchase the necessary land. Although attempts were made to combine the reconstruction of the surface water system with spatial reconstructions in municipal and greenhouse areas, this proved difficult. Political problems arose as space is scarce and land is expensive. In 2008, the Westland municipal council approved the water plan, but not the financial section. The political problems that arose led to mediation attempts by a former minister, but could not be resolved.

The municipalities within The Hague Region and Delfland agreed in 2006 in their Water Framework The Hague Region Covenant that innovative solutions were needed and seized an opportunity that coincidently arose to acquire financial support from the national government to establish a joint knowledge and innovation program aimed at finding innovative solutions for excess rainwater storage. An essential part of the innovation approach was experimentation in experimental areas (in Dutch *proeftuinen*, literally: trial gardens, see Fig. **1**), in which the regional water authority, municipalities, and stakeholders collaborated, and regular policy was temporarily suspended.

Niche Level Developments

Some of the *proeftuinen* aimed at the multiple use of space, working out solutions to store excess rainwater under greenhouses or in parking garages. In one of the *proeftuinen* (Waalblok) and as an outcome of intensive consultations with farmers and the municipality, a water storage cellar was constructed under a greenhouse as a part of a larger plan to purify and recycle drainage water for irrigation of crops. In another *proeftuin* (Midden-Delfland) in a grassland area, parties set their stakes on so-called blue services by farmers: farmers accepting flooding more often than the inundation protection norm in exchange for a predefined financial compensation. In one of the *proeftuinen* in the city of The Hague (the Noordpolder), with a calculated lack of water storage capacity of 50,000 m^3, a new hydrological modeling approach was applied, enabling the mapping of predicted inundated areas, which showed that flooding would occur, but would be limited to sporting facilities and parks. In this *proeftuin*, discussions started about whether the huge public investments needed to achieve extra water storage capacity were legitimate given the forecasted limited effect of inundation at these locations.

Learning Processes and Tensions at Regime Level

In the context of these pilots or niches, but also in more regular settings, such as drawing up the water plan for the city of Delft, or studies on water management in the eastern part of the district, further knowledge development supported by advanced hydrological models provided a better insight into the functioning of the physical system and the effect of inundations. However, in these more regular settings, it proved difficult to apply these new insights to propose and design alternative measures. As all plans, measures, and related investment budgets already approved by Delfland's elected general board were based on the earlier – less advanced – calculations, it was decided after ample deliberations with the responsible alderman to translate the results showing predicted actual inundation back into the inundation norms in cubic meters laid down in the regional water authority's policy, and the measures proposed were subsequently based on these calculations.

At the same time, regional water authority professionals tried to expand the inundation protection policy to include the option of innovative solutions, but this was also met with considerable cautiousness by the regional water authority executives who had been held responsible for the earlier floodings and would rather stick to the robust solution of "*digging for extra water*".

As the costs of the inundation protection program were much higher than initially anticipated – in 2008 the projected investment budget was 280 million euro – because of the complicated solutions that had to be found due to the densely built-up areas, and following better insights into the functioning of the physical system and the effect of inundation, doubts arose among the regional water authority professionals about the legitimacy of investing public resources for measures necessary to comply with the water storage norms *versus* accepting inundation more often when this would not lead to significant damage.

Window of Opportunity and a Paradigm Shift within the Water Authority

In 2009, the water authority's new water management plan for the period 2010–2015 was discussed by the newly elected general board. The discussions took place against a backdrop of financial and economic crisis, and national budget cutbacks that also affected the regional water authorities and municipalities. The new board members argued that Delfland was overstretching its finance-bearing capacity and urged the executive board to reconsider its earlier plan and to come up with solutions to reach a sustainable financial policy. In the framework of this ambition check, mixed groups of policymakers, engineers, fieldworkers, and external inspirers were formed that in two subsequent sessions were encouraged to rethink the regional water authority's tasks fundamentally and freely. In the first session, they tried to answer questions like: What is the very essence, what are the core values and goals of regional water management? What would you do if regional water management had to be re-invented and anything was possible to reach these goals? In the second session, they worked on questions like: If protecting society against flooding due to excess rainwater is such a goal, is the exclusive search for storage capacity the best solution to fulfill this goal? Can measures be designed that are more cost efficient, or better match the needs or interests of specific stakeholders? The experiences with the *proeftuinen* and insights gained in more regular settings were brought into the discussions. During the sessions, a mental shift occurred: increasing storage capacity would no longer be the main policy goal, but was now seen as only one of various possible solutions to obtain the higher goal of protecting society from inundation due to excess rainwater. And, as it was argued that the protection levels were based on anticipated climate conditions in 2050, the deadline of 2015 was deemed too ambitious as well. A new guiding principle to express this shift was formulated: "*from norm-oriented – to effect-oriented*".

The executive board embraced the new approach readily and obtained the support of the general board to adjust the water inundation policy based upon the new guidelines in the framework of the overall adjustment of the water management plan. Annual investment budgets were cut back from 60 to 25 million euro for inundation prevention.

In summary, we have seen that the regional water authority and the municipalities tried to resolve increasing tensions by installing a mutual innovation program including several experimental areas. The innovative solutions found, however, initially remained within the norm-oriented policy paradigm. Only when a policy window opened consequent to severe financial pressures within the water authority, brought to light by the new elected board, new insights developed within the experimental areas and learning processes within the regime became connected, and a policy paradigm shift occurred.

IMPLEMENTATION OF THE POLICY INNOVATION

Although the new policy concept was accepted almost overnight, it took a strenuous effort to implement the new policy paradigm. Regional water authority executives, as well as professionals, had to advocate the policy shift to the executives and professionals from the municipalities and the province. Regulations and existing plans and agreements had to be adjusted, planned investments had to be revised. In this section, we describe the implementation of the new policy paradigm at both niche and regime level, and also how the paradigm shift in its actual implementation was brought into accordance with conditions set by the regional water authority's broader policy landscape.

Implementation at Niche Level

One of the *proeftuinen* – called Oranjepolder – offered an opportunity for the regional water authority to work out this new approach with its partners, the Westland municipality and greenhouse farmers in the area. In a two-day brainstorming session, the partners embraced the new approach. Much to the surprise of the farmers, they were no longer asked to help *"search for the cubic meters of Delfland"*, but to work together with Delfland and Westland to explore all kinds of solutions that would protect the polder and their greenhouses from water damage. Another fruitful coincidence occurred. Delfland had engaged in an innovation network with a.o. an university, a knowledge institute, and the Delft municipality, called Delft Blue Technology. Through this network, an innovative consortium offered a new technique for fast hydrological calculations and 3D visualizations. The consortium advocated this new technique for fast calculations in cases of actual flooding, but the Delfland professionals saw, besides the huge calculation speed advantage, its communications potential. Now, for the first time, the involved parties' suggestions for measures in the polder could be calculated and visualized almost immediately. The visualization technique offered images of areas that would or would not flood consequent to the suggested measures in specific circumstances.

Implementation at Regime Level

While Delfland was working to include the new policy paradigm in its policies and regulations, Delfland and the Westland municipality took on the task of translating the effect-oriented policy and the experience of *proeftuinen* like the Oranjepolder to formulate a joint approach to water management. They worked out an approach for the water plan process called *Follow the Water,* which seeks solutions along the lines of rainwater falling on the houses, greenhouses, streets, and farmlands and running off to sewage systems and surface water. The approach structures the way parties define the problem and seek solutions. In a first phase, parties analyze the physical system (how does it really work) and seek for the best solution, from a technical as well as a financial perspective, regardless of the formal division of responsibilities. The symbol of this phase is a pine cone – project members are to be prickly, to stimulate one another and involved stakeholders to find creative solutions. In later phases, parties negotiate about who does what, and their financial contributions. Several mechanisms are put in place to make the boundaries between the two local governments more permeable and to increase trust, such as low profile conference dinners and the like.

At the level of the regional water authority, numerous investment projects were revised, and regulations adjusted. Some professionals worked out the new guiding principle towards guidelines for prioritizing measures for the bottlenecks in the 70 polders, using practical knowledge from fieldworkers in addition to the modeling results. Field visits requested by farmers were grasped as opportunities to find solutions that would fit with farmers' restructuring plans, such as raising the level of lower lying parcels. Considerable effort went into adjusting the obligatory water advice on infrastructural and spatial projects in such a way that initiators of projects could choose either the original water storage norm or water advice based on functional specifications, in which they had to prove that their projects complied with the inundation protection goals.

Landscape Dynamics

The new water law, enacted by the end of 2009, defined the tasks of municipalities and regional water authorities in the field of water management more clearly – municipalities are responsible for rainwater management and the sewage water system, and regional water authorities for surface water management (and sewage treatment) – but also obliged them to collaborate if otherwise no effective and cost-efficient solution could be found. This supported Westland and Delfland in their search for new ways of working. However, as the provinces supervise the regional water authorities, Delfland also had to convince the province of Zuid-Holland, which monitors its progress in realizing surface water storage expressed in cubic meters, of its new effect-oriented approach. As other regional water authorities in the low-lying part of the Netherlands were facing similar problems, they joined forces to form an alliance to convince provinces as well as the national level that the formerly agreed protection levels would pose problems if they were translated too bluntly into storage capacities expressed in cubic meters or areal percentages, and that innovative approaches were necessary to avoid unacceptable societal costs in densely built-up areas and farmlands alike. The Zuid-Holland province and the regional water authorities agreed to work out the new approach in the framework of their new water agenda that was put in place following provincial elections. Influencing the national level is an ongoing process. In the more elevated, less populated eastern part of the Netherlands where water is scarce, it is much easier to find fruitful combinations with nature development and recreation. The regional water authorities in this part of the Netherlands do not favor adjustment of the national policy.

In summary: to effectuate the new policy paradigm, activities were undertaken at all three levels. The experimental areas were used to experiment with the new paradigm, the Westland municipality and the regional water authority designed and applied a new integrative cooperative governance approach, and lobbying activities were undertaken together with adjacent water authorities to induce a new policy at provincial level.

CONNECTING LEVELS – THE ROLE OF POLICY ENTREPRENEURS

In our case study, we have seen parties in The Hague Region – at regime level – seeking to resolve conflicts by installing an innovation program. The innovation program was actively pursued by an accounts manager for this region at the regional water authority and a staff member of The Hague Region, who also took care that the innovation program was included in the covenant on water between the municipalities and the regional water authority. Once the innovation program was put in place, enthusiastic senior professionals from the regional water authority and the municipalities initiated collaboration at niche level with receptive representatives of farmers, companies, and other stakeholders, searching for opportunities to combine ideas and interests of parties in the experimental areas, involving experts from knowledge institutes, consultancy firms, and so on. Within the regional water authority, these were mostly the members of a spatial planning team that had experienced how difficult it was to realize the inundation protection policy in real life, engaging their more technical- and policy-oriented colleagues in discussions on innovative solutions. For the latter, as we have seen, it was difficult to convert improved insights on the functioning of the water system into alternative solutions that did not fit with the existing inundation policy at regime level. The preferences of the executive board, who had been held responsible for the earlier extensive flooding, for robust *digging for water* solutions played an important role. Professionals did, however, exchange their ideas in knowledge sharing meetings and in informal consultations, thus connecting learning processes at niche and regime level. When the financial tensions within the regional water authority opened a policy window, these professionals linked their ideas to the creative process of rethinking that took place during the sessions. During the policy innovation implementation process, senior professionals from Delfland and the municipalities worked out the new policy together, at niche level, *e.g.* in the Oranjepolder *proeftuin*, linking new technology to the niche level processes, and at regime level in the *Follow the Water* approach for Westland, a process that included relation and trust building, as well as experimentation with a more integrative technical approach. A Delfland professional responsible for investment projects played an important role in translating the rather abstract guiding principle for more practical workers and engineers when revising the measures needed to solve the bottlenecks in the other 70 Delfland polders, thus contributing to learning processes at regime level. A professional from the regional water authority's planning team initiated the process of reformulating regulations to allow compliance with functional specifications instead of water storage norms, linking external expertise and seizing an opportunity for experimentation in a water advice process for new infrastructure.

We conclude that several senior professionals within the water authority and the municipalities, interconnected in formal and informal networks, indeed played an important role in linking learning processes between the different levels and in furthering innovative concepts and solutions. In numerous informal consultations, they exchanged new insights but also conferred intensively about the strategies to obtain political and organizational support. Although we did not categorize their strategies very strictly, we discern idea-generating strategies, seizing emerging opportunities, venue strategies, and relational management strategies.

DISCUSSION

In this section, we summarize the main factors resulting in the observed paradigm shift from a norm-based towards an effect-based approach to regional water management. We show how this innovation was the result of a co-evolution of several developments at landscape, regime, and niche level that were deliberately connected by some entrepreneurs who made use of a policy window created by serious budgetary problems at the regional water authority.

Dominant Policy Beliefs on the Landscape Level

A longer transition towards a more adaptive approach to water management in the Netherlands resulted around the millennium in a national policy called Water Management for the 21st Century. More "*room for water*" had to be created, and excess rainwater should be "*first retained, then stored, and finally drained* ", in that sequence. Inundation protection levels were installed. The regional water systems had to be in order by 2015 for rainfall amounts expected under a midrange climate scenario for 2050. The regional water authorities in the Netherlands translated the inundation protection levels into norms for water storage capacity expressed in spatial variables, such as cubic meters, areal percentages, or square meters. The approach thus depended heavily on climatological and hydrological modeling, and the focus on water storage and the language used coincided with the way hydrological models worked at that time.

Tensions and Anomalies at Regime Level

At regime level, where municipalities and regional water authorities cooperated, this soon led to problems, at least in the low-lying densely populated polders in the western part of the Netherland, where water is abundant and space is scarce. Uneasiness grew about the extent of the calculated measures and the associated huge investment cost in relation to the sometimes relatively small effects in the event of inundation. We thus can distinguish four major tensions on the regional water management regime in the Delfland district:

- Realizing extra space for water storage in densely built-up areas was difficult and expensive.
- The time frame in which the water system had to be in order, 2015 according to the National Water Covenant of 2003, did not fit with the rhythm of reconstruction of housing areas or greenhouses.
- The advent of faster computers and software developments made it possible to calculate inundation patterns and to visualize the effect of the shortcomings in the water system. The new insights into the physical functioning of the water system contributed to the belief that the inundation norms were too rigid.
- Budgets were constrained due to internal and external financial pressures.

Creation of Niches in The Hague Region

Although all municipalities and the Delfland regional water authority had started drawing up water plans following the National Water Covenant of 2003, difficulties connected to realizing more water storage in the densely populated district soon became apparent. The municipalities cooperating within The Hague Region and the Delfland regional water authority drew up their own covenant in 2006, The Water Framework The Hague Region, including an ambitious innovation program for knowledge development and experimentation in experimental areas. In the multilevel perspective language: the regime parties deliberately created the niches where current policies were suspended and innovative solutions could be worked out. Herein we discern an internally induced adaptation path (De Haan and Rotmans, 2011). The collaborative spirit that characterized most of the pilot projects formed an important impetus for their success (van Buuren and Bressers 2013).

In fact, the innovation program itself can be considered as a niche created by the regime to work out solutions in a setting where experimentation, collaboration, and joint knowledge development and innovative idea formation were actively stimulated. The very existence of the innovation program, the collaborative effort of all parties to find solutions that fitted best with the actual problems in the experimental areas, the relative freedom from regular policies, the possibility to engage knowledge institutes and consultants facilitated by a program bureau, and sufficient resources all contributed to new knowledge development and new insights, and a better understanding between parties.

However, in spite of the freedom to experiment, the solutions implemented in the *proeftuinen* before the policy paradigm shift were innovative (*e.g.* the water storage cellar in Waalblok *proeftuin*) but did not deviate from the norm-oriented approach, and it took considerable effort to get the consent of the responsible executive. Only after the policy paradigm shift could the effect-oriented approach be worked out in a.o. the Oranjepolder *proeftuin*. The increased insights into the physical system connected with the development of faster computers and hydrological models and the learning processes at regime level were crucial.

The Paradigm Shift within the Regional Water Authority – A Policy Window

Measures to improve the regional water system itself, such as increasing pumping capacity and canals, were advanced with great speed from 2001, putting significant strain on the regional water authority's budget. The (political) difficulties of realizing water storage "on land" on the one hand, and the better understanding of the functioning of the water system under severe rainfall conditions supported by more advanced modelling and the experiences in the experimental areas on the other hand, led the regional water authority professionals increasingly to doubt the often costly measures taken following their studies. It was not, however, until a newly elected board was installed in 2009 that these problems could be addressed. Following a resolution put forward by the general board that pressed for a sustainable financial policy and the subsequent reconsiderations of the regional water authority professionals and managers, the above-described paradigm shift occurred. Thus, the reconsideration sessions opened up a policy window where several developments – decreasing budgets, implementation problems, experiences in the experimental areas, and increased insights into the functioning of the water system – could be coupled, leading to this policy innovation.

Implementation at Niche and Regime Level

The policy innovation was worked out further in a myriad of actions at different levels, ranging from experimentation in areas such as the pilot project Oranjepolder and more regular regime-level processes like the water plan process for the Westland municipality, to adjusting investment projects, often with other parties, and adjusting policies and regulations. In this phase also, joint experimentation, learning, and gaining insight into the functioning of the water system by combining advanced technologies and field knowledge played an important role.

Several senior professionals from the regional water authority and the municipalities acted as policy entrepreneurs, when they – while interacting informally and intensely – actively sought to develop new insights and solutions that fitted better with real-life situations and interests of other parties, and seized opportunities to connect these to more regular processes and decision making in their own organizations.

Our case nicely shows how collaboration and innovation are strongly entwined. Innovation in policy resulted from focused collaboration between various actors inside and outside the regional water authority. This collaborative innovation took place in niches created by the regime actors in which actors felt more freedom to explore alternative strategies (cf. Van Buuren *et al.* 2014). Niches can contribute to learning processes at regime level as people participating in different niches exchange ideas and knowledge. However, our case also shows that policy entrepreneurs who utilize opportunities and policy windows resulting from emerging tensions in the regime, and connect insights developed in niches to learning processes at regime level, are needed to alter dominant policy paradigms.

CONCLUSION

We started this chapter by asking about the relationship between collaborative innovation at project level (in pilots or niches) and policy innovation at regime level, from a multilevel perspective. We have tried to understand how learning and change processes at several levels (niches, regime, landscape) are interrelated and how policy entrepreneurs link developments at different levels in order to realize cross-level breakthroughs.

When we analyze how Delfland's initial technocratic norm-oriented policy approach towards more water storage developed into a more pragmatic and adaptive effect-oriented approach, we see two main enabling factors. First, there were the collaborative learning processes at niche and regime level. Learning processes at niche level were intentionally provoked by the regime by putting in place an innovation program to overcome some persistent problems in relation to combining water storage and land use planning that were causing significant tensions within and between the involved regime parties. These concerned actors from different governments, stakeholders, and knowledge institutes and consultants. These niches in which collaboration between diverse actors was encouraged resulted in innovative ways of dealing with water retention. Learning processes at regime level occurred as part of the regular work of the water professionals and the growing anomalies with implementing the norm-oriented approach. These anomalies essentially had to do with legitimizing expensive measures and drastic claims on space, which consequent to new insights could no longer be substantiated.

However, the insights gained in these niches and regular projects were able to lead to the observed policy change process only because the regional water authority came under severe financial pressure, with the associated internal political tensions. The learning processes within the niches and at regime level became connected within various visioning sessions, finally leading to a paradigm shift towards another dominant policy paradigm. It is interesting to see that the implementation of the new policy paradigm took shape by (again) making use of niches, *e.g.* the experimental areas, but also several other pilots and experiments within the regional water authority as well as in collaboration with municipalities and stakeholders. A lobby with other regional water authorities to influence the landscape level is ongoing.

We assumed that policy entrepreneurs fulfilled a crucial role in connecting developments at niche, regime, and landscape level. We see that in our case there were indeed active civil servants from the regional water authority who were involved both in several niches and in informal networks within the regional water authority. At the municipalities also, especially Westland, several civil servants acted as policy entrepreneurs. Their entrepreneurial activities seem to have the following components: in their own organizations, they further their experiences and innovative solutions arrived at in the niches by engaging in informal interactions and connecting their insights to formal political decision-making processes. They discuss and align their strategies – idea-generating strategies as well as venue strategies and relational management strategies. They function as boundary spanners between niche and regime and further collaboration between relevant regime players in order to stimulate learning at regime level.

At landscape level, the transition towards a more adaptive water management approach, the growing awareness of the effects of climate change, and the subsequent covenant between the different governments to take adaptive measures are supportive developments. In 2009, the new water law clarified responsibilities in water management and strongly encouraged cooperation between governments. Finally, the financial and economic crisis forced all parties to strengthen their focus on the effective use of public resources.

From our analysis, we can derive three important implications for the governance of collaborative innovation processes in the public domain. They have to do with:

- Strategic niche management in which collaboration and learning is fostered;
- Stimulating learning processes at regime level;
- Supporting policy entrepreneurs connecting dynamics at different levels.

First of all, from our case we can learn that innovation spaces fulfill a valuable role: they provide space for learning processes and testing a policy paradigm in real-life situations. Consequently, they contribute to the reflexive capacity of public organizations and to identifying the problems that the regime is encountering, and enable the improvement and adjustment of policy paradigms. It is important that the various niches get enough freedom to explore new avenues and to apply solutions in practice. The latter is quite difficult and cannot be overstressed, because dominant policy paradigms often steer idea generation and hinder the actual implementation of alternative solutions. The niches should be well managed, in the sense that sufficient diversity (creativity) and cognitive distance are ensured in a context of collaboration and mutual adjustment (Van Buuren & Loorbach, 2009), especially when they are created by the regime, and that the niches are well connected to learning processes at regime level.

Secondly, although there may seem to be a tension with ambitions to improve the effectiveness of public service delivery that is served by a coherent set of rules, procedures, and arrangements, it is important to stimulate learning processes at regime level, especially to flexibly develop and adapt to new insights and reflect upon anomalies and inefficiencies in the dominant policy paradigm. Provisions should be put in place to provide opportunities for executives, managers, and professionals to feel confident to critically discuss current practices and to express their doubts and develop new practices; such provisions could include informal reflection sessions, knowledge sharing meetings, and the like.

Finally, the success of policy innovation is strongly dependent on the extent to which the creativity developed in niches and ongoing learning processes at regime level are synchronized. Entrepreneurial professionals participating at both levels play an important role. Although these professionals are known to have strong intrinsic motivations (Kingdon, 1995), public organizations could support entrepreneurial activities by more explicitly recognizing the importance of this role and offer training to professionals to further develop the specific competences associated with it.

ACKNOWLEDGEMENTS

This article is based on interviews with professionals within the Delfland regional water authority, whose contribution and critical review of the representation of the cases we gratefully acknowledge, and on an evaluation of The Water Framework The Hague Region innovation program.

CONFLICT OF INTEREST

The authors confirm that this chapter contents have no conflict of interest.

REFERENCES

Bekkers, V., Edelenbos, J. & Steijn, B. (eds) (2011). Innovation in the public sector, linking capacity and leadership. In *IIAS Series: Governance and Public Management*, Palgrave Macmillian, UK.

Bennett, C.J. & Howlett, M. (1992). The lessons of learning: Reconciling theories of policy learning and policy change. In *Policy Sciences* 25, 275-294.

Brouwer, S. (2013). *Policy Entrepreneurs and Strategies for Change: The Case of Water Management in the Netherlands.* PhD thesis, Institute for Environmental Studies (IVM), Amsterdam.

Brouwer, S., & Biermann, F. (2011). Towards adaptive management: examining the strategies of policy entrepreneurs in Dutch water management. In *Ecology and Society* 16:4, 5, http://dx.doi.org/10.5751/ES-04315-160405

Castells, M. (1996). *The Rise of the Network Society*. Malden, MA: Blackwell.

De Haan, J. H. & Rotmans, J. (2011). Patterns in transitions: Understanding complex chains of change. In *Technological Forecasting and Social Change*, 78:1, 90-102.

Duijn, M., (2009). *Embedded Reflection on Public Policy Innovation*, Thesis University of Tilburg.

Geels, F.W. (2002). Technological transitions as evolutionary reconfiguration processes: a multi-level perspective and a case-study. In *Research Policy,* 31 (8/9), 1257-1274.

Geels, F.W. & Kemp, R. (2007). Dynamics in socio-technical systems: Typology of change processes and contrasting case studies. In *Technology in Society* 29, 441-455.

Geels, F.W., & Schot, J. (2007). Typology of sociotechnical transition pathways. In *Research Policy* 36:3, 399-417.

Hall, P.A., (1993). Policy Paradigms, Social Learning and the State: The Case of Economic Policy Making in Britain. In *Comparative Politics* 25:3, 275-296.

Hartley, J. (2005). Innovation in governance and public services: Past and present. In *Public Money & Management,* 25:1, 27-34.

Heclo, H. (1974). *Modern Social Policy in Britain and Sweden: From Relief to Income Maintenance.* New York: New Haven.

Huitema, D., &Meijerink, S. (2010). Realizing water transitions: the role of policy entrepreneurs in water policy change. In *Ecology and Society*, 15:2, article 26. http://www.ecologyandsociety.org/vol15/iss2/art26/

Kingdon, J. W. (1995). *Agenda, alternatives, and public policies*. Second edition. New York: HarperCollins.

Leifer, R., & Delbecq, A. (1978). Organizational/environmental interchange: A model of boundary spanning activity. In *Academy of Management Review,* 3:1, 40-50.

Lovell, H. (2009). The role of individuals in policy change: the case of UK low-energy housing. In *Environment and planning. C, Government & policy*, 27:3, 491-511.

Moore, M. H. (2005). Break-through innovations and continuous improvement: Two different models of innovative processes in the public sector. In *Public Money & Management*, 25:1, 43-50.

Rip, A. & Kemp, R., (1998). Technological change. In: Rayner, S., Malone, E.L. (Eds.), *Human Choice and Climate Change*. Columbus, OH: Battelle Press, 327-399.

Rotmans, J., R. Kemp, & M. van Asselt. (2001). More evolution than revolution: transition management in public policy. In *Foresight* 3:1, 15-31.

Sabatier, P.A. (1987). Knowledge, Policy-Oriented Learning, and Policy Change: An Advocacy Coalition Framework. In *Science Communication,* 8, 649-692.

Schot J. & F. W. Geels (2008). Strategic niche management and sustainable innovation journeys: theory, findings, research agenda, and policy. In *Technology Analysis & Strategic Management*, 20:5, 537-554.

Sørensen, E., & Torfing, J. (2011). Enhancing collaborative innovation in the public sector. In *Administration & Society*, 43:8, 842-868.

van Buuren, M.W. & Bressers, N.E.W. (2011). *Waterproeven in polderland. Een terugblik op Waterkader Haaglanden. Evaluation report*. Rotterdam: Erasmus Universiteit Rotterdam.

van Buuren, M.W. & Loorbach, D.A. (2009). Policy innovation in isolation. Conditions for policy-renewal by transition arenas and pilot projects. In *Public Management Review,* 11:3, 375-392.

van Buuren, M.W. van, Eshuis, J. & Bressers, N.E.W., (2014). The governance of innovation in Dutch regional water management. Organizing fit between organizational values and innovative concepts. In *Public Management Review*. Online First: DOI: 10.1080/14719037.2013.841457

van der Brugge, R. (2009). *Transition Dynamics in Social-Ecological Systems*, PhD Thesis. Erasmus University, Rotterdam.

Van de Ven, A.; Polley, D.; Garud, R. & S. Venkataraman, (1999). *The Innovation Journey.* New York: Oxford University Press

Vreugdenhil, H., J. Slinger, W. Thissen & P. Ker Rault, (2010). Pilot Projects in Water Management. In *Ecology and Society,* 15:3, 13 [online]: http://www.ecologyandsociety.org/vol15/iss3/art13/

Williams, P. (2002). The competent boundary spanner. In *Public Administration*, 80:1, 103-124.

CHAPTER 9

European Patent Reforms: Transforming European Patent Governance and Enhancing Collaborative Innovation?

Esther van Zimmeren*

Faculty of Law, University of Antwerp, Belgium

Abstract: The main objective of the current chapter is to examine to what extent the European patent system, the decision-making process on the so-called "Patent Package" and its implementation reflect the conceptual framework of dynamic governance, a framework which aligns closely with the notion of collaborative innovation. In the global patent context, a gradual increase of more dynamic patent governance has been observed. The adoption of fundamental patent reforms in Europe calls for a review of those reforms from a dynamic governance perspective. After decades of negotiations on the European Union (EU) patent, the financial crisis has finally driven the EU Member States and the EU institutions to gain the momentum and to adopt a compromise on the Patent Package. These reforms are aimed at simplifying the European patent system, lowering the costs of patenting, improving legal certainty and limiting forum-shopping in terms of litigation. These objectives were supported widely by stakeholders. However, despite these laudable objectives, the way the decision-making process was spun out and then suddenly rushed through and the actual content of the package are highly controversial. In the end, the reforms will further increase the complexity of the European patent system, patent protection in Europe will probably remain rather expensive and the risk of forum shopping may continue to persist to a certain extent. This raises the fundamental question whether stakeholders have actually been sufficiently involved in the decision-making process.

Keywords: Collaborative innovation, dynamic governance, European Union, governance, patent law, patent reforms, unitary patent.

INTRODUCTION

Patent governance gradually seems to become more *dynamic* (Murray & van Zimmeren, 2011). This means acknowledging the role of more diverse public actors from varied policy contexts, and enabling more interaction between these actors, on the one hand, and stakeholders, on the other hand (Murray & van

***Corresponding author Esther van Zimmeren:** Faculty of Law, University of Antwerp, Belgium; Tel: 00 32 48 63 14 595; Fax: 0032 3 265 54 92; E-mail: esther.vanzimmeren@uantwerpen.be

Annika Agger, Bodil Damgaard, Andreas Hagedorn Krogh and Eva Sørensen (Eds.)

Zimmeren, 2011). Typically, the model of patent regulation has been quite static relying mainly on patent offices as a simple registrar of patents with a limited ability to consider broader patent policy issues and without further interference from other actors or civil society. This static model of governance is clearly deficient. Patent governance systems around the world have been under severe criticism due to considerable backlogs at patent offices, a decrease in patent quality, high patent damages, legal uncertainty and significant patenting costs (*e.g.* Danish Board of Technology, 2007; European Commission, 2007; Gowers, 2006; US Federal Trade Commission, 2003). Some patent offices have also been strongly criticized for serving their "customers" (the patent owners) too much and for ignoring the public interest (Schneider, 2009; Lemley, 2001). A more dynamic reconceptualization of patent governance shows that a broader set of more fundamental governance issues is at play in the patent field. Issues that are central to dynamic governance relate to the appropriate role for the patent community, the constitution of the patent community (*i.e.* only patent experts, or also other (less obvious) civil society actors), the optimal way and tools for the patent community to exercise its role and to participate in the decision-making process in order to contribute to the functioning of the patent system (Murray & van Zimmeren, 2011).

This variety of issues exposes a key challenge to how patent law may be governed in a new era and reveals a need for patent reforms. The main objective of the current chapter is to examine to what extent the European patent system, the decision-making process on the reforms of the European patent system, the so-called *Patent Package* and its implementation reflect the conceptual framework of *dynamic governance*. This framework is closely aligned with the notion of *collaborative innovation* (Sørensen & Torfing, 2011), a cross-disciplinary approach for enhancing public innovation through multi-actor collaboration, the focus of this book. It is important to note that the implementation of the Patent Package is ongoing and that there are several highly controversial outstanding issues (see below). This chapter describes the status of the implementation process until August 2014, the moment of finalization of the chapter.

The European patent system has been in great turmoil. Since the 70s, there have been regular attempts to harmonize the European patent system and to create a *Community patent*, later referred to as a *European Union (EU) patent* (hereinafter EU patent). The EU patent would be linked to a system of centralized patent litigation. The creation of the EU patent is aimed at overcoming the weaknesses of the European patent system, which is renowned for its complexity, costs and the risk of "forum shopping" leading to legal uncertainty (see below). In 2006, the European Commission revitalized its efforts to create an EU patent with a centralized patent litigation system culminating in a political compromise on the Patent Package in December, 2012. The financial crisis offered an excellent opportunity for the participating Member States and the EU institutions to show that they were still capable of deciding on fundamental dossiers that may drive progress and increase welfare (European Commission, 2011c). The package consists of three main components: (1) a regulation creating *unitary* patent protection; (2) a regulation clarifying the associated translation arrangements (giving priority to English, German and French); and (3) an international agreement establishing a centralised patent litigation system, the Unified Patent Court (UPC). The regulation of patent protection is *unitary* as no consensus could be achieved amongst all EU Member States which would have allowed for a proper EU patent label. Being *unitary* the patent will only have effect in the participating Member States as explained later.

The conceptual framework of *dynamic patent governance* is based on the literature on network governance and has been described in greater detail in Murray and van Zimmeren (2011). Dynamic patent governance extends the theoretical framework of network governance (*e.g.* Rhodes, 1997) to explain the emergence of networks and the dynamics for public and private actors in the patent decision-making process. In this respect, it builds on prior work on network governance and patent law (Drahos, 2004 & 2010) and institutional choice theory and intellectual property (IP) law (Tamura, 2009; Lee, 2009; Engelbrekt, 2007; Rai, 2003). In Murray and van Zimmeren (2011), we observe a steady emergence of dynamic relationships between a variety of institutional *formal* actors that play a role in patent systems (*e.g.* patent offices, legislators, policymakers, courts, competition authorities), on the one hand, and interaction and collaboration between these formal actors and the patent community, the *informal* actors, on the other hand. In particular, this second observation fits well with the notion of collaborative innovation. Although the conceptual framework was originally developed in the context of patent law, in principle it could be applied in other contexts as well, which justifies the use of the more general term dynamic governance in the current chapter.

The added value of this conceptual framework in comparison to for instance institutional choice theory is the emphasis on the dynamic nature of the interactions between the formal and informal actors and the capability of the framework to capture the nuances of institutional change. Dynamic governance is, therefore, also particularly apt as a lens to analyse the Patent Package, which is aimed at transforming the European institutional patent infrastructure. The analysis that follows is focused on two main research questions encompassing both a descriptive and a normative component. First, how will the Patent Package transform the institutional infrastructure of the European patent governance system (descriptive)? Second, to what extent does the decision-making process and the implementation of the Patent Package reflect the conceptual framework of dynamic governance/collaborative innovation (normative)? Dynamic governance is, hence, used as a lens to provide a systematic overview as to what extent these dynamics have been part of the decision-making process regarding the Patent Package and to identify lessons for the ongoing implementation process. In the following sections, first, the conceptual framework of dynamic governance will be explained in more detail followed by a descriptive analysis of the recent developments of the European Patent System in the light of this framework. In the final section, a more normative perspective will be taken including a critical examination of the Patent Package.

CONCEPTUAL FRAMEWORK DYNAMIC GOVERNANCE

The framework of dynamic governance was developed to capture the impact of two key developments in patent law: (a) the emergence of a more heterogeneous set of formal institutional actors and (b) the emergence of a more heterogeneous set of informal stakeholders that interacts with the formal actors in the policymaking process. These two changes also acknowledge and reflect the relevance of the concept *network governance* in its diversity and fluidity that has been explored more thoroughly in other regulatory contexts, such as environmental and international law (Burris *et al.*, 2008; Haas, 2004; Lobel, 2004). However, apart from Drahos' work (2004 and 2010), network governance has been left relatively unexplored in the area of patent law and patent reform processes.

Heterogenity of Formal Actors in Dynamic Governance

Many analyses of patent systems have exclusively focused on the role of the patent office in granting patents. This approach largely ignores the impact that other actors – other administrative agencies or subsequent judicial actors – may have on the evolution of patent law (Murray, 2008). Heterogeneity of patent actors suggests that more than one institutional, formal patent actor can and will seek to regulate the grant and enforcement of patents. A heterogeneous perspective of formal actors within the patent governance system starts from the assumption that the roles of institutional actors are consistent across patent systems (Murray & van Zimmeren, 2011). Two kinds of roles can be distinguished: primary and secondary patent actors.

Primary actors are responsible for regulating the system on an on-going basis. Primary actors – the legislator, the executive, and the reviewers – fulfil three key tasks in a patent system. First, the legislative actor has a democratic legitimation and creates the regulatory framework for the other primary actors and for the secondary actors. The legislative actor can also hold the other formal actors accountable for their activities. Second, the executive determines whether the patent should be granted. Finally, the reviewers, including in most patent systems both (internal) administrative review (*e.g.* re-examinations and opposition procedures) and (external) judicial review of a patent after its grant. The roles of these reviewers can possibly overlap, but often they have slightly different duties within the context of a given patent regime.

In many countries several secondary actors are regulating patents as well, by either replicating the role of the primary actors in a narrower content area, or by using their expertise derived from other content areas to influence the development of patent law (Murray & van Zimmeren, 2011). The growing role of secondary actors is due to the increasing diversity of patent law. Patent law affects other fields of law, such as competition law, unfair competition and trade law, and it has incorporated new subject matter, such as biological material, software and business methods. These changes have had the consequence of strengthening the role of secondary actors, such as specialized trade tribunals, ministries responsible for trade, health and agriculture, advisory bodies with a diverse range of expertise. While in principle these actors are meant to supplement the policy determinations of the primary formal patent actors, they can also become regulatory rivals in defining the limits of an issued patent or in guiding the desirable behavior of patent owners. This second set of formal actors is, however, less relevant for the current analysis, as the Patent Package focuses on the introduction and functioning of new primary patent actors. Nonetheless, the functioning of these new actors within the patent governance network will certainly have an impact on the relations between the primary and secondary actors.

Heterogeneity of Informal Actors and Interaction Between Formal and Informal Actors

Within the dynamic governance model the concept of network governance is used to explain how a variety of autonomous formal and informal actors operate in interdependent relationships to govern the systems in which they participate. The underlying idea of network governance is that the effective functioning and legitimacy of the system, as a whole, is more than the mere aggregation of individual formal actors' performances (Borrás, 2006). Network governance differs substantially from classic theories of regulation, which tend to focus solely on the formal governmental actors and less on the interrelationships between formal institutions and informal actors beyond those institutions.

Consistent with the idea of network governance, global patent policy is influenced by a plurality of national, European and international actors that actively pursue legislation and policy-making (Drahos, 2004 & 2010). The network consists of a variety of formal actors, such as national and European regulators, national and European patent offices, national courts, national and European advisory organs, funding organizations and international organizations (*i.e.* World Intellectual Property Organization). They interact with industry and non-governmental organizations (NGOs), such as associations of patent professionals and practitioners, consumer and patient advocacy groups, environmental organizations, human rights organizations, medical associations and scientific organizations. Consumers, patients, physicians, scientists, interested citizens, and other non-patent experts that seek to participate in patent policy-making, are new actors on the patent scene. This *patent civil society* is increasingly playing a disruptive role in patent policy-making, often criticizing the basic norms of the patent system. As a consequence, they have encountered resistance from the more settled stakeholders and experts that traditionally drive the decision-making process for patent policy.

Patent law has typically relied on well-organized and well-informed *epistemic communities*, groups of professionals who share a set of worldviews, common understandings, norms, routines and daily practices that define the interactions among public and private organizations and individual actors (Borrás, 2006). In the patent context the dominant core of these epistemic communities consists of transnational firms with important patent portfolios, technically sophisticated lawyers, legal academics, and legally trained scientific experts and officials (Borrás, 2006). Patent law is generally regarded as a very complex field of law due to its difficult legal framework, procedures and concepts, as well as the inherently technical nature of patents. Therefore, national, European and international regulators tend to rely on the advice of a relatively small group of technical and legal experts constituting the epistemic patent community. The involvement of epistemic communities has proven itself to be a mixed blessing: experts safeguard a level of expertise required by the complex nature of patent law, thus helping to guarantee high quality and efficient decision-making, but at the same time they are associated with *insider governance* due to the continued involvement of a small group of stakeholders (Murray & van Zimmeren, 2011; Drahos & Brathwaite, 2003). Over the past decades, the epistemic community of patent experts has gained a strong grip on the patent system as well as patent policy on the national, regional and international levels (Drahos & Brathwaite, 2003). Despite their improved visibility and increased participation in patent debates, interests of the broader patent civil society and small and medium-sized enterprises (SMEs) are more easily discounted.

A variety of *internal* mechanisms (*e.g.* consultation procedures organized by patent policy makers, opposition procedures at the patent office) and *external* tools (*e.g.* economic pressure, lobbying, social norms) exist within the network that enables informal actors to participate in the decision-making process. However, in the patent context most of these instruments have primarily been used by the epistemic patent community excluding the patent civil society and notably representatives of SMEs. New patent policies are often preceded by consultations, but epistemic participants have been relatively dominant in shaping these policies. Internal review procedures have basically been the playground of competing large corporations.

The implications of instituting a system, which incorporates dynamic governance, are two-fold. First, dynamic governance fosters a greater fluidity between the formal and informal dimensions of governance. A more heterogeneous regulatory environment can be more responsive to newly identified problems and to new informal actors. New patent actors may bring other arguments to the table and open up new opportunities for policy innovation through collaborative processes. Second, dynamic governance has prompted a reappraisal of *internal* transparency and accountability mechanisms. It has fuelled some experimentation with mechanisms to widen institutionalized access for participation by civil society, such as for instance the increased use of the European Patent Office (EPO) opposition procedure by civil society (Murray and van Zimmeren, 2011). In the following section, I will examine to what extent the Patent Package has affected/contributed to the dynamic nature of the European patent system.

Dynamic Governance in the European Patent System

The institutional structure of the European patent system is particularly complex: the European system is a multilevel governance system with regulatory activities at the national, European and international level, but at the European level the system further consists of two autonomous branches.

The multilevel nature of the governance system means in the patent context that patents are regulated at the national level, the international and the European level. At the national level, national patents are granted by the various national patent offices and litigated before national courts. At the international level, treaties such as the Paris Convention, the Patent Cooperation Treaty (World Intellectual Property Organization) and the Agreement on Trade-related aspects of Intellectual Property Rights (World Trade Organization) aim at harmonizing substantive and procedural patent law and at simplifying patent application procedures. At the European level, the existence of two governing branches, the European Patent Organization (EPOrg), on the one hand, and the EU, on the other hand, adds considerable complexity as will become evident when the current European patent system is described below. The depiction of the current patent system is followed by an account of the negotiations for patent reforms and of the adoption of the Patent Package.

The Current European Patent System

The first autonomous branch of the European patent system, the EPOrg, is a supranational organization established in 1977 on the basis of a treaty, the European Patent Convention (EPC) (1973). It is not part of the institutional framework of the EU. EPOrg has 38 Member States and two executive bodies: the European Patent Office (EPO) and the Administrative Council. The EPO is the primary executive actor that issues and refuses patents. The Administrative Council, which consists mainly of representatives of national patent offices, supervises the Office's activities and has some regulatory powers. However, the EPOrg lacks a democratically legitimized body, which could challenge policy changes and hold the executive accountable. This is a fundamental governance deficit of the system. Patent owners and third parties may, however, challenge EPO decisions in individual cases through the internal review process before quasi-judicial opposition and appeal boards. Nonetheless, the decisions of these boards cannot be challenged before an external judicial review actor, an independent judge. This is another vital shortcoming within the first branch of the European patent system.

Once the EPO has granted a European patent, the patent turns into what is commonly referred to as a *bundle* of national patents. This is why some people refer to these patents as *classical European bundle patents* to distinguish them from the new category of patents created by the Patent Package, the unitary patents. European bundle patents need to be validated by patent owners at the national level within each and every designated state. National validation will generally require the involvement of local patent attorneys and translation services. After a certain period, the patent owner will also need to start paying national renewal fees. This brings along significant administrative, translation and renewal costs. Moreover, in case a patent owner wants to start infringement procedures or a competitor or third party wishes to challenge the validity of the bundle of national patents before a court, parties will have to litigate separately before all competent national courts. This often results in high litigation costs, forum shopping (a practice adopted by litigants to have their case heard in the court thought most likely to provide a favourable judgment), and – as a result – legal uncertainty. Moreover, as the EPO is independent of the other autonomous governing branch, the EU institutional framework, the Court of Justice of the EU (CJEU) has no powers regarding European bundle patents. So, currently there is no centralized system for issuing a European-wide determination on the validity and infringement of a given patent.

The advantage of the complex nature of the European patent system is that multiple fora exist for interaction between formal and informal actors. For instance, a number of formal mechanisms described in the European Patent Convention allow third party participation within the executive actor and the internal review procedure of the EPOrg. Firstly, granted European patents can be challenged before the EPO Opposition Division by "any member of the public" (Article 99 EPC). This procedure saves considerable time and money in comparison to challenging the bundle of national patents in a later phase of the life of a patent before the various national courts. Moreover, the broad personal scope has allowed civil society to employ this relatively cheap procedure in controversial patent cases regarding human DNA sequences, stem cells and biological processes (Murray & van Zimmeren, 2011). Second, all third parties can present observations concerning the patentability of a published European application (Article 115(1) EPC). They can also present written statements during the course of proceedings before the Enlarged Board of Appeal (Article 10 Rules of Procedure of the Enlarged Board of Appeal). However, the Board can address these statements as it thinks fit, so no certainty exists that these statements will actually have an impact on its decision.

Apart from these formal participation mechanisms created in the Convention, the EPO remains a fairly closed system for the patent civil society. Through its

Administrative Council the interests of the Member States are taken into consideration. In addition, several advisory bodies and platforms for debate and exchange between the EPO and the epistemic patent community exist. First, the Standing Advisory Committee before the EPO (SACEPO) (1978) was formed in order to give "interested circles" a say in the development of the European patent system. Its membership is comprised of representatives from industry (nominated by BUSINESSEUROPE) and the patent profession (nominated by the Institute of Professional Representatives before the European Patent Office (EPI) as well as some recognized patent experts appointed by the President of the EPO on a personal basis. Second, the European Roundtable on Patent Practice (EUROTAB) (1992) is a mechanism for national patent offices and the EPO to exchange views and compare approaches on matters concerning the patent grant procedure, both from a substantive and formal point of view. Apart from representatives from the national offices, EPI, BUSINESSEUROPE and the International Federation of Inventors' Associations are also invited. Third, the EPO Economic and Scientific Advisory Board (ESAB) (2012) consists of a mix of economists, social scientists and practitioners and was set up as a platform for discussing specific issues of major economic and social importance closely related to the patent system by carrying out studies, presenting the results at publicly available seminars and widely disseminating the results. Several closed (!) workshops were organized on respectively patent quality, patent fees, patent thickets and the economic effects of the Patent Package (http://www.epo.org/about-us/office/esab/workshops.html). ESAB also issued its 2012 Statement with recommendations for improving the patent system (ESAB, 2013). Although the reports of the workshops are very informative, the final recommendations tend to remain relatively vague leaving vital governance questions aside. Finally, the EPO President's Blog was launched (http://blog.epo.org/) that aims at providing greater transparency to the public. While the objective of greater transparency should be applauded, the topics posted on the blog remain quite general and mainly discuss international and European meetings in which the EPO President participated, patent statistics and reports, which are made available publicly anyway. The blog does not appear to trigger considerable interaction with informal patent actors. The lack of interaction is even more obvious, if one compares the EPO President's Blog with the Director's Forum of the US Patent Office (http://www.uspto.gov/blog/), the predecessor of the EPO President's blog, where a broad range of IP policy issues are being discussed and commented upon.

These examples clearly show that the advisory boards and discussion platforms primarily include representatives from the epistemic patent community, patent experts. Apart from some high level expert interest and industry groups, patent civil society and representatives of SMEs are largely excluded from most of these platforms for exchange and interaction with the EPO. This is an important observation in the light of dynamic governance. In particular in contrast with another initiative of the EPO several years ago, the Scenario's for the Future. As part of this exercise, the EPO undertook a consultation of a wide range of academics, other patent experts and members of civil society. It identified different scenarios for the future of the patent system (EPO, 2007). Initially, the scenarios received wide public attention, but it is unclear whether the EPO has given any (internal) follow-up to this process. In particular in the light of the adoption of the Patent Package it would be interesting to revive this type of strategic and forward-looking initiatives reconsidering some of the findings of that exercise.

Reforms of the European Patent System & the Adoption of the Patent Package

Work on a patent system within the context of the second autonomous European patent branch had started as part of the negotiations on the European Communities and been revived in the '70s with the Community Patent Convention followed by the Agreement relating to Community patents in 1989. In the beginning of the 21st Century, the European Commission again launched various proposals to resuscitate the debate. For several decades, all initiatives for an EU patent and centralized court system were doomed (Jaeger, 2010). Interestingly, the reasons for disagreement that stalled these initiatives were never really about the core features of the design of the patent. In the early days, protectionism among Member States impeded progress on the matter (Beier, 1969). More recently primarily discord about formal issues, such as the language and translation requirements, the relationship between the European patent system and national patent systems and the re-allocation of fees between the EPO and national patent offices, significantly slowed down and at times even blocked the decision-making process. This can be explained by the fact that these formal issues often have a strong political component reflected in vested interests of the epistemic patent community (*i.e.* patent attorneys and translators) and national patent offices.

An attempt was made to remedy the gap related to the absence of a centralized court system by proposing the establishment of a European patent litigation system (European Patent Litigation Agreement (EPLA), 2004). EPLA differed from the current Patent Package in that these negotiations were coordinated from the side of the EPO, the other patent branch, rather than from the side of the EU institutions. The negotiations on EPLA were adjourned, because several (EU) countries preferred to integrate the two branches of the European patent system, which was anticipated in the proposal for the EU patent.

In December 2009, the Council unanimously adopted conclusions on an enhanced patent system in Europe (Council of the EU, 2009). Notwithstanding this move forward, the translation arrangements remained a vexed question. The translation arrangements proposed by the European Commission and the compromise solutions offered by the Belgian Presidency in the second half of 2010 could not convince all EU Member States. Notably Italy and Spain strongly resisted any solutions based on the trilingual regime of the EPO (English, French, German). Due to this resistance by Italy and Spain, the proposal had a rather turbulent and unusual course. In fact, in December 2010 twenty-five out of the twenty-seven Member States decided to create a patent with unitary effect in the participating Member States on the basis of the so-called enhanced cooperation procedure. This is a special procedure enshrined in the EU treaty allowing a group of countries to adopt new common rules when EU-wide agreement cannot be reached within a reasonable period of time. At first face, the enhanced cooperation procedure may seem quite fascinating from the perspective of collaborative innovation. It accommodates a diversity of obligations within the EU and allows Member States some degree of differentiated collaborative action. However, this flexibility is at cross purposes with bedrock principles of the EU, such as uniformity and solidarity. Already early on, when the Treaty Amsterdam still referred to *closer* instead of *enhanced* cooperation, the requirements were more onerous and the role of the Commission was more limited (Murphy, 2003), fear for a *multispeed Europe* or *Europe à la carte* led to a lot of criticism (Schrauwen, 2002; Gaja, 1998). In principle, at least nine states must be involved in enhanced cooperation, but the cooperation remains open to any state that wishes to participate later on. The use of this procedure may not result in discrimination between the participating Member States and the other states and it must contribute to the realization of the objectives, to the protection of EU interests and to the EU integration process. Enhanced cooperation may, hence, only be used in limited circumstances and as a last resort. In fact, it was only the second time that it was employed since its introduction in the Treaty of Amsterdam in 1997.

However, for increased multiactor cooperation with informal actors, an important component of dynamic governance and collaborative innovation, the enhanced cooperation procedure clearly does not leave much leeway. With respect to the

Patent Package, the EU institutions actually rushed through the decision-making process on enhanced cooperation leaving little opportunity for opponents to voice their criticism and influence the process. Following the Commission's approval of the plan to use the enhanced cooperation procedure in December 2010 (European Commission, 2010), within a few months the European Parliament approved the use of the procedure (European Parliament, 2011) the Council authorized the use of the procedure (Council of the EU, 2011a) and the Commission adopted the implementation proposals (European Commission, 2011a and 2011b). This short timespan shows the strong support of all three EU institutions. Nonetheless, the use of the procedure was criticized by many legal scholars (*e.g.* Uhllrich, 2012; Lamping, 2011) and challenged by Spain and Italy before the Court of Justice (CJEU, 2013).

Unlike the sudden progress achieved with respect to the unitary patent and the translation regime through the enhanced cooperation procedure, the negotiations on the Unified Patent Court (UPC) remained in a deadlock. As the three components – the regulation creating unitary patent protection, the regulation regarding the translation arrangements, and the international agreement establishing the UPC – had been bundled into one regulatory package, this deadlock position also affected the progress on the unitary patent and the translation regime. The reason for the delay on the UPC was three-fold. Firstly, the UPC Agreement had to be modified after an earlier opinion of the CJEU holding that the original proposal was incompatible with the EU Treaties (Opinion 1/09 CJEU, 2011). Secondly, a political disagreement existed about the location of the central division of the UPC between the UK, Germany and France. Thirdly, a growing number of patent professionals and associations were voicing their criticism against the proposal, in particular with respect to the competence of the CJEU – a non-specialized court renowned for its considerable backlog of cases – in interpreting patent law. In particular this third stumbling block in the negotiations is fascinating from the perspective of dynamic governance. In this late phase of the negotiations, suddenly the interaction between the formal and informal actors increased. However, the informal actors mainly consisted of the epistemic patent community.

In terms of the degree of interaction between formal and informal actors during the negotiations on the Patent Package since the revitalization of the process in 2006, one can identify basically three periods. During the first period between 2006 and 2008, the Commission made considerable efforts to involve both the epistemic patent community and civil society in the debate on the future of the

European patent system. When it became clear in 2009 that the translation regime remained a major hurdle in the negotiations and the enhanced cooperation procedure was invoked, the debate disappeared behind closed doors entering the second period of the negotiations (see above). This situation continued with only a handful of – mostly leaked – documents available to the general public until the UK House of Commons Scrutiny Committee initiated the third period in 2011 opening up the debate for stakeholders with an inquiry inviting stakeholders for feedback and the publication of a very critical report.

In the early years, after the re-launch of the European patent reforms by the Commission in 2006, the *first period*, the EU institutions used a range of methods to address a varied set of public interests and to allow for the participation of a critical layer of citizens. The institutions engaged in an active written and oral dialogue through several consultation procedures, expert studies and public hearings. The Commission organized informal consultations combined with a public hearing on the Future Patent Policy in Europe (European Commission, 2006). On the basis of this extensive consultation round, the Commission adopted a Communication in 2007 (European Commission, 2007), which fostered the patent reform debate in the Council. In its communication, the Commission suggested new avenues to explore regarding the establishment of the centralized patent court and the translation regime. The Commission issued another Communication on An Industrial Property Rights Strategy for Europe in 2008 proposing a horizontal strategy across the spectrum of IP rights (*i.e.* patents, trademarks and design rights) and initiatives on enforcement, support for SMEs and IP quality (European Commission, 2008). The 2008 Communication was meant to complement the 2007 Communication and confirmed the Commission's commitment to the EU patent and a centralized patent court system once more. The communication was followed by a conference in Strasbourg with a full day devoted to the EU patent and patent litigation and a large number of panels populated with a broad range of patent experts and a number of representatives from civil society. The European Parliament obtained some further input from the epistemic community and the general public through studies of the European patent system by independent experts (TNO, 2010; Danish Board of Technology *et al.*, 2007). These studies were accompanied by workshops and conferences for members of the parliament and the general public. Remarkably, these meetings were also partially devoted to broader governance issues, such as transparency and political accountability.

As explained above, during the *second period* the EU institutions shifted to a more closed approach when it became clear in 2009 that the translation regime remained a major hurdle in the negotiations and the enhanced cooperation procedure was invoked. Nonetheless, starting in 2011 gradually the voice of the epistemic patent community grew louder triggering new opportunities for debate and opening up the *third phase* in the reform process. Various experts, including a highly regarded former UK patent judge and a German, well-known patent law professor, and professional organizations had issued opinions opposing jurisdiction of the CJEU in patent cases (*e.g.* Jacob, 2011; Kraßer, 2011; European Patent Lawyers Association, 2011; Intellectual Property Judges Association, 2011). The Court would lack the required expertise and its involvement would result in high costs and considerable delay. Despite increased lobbying efforts at the EU level, the EU institutions turned a deaf ear to the voices of the epistemic community. They pursued their attempts to speedily agree on the Patent Package, but they did not reckon with the fierce resistance of the UK House of Commons.

The European Scrutiny Committee of the UK House of Commons organized various hearings for stakeholders and questioned Baroness Wilcox, Undersecretary for Business, Innovation and Skills, who was the UK representative for the negotiations on the Patent Package. As a result of the scrutiny, the committee published a report (UK House of Commons Scrutiny Committee, 2012) expressing its concerns about the effect of the Patent Package on SMEs, supposedly the main intended beneficiaries. The patent profession overwhelmingly claimed that the UPC would actually increase litigation costs for SMEs and be far more burdensome than the old system. The Scrutiny Committee concluded that the UK Government had to adopt a strong position reflecting the concerns of practitioners. It also indicated that the central division of the UPC should be in London in order to mitigate the most damaging effects of the Patent Package (UK House of Commons Scrutiny Committee, 2012).

As a compromise solution the EU Competitiveness Council decided in June 2012, that the powers of the CJEU in interpreting patent law would be abridged and that the central division of the UPC would have a central seat in Paris and sections in London and Munich distributed on the basis of thematic clusters (London: chemistry, including pharmaceuticals, and human necessities; Munich: mechanical engineering) (EU Council, 2012). However, the European Parliament was irritated by the fact that the European Council had sneaked in these changes without the consultation of the European Parliament, in particular because this unilateral solution would have a serious impact on the powers of the Court. So, despite the compromise in the Council the delegates were back at the negotiation table. Not much happened over the summer of 2012. After the brief upheaval of transparency and interaction institutionalized by the UK Scrutiny Committee, transparency and access to documents ended up being even more limited. In September meetings between the MEPs and the Council were scheduled, but everything happened behind closed doors. Access to Council documents was barred from the general public and comments or participation by civil society was virtually impossible. Moreover, EU officials at public events emphasized that most of the key decisions had already been taken and that there was not much room for negotiations left. It was also acknowledged that due to the challenges involved in political deliberations the outcome would not be ideal, but any deficiencies would be fixed later through the UPC's Rules of Procedure or when the system would be operational (*e.g.* Jorna, 2012).

In late 2012, the Cyprus Presidency broke the deadlock position with a compromise proposing to leave questions related to the scope of protection and limitations outside the scope of EU law and hence outside the scope of the powers of the CJEU. Subsequently in December 2012 a political agreement on the Patent Package was reached. In February 2013, 24 Member States signed the Agreement on the UPC. Italy also signed the agreement even though it is not participating in the enhanced cooperation procedure and even challenged the use of that procedure before the CJEU. Bulgaria signed later. Spain and Poland have not yet signed the agreement.

Especially the resistance of Poland against the Patent Package is another fascinating example of the rise of civil society and – even – the general public in the patent context. The events in Poland are a clear reflection of the growing concerns amongst the general public about the perceived benefits of the Patent Package and the interaction between formal and informal actors within the patent governance network. Poland had initially embraced the Patent Package with significant support of associations of patent professionals, industry and a significant part of civil society. This initial enthusiasm faded, however, when the first draft was considerably amended in the late stage of the negotiation process (AIPPI, 2013; Kupzok, 2013; Zawadzka, 2013). Eventually, a large group of experts, including several well-known Polish IP professors and industry associations, started criticizing the Patent Package. The experts feared that Polish entrepreneurs would be deprived of the opportunity to receive essential patent information in Polish, which would increase the costs of patent clearance, decrease legal certainty and violate the Polish constitution. The translation regime would require translation, not only from English, but also, potentially, from French or German, further increasing costs. Finally, the role of the UPC would deprive the Polish national courts from their constitutionally recognized judicial powers (AIPPI, 2013; Kupzok, 2013; Zawadzka, 2013; Deloitte, 2012). As a consequence, there was a change in the position of the Polish government in December 2012 (AIPPI, 2012). The Ministry of Economy maintained support for the enhanced cooperation procedure but reported reservations to the package in its current shape. Ultimately, the government felt that a wait and see approach would be best for the time being and decided not to sign the UPC agreement in February 2013.

Although the Patent Package has been adopted by the EU institutions and the UPC Agreement has been signed by a majority of Member States, the three components of the Patent Package will only enter into force after a number of outstanding issues will be resolved. The three major outstanding issues relate to (1) the ratification of the UPC Agreement (*i.e.* the UPC Agreement is an international agreement and needs to be ratified by at least 13 Member States, including the three Member States with the highest number of validations of European bundle patents (Germany, the UK and France)), (2) the establishment of the UPC and the negotiations on the implementation rules for the UPC (*i.e.* the set-up of a complete new court system requires new facilities, a governance structure, the election of judges, the recruitment of staff, the training of judges, the setting of a budget and drafting the rules of procedure) (Preparatory Committee, 2014) and (3) the implementation rules for the EPO.

The first and third outstanding issue are crucial in view of the role and interaction of formal and informal actors in the European patent system. The ratification of the UPC Agreement may seem a purely formal requirement. However, in some countries the ratification requires a referendum (*i.e.* Denmark) and, hence, it requires the involvement of the general public and a transparency campaign explaining the importance of the UPC. Such a requirement will contribute to the dynamics and interests of a broader public in the patent system.

The third outstanding issue is particularly relevant from a dynamic governance perspective in view of the necessary interaction between the EPO, national patent offices and (to a limited extent) the European Commission. When the Patent Package will ultimately enter into force, the EPO will continue to play a key role in patent administration of the unitary and European bundle patents. Patent applicants will continue to file patent applications at the EPO as they have been doing for decades. If the EPO decides to grant a European patent, the applicant can request that the patent is given unitary effect for the territories of the participating Member States. The EPO will be responsible for the administration of requests for unitary effect, the management of the register for unitary patent protection, the publication of translations and the collection of fees. For the supervision and governance of these activities a Select Committee of the Administrative Council of the EPO (consisting of representatives of the participating Member States and a representative of the Commission) has been set up. This Committee is tasked with setting the level of the renewal fees for the maintenance of the patent with unitary effect and the establishment of a distribution key for the renewal fee income between the EPO and national patent offices. These matters are very controversial. The controversy is related to the fact that the level of the fees will be decisive for the use of the system and the accessibility for SMEs, individual inventors and universities. At the same time, the level of the fees is important for the participating Member States as 50 per cent of the renewal income will be redistributed amongst them (according to "fair, equitable and relevant criteria"). The rationale for this redistribution of income is the expected shift of patent applicants from the European bundle patent to the unitary patent, which will likely have a significant impact on the budget of the national patent offices, as national validation will no longer be required. The discussion on the level of the renewal fees and the distribution key has started in autumn 2013. In view of the budgetary constraints of many EU Member States in the aftermath of the financial crisis, the discussions on the fees and the distribution key will likely remain one of the potential stumbling blocks for the implementation of the Patent Package.

DRIVING TRANSFORMATION AND COLLABORATIVE INNOVATION THROUGH DYNAMIC GOVERNANCE?

In view of all these outstanding issues and potential stumbling blocks, which lessons can we draw from the European patent reform process through the lens of dynamic governance? To what extent is the Patent Package driving transformation and collaborative (public) innovation in the patent context?

Provided that the various committees will succeed in pursuing the implementation process and the required number of ratifications will be achieved, the Patent Package will lead to the introduction of a new institution, an additional layer of European patent protection, the unitary patent. It will also be the basis for another specialized patent court, the Unified Patent Court, in line with the global trend to create specialized courts in the area of IP law. Whereas many other countries have simply reorganized their judicial system by turning specialized divisions into specialized courts, the implementation of the package entails a complete new judicial system independent from the national courts with its own first instance court (with local and regional divisions and a central division with three locations), an appeal court, a Training Centre for judges and an Arbitration and Mediation Centre.

Therefore, the entry into force of the Patent Package will definitely transform the relationship between the two autonomous European patent branches and the respective formal patent actors: the EPO and the EU institutions, the relationship between the EPO and the national patent offices and the position of the national courts. These transformations will require major policy and governance innovations, many of which cannot even be anticipated at this point in time. Moreover, if indeed the Patent Package will trigger a shift by patent applicants from European patents towards unitary patents this will also involve major changes in private and public patent strategies and organizational behaviour and plausibly entail further consequences for the interpretation of patent law, policy and doctrine.

The criticism on the decision-making process and the content of the Patent Package raises some concerns about the potential impact of the lack of transparency and participation by informal actors in the process of institutional innovation. Openness and public participation are vital in generating trust from the general public in complex governance systems. Moreover, without the necessary level of openness, public participation becomes meaningless. In its White Paper on European Governance the Commission clarified that the institutions and Member States should work in a more open manner and should actively and understandably communicate about the EU activities and decisions (European Commission, 2001). It also acknowledged that the quality, relevance and effectiveness of EU policies depend on ensuring wide public participation throughout the policy chain – from conception to implementation. Improved participation is likely to create more confidence in the end result and in the (new) institutions which drive policy (European Commission, 2001).

The revival of the discussions concerning the Community patent by the European Commission in 2007 was preceded by a broad consultation of all the stakeholders concerned in order to assess the need for a more simple, cost-effective and high quality patent system for Europe. The European Parliament requested studies by experts with workshops and conferences with wide participation by informal actors from the private and public sector. In the later phases of the negotiations, public access to information and working documents was, however, scarce and inadequate. In particular the general public would have difficulties ploughing their way through the different registries of the institutions, Commission website, blogs, *etc*.

The lack of transparency was justified by politicians and bureaucrats by pointing to the political sensitivity and confidentiality of the ongoing negotiations. Nonetheless, experts' part of the closed epistemic community did succeed in passing on their feedback to negotiators and influencing national delegates even in this final, confidential stage. In particular patent practitioners and patent scholars in the UK had considerable impact on the UK position and the final compromise which was reached within the Council in June 2012. Whereas the delegates of the UK had been quite absent from the earlier discussions on the EU patent – and had been rapped over the knuckles for that by the Scrutiny Committee (2012) – the UK suddenly took an extremely strong stance in the final stage of the negotiations. Thus, whereas large companies and local patent experts or professional organizations found ways to get their message across, the voice of less obvious informal actors, individual inventors and SMEs, were largely excluded from the debate. This approach makes the process prone to capture by vested interests and subject to empty promises as the lack of transparency and public participation will likely foreclose proper accountability mechanisms.

I acknowledge that confidentiality may be vital in political negotiations that have reached a critical, final phase. However, then at least the input and results from earlier consultations and reports and the underlying reform objectives (*e.g.* decreasing complexity, limiting costs, protecting interests of SMEs) should have been taken into account by the negotiators in the final negotiation round as well. I also recognize the key role of epistemic communities in the highly technical and legally complex patent environment, but their role may not be used as an excuse to debar the wider public from commenting and participating in the decision-making process. If SMEs, a group of core stakeholders mentioned in all proposals, reports and consultation documents, would have been given a more visible and vocal representation, the final result may actually have enhanced the European patent system for SMEs. At present, several important issues are still open. Many SMEs have, nevertheless, already indicated that even after the entry into force of the patent package, they may simply continue applying for classical European bundle patents instead of requesting the registration of unitary effect with all its associated uncertainties.

The Preparatory Committee that is working on the Rules of Procedure for the UPC has committed publicly to principles of openness and public participation. It has adopted an external communication plan based on transparency and a wide involvement of stakeholders. This plan confirms the importance of the wide availability of information on its website, regular updates of the website, written consultations with stakeholders and hearings for a broad range of stakeholders. The Preparatory Committee indeed carried out a consultation procedure on the draft Rules of Procedure for the UPC. Regrettably, the draft itself had been prepared in a relatively closed process by an expert group of patent judges and lawyers without guarantees of transparency and public participation. The results of the consultation have been published and commented (Preparatory Committee, 2014). The public hearing on the revised draft will normally follow later this year.

For the time being – despite the strong wish of the Commission for the first unitary patents to be granted in 2015 – it is still unclear if and when the Patent Package will be fully operational as there are still so many outstanding issues. We are left to the tender mercies and the wisdom of the Preparatory and Select Committees for the implementation process, on the one hand, and of the Member States for the ratification of the UPC Agreement, on the other hand. The expectations for the Patent Package are high. Even more so, significant institutional transformations of complex governance systems, such as the European patent system, cannot be justified by empty promises on global competitiveness or interests of SMEs or by pledges to improve the system along the way.

Therefore, the way ahead should take due account of the lessons that can be drawn from the perspective of dynamic governance, in particular by improving the actual dynamics of the reform process and the input by all relevant stakeholders going beyond the epistemic patent community *e.g.* in consultation procedures on the Rules of Procedure, the fee schedule and other implementing regulations. The Polish case has shown that even the general public can have a considerable impact on the advances of the Patent Package. In adopting a more *dynamic* approach, an attempt can be made to – at least – make up for the failure to respect principles of transparency and public participation earlier on in the process and in order to sustain public trust in the transformed European patent governance system.

ACKNOWLEDGEMENTS

I would like to thank the participants of the Roskilde University Sunrise Conference "Transforming Governance, Enhancing Innovation" (October 29-31,

2012) for their helpful feedback. Furthermore, the conceptual framework used in this paper is partially based on earlier research together with Prof. Kali Murray (Associate Professor of Law Marquette University Law School) (Murray, K.N. & van Zimmeren, E. (2011). "Dynamic Patent Governance in Europe and the United States The Myriad Example", 19 *Cardozo J. Int. & Comp. L.*, 287-342. Thanks go to Prof. Murray for the interesting and inspiring discussions on patent governance that have triggered my ongoing research project in this field.

CONFLICT OF INTEREST

The author confirms that this chapter contents have no conflict of interest.

REFERENCES

AIPPI Poland (2013). *Whatever happened to Polish support for Unified Patent Package,* AIPPI e-news, No. 30, May 2013, available at https://www.aippi.org/enews/2013/edition30/Marek_Lazewski.html

Borrás, S. (2006). The Governance of the European Patent System: Effective and Legitimate? *Econ. & Soc.'y*, 35, 594-610.

CJEU (2013). 16 April 2013, *Kingdom of Spain and Italian Republic v. European Commission,* Joined Cases C-274/11 and C-295/11 [2013] ECR I-n.y.r.

CJEU (2011). 8 March 2011, *Opinion delivered pursuant to Article 218(11) TFEU* – Draft agreement *European and Community Patents Court, Opinion* 1/09 [2011] ECR I-n.y.r.

Council of the EU (2013). *Agreement on a Unified Patent Court,* [2013] *OJEU* C175/1

Council of the EU (2012a). *Council Regulation (EU) No 1260/2012 of 17 December 2012 implementing enhanced cooperation in the area of the creation of unitary patent protection with regard to the applicable translation arrangements*, [2012] *OJEU* L361/89

Council of the EU (2011a). *Council Decision of 10 March 2011 authorising enhanced cooperation in the area of the creation of unitary patent protection,* [2011] *OJEU* L76/53

Council of the EU (2011b). *Draft agreement on a Unified Patent Court and draft Statute – Presidency text*, June 14, 2011, PI 68, COUR 32

Council of the EU (2009a). *Conclusions on an enhanced patent system in Europe,* 2982nd COMPETITIVENESS (Internal market, Industry and Research) Council meeting, Brussels

Council of the EU (2009b). *Draft Agreement on the European and Community Patents Court and Draft Statute*, Working Document 7928/09 PI 23 COUR 29, 2009

Danish Board of Technology, *et al.* (2007). *Policy options for the improvement of the European patent system,* Brussels, European Parliament, STOA, IP/A/STOA/FWC/2005-28/SC16

Drahos, P. (2004). Intellectual Property and Pharmaceutical Markets: A Nodal Governance Approach, *Temple L. Rev.*, 77, 401-424.

Drahos, P. (2010). *The Global Governance of Knowledge: Patent Offices and their Clients*. Cambridge: Cambridge University Press.

Engelbrekt, A.B. (2007). Copyright from an Institutional Perspective: Actors, Interests, Stakes and the Logic of Participation. *Review of Economic Research on Copyright Issues,* 4, 65-97.

EPO (2007a). *Convention on the Grant of European Patents (European Patent Convention – EPC),* applicable since 13 December 2007, 14th Ed., entered into force in 2010

EPO (2007b). *Scenarios for the future*, available at http://www.epo.org/news-issues/issues/scenarios.html

EPO (2012). *EPO welcomes historic breakthrough on the unitary patent*, Press Release June 29, 2012

ESAB (2013). *2012 Statement – Recommendations for Improving the Patent System*, February 2013

European Commission (2006). *Commission Public Hearing on a Future Patent Policy in Europe,* COM (2006) 170.

European Commission (2001). *White Paper on European Governance*, COM(2001)428 final

European Commission (2007). *Communication form the Commission to the European Parliament and the Council Enhancing the patent system in Europe*, COM(2007)165 final

European Commission (2008). *Communication form the Commission to the European Parliament and the Council and the European Economic and Social Committee-An Industrial Property Rights Strategy,* COM(2008)465 final

European Commission (2010). *Proposal for a Council Decision authorising enhanced cooperation in the area of the creation of unitary patent protection,* COM(2010) 790 final, December 14.

European Commission (2011a). *Proposal for a Council Regulation of the European Parliament and of the Council implementing enhanced cooperation in the area of the creation of unitary patent protection,* COM(2011)215 final, April 13, 2011

European Commission (2011b). *Proposal for Council Regulation implementing enhanced cooperation in the area of the creation of unitary patent protection with regard to the applicable translation arrangements*, COM(2011)216 final, April 13, 2011

European Commission (2011c). *Commission proposes unitary patent protection to boost research and innovation*, IP/11/470, Press Release April 13, 2011

EU Council (2012). *Conclusions 28/29 June*, EUCO 76/12, CO EUR 4, CONCL 2, 29 June 2012

European Parliament (2007). *Interim Legal Opinion - Possible conclusion of the European Patent Litigation Agreement by the Member States - overlap between that agreement and the acquis communautaire*, February 1st, 2007

European Parliament (2011). *European Parliament legislative resolution of 15 February 2011 on the draft Council decision authorising enhanced cooperation in the area of the creation of unitary patent protection* (05538/2011 – C7-0044/2011 – 2010/0384(NLE))

European Parliament and Council (2012). *Regulation (EU) No 1257/2012 of the European Parliament and of the Council of 17 December 2012 implementing enhanced cooperation in the area of creation of unitary patent protection*, [2012] *OJEU* L361/1

European Patent Lawyers Association (2011). *Unitary Patent and Unified Patent Court*, October 29, 2011

Gaja, G. (1998). How Flexible is Flexibility under the Amsterdam Treaty?. *CMLRev*. 35, 855-870.

Gowers, A. (2006). *Gowers Review of Intellectual Property*, London, HM Treasury

International Intellectual Property Institute (2012). *Study on Specialized Intellectual Property Courts*, available at http://iipi.org/wp-content/uploads/2012/05/Study-on-Specialized-IPR-Courts.pdf

Intellectual Property Judges Association (2011). *To all concerned with the project for a Unified Patent Court for the EU and Unitary Patent*, November 2, 2011, available at http://www.eplawpatentblog.com/2011/November/Venice%2020Judges%2020Resolution%20202011%5B1%5D.pdf

Jacob, R. (2011). *Opinion*, November 2, 2011

Kupzok, A. (2013). *Law and Economics of the unitary patent protection in the European Union – a rebels' viewpoint*, EPIP Conference 2013, Working Paper

Kraßer, R. (2011). *Effects of an inclusion of regulations concerning the content and limits of the patent holder's rights to prohibit in an EU regulation for the creation of unitary European patent protection*, Munich, 1 September/18 October 2011

Lamping, M. (2011). Enhanced Cooperation – A Proper Approach to Market Integration in the Field of Unitary Patent Protection?, *42 IIC*, 879-925

Lemley, M.A. (2001). Rational Ignorance at the Patent Office, 95 *Nw. U. L. Rev.*, 1495-532

Max Planck Institute for Intellectual Property and Competition Law (2012). *The Unitary Patent Package: Twelve Reasons for Concern*, October 19th, 2012, available at http://www.ip.mpg.de/files/pdf2/MPI-IP_Twelve-Reasons_2012-10-17_final3.pdf

Murphy, D.T. (2003). Closer or Enhanced Cooperation: Amsterdam or Nice, *Ga. J. Int'l & Comp. L.*, 31, 265-319.

Murray, K.N. & van Zimmeren, E. (2011). Dynamic Patent Governance in Europe and the United States The Myriad Example, 19 *Cardozo J. Int. & Comp. L.*, 287-342.

Preparatory Committee (2014). *Responses to the Public Consultation on the Rules of Procedure of the UPC*, February 2014, available at http://www.unified-patent-court.org/images/documents/rop-digest.pdf

Rai, A. (2003). Engaging facts and policy: A Multi-instutional approach to patent system reform, *Colum. L. Rev.*, 103, 1035-1135.

Rhodes, R. A. W (1997). *Understanding Governance: Policy Networks, Governance, Reflexivity and Accountability*, Buckingham/Philadelphia: Open University Press

Schneider, I. (2009). Governing the patent system in Europe: the EPO's supranational autonomy and its need for a regulatory perspective. *Science & Pub. Pol'y*, 36, 619-629.

Schrauwen, A. (ed.) (2002). *Flexibility in Constitutions: Forms of Closer Cooperation in Federal and Non Federal Settings*, Europa Law Publishing

Sørensen, E. & Torfing, J. (2011). Enhancing Collaborative Innovation in the Public Sector. *Administration and Society,* 43, 842-868.

Tamura, Y. (2009). *A theory of the Law and Policy of Intellectual Property - Building a New Framework*, NJCL, available at http://www.njcl.utu.fi/1_2009/article1.pdf (translated by N. Lee)

TNO *et al.* (2010). *Current policy issues in the governance of the European patent system*, Report commissioned by the European Parliament Science and Technology Options Assessment, IP/A/STOA/IC/2008-188, available at http://www.europarl.europa.eu/RegData/etudes/etudes/join/2009/424763/IPOL-JOIN_ET(2009)424763_EN.pdf

UK House of Commons Scrutiny Committee (2012). *The Unified Patent Court: help or hindrance?*, April 25, 2012, available at http://www.publications.parliament.uk/pa/cm201012/cmselect/cmeuleg/1799/1799.pdf

US Federal Trade Commission (USFTC) (2003). *To Promote Innovation: The Proper Balance of Competition and Patent Law and Policy*, USFTC, Washington, D.C., available at http://www.ftc.gov/os/2003/10/innovationrpt.pdf

Zawadzka, Z. (2013). *The unitary patent protection: a voice in discussion from the perspective of Poland*, EPIP Conference 2013, Working Paper.

CHAPTER 10

Case Study: Lead User Innovation in the Danish Tax Ministry

Helle Vibeke Carstensen*

Advisor on Human Resources and Enhanced Innovation Capacity, Denmark

Abstract: The aim of this chapter is to examine how the lead user approach successfully can be applied in the public sector and how it can contribute to collaborative innovation. This chapter is based on a case study of lead user innovation in the Danish Ministry of Taxation. In the last decade, the Ministry has increased the participation of citizens and thereby strengthened the role of the users in the innovation process. Encouraged by studies showing that users contribute more to the innovation than producers, the Ministry wanted to examine whether lead users could also contribute to public innovation on complex problems. This was done by doing a lead user study concerning bookkeeping. On the basis of the project, it is described and discussed how the lead user approach can be used to make collaborative innovation happen and increase the outcome of the innovation process. The conclusion is that the lead user approach can be used in the public sector and it increases the possibility for radical innovation. However, development of the lead user approach is needed. Firstly, by adding a fifth phase to the existing lead user approach to be sure innovation happens in a collaborative way, and secondly, by expanding the bottom lines to the complexity in the public sector and thirdly, by updating the methods used to engage citizens.

Keywords: Bookkeeping, bottom lines, collaborative, complex, innovation, involvement, lead user, methods, participation, power, public sector, taxation, trends, user needs.

INTRODUCTION

The Danish Ministry of Taxation has for a long time faced a political demand for increased efficiency, increased compliance and deliverance of better services. In order to meet these demands and at the same time maintain a high standard in law production, as well as administration and services the Ministry has strengthened the role of the users in the innovation process (Carstensen, 2010).

Encouraged by studies (*e.g.* von Hippel, 2010) showing that users contribute more

***Corresponding author Helle Vibeke Carstensen:** Head of Office for Organizational Development at the Social Services Department in Copenhagen Municipality, Denmark; E-mail: BQ4R@sof.kk.dk

Annika Agger, Bodil Damgaard, Andreas Hagedorn Krogh and Eva Sørensen (Eds.)

to the innovation than producers the Ministry wanted to examine whether lead users could also contribute to public innovation on complex problems. The aim of this chapter is to answer this question by analyzing a process of lead user innovation in the Ministry concerning bookkeeping. The chapter will clarify how lead users can contribute to public innovation and will also inform efforts to develop a distinctly public model for lead user innovation. This is being done by testing the impact of a lead user approach to innovation as described in the handbook (Churchill, 2009).

The chapter begins with a presentation of the innovation work in the Ministry and the different theories behind their innovation processes. The main part of the chapter is a presentation of the lead user project in the Ministry, why bookkeeping was chosen, how the users were involved, and the outcome of the collaborative innovation process. Lastly, it is discussed whether the lead user approach is useful and efficient way to enhance collaborative innovation in the public sector, and how it can be developed to a public context. Behind the term *the Ministry* is of cause civil servants doing a lot of different innovation projects. The deep insights and knowledge about the Ministry's innovation work was gained through my position as Director of Innovation in the Ministry. My position allowed me in the lead user project to allocate resources to document the process and as an innovation expert discuss the process with the Ministry's research group. This implicates that I'm not an objective researcher, but a theoretical based practitioner with insights on how to make public innovation happen.

INNOVATION IN THE MINISTRY OF TAXATION

The Ministry works with both expert driven innovation and user involvement in the innovation process. The language and terms used about innovation are very inaccurate (which does not suit tax people) and the Ministry has found it necessary to be explicit about the definition of user involvement and the degree of power handed over to the users in the innovation process. Therefore the Ministry has defined three different user roles in the innovation process (Fig. **1**).

In the *expert driven* innovation processes the Ministry uses the knowledge of the employees from their formal training and practices, and the huge amount of data from the tax systems. The users are not directly involved, but the Ministry changes their behaviour *e.g.* through nudging (Thaler & Sunstein, 2009).

In the *user centred* innovation processes, the users are studied – directly or indirectly – in order to learn about their routines, behaviour, attitudes, and thoughts regarding the activity in focus. The Ministry bases this kind of innovation on methods and theories from sociology and anthropology and uses interviews, observations, or personas in the innovation process (Hastrup *et al.* 2011, Bason 2009, Kvale 2003, Gjerde 2006).

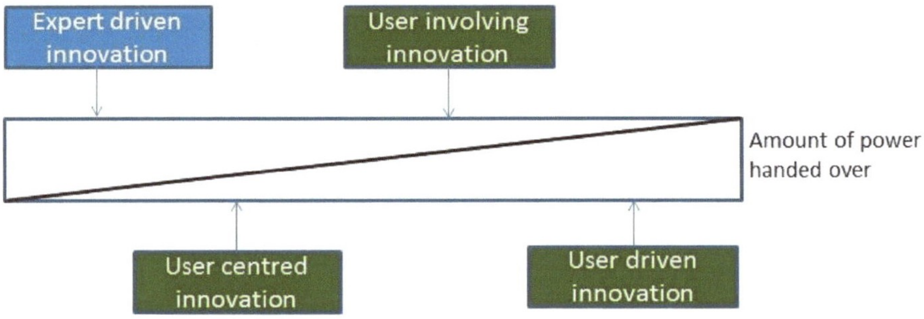

Figure 1: Different user roles (The Danish Ministry of Taxation, 2007).

In the *user involving* processes the users are actively and systematically involved in developing new services or administration processes. The Ministry bases this kind of innovation on design and co-creation theory (Bason, 2010; Sørensen & Torfing, 2011).

User driven innovation is innovation by users, where citizens have (radical) innovative solutions that the Ministry can use directly or refine. The Ministry bases this kind of innovation on theories about open innovation (Chesbourgh, 2006) and lead user innovation (von Hippel, 2005).

Which kind of innovation process the Ministry chooses to use depends on the context and the desired shared amount of power.

DEFINITION AND PROCESS

The Ministry defines innovation as "*a new idea that creates value, when implemented*" (Bason, 2007). This implicates that the idea has to be new (to the Ministry). It has to be implemented, hence creativity is not enough. Finally, it has to create value, and this value is measured on the Ministry's bottom lines and has to be neutral or positive on all bottom lines.

The value of an innovation has for several years been measured on four bottom lines in the Ministry: It has to be cheaper (the administrative bottom line), give a better service to the citizens (the service bottom line), meet political demands *e.g.* by reducing the tax gap (the policy bottom line), and secure due process, high legitimacy and involve the users (the democracy bottom line) (Bason 2007). A fifth bottom line has been added lately and is about enhancing the organization's innovation capacity. It is not easy to measure the value on the bottom lines but it is possible (Carstensen, 2013). To make innovation successful (in a New Public Management ruled world) with limited resources, it is the Ministry's experience that measurement is necessary.

The process of constantly and systematically learning about, from and with the users ensures that the problem solved is in fact the right one, and that the solution developed is the best one. The process (Fig. **2**) consists of three main steps and is iterative and centred around the user (Carstensen & Dahl, 2013).

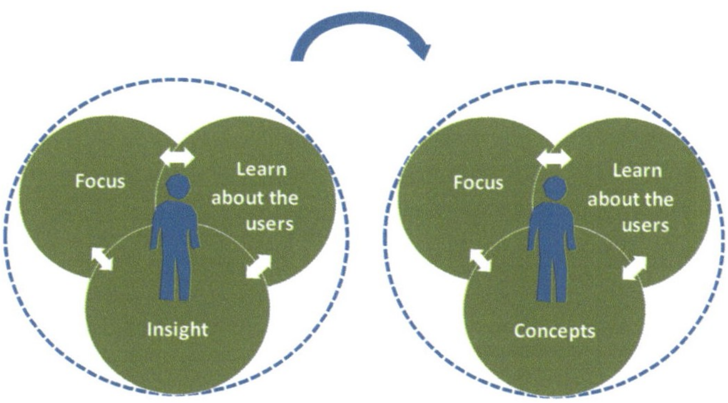

Figure 2: The users in the innovation process. (The Danish Ministry of Taxation, 2011).

It consists of two separate turns, where you focus on the problem, learn about the users and gain insights (first turn) or develop concepts (second turn). A concept is an illustration of a solution with descriptions of key elements, a pretotype (Savoia, 2011) or prototype of the solution. To develop a usable concept (used by the Tax Ministry) a profound understanding of the Nordic welfare model and the high degree of digitalization of the Danish tax administration was necessary.

This innovation process model is highly relevant and useful when users are engaged in user centred or user involving processes (Fig. **1**). The process is partly open as the Ministry invites the users to hand over knowledge or participate in the innovation process at given times. When it comes to user driven innovation the process model has to be supplemented to have a more or constantly open innovation process and to find the lead users (von Hippel, 2005).

So far the term *lead users* has been used in private sector innovation and are citizens who develop innovations long before commercial products are available on the market (von Hippel, 1999). The curve illustrates a market trend (Fig. **3**). Lead users have needs that are well ahead of the trend and over time more and more users will feel the same need. Lead users can also develop services to be used in the public sector or to meet demands from authorities *e.g.* the Ministry but so far the public sector in Denmark has not applied this form for innovation, which probably has something to do with handing over power to the citizens (Fig. **1**).

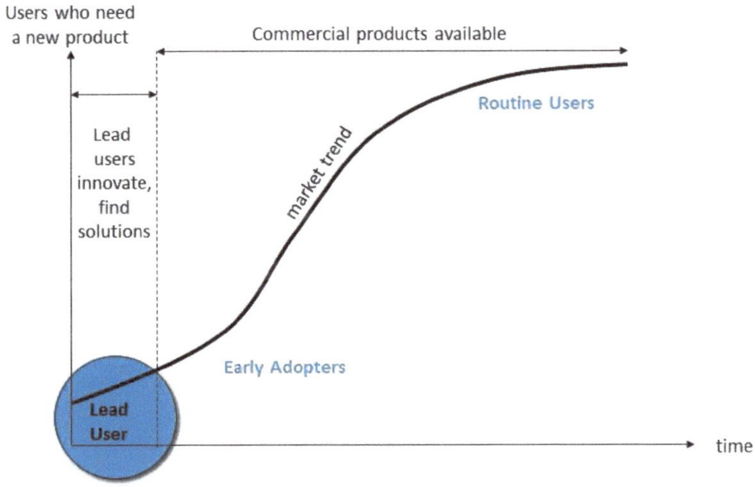

Figure 3: The lead user curve. (von Hippel *et al.* 1999).

Studies of lead user innovation have shown that users contribute more to the innovation than producers (von Hippel, 2010) and the Ministry wanted to examine whether lead users could also contribute to public innovation. The Ministry has very good experiences with opening up the innovation process at well-defined points (Chesbourgh, 2006) and learning from and with private companies (Bessant, 2005). At the same time the Ministry assumed that lead user innovation could lead to a higher effect on the bottom lines and encourage radical solutions better than user centred or user involving innovation would be able to (The Danish Ministry of Taxation, 2010).

THE CASE: INNOVATION AND SMES

The Ministry experiences decreasing compliance from the small and medium sized enterprises (SMEs). Of the 1.15 billon euro tax gap in 2012 (defined as the difference between the possible tax revenue and the actual collected tax revenue) 0.85 billion euro is missing from SMEs with less than 10 employees. A substantial amount comes from errors in bookkeeping although it is not known exactly how much.

The Ministry has done quite a lot of user centred innovation (Fig. **1**) concerning SMEs. In one of the first major attempts to discover the root of the problem with decreasing compliance among SMEs, user centred approaches were used (Bason *et al.*, 2009). Entrepreneurs were interviewed and filmed while doing their accounting and reporting Value Added Tax (VAT). The routines were mapped in order to identify where in the process system failures or breaches in communication occurred. Both VAT and innovation experts participated in the mapping process, and later used the knowledge to improve the registration and administration process *e.g.* making instructional videos on how to handle business registration and VAT accounting digitally. From this and other cases the Ministry also gained the insight that the majority of the SMEs and start-ups want to do things right and be compliant but they need help to achieve that.

However, the Ministry's knowledge of the entrepreneurs' bookkeeping routines and helpers was limited. The Ministry decided to do a project concerning increased tax and VAT compliance of small businesses by better bookkeeping, using von Hippel's lead user approach (von Hippel, 2005). The Ministry chose user driven innovation (Fig. **1**), since there was a need for radical innovation in a complex problem involving many different stakeholders. The Ministry also expected a higher effect on the bottom lines using this approach.

The case suitably illustrates how lead user innovation can contribute to innovation in the public sector since it was designed using the Lead User Project Handbook (Churchill, 2009) and involved users throughout the innovation process and the innovation is about taxation, which is exercise of authority and highly regulated by law. The case also provides useful insights on the role of facilitators in the innovation processes – in the case done by the research group.

The Lead User Approach – Project Design

The Ministry decided to use the lead user approach as described in four phases in the Lead User Project Handbook. During the project a fifth phase was added based on the Ministry's experience (Fig. **4**) and other studies of innovation with users (Sørensen & Torfing, 2011). The Ministry also supplemented the user driven innovation process with the two other kinds of user innovation in Fig. **1** to enhance collaborative innovation. Throughout the project the research group consulted Professor Christoph Hienerth, CBS and Professor Eric von Hippel, MIT and is grateful for their contribution.

A lead user project takes departure in the definition of a challenge that needs to be solved. It has to be a challenge representing a business potential, just as described in the Olympic Snack study when a major food company made a lead user project to find the future snack (Churchill, 2009). The starting point for the Ministry's project was the following challenge: *How can bookkeeping become easier for SMEs (less than 10 employees) and thereby become more correct and help SMEs to be in compliance?*

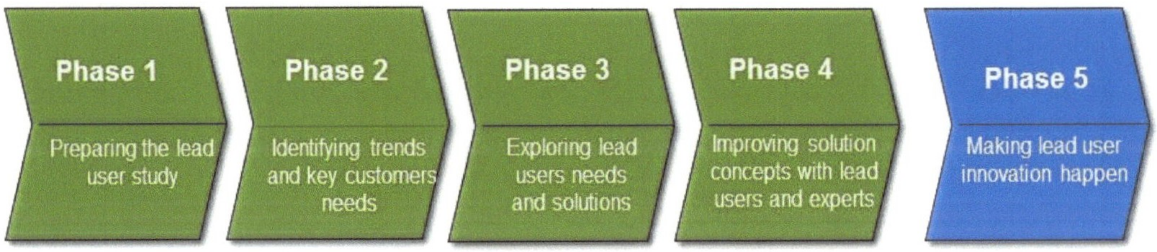

Figure 4: The lead user project phases (Source: The Danish Ministry of Taxation, 2012).

The business potential measured on the bottom lines was set out to be (radically) better services or products, better and cheaper processes, more compliance, easier understandable tax and VAT rules (implying higher legitimacy and securing due processes), and involvement of the users. Compared to the private sector's purpose of using the lead user approach the public sector's purpose is more complex since the bottom lines are always multiple.

A cross-disciplinary research group (Darsø, 2001) with five members was formed to facilitate the project. They had very different competencies and knowledge about design, innovation methods, compliance, communication, economy, bookkeeping, VAT and taxes. Many of the competencies are core competencies in the Ministry (Prahalad & Hamel, 1990).

A master plan for the project was developed and combined the Ministry's project model with a journey into the unknown. The project model is a classical stage gate model with phases that give room for both divergent thinking to open up the innovation process and getting ideas; and convergent thinking to focus on solutions to be implemented (Leonard & Strauss, 2000; Darsø, 2001). By using the project model the research group followed the Ministry's normal procedures but adapted it to the fact that no one could know what the solution would be and therefore could not quantify the expected effects on the bottom lines in the beginning of the project.

Who Were the Users and How Were They Involved?

The users were involved in the process in three different ways: As stakeholders, as knowledge keepers and most important as lead user innovators.

As Stakeholders

A stakeholder analysis identifying key stakeholders internally and externally, were made in phaseone. All the stakeholders have a major interest in the concept being innovated, but not all of them are direct users. The primary stakeholders were – besides the lead users – user SMEs and accounting firms, and indirect users such as civil servants working with law, processes or IT in and outside the Ministry. The stakeholders were involved through meetings with the research group and facilitated co-creation processes through all phases of the lead user project (Fig. **4**).

As Knowledge Keepers

The research group grounded themselves in the field as suggested in the Handbook by reading about bookkeeping to find more relevant literature and people to interview. They interviewed company owners, bookkeepers and experts in the target markets (finance, accounting, and bookkeeping) and analogue markets (medicine, health, insurance, and traffic) to identify user needs and lead users.

Identifying trends and user needs is a very important part of a lead user project. Trends are what are starting to happen or emerging in the market and user needs are problems with existing products and what is talked about and searched for.

The research group found users who had innovated systems to accomplish the tasks as easily as possible and found a variety of non-tech solutions as pens in different colours depending on VAT rates or four coffee cans depending on who drinks the coffee (important for applying the correct the VAT rate). The target group for the lead user innovation was then defined in phase two by using the personas method and six personas were identified as the potential target group for the lead user innovation.

Based on an analysis of mega-trends in phase two the group looked for experts in different fields that might be helpful in identifying trends and user needs. They found experts:

- In other countries that might have a simple solution *e.g.* Sweden with one standard plan for accounting or tax authorities' with knowledge on uses of technology *e.g.* UK (payment), Mexico and Brazil (upload of invoices).
- On regulation *e.g.* which errors happen and why errors happen.
- At the forefront of quality-management systems.
- In network economies.
- On compliance in other fields *e.g.* health-care.
- On integrated solutions, intuitive solutions, mobile apps, level 3 data, and e-invoice.
- In linguistics about the importance vocabulary in the target market.
- On learning individually while doing a task.
- On motivation, commitment, and knowledge sharing.
- On use of micro-time and gamification.

The experts were interviewed and the purpose of interviewing was to obtain knowledge about the field, the trends and user needs. The interviews and analysis of data resulted in the identification of five trends and user needs to be explored in phase three:

- Motivation – the concept had to motivate the use of it.
- Confidence – the concept had to make the users confident while using it.
- Free of charge – the concept had to be free or cheap.
- Learning by doing – the concept had to ensure increasing competencies.

- Automation – the concept had to be integrated with other business processes.

As Lead User Innovators

The lead users were expected to (have) innovate(d) a useful concept that the Ministry could copy or refine.

The lead users in phase three were found by pyramiding (von Hippel, 2009). "Pyramiding is a search process based upon the idea that people having a strong interest in a given attribute or quality, for example a particular type of expertise, will tend to know of people who know more about and/or have more of that attribute than they themselves do" (von Hippel *et al.* 1999). Pyramiding turned out to be useful to identify people with higher knowledge levels of a given attribute in a quite simple way. The research group asked the people they interviewed to identify one or more others who knew more about of the sought-after attribute. They then asked the same question to the next interviewee and continued the process until individuals with the desired high levels of the attribute had been identified.

Fourteen lead users were identified – all at the top of the pyramid. Not all of them were willing to identify themselves as experts but at the same time admitted that they could not think of anyone, who knew more than they did on the given trends or user needs. The 14 identified lead users represented the five trends and some of them represented more than one trend, and some were also identified as SME lead users.

How Was the User Involvement Organized and for What Purpose?

Stakeholder Nursing

Often in public innovation processes there are many stakeholders and there is a need for the research group to nurse them by engaging them to ensure their ownership of the innovation and thereby increase the possibility for innovation to happen. In the lead user project the stakeholders have been involved in all five phases – also in changing the regulation, processes and IT, and have been positive and willing to co-create, facilitated by the research group.

The lead users continued to be part of the process in phase five – some being informed about the progress, others more actively as co-creators (target market participants), and others have continued to innovate different parts of the concept for their own business purposes. The strong relations built between the civil servants and the lead users helped the work with the innovation.

Interviewing the Knowledge Keepers

The purpose of interviewing users was to identify lead users and lead user experts. In the Handbook this is traditionally done by telephone interviews, but instead the research group used the pyramid method (von Hippel *et al.* 2009) and the broadcasting method using the Ministry's profile @skattefar on Twitter and online communities to find the lead users.

The broadcasting method (Eisenberg, 2011) means "seeking lead users by posting to websites, online forums, or discussion groups lead users are likely to visit and asking lead users to identify themselves or their colleagues". Broadcasting has become made possible with the common use of the internet. Finding the lead users are now easier than through the preliminary interviews *via* individual telephone calls as the Handbook describes. Also netnography could have been used to find lead users. Netnography is a combination of use of the web and ethnography. It identifies online communities of interest and compares posts by the most active community members to a set of lead-user characteristics (Belz & Baumbach 2010).

This reduced the time used on finding the lead users. The research group both operated in the target and analogue markets. The research group used semi-structured interviews and research group members, who needed so, were trained in interviewing techniques.

To find the lead users the research group identified and interviewed 15-20 experts in the target market who were bookkeepers, IT developers, accounting experts, audit experts, and foreign tax experts. The research group used already collected knowledge of company owners and entrepreneurs from earlier user centred projects and supplemented it with interviews of 20 users representing the 6 personas.

The group also found and interviewed 10 experts in analogue markets: Doctors treating HIV positive patients (compliance with medicine), gaming experts and experts on regulating traffic in an intelligent (changeable) way.

The interviews resulted in identifying the final 14 lead users.

The Lead User Workshop

The lead user workshop is a core activity in a lead user project because it is here the lead users are together to innovate and the Handbook describes how to plan and facilitate the workshop but with very traditional methods and the research group therefore diverted from this.

The lead users were invited for a 24 hour seminar. The location was chosen to be INSP! which is a citizen driven inspiratory to increase creativity, social inclusion, and entrepreneurship and situated in heart of Roskilde in abandoned old slaughter house school buildings. This location was chosen to encourage radical different ideas, which traditional meeting rooms do not.

The workshop was scheduled to take place from two pm until two pm the next day. The activities and process were carefully planned by the research group using the New Room Method. The New Room Method is based on the artist studio, creative thinking, and Otto Scharmer's U-theory (Scharmer, 2009). The method has been developed by The Ministry and draws on the Ministry's experience having users as participants in the innovation processes through workshops (Owen, 1997; Brown & Isaacs, 2007) or using participatory design (Buur & Mathews, 2008).

The program was divided into sections: knowledge creation, ideation, concept development, and concept presentation (Fig. **5**).

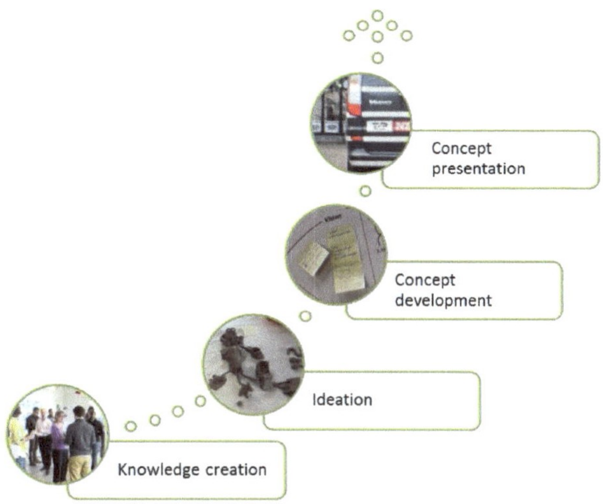

Figure 5: The phases of the workshop (The Danish Ministry of Taxation, 2012).

The workshop participants were welcomed by me as the Director of Innovation and the research group were introduced with specific roles: Listen-Lisa, who would write notes on what she heard; Camera-Carl, who would document the workshop by filming; Tax-Tom, who could be asked about taxes and VAT for SMEs; Practical-Paula, who could and would help with all practical stuff; and the three very skilled and experienced facilitators, who would also have the role as Question-Queens to get as much knowledge out in the open as possible.

The first hours were used to get the participants to know each other and introducing them to the field and the trends identified through the research group's analysis. This was done by storytelling and by creating a market place of knowledge which consisted of five pitches where the participants could:

- Be introduced to the five trends and the research group's analysis.
- Listen to interview sound bites of SMEs talking about bookkeeping and taxes.
- Write down the thoughts and ideas they already had.
- Try bookkeeping and accounting and the digital reporting of VAT and taxes.
- See and read about the bookkeeping personas and SME personas.

The market place was a success and gave the participants an opportunity to present their ideas, which especially was the case for participants from the target market, who needed to get their ideas out of their mind and down on paper (as a brain dump exercise). To the other participants the market place gave an introduction to the field, which was a prerequisite for the rest of the workshop.

After the market place the five trends were examined in a facilitated process and each participant related to the trends by telling their story of how they interacted with these trends on an everyday basis. Then the participants went for a walk in order to reflect on what they had seen, read, and heard, and returned for a tapas snack before concept ideation began.

The research group had decided that the concept should be developed around the following model, which was presented to the participants (Fig. **6**). The top of the figure illustrates the bites of knowledge held by the lead users, which need to be connected into an idea. Then the idea is matured and developed in details in order to obtain the highest possible effects on the bottom lines. The bottom of the figure starts with the matured idea and shows the development into a concept with description of key elements (the idea with and the idea in) and from the user perspective.

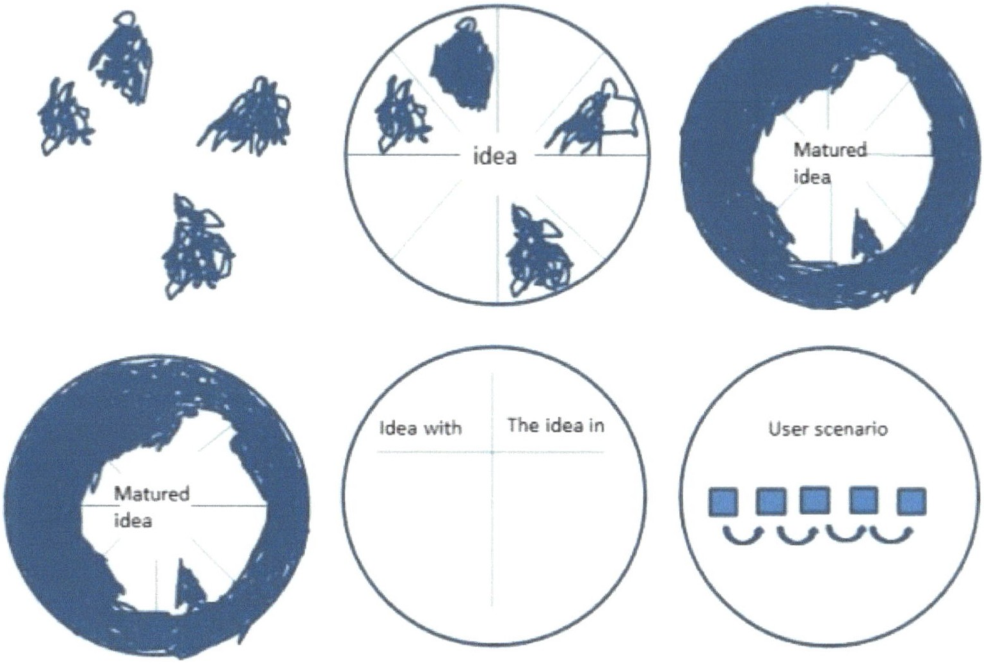

Figure 6: Concept development – from knowledge to idea to concept (The Danish Ministry of Taxation, 2012).

The research group framed a concept based on the trend and user need analysis of the challenge to innovate that meant SMEs would:

- Become more confident.
- Become motivated and better able to do bookkeeping.
- Experience an administrative relief in daily life.
- Find it easier to get the proper deduction.
- Get a good start with taxes/VAT and learn along the way.

- Feel that they are better able to operate their business without high costs.

The participants worked in two facilitated groups having all five trends represented. The experience was that the participants at first did not really need a facilitator, since they were highly capable of ideation processes. Later on facilitation was needed to encourage radical innovation, clarify concept descriptions and pushing the participants to go forward and not fall into too many sub-discussions.

The participants worked on the generated concepts for a couple of hours and afterwards it was time for five course dinner designed around the five trends. During dinner young people from *INSP! Play* entertained by playing the five trends as improvised jazz music.

The next morning the two groups continued to develop the concept in detail and preparing to tell about their concept. A new member (lead user) was introduced to each group to spur energy in concept development and hopefully make it even more radical. The member was integrated in the process and added on to and twisted the developed concepts. The result was a delay in the process making the time constraint more severe.

At the end of the workshop stakeholder representatives from the Ministry of Business Affairs and Growth and the Ministry of Taxation showed up to have a dialogue about the concepts and to ensure their ownership in developing and implementing the concepts in phase five.

What Was the Outcome of the Involvement of Lead Users?

The concepts developed were very different and in line with the five trends and meeting the challenge: How can bookkeeping become easier for SMEs (less than 10 employees) and thereby become more correct and help SMEs to be in compliance?

The first concept, named the Company Control Room, was built on existing regulation using ideas from existing IT platforms and apps but putting it together in a new way to make the business owner more competent. The concept has been handed over to different stakeholders within the ministries, who have used the concept to improve their existing services to SMEs.

The second concept was more radical both in regulation, services and IT. It consisted of two parts, the first part being about bookkeeping and accounting (named The Three Step Solution) and the second part being Getting Started Successfully. It has been further developed together with the lead users in two different projects.

The work with the concept's two parts has continued with (paper) prototyping the concept *The Three Step Solution* together with the stakeholders and lead users to solve any challenges and to be more specific on the necessary changes in IT (public and private) and regulation. The first step of the concept is for starts-ups with very simple business economy. Taxes (standardised) and VAT will both be automatic and based on real time transactions with the purpose of making life easier for company owners and hence making it easier to be in compliance. The second step for the more experienced entrepreneur is a bookkeeping guide and an integration of the company's bank account, accounting (bookkeeping) system and tax/VAT payments. The third step is for the skilled and experienced company owner, who can benefit from an integrated system to reduce the administrative burdens.

The first year after the workshop has been concentrated around prototyping the first step. The time span indicates that radical innovation in the public sector takes time because of the many stakeholders and the complexity of the bottom lines.

Although the concept is not fully developed yet it is expected to have positive effects on the bottom lines with an increase in service without using more resources and a high possibility of being in compliance and understanding the rules.

The concept of *Getting Started Successfully* has also been prototyped not on paper, but in real life in the autumn of 2012. It turned out there was a lack of information from the central government responsible for regulation and digitalization to the local municipal government, who has the direct contact with start-ups. Therefore the concept was co-created and prototyped together with three different local governments. New start-ups within the local government area were contacted to ensure they are registered correctly and know what to do in order to be in compliance. Some of it was done by the use of existing local information meetings or contact by phone. Others were done by creating new local services to start-ups by facilitating collaborative learning processes B2B rather than just presenting (more or less) relevant government information. Start-ups were invited to a series of meetings, where networking and knowledge from the ministries, local government, non-government organizations and experienced business owners were available. Focus was to create a learning space and to get the local community to support the start-ups. The prototyping had the starting point in the lead user developed concept but allowed for local variation depending on types of start-ups, the entrepreneurs, and their needs.

All three local governments have changed the way the introduce start-ups to become successful SMEs and the concept has also changed the collaboration between the ministries and the local governments.

This concept's effect on the bottom lines was positive with an increase in service without using more resources; that start-ups get a better introduction and therefore has a better chance of being compliant; and on the democratic bottom line – one of the developed concepts was highly based on collaboration with SMEs.

Reflections on the Involvement of Users in the Lead User Method

In a lead user project users are involved differently in the five phases. In phase one they are problem holders having needs that the market does not fulfil, which *e.g.* brings them in incompliance. In phase two and three, the users deliver knowledge about their needs and their solutions. In phase four and five they are innovators. Some of the users are involved in all five phases.

In the public sector, a lead user project is initiated by a problem or a challenge *e.g.* with lack of compliance. The users are identified as problem holders or having a need (forced by the authorities) that has to be solved and this project shows that even in the tax field there are lead users. Since, a lead user project is very time consuming the challenge to be solved must be complex: a wicked problem.

The research group was several times tempted to start developing concrete solutions by themselves or together with the lead users. It is always a temptation to act and that is why the Ministry has developed the innovation process model (Fig. **2**) that requires focusing on the problem and learning about the users before acting. Staying in the search phase in the lead user project and thinking divergently at times became an almost physical pain for civil servants. Since, the lead users' solutions found in the first phases only partly met the given challenge and because all the key requirements were not completely clear the lead user project continued.

In phase three, the research group challenged the Handbook's way of finding the lead users and since the Ministry is much digitalized and uses social media, it was decided to use social media instead of telephone interviews only. Already established profiles on social media and a profound understanding of social media helped the research group.

In phase four, the facilitation challenges could have been to get the lead users to participate in the workshop. The Handbook mentions that it is probably necessary to pay the lead users to do so. This was not the Ministry's experience, since all the identified lead user participated for free. The lead users said that the time given was to benefit the businesses (*not* the Ministry) and they wanted to make it easier and better for the businesses. They were also intrigued about the lead user approach and the fact of sharing their expert knowledge with other experts and developing concepts to be used to something most of them did not know much about – bookkeeping. Finally, they were taken by surprise that the Ministry invited to this kind of event and that aroused their curiosity and willingness to participate. No one asked about IP rights but since the Handbook highlights this as a potential problem, the research group decided to state very clearly that all knowledge shared and created as well as the concepts would be public.

In phase five, the challenges were among the stakeholders. It came to a competition between the civil servants concerning which minister should be credited for the innovation. This was due to change of management in the Ministry and their ambition to successfully serve their minister and their lack of positive personal relations. The research group was ordered by the new director not to involve the other ministries any longer or tell them about progress of the concept. This destroyed the collaboration between the ministries and the Ministry closed the innovation process and continued to work bilaterally with chosen stakeholders *e.g.* lead users. It became very obvious that power play and positive personal relations are very important for the possibilities for collaborative innovation.

DISCUSSION

The Ministry wanted to examine whether lead users could contribute to public innovation on complex problems such as bookkeeping and compliance for SMEs. To conclude on this, positive effects on the bottom lines need to be realized.

In the challenge, both the service bottom line (bookkeeping becoming easier) and the policy bottom line (being in compliance) are highlighted but the effect on the administrative and democratic bottom line also has to be neutral or positive.

The Three-Step-Solution will be cheaper to administrate for the Ministry as well as the SMEs and therefore have a positive effect on the administrative bottom line. It will provide better services for the SMEs by digitalisation and automation of the bookkeeping and tax/VAT processes and increase compliance because fewer mistakes are made both by simpler regulation but also the automation. Hence, it has a positive effect on the service and policy bottom line.

The democratic bottom line is about due process, legitimacy and actively involving the users (Langergaard & Carstensen, 2014). The effect on the democratic bottom line is both positive and negative. The Three-Step-Solution will empower the SMEs to do the bookkeeping and thereby increase the due process and the legitimacy, but the high degree of automation can decrease the awareness of how VAT and taxes are calculated and then make the SMEs less competent concerning the regulation. One of the lead users the research group found in phase one has together with the Ministry prototyped the bookkeeping guide and the prototype will be integrated in the step two. To ensure a positive effect on the democratic bottom line this guide needs to explain the regulation as well as guiding the SMEs to use the correct rules.

The third element on the democratic bottom line is about how the users are actively involved. In the lead user approach lead users develop innovations long before commercial products are available on the market (von Hippel, 2005). This means a positive effect on the democratic bottom line, if the Ministry copy or refine the lead user innovation. Especially when it is done together with the lead users as is the case with the bookkeeping guide innovated by the SMEs having the problem.

In the lead user workshop, the SMEs having the problem with bookkeeping was not the majority and there was not a single lead user made concept to refine but different lead user concepts presented in the marketplace. Most of the participants were lead users in the trends and user needs. The effect on the democratic bottom line can be different depending on whether it is enough to actively involve citizens (people not hired by the Ministry or other authority *e.g.* lead users in trends) or if it is necessary to actively involve the lead users having the actual problem (the SMEs) in solving it. In the Ministry's project the effect is positive either way.

Even though the Ministry has not launched the Three-Step-Concept yet the lead user approach can without doubt be used successfully in the public sector. It is a meaningful approach to enhancing collaborative (radical) innovation in the public sector. The Ministry has gained the following insights with the lead user approach:

- Do not be tempted to act too early: The first interesting ideas are not the (best) lead user ideas.
- Do not abort the lead user approach to work on your own – then you will only make incremental innovation.
- Do not worry: you will not be empty handed at the end of the process.
- Involve stakeholders early-it increases ownership and improve relations.
- The research group's competencies, knowledge, and ability to abstract and divergent thinking are extremely important – and the group might change during the phases.
- Get the management to accept that you cannot make a traditional business case at the beginning of the lead user project because you do not know what you will end up with.
- Stay in touch with the management during the progress of the project.
- Relations and interviewing are crucial skills-nurse the stakeholders and the lead users.
- Use the web! It is a gift for lead user studies.

The lead user approach has to be clarified and developed further, since the goal of the lead user process is quite different in a public organization compared to a private company, thus the concept of lead user must be adapted to the particular context of the public sector (Bason, 2010).

Difference Between Private and Public Sector Lead User Innovation

The research group refrained from constructing preliminary concepts as described in the Handbook because it was not a given that it would or should end with a product or service the Ministry should produce, supply or sell. Here the difference between using the lead user approach in the private and public sector became obvious.

In the private sector, the company wishes to develop a concept which they can produce, sell and be in complete control of. In the public sector, the developed concept has to have certain effects but the public sector is not in it for the possible profit gain and business opportunity.

The complexity of the public sector's bottom lines also makes a difference in constructing preliminary concepts. None of the SMEs' lead user concepts embedded all of the wanted effects. Most of them were about making it easier and coping with the complexity of the rules. A lot of them were not digital but very individual based solutions (*e.g.* colour pencils, yellow notes). So where the lead user approach in the private sector means finding a lead user with a prototype that can form the base for developing an innovative and commercially successful product, the lead user approach in the public sector is more about finding lead users with prototypes that can be combined with the Ministry's needs as an authority (*e.g.* due process, legitimacy, control) and satisfy the complexity of the bottom lines.

Also it seemed contradictory to turn a lead user innovation project into expert-driven or user centred innovation (Fig. **1**) by constructing preliminary concepts.

The Needed Development of the Lead User Approach

The needed development of the lead user approach as described in the Handbook is:

- In phase two, considerations should be made about who the lead users in a public sector context are – since it is difficult to find lead users, who embed the whole complexity of the public sector bottom lines in their prototypes.
- In phase three, the Ministry's experts should not make concepts to be worked on by lead users (which would be expert innovation based on user input or user centred innovation in Fig. **1**) but *only* specify the framework the lead users should work within at the workshop. The framework has to contain the lead user solutions found in the search process (even though the solutions only address some of the bottom lines). This would give a much richer collaboration between the lead user and the civil servants.
- In phase four, the focus should be open innovation – not closed innovation, when lead users have shared their knowledge (after the

workshop). In the public sector knowledge is owned by the public and it does not make sense to try to close the innovation process.

- The focus and challenges around IP are different as they are not as important in the public organisation, since whatever created normally belongs to the public and not to the individual.

- In the public sector, the value of the lead user innovation is not only measured on the economic bottom line. The lead user approach will always make services better for the citizens. The administrative and policy bottom line can be met by the correct framing of the lead user workshop. The democracy bottom line is a bit more difficult to conclude on since the lead users who are actively involved not necessary are the citizens with the need or problem and the lead users might not be concerned about due process or the legitimacy of the authority (Langergaard & Carstensen, 2014).

In general, the Handbook is outdated or at best very conventional when it comes to methods of engaging and involving users and the use of the web to find lead users and there is a need to find ways to reduce the cost and time span of a lead user study (Ebel, Bretschneider & Laimeister, 2013).

The lead user approach seems at first sight time-consuming (expensive). The Ministry has used around 47.000 euros (salaries) and 6.500 euros (transport, hotel, food) on the lead user project (the total amount of expenses in the four phases). To compare the expenses the Ministry has documented the cost of similar project aiming for radical innovation to increase the compliance of SMEs, which was started January 2012. This project was carried out solely by the Ministry's civil servants in a traditional way. Their costs for workshops have been around 47.000 euros (salaries) and 30.000 euros (hotel, transport and food). The Ministry has not recorded the project's salary cost for the work done between workshops.

The output of the two projects can also be compared since they tried to meet the same challenge. The proposals of the civil servant group were well-known ideas from the past: to increase the control of businesses, increase punishments for violating regulation and re-introducing the business license – like a driving license.

The lead users came up with radical innovation, which the civil servants did not. Lead users often do so (Agger & Lund, 2011); although the Ministry's experience with the lead user workshop was that they needed to push the lead users to be radical (they had a tendency to limit themselves and not challenging *e.g.* the regulation). Since the lead user approach takes quite some time it should primarily be used in the public sector on complex and wicked problems, where solutions are not easily found. When radical innovation is needed the lead user approach is strongly recommended.

The lead user approach with the all the questions it raises can when applied in the public sector give us important insights about collaborative innovation. There is a power relation between the public sector and the lead users – and the power shifts from the civil servants to the citizens, when the lead user approach is applied. It is necessary to acknowledge that and to find ways to handle it continuously through the innovation process. There is also a power relation between public authorities which can hinder the implementation of the lead user innovation and which need to be handled. Strong personal relations (*e.g.* between civil servants) and positive relations between lead users and civil servants turn out to be very important and spur the collaborative innovation.

CONCLUSION

The aim of this chapter has been to examine how the lead user approach successfully can be applied in the public sector and how it can contribute to our understanding of collaborative innovation in the public sector.

Using a lead user approach project about bookkeeping from the Danish Ministry of Taxation it has been shown that the lead user approach as described in the Handbook can be used in the public sector and that this collaborative innovation approach increases the possibility for radical innovation. However, adjusting the lead user approach to the public sector is needed. Firstly, by adding on a fifth phase to the existing lead user approach to be sure innovation happens in a collaborative way. Secondly by expanding the bottom line to the complexity in the public sector and thirdly by updating the methods used to engage lead users.

The project shows that collaborative innovation needs to handle the power relation between authorities, and between authority and the lead users. Relation building and strong personal relations can spur collaborative innovation, and the lack of them risk hindering innovation.

The project also shows that public collaborative innovation can have a weakness internationally at least in the lead user approach. In the case the Ministry needed lead users to understand the Nordic Welfare Model with the high tax level and the high degree of digitalization and that limited the lead user search. If the innovators do not understand the context due to cultural differences international collaborative innovation becomes difficult.

ACKNOWLEDGEMENTS

Declared None.

CONFLICT OF INTEREST

The authors confirms that this chapter contents have no conflict of interest.

REFERENCES

Agger, A. & Lund, D. H. (2011). Borgere og brugere i samarbejdsdrevne innovationsprocesser. In Sørensen E. & Torfing, J. (eds.) *Samarbejdsdrevet innovation i den offentlige sektor*, (pp. 177-194). Copenhagen: Jurist og økonomforbundets Forlag

Bason, C. (2007). *Velfærdsinnovation*, Copenhagen: Børsens Forlag.

Bason, C. m.fl. (2009). *Sæt borgeren i spil. Sådan involverer du borgere og virksomheder i offentlig innovation*. Copenhagen: Gyldendal Public.

Bason, C. (2010). *Leading Public Sector Innovation: Co-creating for a Better Society*, Bristol: Policy Press.

Belz, F-M., & Baumbach, W. (2010). Netnography as a method of lead user identification. In *Creativity and Innovation Management*, 19:3, 304–313.

Bessant, J. (2005). Enabling continuous and discontinuous innovation: Learning from the private sector. In *Public Money & Management*, 25:1, 35-42.

Brown, J. & Isaacs, D. (2005). *The World Café*. San Francisco: Berrett-Koehler Publ., Inc.

Buur, J. & Matthews, B. (2008). Participatory innovation. In *Int. Journal of Innovation Management*, 12:3, 255-275.

Carstensen, H. V. (2010). Skatteministeriet – et innokrati [The Ministry of Taxation: An innocrati]. In *Administrativ Debat*, 2, 16-19.

Carstensen, H.V. (2013). Effektmåling og evaluering af innovation i SKAT. In *Økonomistyring & Informatik* – 28. årgang 2012/2013 nr. 5.

Carstensen, H.V. & Dahl, S. (2013). Case study: Strengthening the role of the users. In Augsdörfer, P., Bessant, J., and Mosslein, K. *Discontinuous Innovation (Series on Technology Management)*.

Chesbourgh, H. (2006). *Open Innovation: A new paradigm for understanding Industrial Innovation*, Oxford.

Churchill, J. *et al.* (2009). T*he Lead user handbook. A practical guide for lead user project teams*. http://web.mit.edu/evhippel/www/Lead%20User%20Project%20Handbook%20(Full%20Version).pdf

Darsø, L. (2001). *Innovation in the Making*. Frederiksberg: Samfundslitteratur.

Eisenberg, I. (2011). *Lead-user research for breakthrough innovation*. In *Reseach-Technology Management* 54:1, 50-58. http://www.iriweb.org/Public_Site/RTM/Volume_54_Year_2011/Jan-Feb2011/Lead-User_Research_for_Breakthrough_Innovation.aspx

Ebel, P., Bretschneider, U. & Laimeister, J. M. (2013). *The lead user Method for SME. A Guidebook for Practioners and Facilitators*. http://leaduserhandbook.eu/handbook.pdf

Gjerde, S. (2006). *Lytning på forskellige niveauer. In Coaching – hvad, hvorfor, hvordan,* (pp. 124-133). Frederiksberg: Samfundslitteratur.

Hastrup, K., Rubow, C. & Tjørnhøj-Thomsen, T. (2011). *Kulturanalyse. Kort fortal*t. Frederiksberg: Samfundslitteratur.

Kvale, S. (2003). *InterView. En introduktion til det kvalitative forskningsinterview*. Copenhagen: Hans Reitzels Forlag.

Langergaard, L. & Carstensen, H.V. (2014). Democracy innovation and public authorities: Learning from the Danish Ministry of Taxation. In *The Innovation Journal, Special issue on Democracy*, vol. 19:1.

Owen, H. (1997). *Open Space Technology: A user Guide.* San Francisco: Berrett-Koehler Publ., Inc.

Prahalad & Hamel (1990). *The core competences of the Corporation*, HBR.

Savoia, A. (2011). *Pretotype it.* http://www.albertosavoia.com/

Scharmer, O. (2009). *U Theory.* San Francisco: Berrett-Koehler Publ., Inc.

Skatteministeriet, 2010. *Innovationspotentialeanalyse* (working paper).

Sørensen, E. & Torfing, J. (2011). *Samarbejdsdreven innovation i den offentlige sektor.* In E. Sørensen & J. Torfing (eds.) Samarbejdsdrevet innovation, chapter 1. Copenhagen: Jurist og økonomforbundets Forlag.

Thaler, R.H. & Sunstein, C.R. (2009). *Nudge.* London: Penguin Books.

von Hippel, E., Thomke, S., & Sonnack, M. (1999). *Creating Breakthroughs at 3M. In Harvard Business Review*, 77:5, 47-57.

von Hippel, E. (2005). *Democratizing Innovation*, Cambridge, MA: MIT Press (April).

von Hippel, E., Franke, N. & Prügl, R. (2009). Pyramiding: Efficient identification of rare subjects. In *Research Policy*, 38, 1397-1406.

von Hippel, E. (2010). The role of lead users in innovation. In B. H. Halland & N. Rosenberg (eds.) *Handbook of the Economics of Innovation*, Vol. I., (pp. 411-28), Burlington: Academic Press.

CHAPTER 11

Public Innovation, Civic Participation and the Third Sector – A Psychosocial Perspective

Lynn Froggett*

University of Central Lancashire, UK

Abstract: Third sector organisations (TSO's) increasingly provide alternatives to public services, manage community ownership of local assets, and offer relational models of production and exchange. Many TSO's have relatively flat structures, valorise peer relations and are seen as a democratic alternative to local state bureaucracies. This chapter draws on two empirical case studies to argue that a psychosocial understanding of lateral peer relations is essential if displacement anxiety and rivalry are to be avoided and conflict used as productive feedback for organisational development. Taking the UK as an example, and a context where the functions of local authorities have been sufficiently curtailed, it concludes that TSO's may still need the vertically organised mediating functions of the local state if they are to carry out their roles effectively.

Keywords: Third sector Organisations, psychosocial perspective, conflict, vertical leadership, democratic participation.

Third sector organisations are increasingly seen as important partners for public authorities in innovating, producing and delivering public services. These partnerships are advocated by opposing political tendencies, reflecting a neo-liberal assumption that the state is incapable of innovation and a neo-communitarian assumption that the Third Sector is a vital guarantor of community identity and democracy. Increasingly collaborative arrangements between Local Authorities and Third Sector Organiations (TSO's) are regarded as a form of co-production (Pestoff *et al.* 2014, Hulgård *et al.* (forthcoming)), implying close, often complex, and above all harmonious working relationships. Furthermore, these arrangements are required to deliver *relational goods* which have been recognised as economically vital in the not-for-profit sector (Mosca *et al*, 2007). Yet psychosocial dimensions of organisations and communities have been overlooked in research on TSO's. There has as yet been little attempt to analyse the relational dynamics between social enterprises and the communities in which

***Corresponding author Lynn Froggett:** University of Central Lancashire (UCLAN), UK and University of Stavanger, Norway; E-mail: Lfroggett@uclan.ac.uk

Annika Agger, Bodil Damgaard, Andreas Hagedorn Krogh and Eva Sørensen (Eds.)

they are embedded, or to foreground the voices of beneficiaries (Curtis 2008). Yet collaborative ethos, participatory methods and democratic decision-making are often emphasised and interpersonal relations and goodwill are of vital importance in enabling agencies oriented to community-level innovation to function effectively. Surprisingly, there have been few studies of the tensions that can afflict such organisations. They are often idealised as conflict-free entities, living in harmony with their environments while pursuing a co-operative social mission and economic sustainability.

This chapter is a development of a paper given jointly with Linda Andersen at the EMES conference hosted by the University of Roskilde in 2010 (Andersen & Froggett 2010). The thinking behind it is derived from a shared interest in developing psychosocial and psychosocietal approaches to third sector research. The examples used here are taken from the UK. However, they illustrate the relational and leadership problems that arise for community-based TSO's within a European context, especially where they are seen as cost-effective replacements for public services provided by local authorities, and as a democratic alternative to the local state. In Europe, the innovatory potential of social enterprises in the public sphere has been seen as intrinsically related to their relatively flat structures, reduced internal bureaucracy, closeness to the communities in which they are located, and the egalitarian nature of their collegial relations, united around a common social mission.

This chapter develops a psychosocial analysis of the conflicts that can afflict such TSO's, illustrated by case vignettes taken from empirical studies conducted by the author. It argues that the current context in which European TSO's operate, in the wake of the 2008 financial crisis, creates particular tensions between the hierarchical (vertical) leadership needed for effective decision-making, and the internal democratic (lateral) peer relations which carry their democratic and community-oriented remit. It is often assumed that as far as social enterprises are concerned, creativity and vigour depends on their being freed from the shackles of local government. However, the chapter concludes that while their position within the third sector confers a certain room for manoeuvre as social businesses, they can also become mired in problems of local democracy and community politics, and in this respect they do not necessarily have an advantage over elected local representatives. Indeed Local Government may yet have an important role in maintaining an environment in which public innovation can flourish.

ORGANISATIONAL AFFECT AND BEHAVIOUR

Rather than taking a reductively psychological or sociological perspective, this chapter departs from psychosocial theory applied to the public realm (Hoggett 2000, Froggett 2002, Stenner *et al.* 2008) that regards personal desires and anxieties, interpersonal relations, organisational structures and cultures, and societal drivers as mutually constitutive. Hence, mind-sets and behaviours are seen as being produced, but not wholly determined, within a particular institutional and socio-political context (see Froggett & Chamberlayne 2004 for an extended case study).

Psychosocial Studies are a strongly emergent but relatively recent approach in the UK,[1] with cognate areas of activity in Germany and Scandinavia.[2] Many psychosocial researchers who have studied organisations have drawn on an Object Relations theory base, rather than on organisational psychology.[3] A few have integrated Lacanian approaches (Kenny 2010, Fotaki 2010) or other psychoanalytic perspectives (Gabriel 1999; Frosh, 2010, Froggett 2014). In object relations theory human subjects are seen as agents who interact with their environment by internalising the relations and objects which constitute it. They then modify and reproduce those relations in accordance with their own anxiety, desire, creativity and values. In this perspective, the dynamic between actors and their organisations is also understood systemically so that individuals, cultures and structures are always in interaction, and often in tension (Fotaki & Kenny 2014, Froggett 2014).[4] Individual behaviours are influenced, but not determined, by beliefs and assumptions related to the socio-cultural context, the social relations of the organisation, and the field in which it is located, as well as life historical experience and personal dispositions. The relational dynamics of third sector organisations can thus be explored using a psychosocial micro/meso/macro framework that will be explained further below. The issues discussed are illustrated with vignettes from two empirical studies carried out by the author, one of them an in-depth study of a flagship social enterprise which has been through various phases of development (Froggett *et al.* 2005), and the other, a small case study of a Local Authority's attempts to transfer publicly owned assets to a community association (Froggett 2014).

---

[1] http://www.psychosocial-studies-association.org

[2] The International Research Group for Psychosocietal Analysis is a forum for researchers in cross-national dialogue and collaboration in this area http://internationalresearchgroupforpsychosocietalanalysis.com

[3] http://www.tavinstitute.org

[4] See also the Journal of organizational and Social Studies for a selection of articles for a selection of articles with a psychosocial approach

In earlier work (Froggett 2002), I provided a theoretical model for psychosocial analysis in a policy and organisational context. Four different dimensions of organisational functioning can be depicted as concentric circles *nested* within each other as in Fig. **1** above. The model is thoroughly relational and draws on

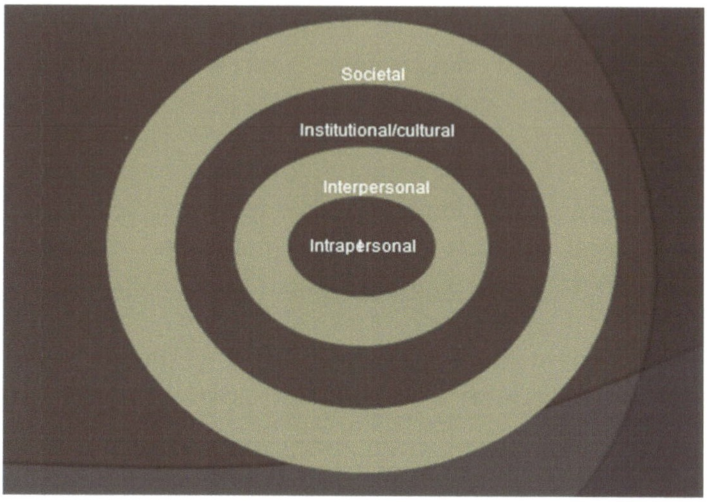

Figure 1: A psychosocial Model: Interlinked dimensions of analysis.

Object Relations Theory to explain how individuals internalise a particular institutional and societal order. This influences how they feel, think and interact with other. Both individuals and organisations exist within a societal framework (political, social, economic) which they either reflect or resist. Sometimes, given the conflicted and irrational propensities of human beings, they do both at the same time. The key point - and this is often ignored - is that affect runs through the whole system, including the societal (macro-level policy making, for example). If we consider by way of illustration a Local Authority Department – there is clearly an interpersonal affective *ecology* in which individual relationships between members of staff and public can be relatively harmonious or discordant. These relationships are likely to be affected by the organisational culture which may remain solidary, and united by a sense of public service, or beleaguered and fractious as purpose is undermined by dwindling resources, job insecurity and a loss of public confidence. These alternative scenarios are typified as much by an *affective climate* that pervades the organisation, as they are by emotions felt by individuals, modes of behaviour and expectations regarding cooperation or competition. They will of course be influenced by wider socio-political discourses which determine whether staff see themselves as serving the public as clients, or customers, or people they care for.

Each of these positions in relation to the public imply a different mind-set and require a different set of organisational supports and emotional resources in order to carry out the required roles. Much has been written - for example in studies of emotional labour (Hochschild 1983) about the potential for dissonance between and within workplace roles and the toll this takes on staff. However, the emotional climate within which people and organisations operate is also re-produced by public states of mind or flows of affect that have varied historically (Froggett 2002). For example, a national *mood* can be reparative, as in the post-war period of welfare state construction where local authorities were generally expected to embody and administer a solidary sense of social responsibility. It can also be divisive, as in the neo-liberal settlements which have followed across Europe and beyond, favouring attacks on the workless and *workshy*. The coalition government in office in the UK at the time of writing has, in its efforts to reduce support for the unemployed, sustained a polemic against the so-called *shirker* scapegoat who lives off welfare and the generosity of the taxpayer. Discourse is not emotionally neutral - if impelled by divisive and blaming impulses it shapes institutional responses that reinforce mistrust and righteous indignation among front-line staff infecting them with suspicion that recipients of their *service* are seeking *something for nothing*.

Government rhetoric in the UK has positioned Third Sector Organisations on the side of the angels for over two decades as political parties have sought alternatives to state and market led provision for the needs of communities. There have been dramatic reductions in the scale of local government services and an expectation that public authorities will engage in partnership with the private and third sectors to provide community services. TSO's are increasingly expected to take on cultural, civic and care functions. They must also compensate for the de facto disenfranchisement of communities as the remit of elected local authorities reduces. TSO's are not only required to address a *democratic* deficit by encouraging direct participation in decision-making, they have been accorded *moral* role of giving voice to a diversity of interests within place-based communities. It is often assumed that where they are rooted in localities they will be more responsive to a full range of local needs than either private or public sectors. At the same time they are thought to be immune from capture by the professional interests that can influence decision making in local government bureaucracies.

The specific political context of these ambitions for the third sector in the UK is a *neo-communitarian* (Fyfe 2005) tendency that finds expression in various forms across the political spectrum. Neo-communitarianism seeks to strengthen community based organisations and solutions to social problems. It appeared as one among several competing political strands in the guise of *The Third Way* (Etzioni

1997, Giddens 1998) when the Labour Government led by Tony Blair was elected in 1997. It then informed a policy agenda in which local government was encouraged to *partner*, social enterprises and voluntary organisations. With the election of the Conservative-led coalition government in 2010, it appeared in the guise of the *Big Society* (Norman 2010, Corbett & Walker 2013), an aspirational concept which caused head-scratching in policy circles and failed to ignite public enthusiasm for a while, before being quietly dropped from political discourse. Nevertheless an institutional contraction of the local state has remained very much on the agenda, together with a handing over of functions, and indeed public assets, to communities and third sector organisations (Wyler & Blond 2010). Under both Labour Governments and the Conservative-led coalition neo-communitarianism has developed in parallel with neo-liberal inspired policy programmes. Indeed it could be said to have had the effect of providing an *acceptable face* to a society driven by global capitalist competitiveness, with consequent steep rises in social and economic inequality (Wilkinson and Pickett 2009, Picketty 2014) and a general preference for non-state solutions to its amelioration.

Third sector organisations have been beneficiaries of this process insofar as they are seen to be closer to communities, unconstrained by political self-interest or profit motive and better able to focus on *the common good.* Despite these supposed virtues, however, financial resources available to TSO's, especially from local government contracts, have dwindled in the wake of the 2008 global economic crisis. This has forced many into an economistic logic to ensure their own survival, entangling them in a set of contradictions corrosive of their moral and social mission. At the same time it has offered them the opportunity for increased independence from public sector contractors. In terms of the psychosocial model depicted in Fig. **1**, it is easy to see how these contradictions can set up tensions within and between TSO's and communities as members position themselves in relation to conflicting imperatives.

Anecdotally, stories circulate about how fractious community organisations can be, but very little has been written about this. An exception is Milbourne (2009) who writes of how "*the rhetoric of collaboration and partnership suggests something open, equal and democratic*" (2009, 290) whilst struggling with competitive funding regimes and non-negotiable funding targets, more easily accommodated by professionalised and corporatist agencies. Third sector organisations are also subject to competition for funding with one another. Corporate management practices are often seen to give them a competitive edge and raise their credibility with public sector partners on whom they often depend for contracts.

Chapman *et al.* (2010) draw on a research programme in the North East of England which took evidence from a series of policy seminars to look at the weaknesses of inter- and intra- sector relationships – in particular the tensions that arise between public sector officers (PSO's) and what they term Third Sector Champions (TSC's). PSO's reported finding TSC's *troublesome*, *amateurish*, *undiplomatic* and unwilling to adopt professional standards, while TSC's often found PSO's to be overly bound by protocol. Although there was reported recognition among TSC's that the lack of corporate identity meant they often acted as a disparate group: "*we don't even know who we are*", there was also a feeling among them that they needed to take themselves more "*seriously*" if partnership with the public sector was to be viable.

While some TSC's held on to an idealism in which they sought a community of values for the common good - others valued the relative freedom to adopt a combative style both in intra- and cross-sector disputes – "*we unite around common enemies out of pure self-interest*". The authors suggest there is further work to be done to understand why the third sector is so riven with antagonisms that appear to belie its co-operative values. In part, they may be structural – reflecting disparities in power and influence in relation to the public sector. In part, they may reflect community level divisions arising from real differences in culture, ethnicity, class and income. It is possible that the third sector attracts individuals who are innovative, abrasive and ill-suited to co-operation or even to protocol compliance. It may also be that the more *grass-roots* they remain the more prone they are to friction, precisely because of the lack of mediating hierarchical structures which can counterbalance the influence of personalities and take the heat out of personal conflicts. Social Enterprises are often initiated by charismatic individuals with drive and imagination who generate as much friction as they do loyalty (see Froggett *et al.* 2005 for a detailed case analysis). However, the structural positioning and motivations of organisations and individuals still offer only a partial explanation for their collaborative or competitive potentials and the behaviours these generate.

The Third Sector is being asked to deliver economic efficiency, entrepreneurial energy and relational goods (Mosca *et al.* 2007) in the form of community engagement and decision-making, generation of social capital and re-invigorated social bonds. It is in understanding the relational conditions of production of these relational goods that a psychosocial perspective is of value. It aims to explain how individuals, communities, institutions and social policy intersect at any given moment to produce a historically and culturally specific configuration of fantasy, anxiety, desire and conflict which can make relationships within and between third sector community based organisations and public authorities very fraught. The psychosocial analysis offered here takes seriously the more primitive fantasies aroused within any overt *community of values*.[5] It recognises that the challenges facing TSO's in communities can be productive in that *lateral* relationships are highly valorised and can give rise to participatory and egalitarian practice. However, TSO's are also obliged by government and funders to enter into partnerships where relationships are structured by *vertical* hierarchies such as local government bureaucracies. The contradictions between vertical and lateral relations go some way to explaining why they can fail to fulfil the expectations surrounding them as key institutions of community solidarity and socially responsible market behaviour. Two vignettes taken from empirical studies conducted by the author serve to illustrate the relational problems that may beset them.

ASSET TRANSFER AND THE COMMUNITY ASSOCIATION

The first example arises from a study of 500 strong elected community associations in a small town in England (Froggett 2014, forthcoming) which was offered the option by the local council of taking over two key assets to run as social enterprises: an independent cinema in the town – much loved by the local population; and the former Town Hall Offices which were undergoing re-development to make them available for community use.

Within a short time, the project became mired in conflict and factionalism and suspicions were aired publicly on the town blog about the motivations of some within the community association along the lines of "*who do they think they represent? Taking over 'our' assets for whose benefit?*" As a result the Council was obliged to abandon plans for the transfer of the cinema to community ownership in favour of a *partnership* where the council retained direct oversight. The management of the town hall redevelopment – equally riven by conflict – passed into the hands of a *professionalised* group (a series of sub-committees run by specialists) nominally under the direction of the Community Association. It nevertheless continued to experience a succession of problems related to operational and strategic decision-making; it failed to complete on time and within budget, and the subsequent process of launching it as a viable business was halting. These difficulties were in part related to tensions between the lay Community Association Directors and the

[5] Andersen (e.g in Andersen and Froggett 2010) has particularly stressed the tendency to idealisation within the third sector itself when they describe their own work. She points out that idealisation operates at both a conscious and unconscious level and that although it generates an overt self-confidence it is always accompanied by an unconscious anxiety that the organisation fails in reality to live up to the perfection it attains in fantasy.

professionals they contracted to undertake the work – in other words it manifested as a conflict between a community-political and a technical-rational logic. As with the cinema, there were ongoing conflicts within the community milieu over who had the authority to speak for whom.

As a social enterprise taking over the Local Authority assets the Community Association benefitted from a wider policy agenda: governmental approval for asset transfer in the context of *localism*. It received preferential treatment for its business plan, with the expectation that it would develop entrepreneurial vigour while reflecting community solidarity. It was hoped that positive affect would then flow in a virtuous circle as optimism and purposefulness was fed back into the system buoyed by the sense that everyone in the organisation was collaborating in the happy *co-productive* realisation of social purpose and economic sustainability;[6] except that it did not. The second diagram (Fig. **2**) depicts the rivalrous and fragmented relational environment observed in the early key phases of the asset transfers. This manifested in an apparent fear of personal *displacement* among people jockeying for position and mistrustful of each other's intentions. The mind-set and emotional atmosphere was conflictual and embattled, prejudicing ability to carry out organisational tasks and manifesting in acrimonious inter-personal rivalries. Fear of fragmentation pervaded the institutional mind-set as the organisation struggled to contain factions and cliques, and found itself in conflict with a Local Authority whose responsibility was to ensure a smooth transfer and good governance, but whose mediating vertical authority was being withdrawn.

Figure 2: Dimensions of Psychosocial conflict, in the absence of mediating vertical structures.

---

[6] Market behaviour is clearly dependent on aggregate emotion, often irrational, but oddly enough, this is generally only acknowledged at a level of systemic abstraction – it rational choice theory it is markets that panic, get depressed or over-heated, rather than the people within them.

At this point in its evolution macro-social neo-communitarian discourses were less salient than the rhetoric and reality of schizmatic neo-liberal ground level effects. In conflicts over power and responsibility between the local state and the third sector, the latter was favoured by government for the ideological reason that *statism* is supposedly bad for social and economic responsibility, and that the operations of Local Authorities needed to be severely restricted.

It is worth highlighting here that the Big Society version of neo-communitarianism that so aggressively disparaged Local Government, at times amounted to a political attack on its very legitimacy. Fundamental questions were being raised about how local democracy was to be configured in the future, on what representative basis, and what role the community sector was to play in its revitalisation. However, the problems experienced in the Community Association appeared to derive at least in part from local unease over that organisation's democratic intent, despite the fact that leaders were elected, all proceedings were published openly on the town web and there were opportunities for direct participation in local public forums. The progressive withdrawal of the Local Authority from the field of public deliberation had left the Community Association and various town factions without any mediating vertical structures of conflict resolution, and without any institutional psychological *containment*[7] which might have moderated personal and collectively held anxieties. The eventual outcome was that the Local Authority had to step back in and forge a new partnership with the community in which it retained a management oversight of the cinema. The re-furbished Town Hall floundered as a business and was under-used as a public resource until it managed to evolve a professional bureaucracy of its own.

THE COMMUNITY CENTRE

The second example is taken from a three year study which has been widely publicised (Froggett *et al.* 2005). It concerns a flagship social enterprise, the Bromley by Bow Centre, in the East End of London. The point of interest for the purposes of this chapter is that in the period in which the study was under way - a mid-stage in the Centre's development - it had succeeded in establishing a relatively harmonious internal environment, but was having to work hard to overcome a history of external friction, both with the Local Authority and with other organisations in the voluntary sector. Moreover, dissenting staff tended to leave very

[7] Containment in a psychosocial theory of organisations refers to the ability of an organizational culture to hold and moderate unconscious anxiety among its members – thus enabling, for example, a tolerance of frustration and a capacity for reflection.

quickly and members who were disruptive of the wished for internal harmony, the youth section in particular, had been encouraged to occupy a semi-detached position in a separate building at some distance from the Centre itself. At the time of the study a strong leadership had emerged which was still protective of the organisation's internal culture but very aware that sustainability would depend on proactive, *listening* conflict resolution. The potentially fraught lateral peer relations within the Centre could then be mediated by the vertical authority of the leadership while conflict with the youth section, and indeed with other personnel ill at ease with the internal work culture, was *exported* to the wider environment.

The Centre in its early life had positioned itself as a flagship *can do* social enterprise which had considerable influence in New Labour Government thinking on the innovative nature of the third sector and the potential for a *compact* between the third sector and local government. Its internal cohesiveness had in part been achieved by defining itself in its formative years in opposition to what it saw as an obstructive local council bureaucracy, obsessed with formal equality mechanisms, at the cost of genuinely responsive approaches to diversity. In this situation the internal culture was characterised by organisational identities in which people found their position in the organisation which they cared for as a place. There was strong internal cooperation between people who used it and contributed to it. Harmonious relations and mutual respect were sustained even between those with diverse cultural backgrounds and interests (for example between Bangladeshi and other migrant users and a local white working class East End population who have historically been suspicious of *foreigners*). There was also excellent collaboration with favoured partners like the local housing trust, and a general sense that the Centre was showing the way in developing a social enterprise model for cohesive and equitable communities.

On the other hand, there was friction with external agencies who did not accord with the Centre's way of doing things and in some of the interviews we conducted people professed themselves maddened by what they saw as familism and favouritism. As has already been pointed out the rebellious youth section had to be re-located elsewhere to maintain internal cohesion and individual staff who did not buy into the Centre's ethos quickly moved on. It would not be realistic, and perhaps not even desirable, to propose a conflict free model for an innovatory social enterprise, the question is how conflict is owned, managed and distributed throughout the organisational system and between the system and the external environment so as to build diplomatic skills and resilience. There is virtue in all parts of the organisation being able to use conflict as a form of feedback to ensure responsive evolution as they negotiate the tensions between themselves and their surroundings (as shown in Fig. **3**). Mature distributed conflict negotiation does not pre-suppose the paternalistic solution whereby the leadership takes on the role of *parental* arbiter within the organisation, or *buffer* against the harsh realities of the external world. An workable model might depicted within the diagram below.

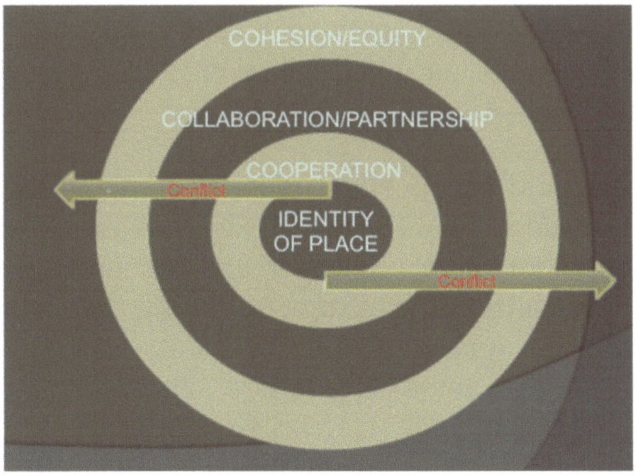

Figure 3: Lateral relations with mediation by vertical authority and distributed conflict management (ideal type model).

CONTRASTING MODELS OF DEMOCRATIC PARTICIPATION

In both the community association led organisations (CAO's) and the Bromley by Bow Centre affective and ideological dispositions to neo-communitarian *versus* neo-liberal solutions appeared to be played out through public consultations. In the CAO's tensions emerged between *community solidarity* and anxieties that some *control-freaks* were simply in it for their own individual advantage. The Bromley by Bow Centre became increasingly unwilling to support formal mechanisms of collective local consultation and decision-making arguing that "*local people don't want to talk like that*" and proposing instead to "*work alongside them*" (Brickell 2000). At stake, though not expressed in these terms, was a tension between the agonistic mode of deliberative democracy (Benhabib 1996), and the communicative democracy advocated by Young (2002). In deliberative democracy conflict is expected and negotiated through a formally constituted participatory public forum that retains some vertical moderation for the exchange of opposing views. In the communicative alternative there is a reliance on the laterally enacted forms of everyday social exchange which recognise the ultimate identity of interest and values of a moral community (Young 2002).

At the most general level we see that the struggles in which these organisations were engaged, especially with the local state, were concerned with equality of participation, voice and access to local goods and services, that are highly relevant to the nature of the (still evolving) relations between the Third Sector and Local Government. They are socio-economically located within policy regimes and use their discursive resources to interpret and articulate policy whilst also relating to communities and networks on the ground who have competing priorities more or less antagonistic to government. They are obliged to negotiate the tensions thus produced without mirroring them internally in such a way as to bring about their own fragmentation.

The report on the Bromley by Bow Centre (Froggett *et al.* 2005) details the ways in which successive phases of leadership struggled with these difficulties. They passed from an *initiatory* phase characterised by high external and internal antagonism under a charismatic leader, to a *reparative* phase under a Director who saw the role as being to mend *broken bridges* with the Local Authority and other agencies, and who laid strong emphasis on lateral communication and decision-making, but found it difficult to resolve conflicts arising from a clash between the imperatives of economic survival and full community participation. Eventually, with a further change of Director, the Centre arrived at a sustainable model of handling internal and external conflict which may well have ensured the survival and growth of the organisation (see Halton 2004 for an elaboration of these leadership tropes). In this version a strongly containing vertical executive was instituted, capable of balancing emotional intelligence, effective delegated structures and business acuity. The Centre evolved this model through a process of trial and error, and *matured* into a vertical-lateral settlement, which moved beyond the initatory phase of charismatic, paternalistic inspirationalism and a middle phase of distributed peer led decision-making. It also generated a strong culture of internal loyalty by developing a organisational memory fit for its collaborative purposes: a creation myth to honour *the founding father* whilst evolving from his iconoclastic and rebellious legacy a style that facilitated community partnerships. Within the organisation this helped to consolidate a sense of attachment to its own tradition whilst maintaining emotional responsiveness towards its weaker and more vulnerable members.

By contrast The Community Association has found it difficult – it may still be too soon at the time of writing (some two years after the opening of the new Town Hall offices) - to develop a coherent and purposeful narrative, or a leadership which has the authority to represent and mediate diverse voices. Instead, it has rather slowly recruited its own professional bureaucrats while the secretariat remains weak and without a well-formed strategy to negotiate the tensions produced from being a community resource while developing as a viable social business. It is still vulnerable to debilitating factionalism and schismatic cliques.

In summary, the innovatory potential of the organisations described here was imperilled for key periods of their development: The Community Association led projects (social enterprises in formation) were riven with internal peer conflicts which jeopardised both their planning and development as viable businesses and their ability to carry out their social role. Within a short space of time it became clear that internal relations between peers needed some sort of vertical bureau-professional mediation. The point about such mediation is that it is psychosocially multi-layered. In the case of Local Authorities it depends on democratic legitimacy, institutional trust (one reason why corruption free public administration is so vital) and psychological containment. The Bromley by Bow Community Centre, on the other hand, appeared for a key phase in its development to maintain lateral internal harmony by extruding disruptive elements and *exporting* friction to the periphery. A strong *vertical* leadership eventually emerged (in this case in the person of a Director with a *mandate* to lead, a high degree of personal trust and the capacity to contain organisational anxiety). This helped to generate equilibrium between lateral peer relations and external partners and a responsive but firmly directive executive.

In order to give an adequate account of these kind of tensions - it has been necessary to trace the connections between individual, institutional and societal relations in order to understand how these are structurally, discursively and affectively constituted in any one organisation. Of particular interest in the cases I have just described is a clarification of the *contradictions* between interlocking dimensions of organisational life. This must include the affective environment as well as how individuals are structurally positioned in particular relations of power and influence in relation to the leadership and membership, and located within the organisational discourses which intersect with their wider external political, cultural and personal interests. These individuals also have an emotional relationship to the organisation and to each other characterised by unconscious fantasy and projection as well as differences in perspective, interest and opinion.

LATERAL RELATIONS AND ORGANISATIONAL ANXIETIES

The dimension of interpersonal solidarity and rivalry is often the least explored in analyses of TSO's and risks being reductively dismissed as *personality conflicts*.

In the paper referred to previously (Andersen & Froggett 2010), we were struck by the fact that in these organisations where the quality of lateral peer relations and peer led decision making was key to their identity, there appeared to be the need for a vertical authority able to mediate conflict or capable of *holding* the tensions it generated. We asked what was the dominant form of anxiety produced by lateral relations and a plausible answer was suggested by work on the paradigmatic lateral relationship – the sibling (Mitchell 2000), where the anxiety is that of displacement – of failing to be the pre-eminent object of parental affection and approval. Displacement anxiety, which may have been unconscious, certainly offers some explanation for the jostling for position and influence observable in the Community Association, as it arguably does in many participatory contexts where the dynamics appear to be especially vulnerable to imposition by powerful personalities. Of course the lateral or sibling relation can also be force for shared enterprise. It can even be a shared attempt to creatively usurp vertical authority as it was in the highly combative, early days of the Bromley by Bow Centre in which members allied in a flamboyant *juvenile* rebellion against the deadeningly measured protocols of the *parental* local state. The opportunity to unite against authority in the initiatory phase of development served to strengthen a self-belief among Centre members that they represented a radically innovative emergent order, and a tendency to dismiss any legitimate role for democratically elected local public bodies.

CONCLUSION

Much research on Third Sector Organisations takes the form of de-contextualised case studies, which are often uncritical *good news* stories, unable to offer a convincing explanation of conflict, or even an acknowledgement of its existence. On the ground, conflict is often assumed to derive from the deficits of individuals, and so no public account of it ever surfaces. TSO's may be particularly vulnerable to tensions which manifest as interpersonal because they lack developed bureaucratic forms of mediation. A psychosocial analysis can offer a non-reductive understanding of conflict in terms of the integration of societal, institutional and personal dimensions of organisational functioning. It can also clarify how these different dimensions interact with each other to favour a collaborative ethos arising from the fact that these organisations are to a degree peer-led and valorise in principle, though not always in practice, lateral peer relations. There is often a lack of acknowledgement of the proper role of vertical leadership in the community sector, since its *democratic* credentials rest on relatively flat internal structures, which allow ground level decision-making.

The empirical material here is UK based, and contextualised in terms of UK Government policy where it is assumed that public innovation at local level will flow from a contraction of local government and the direct transfer of assets and resources to TSO's able to manage them on behalf of communities. In the face of continuing Europe-wide austerity the contraction of Local Government appears to offer an attractive economic solution to the management of public finances. However it may also involve, as in the UK, a programmatic intention to by-pass or reduce the role of democratically elected vertical local government bodies. As a political project *Big Society* lost any initial credibility it might have had, partly because it was hostage to the sharpening inequalities produced by austerity politics, and partly because divesting the Central and Local State of control of public assets has not proved to be a universally popular or conflict free move. It is as yet unclear who will take over the role of mediation between competing community interests, and of ensuring that the most disadvantaged and excluded attain a voice as Local Authorities downsize. An implication of the analysis presented here is that there is a case for recognition and defence of the democratic function of 'vertical' Local Authorities by Third Sector Organisations themselves.

The chapter has argued the case for a psychosocial approach in understanding the relational dimensions of social enterprise and the enduring importance of containing and mediating vertical structures if models of leadership are to be evolved adequate for their increasingly complex civic roles. This is especially pertinent where trust in both market and state institutions to provide for local needs and promote community solidarities is at a low ebb and the third sector is being invoked as an alternative.

ACKNOWLEDGEMENTS

Declared none.

CONFLICT OF INTEREST

The author confirms that this chapter contents have no conflict of interest.

REFERENCES

Andersen, L. & Froggett, L. (2010). *The Psychosocial in Social Enterprise and Social Entrepreneurship.* Unpublished Conference paper, EMES 3rd International Conference, University of Roskilde, Denmark, 2010.

Brickell, P. (2000). *People before structures: engaging communities effectively in regeneration*, London: Demos.

Benhabib, S. (1996). Towards a deliberative model of democratic legitimacy. In S. Benhabib (ed), *Democracy and difference*, Princeton/NJ: Princeton University Press, (pp 67-94).

Chapman, T., Brown, J., Ford, C., & Baxter, B. (2010). Trouble with Champions: local public sector-third sector partnerships and the future prospects for collaborative governance in the UK. In *Policy Studies*, 31:6, 613-630.

Corbett, S. & Walker, A (2013). The big society: Rediscovery of the social or rhetorical fig-leaf for neo-liberalism. In *Critical Social Policy* 33, 451- 470.

Curtis, T (2008). Finding that grit makes a pearl: A critical re-reading of research into social enterprise. In *International Journal of Entrepreneurial Behaviour and Research*, 14:5, 268-275.

Froggett, L. (2002). *Love, Hate and Welfare: psychosocial approaches to policy and practice*, Bristol: Policy Press

Froggett, L. & Chamberlayne, P. (2004). Narratives of Social Enterprise: from biography to practice and policy critique. In *Qualitative Social Work*, 3:1, 61-77.

Froggett, L., Chamberlayne, P., Buckner,S. & Wengraf, T. (2005). *The Bromley by Bow Research and Evaluation Project.* Research Report, Preston: University of Central Lancashire, http://clok.uclan.ac.uk/3386/

Froggett, L. (2014). Community, communitarianism and Displacement anxiety. In M. Fotaki and K. Kenny (eds*), Psychosocial and Organisation Studies: Affect at Work*, London: Palgrave

Etzioni, A. (1997). *The New Golden Rule: Community and Morality in a Democratic Society*. New York: Basic books

Fotaki, M. (2010). Why do public policies fail so often? Exploring health policy making as an imaginary/symbolic construction. In *Organization,* 17:6, 703–720.

Fotaki, M. & Kenny, K. (2014 forthcoming). *Psychosocial and Organisation Studies: Affect at Work*, London: Palgrave

Frosh, S. (2010). *Psychoanalysis Outside the Clinic: Interventions. In Psychosocial Studies*. London: Palgrave.

Fyfe, N. R. (2005). Making space for neo-communitarianism? The third sector, state and civil society in the UK. In *Antipode*, 37:3, 536-557.

Gabriel, Y.(1999). *Organizations in Depth.* London: Sage.

Giddens, A. (1998). *The Third Way*, Cambridge: Polity Press

Halton, W. (2004). By what authority? Psychoanalytical reflections on creativity and change in relation to organisational life. In C. Huffington, D. Armstrong, W.Halton, L. Hoyle & J. Pooley (eds), *Working below the surface: the emotional life of contemporary organisations*, London: Karnac, (pp. 107-122).

Hochschild, A.R. (1983). *The Managed Heart: The Commercialization of Human Feeling.* Berkeley: The University of California Press. Reprinted with new afterword in 2003. Reissued in 2012 with a new preface

Hoggett, P. (2000) *Emotional Life and the Politics of Welfare.* Basingstoke: Macmillan

Hulgård, L., J. Defourny & V. Pestoff (eds) (forthcoming 2014). Hybridity, Innovation and the Third Sector: the co-production of public services. In *Social Enterprise and the Third Sector. Changing European Landscapes in a Comparative Perspective*. London & New York: Routledge.

Kenny, K. (2010). Beyond ourselves: passion and the dark side of identification in an ethical organization. In *Human Relations,* 63:6, 857–873.

Milbourne, L. (2009). Remodelling the Third Sector: Advancing Collaboration or Competition in Community-Based Initiatives? In *Journal of Social Policy*, 38:2, 277-297.

Mitchell, J. (2000). *Mad Men and Medusas*, London: Penguin.

Mosca, M., Musella, M. & Pastore, F. (2007). Relational Goods, monitoring and non-pecuniary compensations in the nonptofit sector: the case of the italian Social service. In *Annals of public and Cooperative economics*, 78:1, 57-8.

Norman, J. (2010). *The Big Society*, Buckingham: Buchingham University Press.

Picketty, T. (2014). *Capital in the Twenty First Century*, Cambridge MA: Belknap Press.

Stenner, P. Barnes, M & Taylor, D. (2008). Psychosocial welfare: contributions to an emerging field. In *Critical Social Policy*, 28:4, 411-414.

Wilkinson, R., & Pickett, K. (2009). *The Spirit Level: Why equality is better for everyone.* London: Penguin.

Wyler, S. & Blond, P. (2010). *Housing, Health and Environment Unit To Buy, To bid, To Build, Community Rights for an Asset Owning Democracy*, London: NESTA/Res Publica http://www.seeewiki.co.uk/~wiki/images/0/0a/ResPublica_-_Buy,_Bid,_Build_(web)_0.pdf accessed October 2013

Young, I. M. (2002). *Inclusion and Democracy*, Oxford: Oxford University Press

CHAPTER 12

Micro-Processes of Collaborative Innovation in Danish Welfare Settings: A Psychosocial Approach to Learning and Performance

Linda Lundgaard Andersen*

Centre for Social Entrepreneurship, Department of Psychology and Educational Studies, Roskilde University, Denmark

Abstract: This chapter explores micro processes of collaborative innovation from a learning perspective. The point of departure for the chapter is my ongoing research with welfare service professionals who display considerable ambivalence towards innovation, feeling both enthusiastic towards it and burdened by it. I start by framing the Danish discourse of public collaborative governance in two empirical fields: site-based management and democracy in the 1990s, and social entrepreneurship and social innovation in the 2000s. I demonstrate how the prevailing discourses offer a number of scripts for action, performance and learning, which can produce important results. However, by analysing learning in collaborative innovation processes from a psychosocial perspective I also demonstrate how identification, ambivalence, idealisation and defence are significant features of the professionals' learning and performance and consequently how contemporary collaborative innovation can lead both to constructive and destructive processes.

Keywords Public innovation, collaborative governance, discourses, learning, micro processes.

LEARNING AS AN AMBIGUOUS AND AMBIVALENT TOOL

Social work, health care, work integration and social enterprises all consider human, professional and organisational development to be core activities and objectives in many different collaborative settings. Learning is, thus, an inextricable part of public welfare services, which aim to support human development, strengthen people's ability to cope and ensure a higher life quality for them. This is, however, a challenging task for a public sector dominated by the New Public Management approach. Research indicates that NPM provides limited

***Corresponding author Linda Lundgaard Andersen:** Center for Social Entrepreneurship and director of the PhD School of Lifelong Learning and Socialpsychology of Everyday Life, Roskilde University, Denmark; Tel: +4526701640; E-mail: lla@ruc.dk

Annika Agger, Bodil Damgaard, Andreas Hagedorn Krogh and Eva Sørensen (Eds.)

space for transformative types of learning, such as those outlined in experiential and collaborative learning theory (Mezirow, 1996; Barckley, Cross & Major 2005), social learning theory (Lave & Wenger 1991; Becker-Schmidt & Knapp, 1987), situated or action learning theory (Dilworth & Willis 2003; Cho & Marshal 2010) as well as more critical approaches like the sociological imagination and critical pedagogy perspectives (Negt, 1975, 1985; Ziehe & Stubenrauch 1996; Ziehe 2001). But learning can be a potent tool for implementing change paving the way for new welfare strategies and societal transformations (Andersen & Dybbroe, 2014; Diochon & Anderson, 2011; Dybbroe & Kamp 2013, Poder, 2009). Research shows that learning can be ambiguous and ambivalent; on the one hand it can transform human lives, social structures and organisations but it can also function as an effective tool in the service of political, professional and societal imperatives. In this chapter, I present two examples of collaborative innovation from the 1990s and 2000s, respectively, with a view to illustrating how public welfare innovation can bring about progressive learning and positive welfare results. However, if we flip the coin we also find demotivation, defensive reactions and ambivalence. We need to deepen our understanding of collaborative innovation and learning. My extensive data, which I will present shortly, suggests that if we do not acknowledge, and compensate for, the strains on staff, we risk that collaborative innovation processes will become counter-productive, thus constraining their potential.

LEARNING IS CHALLENGED IN CONTEMPORARY WELFARE SETTINGS

Everyday work in public welfare services has increasingly put learning and organisational development on the agenda, for a number of historical reasons. Firstly, the replacement of industrial society by the knowledge society has necessitated increasing involvement of personal qualities and competencies in learning and performance in welfare jobs. Secondly, the knowledge society is founded on increasingly differentiated forms of welfare work and welfare knowledge production, organisation and performance, where the emphasis is on enabling independent, problem-oriented employees to develop their skills and qualifications (Salling Olesen 2006). Thirdly, the relationship between professional and client has evolved from a subject-object to a subject-subject relationship, which has intensified the need for professionals – and also clients and citizens - to engage in self-reflection and introspection (Andersen & Dybbroe 2011). Finally, the trend towards learning organisations, the growth of collaborative work formats and the blossoming of theories of reflective management and leadership have led to a growing recognition that public sector services work involves both internal and external interactions and processes.

These developments have been the subject of critical analysis. As I will briefly outline in the following, research into working life, organisational sociology and education has documented that although modern workplaces are characterised by the recognition of feelings, the processes involved in this also exclude, differentiate and discipline: employees constructing an emotional discourse of love and demanding that they invest emotional capital in their jobs (Åkerstrøm Andersen & Born 2001); employees are urged to attend personal development courses, which take place in a setting seemingly devoid of power (Bovbjerg 2010, 2011); developing work places lead to differences in how much employees actually want to develop creating 'A and B' teams (Siig Andersen *et al.* 2001); efficiency, rationalisation and democratisation in welfare work, putting multiple pressures on employees and clients leading to an ambivalent, stressful and (over)emotionalised work culture (Andersen 1999, 2012). The increasing requirements for monitoring and documentation result in work cultures sustained by goal- and efficiency-oriented work tasks results in less emphasis on professional and practically based knowledge, reflection and action; and it also means that *messy*, less flattering, bothersome and irritating problems and work processes become less visible and articulated. From a learning perspective, we also see a paradox concerning, on the one hand, greater interest in workplace- and problem-based learning and collaboration in different formats; and on the other, a learning crisis involving de-qualification, stress, burnout and demotivation (Andersen & Dybbroe 2011). Thus, public employees in welfare services are required to invest their professional and personal knowledge and commitment in their jobs, but at the same time these intensified and subjectified forms of work conceal a darker side.

FRAMING COLLABORATIVE INNOVATION IN GOVERNANCE DISCOURSES

I now turn to framing collaborative innovation in the Danish context, with a specific focus on two empirical fields. The first welfare scenario began in the late 1980s and resulted from the implementation, by the Danish public sector, of the first of a number of modernisation programmes driven by the New Public Management philosophy. All these programmes addressed public service delivery, managerial tasks and objectives and led to a quasi-market in welfare services and the implementation of information technology in various contexts. The objectives were to improve professional service deliveries, to focus on prevention, to decentralise power from the state to the county and local government levels, to move from centralised administrative and financial systems to local financial frameworks and site-based management, and finally to develop a more democratic structure that would engage personnel as well as service recipients (Andersen 1988; Høyrup 1988; Andersen, 2003).

The multitude of goals often gave rise to personal and professional difficulties and frustrations in the institutions in question. Yet this tension was rarely articulated to managers, administration or politicians (Andersen 1999). Research (to which I shall return later in this chapter) has shown that in many cases this state of tension was symbolised by, and transformed into, a diffuse sense of frustration, fatigue, mild burnout, overwork and professional doubts (Andersen 1999). However, this data must be seen in context, and various aspects of the Danish public sector have since evolved, including its governance format (*e.g.* Reff, Sørensen & Sehested, 2011; Hjort & Raa, 2011; Buch & Andersen, 2013; Wihlman, Hoppe, Wihlman & Sandmark, 2014). Nonetheless, my point in this chapter is to document a hitherto understudied perspective, namely how a micro-process perspective on governance and institutional innovation reveals both constructive and destructive processes.

As shown in Table **1**, the first welfare modernisation programme comprised service and governance innovation (Hartley, 2005), institutional in-house collaboration, democracy, and co-creation of local budgets; leading to more *in-house* innovation but only years later did a more inter-organisational, inter-sectoral and open innovation form of practice emerge (Hartley, Sørensen & Torfing, 2013). Related to this, the programme focused on workplace learning and a more qualified professionalism, but also on strengthening a multi-actor learning approach to foster more and better collaboration among employees, managers and users. Another challenge involved better collaboration with local administrations, which were supposed to support the above-mentioned organisational, financial and professional changes, though this proved to be a long, difficult and ambivalent process (Andersen, 1999; 2003).

The second, more recent welfare reform programme focused on social entrepreneurship and innovation, both examples of a new influential discourse in Danish welfare politics. Social entrepreneurship may be defined as follows: when one or more individuals or groups identify an unresolved problem at the societal or individual level, developing innovative services or products with a social and economic value, and manages to involve civil society in the innovation

Table 1: Collaborative governance discourses and practices in Denmark

Collaborative Governance Discourses and Practices in Denmark			
Welfare Scenarios	***Governance***	***Forms of Innovation***	***Learning Arenas***
New Public Management in the 90s: ***Site-based management, efficiency and democracy***	Top-down, government initiated Performance management Decentralisation: autonomy to local managers & committees Local budgeting Quasi-market competition	Service and governance innovation Institutional 'in-house' collaboration: Institutional democracy: user-organised committees & co-creation of local budgets	Workplace learning and increased professionalism Multi-actor collaborative learning Co-creation by staff, management and welfare recipients
Social entrepreneurship and social innovation in the 00s	Bottom-up & multi-actor driven: social entrepreneurs, citizen groups, local communities, civic society politicians Co-production & partnerships Social enterprises and network	Social innovation Collaborative innovation Open innovation Multi-actor collaboration Inter-sectorial and inter-organisational innovation	Blended learning: Action learning Vocational training Participative and network learning Co-creation and empowerment

(Andersen, Bager & Hulgård 2010; Hulgård 2007). Internationally, the concept of social entrepreneurship first emerged around 15-20 years ago, but it came to Denmark somewhat later, around 10 years ago (Defourny & Nyssen 2010; Mair 2010; Hulgård & Andersen, 2009). The early Danish cooperative movements provided a solid foundation for these new social enterprises, just as it had for the Danish self-governing institutions and socio-political experiments that proliferated in the 80s (Andersen, Hulgård & Bisballe 2008).

As indicated in Table **1**, in Denmark this phenomenon has taken a bottom up form, with individual social entrepreneurs, former politicians, non-governmental organisations and public and private funding paving the way for organising, educating and developing social entrepreneurship capacity (Andersen & Hulgård 2014). Only recently has the government noticed the potential of this phenomenon, with the result that it has developed a legislative framework and provided social venture capital and capacity development support. (Hulgård & Andersen, 2014). The number of social enterprises in Denmark has been estimated at around 300, indicating that it is still a niche phenomenon, however (Thuesen, *et al.*, 2013).

Social entrepreneurship is predominantly multi-actor driven, involving social entrepreneurs, groups of citizens, local communities, public sector employees and NGOs. Organisational formats include co-production, co-creating and network learning as well as service production. In general, a vast range of types of innovation may be identified in the social economy sector: social innovation, collaborative innovation, open innovation, inter-sectoral and inter-organisational innovation. They take the form of social enterprises which seek to develop sustainable jobs vulnerable citizens. For instance, one social enterprise called *Bybi* ('City Bee') trains homeless people to set up beehives on public roofs so that they can produce and sell honey; a second enterprise named *Kaffegal* ('Coffee mad') organises a cafe that hires and trains people with psychiatric problems to work alongside volunteers; a third, *Baisekeli* ('Bicycly') buys and restores second-hand bicycles and sends them to Africa where locals have been trained to run bicycle repair shops; a fourth, *Place de Bleu*, trains and educates ethnic women to produce exclusive designs adapted from their own cultural traditions; a fifth, known as *Maternity Worldwide*, provides a bridge between Danish health professional volunteers and Ethiopian mothers through local obstetric and mother and baby health services; and finally *The Specialists* hire and train young adults with autism spectrum disorder to test information technology products.

These social enterprises develop their products and social economy, and are characterised by the participation of many partners and networks. They have been labelled *schools of democracy*, applying *mixed resources*, *i.e.* to do business on the basis of income both from the market and from various forms of public funding and procurement and often manage to create a basis for greater vitality, skills development and co-ownership (Andersen & Hulgård 2008). This requires a particular competence profile featuring skilled businessmen and civil society actors as well as a profile of *extraordinary* ordinariness since they must compete and produce on market terms but be *extraordinary* in terms of their social mission, value creation and involvement in civil society (Amin 2009). Critical analyses point out the challenging nature of these objectives, notably that the difficulties involved in implementing inclusive strategies under market conditions make it hard for many social enterprises to survive in the longer term (Levander 2011, Andersen & Hulgård 2010).

TRANSFORMATIVE LEARNING AND ORGANISATIONS AS PSYCHOSOCIAL AND INTERACTIONAL PHENOMENA

In Table **1** I demonstrate that decades of transforming the public sector and welfare services have actually led to substantial changes: from mono-professional and in-house human service organisations to multi-professional and cross-organisational entities; from conventional social work or disease approaches towards a stronger preventive effort; from public professionals as sole caregivers to professional-user co-production steered by NGOs and the local community; from conventional work integration and community activities to social enterprises and public-private-civic partnerships. These changes have also impacted the welfare professions and personnel, where parallel transformations are evident: from mono to plural functions and competences; from sole authority to co-production and shared responsibility; and from working *for* to working *with* (Andersen, 2014).

The concept of expertise defined by Engeström and Middleton is central to understanding welfare employees' role in transforming task deliveries and everyday innovations pointing to "*collaborative and discursive construction of tasks, solutions, visions, breakdowns and innovations within and across systems*" (Engeström and Middleton 1996: 4). Karvinen-Niinikoski (2004: 23) further claims that "*today the trend is towards de-institutionalisation, hybrid forms of organisation and co-operative mastery of knowing and knowledge production, towards open expertise produced in multi-actor networks*" and it becomes clear that collaborative public welfare work rests on new forms of knowledge and professional work. Finally Anne Edwards points to "*the centrality of knowledge to fluid responsive practices*" and "*relational agency by asserting that professional practices are driven by professional values and interaction*" (Edwards 2010). Consequently, we may speak of a relational turn where professional learning nowadays involves working with others to interpret a problem of practice and figuring out how to respond to it, thereby gaining insight into how others see the world (Edwards 2012).

Adding to these newer understandings, my research is concerned with the psychosocial turn in learning and organisational research that has also been addressed by *e.g.* Redman, Bereswill & Morgenroth (2010); Andersen and Dybbroe (2011); Salling Olesen (2012) and Froggett (2002). When investigating collaborative public innovation we need to understand agents as learning, emotional & cognitive subjects with their own history and experiences. My research documents how professionals individualise themselves when engaging in collaborative processes. Some are enthusiastic, finding it easy to negotiate and engage in service delivery and user collaboration; others are burdened by the demands and complexity; and still others experience this as yet another brick in the wall of a hyper-optimised, overloaded and demotivating work situation (Andersen 1999 & 2005; Andersen & Dybbroe, 2011). The psychosocial approach enables us to conceptualise the social in the subject and the subject in the social, *i.e.* how human beings' conscious and unconscious worlds form and are formed by the societal world (Froggett, 2002; Hoggett, *et al.* 2010; Salling Olesen 2012; Hollway 2008; Leithäuser, Meyerhuber & Schottmayer 2009; Andersen, 2012). Notably, the three dimensions of identification, idealisation and ambivalence constitute a pertinent analytical grid through which to study welfare services. Social research which applies these concepts creates representations of social life that are characterised by diversity, depth and dynamics that might otherwise be difficult to access. In this way, we are able to move beyond traditional binary notions of subject and object, rational *versus* irrational behaviour in organisations, learning and social interaction and to discern how people's inner and outer lives are connected and interdependent and therefore liable to elude rational, linear empirical approaches (Brock 2011; Britzman 2011; Yannis 2002; Andersen 2006, 2012). The psychosocial understanding of identification emphasises that these processes are essential to our personality and professional development where we adapt and model ourselves based on the desirable qualities and actions exhibited by another person or persons or desirable causes. Sandor Ferenczi states that "*the ego is always in search of objects, i.e. individuals or 'desirable causes', to identify with in order introject, grow and mature*" (Ferenczi 1994; A. Freud 1966). Professional and personal performance thus involves both intrasubjectivity and intersubjectivity which are shaped by societal, cultural and organisational contexts (Benjamin 1995). My point here is that the *grand narratives* of site-based management, democracy, public collaboration, social sustainability and social entrepreneurship, *etc.* require professionals and citizens to identify with these narratives in order for them to be implemented and developed. Employees who identify professionally and personally with these objectives constitute the 'engine' of welfare services but these identification processes can, at the same time, produce idealisation, ambivalence and anxiety depending on the concrete societal, organisational and financial framing of the welfare service at hand.

ANXIETY, DEFENCE AND AMBIVALENCE ASSOCIATED WITH SITE-BASED MANAGEMENT IN HUMAN SERVICES

During the early 90s, I carried out a number of studies on how employees, management and clients fulfilled the objectives and requirements of the early

Danish modernisation programmes[1] (as outlined in Table **1**) (Andersen, 1999, 2003). The early decentralisation in Denmark addressed three public service dimensions: economy and finance, service deliveries and professionalism, personnel and administration. My studies took place in a traditional bureaucratic public administration with a working climate characterised by a dichotomous mindset - us *versus* them - between local administration and the human service institutions providing a difficult point of departure. The economic results of delivering in a quasi-market were minimal; half of the institutions had begun to develop an institutional strategy. The pedagogical results had led to greater professional satisfaction and prevention activities among employees and management. The personnel and administration results were mixed – institutional managers were typically more satisfied than employees, who felt peripheral, tired and uninvolved (Andersen, 1999).

My analytical and theoretical understanding was spurred by an initial encounter of a particular kind and which seemed to repeat itself during my later interactions in the research field. By applying a psychosocial approach I was able to examine and interpret my interactions and feelings through institutional transference, enabling me to develop an analytical model. The research process was kick started at a meeting with union representatives and employees of the participating social and health care institutions, in a turbulent and contentious atmosphere. I was invited to talk about my research project, its objectives and methods – and my wish to collaborate and contribute to co-development. Their reaction to this was extraordinary: they were hostile and negative, casting doubts upon my motives, and tired of the endless politically motivated initiatives to improve and rationalise their work.. When I left the meeting, I felt shaken up, a bit of a failure, rejected, confused and frustrated by the fact that a host of factors and experiences that had nothing to do with my research could exert such a powerful influence. This initial meeting served as a kind of knowledge catalyst for how modernisation scenarios at that time, in the early 90s, were playing out, and ultimately it led to my psychosocially informed approach to site-based management and democracy.

[1] One four year research project investigated a decentralisation experiment with site-based management and financial frameworks that was carried out over three years. The experiment involved 30 social and health care institutions and focused on results, barriers and potentials – and involved around 700 persons. Data gathered included fieldwork observations at the human service institutions, 35 semi-structured interviews with managers and staff, eighteen months of observations of management meetings and a semi-structured questionnaire to managers of participating institutions.

As the participants at the meeting did not know me, their reactions had to be rooted in various other experiences. I was later able to explain the encounter by applying the concept of *institutional transference and counter-transference*, developed by the German organisational analyst Franz Wellendorf. Institutional transference refers to what a researcher produces in relation to a specific organisation or field, and which is coloured by her personal life history and previous experiences of organisations. Institutional counter-transference refers to the researcher's reactions to transference from the members of the organisation (Wellendorf 1986:58). Wellendorf posits that the concept of institutional transference is useful for understanding the particular dynamics and positioning of the researcher towards the field or organisation, and that it has predictive power. Any institution affects the researcher and the dynamics of institutional life will attempt to incorporate her into its structures in order to eliminate her as a disruptive foreign body. How the participants in the field reacts towards the researcher are of great importance for the analysis of the field and the organisation in question (Wellendorf 1986).

In order to understand the participants' powerful emotional reactions towards me we need to turn to the psychoanalytic concept of displacement, where an emotion can be transferred from one object or phenomenon to another. Consequently, this led to an understanding of the participants transferring experiences and feelings from their somewhat disillusioned experiences of management, politicians and consultants to my research project and my person. Displacement as part of processes of transference takes place when there is one common element between the original and the current situation hereby creating a channel for the transference. Following from this, my presentation offered key words and images that resembled the political rhetoric and interaction in the field of site-based management and user democracy, monitoring and resource cuts. In recent years, their work situation had been full of ambivalent experiences and consequently, their emotions were seething just under the surface. During subsequent field work, I was able to detect a similar culture of hostility in collaborations between various institutions and the central administration. Corresponding to the logic of the research field and the institutional transference I – as a researcher - was perceived either as biased, or as someone who should be won over or rejected. My initial feelings of inferiority, anxiety and rejection were, I later learned, mirrored by many of the staff members in the institutions. Consequently, the employees at the meeting performed an institutional transference where they transferred the same mix of emotions to me (the researcher) that they themselves had been carrying for some time – emotional responses that were closely related to the work-related pressure from politicians and human service administration.

By examining and interpreting my own reactions and feelings through the institutional transference lens, I was able to develop a psychosocially informed analysis of these encounters. I subsequently validated these findings through a large amount of qualitative data.[2] Based on these empirical findings, I was able to conclude that development and change processes related to administrative modernisation programmes had resulted in significant levels of anxiety and unrest, defensiveness and ambivalence among employees and management. The management response to the anxiety and defensiveness prevalent among the staff and institutions often involved rational, instrumental initiatives such as one-way communication seminars, an increased flow of instructional information sheets or brief formal meetings with local politicians – which did not improve the situation – instead of fostering a more reflective and receptive work climate that prioritised dialogue, co-decision, co-creation and gradual change. Analysis of transference between the researcher and the field thus provided insight into organisational and human dynamics that could enrich prevailing understandings of change and modernisation. The analysis thus showed that the economic, political and cultural context had great significance for the intensity and extent of the defence mechanisms mobilised by employees, for example when political decisions about cuts, deteriorating conditions for social work or broken promises from politicians and management led to more criticism, discontent and unrest from the staff, thus increasing defensive behaviour both among staff and management (see also Andersen, 1999, 2003, 2012).

IDEALISATION AND AMBIVALENCE IN SOCIAL ENTREPRENEURSHIP AND SOCIAL INNOVATION

The second empirical case analyses a social enterprise, the Bridge - a typically Danish example of social entrepreneurship aimed at training and hiring socially vulnerable citizens and bringing them into the workforce. It combined a high degree of innovation, collaboration and participation with a considerable amount of public funding and a smaller market income.[3] The enterprise displayed both

---

[2] The empirical study consisted of a semi-structured questionnaire involving 30 social and health care institutions, qualitative interviews with 35 employees, clients and management representatives and fieldwork focusing on client and employee democracy in four social and health care institutions, meeting-observations involving the managers of human service institutions and managers in public office for a periode of eighteen months.

[3] The case is an excerpt from empirical research material collected by Lars Hulgård and research assistant Thomas Bisballe in 2004 in one of several sub-projects within the EMES European Research Network, a European research project on third sector issues, including social enterprises and social entrepreneurship. A number of semi-structured qualitative interviews were carried

organisational strengths and weaknesses but also reasonable results. The Bridge began as an innovative community centre and local environmental project in a minor city in Jutland, and succeeded not only in attracting and activating socially vulnerable groups, but also reaching out to ordinary citizens from the local community. At its peak, the Bridge consisted of a recycling shop, a textile workshop, a rental shop, a café with reasonably priced meals, various social activities for short and long term welfare clients, a fixed venue for cultural activities for local Turks and Kurds, and educational programmes for early retirees.

The overall objective was community development in combination with upskilling, personal development and participatory collaboration and democracy. The initiator and central figure at the Bridge was the manager, a social entrepreneur who had come up with the original idea and gathered a small group of people to start the enterprise. The manager identified strongly with the Bridge and had formed her own vision for it. Although she had successfully attracted a small group of employees, she was also able to clearly articulate the problems facing the enterprise. In a semi-structured interview, she revealed the difficulties involved, notably that despite her intentions to create a bottom-up environment she observed that when she was absent the cohesion and momentum faded. Her employees became more passive and were not able to run the enterprise as planned.

> *"In my early days in this project I thought that we could turn it into some kind of centre where people would feel an emotional sense of belonging. But I gradually became aware of my disappointment when people left the place or didn't accept what was on offer. This was because I didn't realise that I was in fact their employer. I provided good working conditions and good experiences, since I personally run things here. I was at the front of all of it. I truly didn't believe that a private or public enterprise would take on the tasks that I sometimes had to do. But that's part of the way things work here. That's why I'm not only the boss. I'm just as much a social worker."* (Interview, manager).

During the interview the manager talked of the difficulty of implementing several of her managerial philosophies and practices. It was very evident in her accounts of the daily running of the enterprise that she had taken on a prescriptive

out with the manager of the Bridge, focusing on the organisation's social capital and its significance for activities, development potential, strategy, participant group and composition, collaboration partners and conceptual basis.

leadership role, and this seemed to be fuelled by her physical, moral and personal presence. In the manager's absence, however, the staff's unity and focus on the activities immediately weakened, which was problematic because one of the Bridge's aims was to empower its users. The leader also defined herself as a different kind of leader: a hybrid between a social worker and a manager. At the same time, she aspired towards an ideal leadership practice involving delegation and democratic activation, which was difficult to live up to in practice because the group of users and volunteers was so heterogeneous and complex. The manager also made it clear that the running of voluntary activities was based on work based on relationships - and required both emotional and professional investment - and that the latter sometimes got in each other's way. As described below, however, the enterprise did help transform marginal citizens into active volunteers and staff, and it provided learning that lead to empowerment:

> *"The Bridge is part of the Danish 'Folkehus' (People's House) tradition, and has a similar atmosphere and group identity. We are also a 'community house' for local people. And this is an obstacle. When people join us and want to be part of the Bridge, they are immediately faced with many practical challenges. For one thing, to make this café work every day...what happens is that they quickly become volunteers. In reality they are users, but as individuals they feel better being volunteers. This means that some of the newcomers immediately become part of the staff, whereas others become users – for instance if they use the sewing workshop to sew their clothes. Some want to fix something; others want to learn something. All in all, around 54 people come to the house every day."* (Interview, manager).

Social enterprises including a strong voluntary dimension often focus on grass-roots democracy and co-decision making and this was also the case at the Bridge. But such organisations are also quite dependent on various forms of social sustainability. Social sustainability refers to the social cement that binds social enterprises together and is the reason that they can continue to develop their activities. Local project sustainability ensures a continued local interest and a real user need for the organisation. In the case of the Bridge, as described by the manager, its *social*, *local* and *project* sustainability was relatively well anchored, while the weak point was its *economic* sustainability (Andersen, Neerup & Cauchi, 2007). However, social sustainability also caused problems within the organisation. As mentioned, the clients and volunteers had difficulty taking responsibility in the manager's absence - even though they had been active in formulating and developing activity goals and labour tasks. However, the manager put this into perspective in terms of the Bridge's objectives, working methods and participants, all of which she described as heavily dependent on a long-term commitment. She positioned the Bridge as a project that involved both personal and professional development and empowerment for the individual users and volunteers; developing professional identities and work practices; offering an inclusive workplace with high expectations of its staff. But she also voiced openly her disappointment and sense of failure. This was particularly evident when she spoke of the most vulnerable group of employees/clients who often had difficulties achieving the project's objectives. The constant, ongoing struggle to obtain financial support and income also tired her.

The conceptual framework of the Bridge encompassed a number of different focus areas, namely: creating social political awareness; fostering learning in the Grundtvigian[4] sense: shared knowledge, learning and enlightenment, empowerment and democracy, skills development, vocational training and personal growth. The manager explained that the project's juxtaposition of a process perspective with a product perspective made it complicated to use indicators and measurement criteria to evaluate the project results. This placed the manager in a very difficult dilemma, namely that the project's entire conceptual basis, objectives and methods were completely dependent on the availability of a considerable amount of time as well as sufficient human, professional and financial resources. Her account provided insight into the complicated emotional and professional spectrum involved in running a social enterprise, which indicated how such enterprises can be driven by identification and idealisation but are also jeopardised by ambivalence and defensiveness.

The processes involved are illustrated in Fig. **1**, above. Social enterprises combine challenging goals at the individual level with broader societal objectives and visions. furthermore, these are always implemented in a given social context which exerts a strong influence over the project. In some cases, the context may facilitate the enterprise but in others it can create obstacles and barriers. The point is that the dynamic reciprocal interaction between the many objectives and visions of social enterprises is played out in a specific societal framework which can lead to particular psychosocial manifestations. These include professional and personal fulfilment through identification, but also dilemmas and difficulties which are expressed through ambivalence and defensive attitudes and behaviours. In order to fulfil the *grand vision* of social enterprises, managers and volunteers must

[4] The influential, nineteenth century Danish Lutheran pastor and thinker who espoused, inter alia, an ideal of learning for life'.

identify with the enterprise's objectives and express this through a strong commitment, professional skills and strategic management.

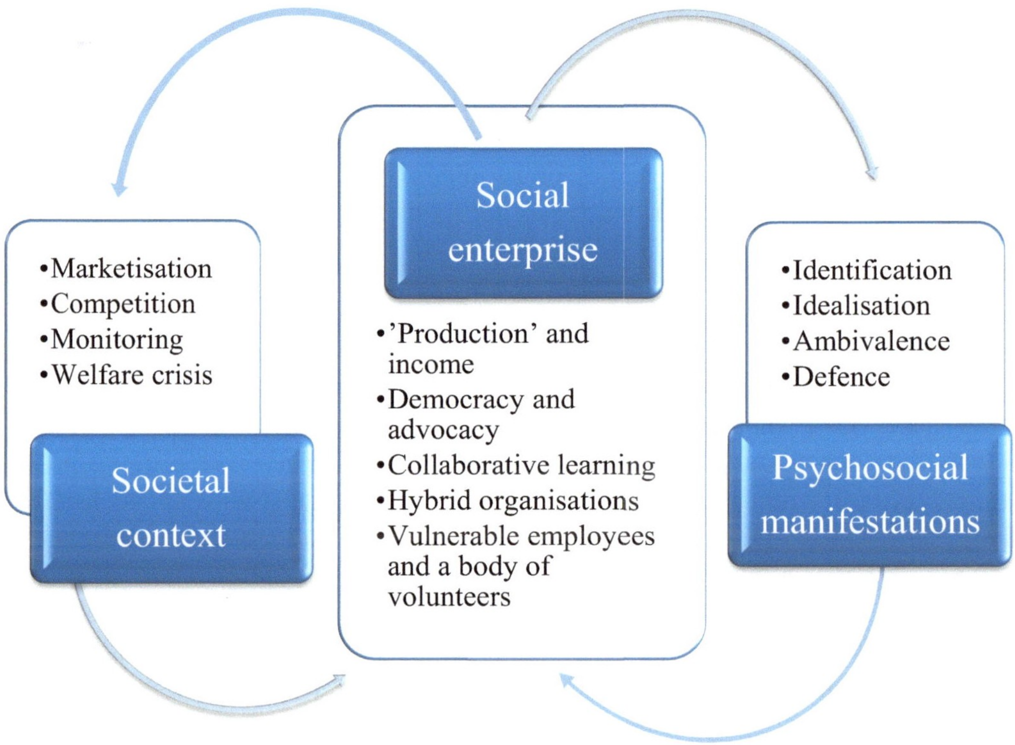

Figure 1: A psychosocial framing of a social enterprise: psychosocial manifestations in a societal context.

One might also ask whether the profile of social enterprises as work integration activities has been idealised in societal and labour market discourse, due to the very high objectives and expectations set out in labour market policy and local government socio-economic strategies. These societal framings influence intrasubjective and intersubjective work processes, as illustrated by the manager's telling account of overinvestment, feelings of powerlessness and being overwhelmed. From a psychosocial perspective, idealisation may be understood as a libidinous, instinctively energetic investment in a person or case, and is typically exaggerated and overstated. People do not always acknowledge that they are idealising. Idealisation is therefore an over-investment that has various consequences. Notably, an ambivalent hierarchy is established between the person and the idealised object, which creates a power relationship where individual is reduced to a smaller subject feeling, overwhelmed and rendered powerless by the idealised object (person or matter). The idealisation therefore hampers the satisfaction of professional or emotional needs since it may lead to states of fascination or destructive rage (Ferenczi 1994; A. Freud 1966). This concept therefore offers a thought-provoking understanding of how attractive visions and objectives, such as social entrepreneurship and social enterprises, may in some cases become a yoke around the neck of the dedicated people who become involved. Where there are elements of idealisation, being unable to realise one's grand vision leads to ambivalence, shame and a tendency towards aggression. It may also mean that individual social entrepreneurs bear an excessive sense of responsibility for the enterprise's processes and goals.

CONCLUSION

In this chapter, I have explored two different scenarios of collaborative innovation from a psychosocial, micro processual and learning perspective. My point of departure has been that public collaborative innovation projects are often characterised by considerable ambivalence on the part of the involved professionals, who may feel both enthusiastic and burdened. By analysing two empirical cases involving site-based management, and democracy and social enterprises, respectively, I have shown how public welfare innovation projects in different scenarios feature similarly positive learning and welfare results. However, if we flip the coin we discover demotivation, defensive reactions and ambivalence. I call for an understanding of agents as learning, emotional and cognitive subjects with their own histories and experiences. Professionals individualise themselves when engaging in collaborative processes. My point is that if the *grand narratives* of site-based management, democracy, public collaboration, social sustainability and social entrepreneurship, *etc.* are to deliver, this requires that professionals and citizens identify with them. Professional and personal identification with these objectives constitutes the very *engine* of welfare services, but these processes can also lead to idealisation, ambivalence and anxiety, depending on how they are framed in social, organisational and financial terms. We need to deepen our understanding of collaborative innovation and learning in public welfare service delivery, and to acknowledge the fact that setting up working teams to engage in these processes is a very delicate matter. My data suggest that if we do not compensate for, and acknowledge, the strains on staff, collaborative innovation initiatives risk becoming counter-productive, thus constraining their potential.

ACKNOWLEDGEMENTS

Declared none.

CONFLICT OF INTEREST

The author confirms that this chapter contents have no conflict of interest.

REFERENCES

Amin, Ash. (2009). Extraordinary Ordinary: Working in the Social Economy. In *Social Enterprise Journal*, 5:1, 30-49.

Andersen, Linda (1999). *Facader og facetter. Modernisering og læreprocesser i socialpædagogik og forvaltning*. [Facades and facets. Modernisation and learning in social pedagogy and administration], Frederiksberg: Roskilde University Press.

Andersen, Linda Lundgaard (2003). When the Unconscious Joins the Game: A Psychoanalytic Perspective on Modernization and Change. *Forum Qualitative Sozialforschung / Forum: Qualitative Social Research* [On-line Journal], 4:3.

Andersen, L. Lundgaard (2005). The Long Gone Promises of Social Work. Ambivalence and Individualisation in a Social Services Administration. *Journal of Social Work Practice*. 18:1.

Andersen, L. Lundgaard (2012). Interaction, transference, and subjectivity: A psychoanalytic approach to fieldwork. *Journal of Research Practice*, 8:2, Article M3. Retrieved from http://jrp.icaap.org/index.php/jrp/article/view/331/271

Andersen, L. Lundgaard (2012). Inner and Outer Life at Work. The Roots and Horizon of Psychoanalytically Informed Work Life Research. In *Forum Qualitative Sozialforschung / Forum: Qualitative Social Research*, 13:3, Art. 26.

Andersen, Lundgaard L. & Dybbroe, B. (2014). Introspection as intra and inter professionalism in Danish social and health care. In *Journal of Social Work Practice*. London: Routledge.

Andersen, Lundgaard L. & Dybbroe, B. (2011). Social Work, Health Care and Welfare undergoing Transformation in Scandinavia. In *Journal of Social Work Practice*. London: Routledge

Andersen, L. & Hulgård, L. (2010) Socialt entreprenørskab - fyrtårne og kuldsejlede projekter [Social entrepreneurship – lighthouses and capsized projects]. In Andersen, Lundgaard L., Hulgård, L. & Bager, T. (eds.) *Socialt entreprenørskab* [Social Entrepreneurship] (pp. 169-177). Odense: Syddansk Universitetsforlag.

Andersen, L., Hulgård, L., & Bisballe, L. (2008). Socialt entreprenørskab i Danmark: et aktuelt signalement [Social entrepreneurship in Denmark – a contemporary description]. In Lundgaard Andersen, L., & Hulgård, L. (eds.). *Socialt entreprenørskab - et aktuelt signalement*: CSE årsrapport *2008* (s. 7-26). Roskilde: Roskilde Universitetscenter.

Andersen, L., Neerup, S. & Cauchi, P. (2007). *Paragraf 18. En casebaseret analyse af samarbejdet mellem kommunerne og de frivillige sociale foreninger* [Paragraf 18. A casebased analysis of the collaboration between the minicipalities and the volunteer social organisations]. København: Velfærdsministeriet, Frivilligenheden.

Andersen, M. M. (1988). Administrationspolitikkens nyorientering - et erfaringsbaseret syn på ændringer i organisation og ledelse [The new orientation of adminstrative policy – an experience based perspective on changes in organisation and management]. In K. H. Bentzon (Eds.), *Fra vækst til omstilling - moderniseringen af den offentlige sektor* [From growth to readjustment – on the modernisation of the public sector] København: Nyt fra Samfundsvidenskaberne.

Buch, A. & Andersen, V. (2013). (De)stabilizing Self-Identities in Professional Work. In *Nordic Journal of Working Life Studies*, 3:3, 155-173.

Benjamin, J. (1995). *Like Subjects, Love objects. Essays on recognition and sexual difference*. New Haven: Yale University Press.

Bovbjerg, K.M. (2010). Ethics of sensitivity: Towards a new work ethic: New age in business life. In Rendtorff, J. D. (Ed.), *Power and principle in the market place: On ethics and economics,* (pp.169-179). Surrey: Ashgate.

Bovbjerg, K. M. (2011). Personal development under market conditions: NLP and the emergence of an ethics of sensitivity based on the idea of the hidden potential of the individual. In *Journal of Contemporary Religion*, 26:2, 189-205.

Brock, M. (2011). Psychoanalysis outside the clinic: Interventions in psychosocial studies. Stephen Frosh. In *Psychoanalysis, Culture & Society* 16, 107–109.

Becker-Schmidt, R. & Knapp, G.-A. (1987). *Geschlechtertrennerung – Geschlechterdifferenz. Suchbewegungen sozialen Lernens* [Gender tensions, gender differences. The search for social learning] Bonn, Verlag Neue Gesellscharft GmbH

Britzman, D.P. (2011). *Freud and Education*. New York: Routledge

Cho, Y. & Marshal, T. E. (2010). *The State of the Art of Action Learning Research. In Advances in Developing Human Resources,*12:163. Sage Publications. DOI: 10.1177/1523422310367881

Defourny, J. & Nyssens, M. (2010). Conceptions of social enterprise and social entrepreneurship in Europe and the United States: Convergences and divergences. In *Journal of Social Entrepreneurship*, 1:1, 32-53.

Dilworth, R.L., & Willis, V.J (2003). *Action learning: Images and pathways.* Malabar, FL: Krieger.

Diochon, M. & Anderson, A. R. (2011). Ambivalence and ambiguity in social enterprise; narratives about values in reconciling purpose and practices. In *International Entrepreneurship Management Journal*, 7, 93–109.

Dybbroe, B. & Kamp, A. (2013). What counts? Who counts? Standardization and emotional labour in psychiatric care. Paper presented at 2013 International Labour Process Conference, New Brunswick, USA.

Edwards, A. (2012). The role of common knowledge in achieving collaboration across practices. In *Learning, Culture and Social Interaction*, 1, 22–32.

Edwards, A. (2010). *Being an Expert Professional Practitioner: the relational turn in expertise,* Dordrecht: Springer.

Ferenczi, S. (1994) *Final Contributions to the Problems and Methods of Psychoanalysis*, London: Karnac Classics

Freud, A. (1966 (1936). *The ego and the mechanisms of defence*. London: Karnac Books

Froggett, L. (2002). *Love, Hate and Welfare: psychosocial approaches to policy and practice*, Bristol: Policy Press

Hartley, J. (2005). Innovation in governance and public services: Past and present. In *Public Money & Management*, 25:1, 27-34.

Hartley, J.; Sørensen, E. & Torfing, J. (2013). Collaborative innovation: A viable alternative to market competition and organizational entrepreneurship. In *Public Administration Review*, 73:6, 821–830.

Hjort, K. & Raa, P. H. (2011). Strategic self-management: Danish gymnasium management between playing solo and showing solidarity. In *Journal of Public Administration and Governance*, 1:2, 186-202.

Hoggett, P.; Beedell, P.; Jimenez, L.; Mayo, M. & Miller, C. (2010) Working psycho-socially and dialogically in research. In *Psychoanalysis. In Culture and Society*, 15:2, 173-188.

Hollway, W. (2008). The importance of relational thinking in the practice of psycho-social research: ontology, epistemology, methodology and ethics. In: Clarke, S.; Hoggett, P. & Hahn, H. (eds). *Object relations and social relations: The implications of the relational turn in psychoanalysis. Exploring Psyco-Social Studies*. (pp. 137–162). London, UK: Karnac.

Hulgård, L.; Andersen, L. L.; Spear. R. & Bisballe. L. (2008). *Alternativ beskæftigelse og integration af socialt udsatte grupper: erfaringer fra Danmark og Europa.* [Alternative employment and integration of socially excluded groups: experiences from Denmark and Europe] CSE Publications; (02:08). Frederiksberg: Roskilde Universitets Forlag

Hulgård, L., (2010). Public and social entrepreneurship. In Hart, Laville & Cattani (eds.) *The Human Economy*. London: Polity Press

Hulgård, L. (2007). *Sociale entrepenører – En kritisk indføring*. Copenhagen: Hans Reitzels Forlag.

Karvinen-Niinikoski, S. (2004) Social work supervision contributing to innovative knowledge production and open expertise. In Gould, N & Baldwin, J (ed.) *Social Work, Critical Reflection and the Learning Organisation.* (pp.23-39). England: Aldershot.

Lave, J., & Wenger, E. (1991). *Situated Learning: Legitimate Peripheral Participation.* Cambridge: Cambridge University Press.

Leithäuser, T.; Meyerhuber, S.& Schottmayer, M. (Eds) (2009). *Sozialpsychologisches Organisationsverstehen* [A social psychological perspective on organisations]. Wiesbaden: VS Verlag für Sozialwissenschaften

Levander, U. (2011). *Utanförskap på entreprenad. Diskurser om sociala företag i Sverige.* [Marginality in the entrepreneurial way. Discourses on social enterprises in Sweden] Stockholm: Daidalos

Mair, J. (2010). Social entrepreneurship: taking stock and looking ahead. In Fayolle, A. and Matley, H. (Eds.) *Handbook of Research on Social Entrepreneurship.* Cheltenham: Edward Elgar.

Negt, O. (1975). *Sociologisk fantasi og eksemplarisk indlæring* [Sociological imagination and examplary learning] Frederiksberg: Roskilde Univeristets Forlag.

Negt, O. (1985). *Det levende arbejde - den stjålne tid. De politiske og kulturelle sider af kampen for nedsat arbejdstid* [Living labor work – Stolen time. The political and cultural dimensions of the fight for reduced working hours]. København: Politisk revy.

Poder, P. (2009). The Political Regulation of Anger in Organisations. In Vandekerckhove, M.S. & von Ismer, S. C (Eds). *Regulating Emotion: Culture, Social Necessity, and Biological Inheritance.* NJ USA: Wiley-Blackwell

Redman, P.; Bereswill, M. & Morgenroth, C. (2010). Special issue on Alfred Lorenzer. *Psychoanalysis, Culture & Society* (2010) 15

Reff A. P.; Sehested, K. & Sørensen,E. (2011). Emerging theoretical understanding of pluricentric coordination in public governance. In *American Review of Public Administration*, 41:4, 375-394.

Salling Olesen, H. (2006). Work Identification - Inhibition or Resource for Learning? Promoting lifelong learning for older workers. In Tikkanen, T. & Nyhan, B. (Eds). *An International Overview.* Luxembourg: CEDEFOP, p. 164-176 (Cedefop Reference series; Nr. 65).

Salling Olesen, H. (2012). Cultural analysis and in-depth hermeneutics — Psycho-societal analysis of everyday life culture, interaction, and learning. In *Forum Qualitative Sozialforschung / Forum: Qualitative Social Research*, 13:3 http://www.qualitative-research.net/index.php/fqs/issue/view/41

Thuesen, F.; Bjerregaard Bach H.; Albæk, K.; Jensen, S.; Lodberg Hansen N. & Weibel K. (2013). *Socialøkonomiske virksomheder i Danmark. Når udsatte bliver ansatte.* [Social Enterprises in Denmark. When marginal citizens become employees] 13/23. København: SFI – Det nationale forskningscenter for velfærd

Wellendorf, F. (1986) Supervision als Institutionsanalyse,[Supervision as institutional analysis] in H. Pühl & W. Schmidbauer (eds.): *Supervision und Psychoanalyse – Selbstreflexion der Helfenden Beruf*, [Supervision and psychoanalysis – autoreflections by the helping profession] Fischer Taschenbuch

Wihlman, T.; Hoppe, M.;, Wihlman, U. & Sandmark, H. (2014). Employee-Driven innovation in welfare services. In *Nordic Journal of Work Life Studies,* 4:2.

Ziehe, T. & Stubenrauch, H. (1996). *Ny Ungdom og usædvanlige læreprocesser.*[New Youth and Unusual Learning Processes]. København: Politisk Revy

Ziehe, T. (2001). Modernitets- og ressourceperspektivet læring i et hypermoderne samfund mentalitetsforandring, læringskultur og fremmedfølelse. [Modernity – and the resource perspective in learning in a hypermodern society: changes in mentality, learning culture and alienation] In *Sociologisk Arbejdspapir,* Vol 8, Ålborg University

Åkerstrøm Andersen, N. & W. Born, A. (2001). *Kærlighed og omstilling. Italesættelsen af den offentlige ansatte* [Love and readjustment. The discourses of the public employee], Frederiksberg: Nyt fra Samfundsvidenskabern.

CHAPTER 13

Making Sense of Public Policy Innovation in a Fragmented World: The Search for Solutions and the Limits of Learning

John Fenwick* **and Janice McMillan**

Newcastle Business School, Northumbria University & Business School, Edinburgh Napier University, UK

Abstract: This chapter considers learning, change and innovation in a public sector where the certainties of 'New Public Management' (NPM) have been replaced by uncertainty and flux. In this setting, policy actors may resort either to innovation or retrenchment. New solutions to policy problems may be generated or actors may revert to foundational approaches. This impacts upon practice as stakeholders search for meaning and engage in sense-making. Drawing from the authors' research within the UK public sector, this theoretical paper argues that rapid change and the failure of old solutions (for instance, to the global financial crisis) do not necessarily generate positive innovation. There may indeed be a retreat to previous failed responses, with entrenched learning producing negative results. The chapter concludes that innovation requires the core component of creativity if it is to be of value. As the modernist conception of gradual mastery of the world has fallen away, different theoretical tools are needed in understanding this changed policy environment. It is suggested that established governance and network theories are of limited assistance. It is more useful to adopt an anti-foundationalist position, using sense-making perspectives informed by both Weberian and critical approaches while avoiding grand meta-narrative.

Keywords: New Public Management, active learning, sense-making, creativity, street level and high-level policy.

INTRODUCTION

This chapter explores innovation, learning and change in an environment where the historical moment of New Public Management (NPM) has given way to unprecedented fluidity in public policy and decision-making. To begin, we examine the broad features of NPM and the key elements of the post-NPM environment, where foundational approaches (in theory and practice) may be challenged either by innovation or, by default, revert to previously established

***Address correspondence to John Fenwick:** Northumbria University, Newcastle upon Tyne, UK; E-mail: john.fenwick@northumbria.ac.uk

Annika Agger, Bodil Damgaard, Andreas Hagedorn Krogh and Eva Sørensen (Eds.)

positions. Both trends (*i.e.*, innovation or retrenchment) are evident in the incoherence of policy responses to the global economic crisis. We then consider the search for meaning and sense-making by policy actors at all levels who seek new solutions to cope with intractable problems. Employing an anti-foundational perspective and to some degree rehabilitating elements of Weberian thought, we discuss possible problems of innovation and the differing narratives of policy actors. In a highly uncertain public policy environment it is impossible to enumerate every possible response or proposed solution, but examples include the growth of Third Sector (voluntary community organisation) involvement in public services rather than exclusive reliance on the state, the rediscovery of a public service ethic amidst the economic crisis and near-collapse of the banking sector (including citizen withdrawal from multi-national banks in favour of ethical or mutual providers) and the realisation that conventional economic models (governing, for instance, interest rates, employment and tax levels) no longer *work* with the predictability they once possessed.

In this condition of flux, we will go on to suggest that learning does not necessarily generate innovation. Although there is a certain inevitability to the process of change in an era which has moved beyond modernist and foundationalist solutions, this does not necessarily generate positive and desirable innovation. Change may instead involve a retreat to failed responses of a previous era. It is as though a familiar script is still recited by policy actors even though the overall storyline has fundamentally changed. In this sense, entrenched learning may produce negative results even though *reverse organisational learning* (*i.e.* organisational amnesia) may accord a superficial appearance of novelty. This may be illustrated by examples from recent economic and public policy where innovative thinking (such as that associated with Thomas Piketty's (2014) powerful if unfashionable focus upon inequality) or a retreat to familiar, albeit failed, policy responses (such as those based on austerity) may readily be identified.

In an era where the modernist conception of gradual mastery (of the world, and of theory) has fallen away, the third section of this chapter will consider the failure of received models of public policy to make use of actors' active learning. We also review the kind of analytical tools that may assist in the theoretical understanding of a changed public policy environment. We advocate an anti-foundationalist position, drawing from sense-making perspectives that eschew grand narrative but are rooted instead in both historical Weberian approaches and contemporary critical perspectives which recognise the failure of previously learned responses.

INNOVATION THROUGH A POSTMODERN LENS

Beyond New Public Management

The New Public Management (NPM) arose from a specific historical moment as old patterns of centralist public administration in Europe gave way to an ostensibly flexible public policy and management characterised by competition, managerial devolution, performance measurement and public participation. We make the assumption that this moment has gone and that the currency of policy solutions offered under NPM has passed. The global economic crisis continues to last much longer than its (now rather touching) description by government as a temporary economic *downturn* suggested. To invert a term used in the UK by New Labour in its election campaign of 1997, things may not 'only get better'. They could get worse, for us all, for a long time. The policy assumptions and prescriptions of NPM have nothing to say to this state of affairs (Fenwick and McMillan 2010). This is partly because NPM gained prominence at a time of relative economic and political stability in Europe and beyond. The policy world was still, it seemed, predictable: the new tools of NPM would simply make it work better. Instability in civil and political society – evident in national and European elections in 2014 for instance – denote the fading away of such certainties.

We live in postmodern times. This proposition does not denote a contemplative withdrawal from the messy world of policy choices, nor a fruitless discussion of pastiche and reinvention, nor does it deny the real hardships currently being suffered by real people in Europe and beyond. By postmodern times, we mean, first, that, on a theoretical level the certainties of the old foundationalist paradigms have given way to an era of flux and fluidity in which there is no convincing dominant explanation of the changing nature of public policy. Any attempts at theoretical understanding must henceforth be based in the recognition that this state of flux has become the norm. NPM is now wholly inadequate as either theoretical tool or descriptive category. Secondly, the political and policy implications of living in a postmodern era are that *modernisation* as the basis of international public sector reform has outstayed its welcome as a policy framework. The moment of modernisation, as a superficially progressive but essentially neo-liberal perspective predicated on competition, *customer* orientation, performance measurement and labour market flexibility in public services (see, for instance, Massey & Pyper 2005) has passed. Thirdly, at the level of public sector practice, the consequence of living in a postmodern era is that individual actors – public servants and citizens – can no longer access any plausible coherent explanation of the changes going on around them (especially at a time of global economic crisis) or any clear guide to action. Hence policy actors increasingly employ their own methods of sense-making, based upon the tools of understanding at their disposal.

We argue that actors now make sense of the public policy environment through the practical and anti-foundational responses available to them. With no simple policy tools or answers, the future (if it is to go beyond the stock remedies of the IMF and the EU) will derive from the lived experience of policy actors and the meanings and interpretations they assign to events, individually and collaboratively. Consequently, we argue that the obsessive desire of national governments to provide a definitive *Plan A* for public service reform is wholly misconceived. It is understandable that governments in troubled times do not stand before their electorate proclaiming that they, as a government, have no idea what to do. It may even be that such governments have members with the insight to recognise the fact that - post NPM and post-modernisation – there is no plan. Our argument is that this is a policy opportunity not a problem. It propels us back toward actors' sense-making which forms the basis of innovation, positive or negative.

But, in making sense, from where do actors – at all levels - *learn*? We intend *actors* to include citizens and public servants as well as those normally regarded as policy makers, and clearly some actors have greater influence than others. For all actors, we suggest that learning is central to the processes of sense-making and practical non-foundational responses, but the sources of learning are numerous and unpredictable. Private sector experience, overseas examples, personal contacts or local networks are all possible sources of learning. In a study of public sector organisational learning (Fenwick & McMillan 2005, 44) a senior strategic manager in local government suggested that the organisation concerned learns "*from all these*", and yet from "*none*". What is meant here is that the potential sources of learning are everywhere but the public organisation may not be able to take advantage of them. True learning cannot be managed – it is an essentially creative unbounded process. That is both its promise and its challenge.

This perspective goes beyond placing importance on the everyday problem-solving of street level bureaucrats (Lipsky 2010), important though that is. Our argument is that actors as individual members of civil society, local communities and other groups are also potential *policy makers* with solutions to offer. How then can actors be supported in finding their own solutions to complex problems?

Centrally imposed reform programmes, even when carried out by self-defined progressives in Europe or the global South, essentially offer a variant of foundationalism, a guide to how it *must be done*. This is most depressingly evident in the advocacy of *policy transfer* (for instance in the global remit of the IMF), whether from rich to poor countries as in the history of centrally-prescribed neo-liberal interventions, or from one Western economy to another as in the chaotic attempt to transfer financial arrangements for child support in the case of absent fathers from the USA to the UK. These are just further versions of the modernist notion of *one best solution* in a world where things are only getting better. Local solutions may of course be derived from examples provided by international policy prescriptions, provided these are informed by local conditions and local needs: the key is flexibility and adaptation. The task for practice is not to provide a grand plan of *how to do it*, but to arrange governance in such a way that 'it' – public policy – can be done. Here, learning remains crucial: it is central to the process of translating actors' sense-making into practical action.

Making Sense

Henrik Bang (2010) has provided a convincing account of everyday makers and expert citizens: the sense-makers of civil and political society. He argues that in a policy context where the old approaches and solutions have failed, there are creative ways of making sense located in the expertise and activism of lay people. In terms of practice, this focuses upon lived experience. From this, learning is derived. In terms of theory, it revisits the question of whether public administration is art or science. In a discussion which takes in Aristotle, the Obama presidential campaign, globalisation and public participation, Bang shifts our attention to the central theoretical issues: the eclipse of old habitual ways of working, the choices facing scholars and practitioners, and an optimistic emphasis on *everyday* sense making by active individuals who cannot fall back on the foundationalist solutions of modernism. The use of social networks and new forms of electronic interaction provide innovative and accessible means for extending activism, which may produce innovation when not confined to narrow sectional interests. For example, against the backdrop of the neoliberal economic agenda, Walliser (2013) discusses mobilisation and social activism in a Spanish context, identifying a key role for information and communication technologies (ICT) in facilitating new forms of social action. To some extent these form a contrast with more traditional views of social movements. "*The origin, participants, and dynamics of these more contemporary mobilisations.are new, the outcome of recent changes in how politically active citizens interact, network, cooperate, think and produce*" (Walliser 2013, 330).

Central to the sense-making process is the domain of values, as the process involved is really a search for meaning. In European public policy, voluntary and community organisations – the *Third Sector* – have long had a role in public provision. Third sector provision has expanded in the UK, reaching areas formerly covered by the local state. This is an example of where local people and local policy actors may find their own solutions to local needs, outwith the prescribed choices set by government, and supported by (not commanded by) local or national state organisations.

But what is the bridge between global-scale problems – principally, the continuing economic crisis – and micro-level solutions based on everyday sense-making? We see four principal ways of linking the micro and the macro levels. First, we suggest that everyday sense-making must be predicated on the values of public service (responding on the basis of need, assuming collective responsibility for, *e.g.*, health care and education, recognising that society is not merely a grouping of atomised individuals) upon which State intervention was originally based but which has been undermined by neo-liberal State reforms. Secondly, new varieties of collective solution (which may range, for instance, from long-standing initiatives such as credit unions through to more recent ICT-based social activism, as discussed above) serve to link individual values to those of the group. Thirdly, on the theoretical level, we argue that postmodern and anti-foundational critiques permit an influence for individual and group perspectives which is excluded from modernist top-down models. Fourthly, in a democratic society, formal representative institutions remain essential guarantors of accountability. However, we would identify a crucial link to policy-making in the ability of governing actors and institutions to *let go* by unleashing creativity and facilitating bottom-up solutions without regarding these as a threat to established ways of formulating and implementing policy.

ANTI-FOUNDATIONALISM AND INNOVATION

Habitual Responses or Positive Innovation?

Foundationalism has been the core of both theory and practice in public policy, offering both a theoretical account of the world around us and a guide to action for policy actors. However, the many instances of policy failure and well-documented policy disasters in western democracies - see for example Gray and ‘t Hart (1998) - point to the negative impacts of foundationalist understandings of the world and the assumed causal relationships that go with them. Our definition of foundationalism is the one offered by Bevir and Rhodes (1999). It is a positivist perspective that "*adopts some variant of the natural science model; tries to discover 'pure facts', and strives after successive approximations to given truth*" (Bevir and Rhodes 1999, 216).

Thus anti-foundationalism, in terms of public policy and governance, presents a picture where interpretations of and practice in governing systems can only be explained through reference to the lived experiences of actors within these governing systems. Anti-foundationalism encourages the consideration of *situated agency* where it is argued that the behaviour of individuals within governing systems cannot be determined by institutions, conventional practices and socialisation alone. Instead, behaviour and individual responses are the outcomes of individual choice, contingent upon context, meaning and adaptive processes as well as institutions and habitual responses (see Bevir, Rhodes & Weller, 2003). Innovation in governance from an anti-foundationalist approach is created through agency; through the individual governance actor (in this case local level actors) and their sense-making of and responses to governance dysfunctions. Innovation is thus an outcome not only of a knowledge process but of the approach of individuals to that process - usually based on pragmatism and context driven interpretation of local concerns. Such innovation eschews a top-down, centralist approach to public service change and sees actors' sense-making as the basis of innovation. To put it another way, innovation is the fulfilment of learning and sense-making.

If we follow Jacobs (2009) in suggesting that people have a preference for narrative as a way of making sense of the world around them – a narrative based on our "*personal versions of reality*", often emotionally and experientially based - it is not surprising that public policy has taken up the discourse of foundationalism as it offers the promise of an overall meta-narrative. However, the status of learning and knowledge within such foundationalist perspectives has largely remained implicit and unchallenged. It is such assumed knowledge – *i.e.*, accepted foundational narratives - that has provided problems for public policy. There needs to be recognition of the status of different types of knowledge and, in particular, the fundamental differences between tacit and explicit forms. According to Nonaka and Takeuchi (1995) knowledge-creation depends on complex interactions between tacit and explicit knowledge, mediated through individual and organisational learning. In their analysis, tacit knowledge is uncodified, subjective, difficult to record, dependent upon the individual, context specific, not widely understood, difficult to pass on, difficult to emulate and only accessible through experience: in short, it is rather elusive. In contrast, explicit knowledge is codified, objective, documented, independent of the individual, context free, widely understood, easy to communicate, codified and can be learned through study and emulated. Knowledge of either kind is predicated upon learning which is, in essence, a shared process.

In foundationalist perspectives the interactions identified here as central to knowledge creation are minimal. Hence the resultant *knowledge* is either unchallenged or is positivistic in nature, creating given truths - for instance in the knowledge and policy solutions generated by governments. This kind of knowledge has underpinned historic understandings of public policy. It is antithetical to innovation.

To illustrate our perspective, we have elsewhere discussed how the foundationalist tradition has compounded the recurring problem of English sub-national governance in a devolved UK. We have argued that "*the solution to English governance cannot reside in a top-down government imposed solution, but, if it is addressed at all, will be built up from the local level through those perspectives seen as important by local actors*" (Fenwick & McMillan, 2008, 3) and, further, that this approach "*can be subverted by the systems of governance themselves propelling actors back toward known foundational positions. Current governance systems cannot match the rhetoric of third-way pragmatism and associated systems. Governance itself imposes a foundational logic on patterns of public policy and management*" (Fenwick & McMillan 2008, 2). We suggest that this perspective has a wider application.

At present, European governments, especially in the Eurozone, are locked into the old policy solutions partly through lack of innovation, but also, in more concrete terms, through international institutional constraints. These supra-national prescriptions (and proscriptions) are based on collaborative relations between States and major institutions but may be far from positive in their consequences. Collaboration amongst the powerful may produce policy innovations which are unknown and potentially unwelcome to ordinary citizens, for instance in the hidden co-operation between Western State security organisations revealed in 2013. Financially, European governments receiving *bail out* funding are quite explicitly required to adhere to policy solutions specified by other governments and by financial institutions. This permits of no learning and no innovation amongst the recipients. Habitual responses based on assumptions – for instance about the relationship of austerity measures to growth – increasingly appear to be based on faulty maths as well as sheer lack of imagination.

There may also, of course, be negative consequences of abandoning the certainties of modernism and foundationalism. Centrally defined public policy solutions certainly generate negative impacts, not least in the uncertain governmental response to the economic crisis, and there is no reason to suppose that a *letting go* in policy terms will always produce positive and successful results. Actors may default to the old habitual responses instead of coming up with innovative new ones. Things can be un-learned as well as learned: alongside organisational memory, there may well be organisational amnesia.

Innovation May Not be Positive

Osborne and Brown (2013) identify three *flaws* that may inhibit the understanding of public innovation. Firstly, they suggest that innovation has hitherto been understood in several inconsistent ways, including innovation as a *product*, innovation as a more general developmental change, and innovation as a process of continuous improvement, with no clear agreement around these different meanings. Secondly, innovation has been seen as a taken-for-granted *good* but in fact reality is more complicated: although innovation has indeed been central to public service improvement it does not follow that every innovation must itself be positive. Thirdly, that models of public innovation tend to use the inspiration of manufacturing industry rather than the service sector, skewing the understanding of what innovation means.

The crucial point here is that innovation (especially, we would suggest, when initiated by the powerful who possess the political ability to guarantee its implementation) may be negative in its effects. This is evident in the very components of NPM which, in the name of public service innovation and the narrative of modernisation, reflect the neo-liberal agenda of performance, privatisation and managerialism.

Learning and Change in a Fragmented World

There is now no single coherent narrative about public policy – theory and practice – and the task is therefore to capture this theme of constant unrelenting change, and to assess its importance for all the actors involved: citizens, scholars, managers and employees. Yet there is still a tendency to fall back on the old assumptions. As practical actors, we tend to take refuge in reification and the search for realist explanations and rational planning.

This search for order and predictability is understandable. Policy-makers (and academics involved in training, consultancy or management development programmes) like to give the impression (to themselves and others) that there is order not chaos. It is a way of making sense of our professional lives. On the political level it would be entirely reasonable, in response to the global economic crisis, to say that we have no idea what will happen next and don't really know if a particular policy response will work or not: let's see what happens. Yet it is impossible to imagine it being articulated in this way. This applies to academics as well as politicians. We are all bound to pretend that we know.

Anti-foundational approaches allow for such chaos and emphasise that for individual actors (sense-makers) there may be order in chaos. This order is however `their` order and not that imposed by central power elites in the form of politicians and public policy makers. Within the world of policy making then anti-foundationalist approaches re-engineer the traditional top-down models of knowledge creation, organisational learning and policy formulation in favour of practical responses that are developed on the ground and are context specific. The challenge in the post NPM world is how the top-down and bottom-up can be reconciled to allow meaningful solutions to emerge and satisfy the demands for change and `getting better` that are the stock in trade of politicians and the expectations of the voting public.

Weberian thought has a part to play in giving theoretical substance to this position. Weber has of course been read in many different ways: the (critical) exponent of modernist thought, the advocate – and critic – of rational bureaucracy, the exponent of interpretive understanding. Gregory (2007) explored aspects of Weber's continuing relevance, seeking to reconnect Weberian thought to the understanding of public sector and governmental reform, arguing that NPM was itself a stage in Weber's process of rationalisation - part of the continuing search for "*greater calculability and precision in the management of human affairs*" (2007, 222). Gregory suggested that NPM embodied a separation of means and ends, and of facts and values, reflected (for example) in the practical separation of *funders* and *providers* or *owners* and *purchasers* central to the public sector. He considers that the link between NPM and the political context of its formulation resembles Weber's *problematic relationship* between instrumental and substantive rationality. What contribution then can be offered by Weberian thought in a post-NPM environment? Peters (2010) has drawn attention to the relevance of a neo-Weberian approach in understanding the post-NPM environment. If we are to accept that Weber retains an immediacy in helping us to comprehend both NPM and post-NPM developments then our focus on individual actors' ways of making sense becomes crucial in an era beyond foundationalism.

It is also evident that governments themselves may employ the language of participation, citizen-centeredness and public engagement as another form of top-down foundationalism rather than as an alternative to it. The *consumer driven* public policy initiatives of successive UK governments have been defined and led from the centre. A government emphasis upon placing the citizen at the heart of local public policy in Wales, for instance, clearly reveals the tensions involved (see Guarneros-Meza, Downe, Entwistle & Martin 2014).

The narratives offered by the powerful - such as those provided by policy makers – are bound to gain power if we have no narrative of our own. They become the dominant narratives, framing the *problem* and its possible solutions through definition of the language we are obliged to use. This has long been the case in public policy, whether the matter at hand is the economy, defence, immigration or foreign policy. In these and other areas the terms of debate are themselves contestable: they embody assumptions and already limit the possible terms of any discussion. They open the illusion of a debate and already through language close down that debate. Influential actors endeavour to control this process: current discussions around austerity and the range of policy solutions constructed for Europe by powerful actors illustrate precisely this point.

LEARNING AND SENSE-MAKING

It is puzzling that politicians and other dominant policy actors are still surprised that what they do has so many unintended consequences, when the reasons why events should not turn out as intended are so numerous. It seems that predictability is assumed, and aberrations from that predictability are seen as highly unexpected. Yet of course it is predictability itself that is unusual. Policy outcomes can hardly ever be predicted, but, again, there are strong reasons why this is rarely articulated. There are some parallels here with Geyer's chaos theory. Geyer (2003) described how the linear paradigm in post-Enlightenment natural science was based upon assumptions about rationality and progress that promised a limitless control of the natural world. This began to be questioned in the twentieth century as probability superseded certainty within scientific method, which is still the case today. Yet there remains a tendency in everyday life, and in social science theory, to default to a linear rationalist model. Geyer explores complexity theory - "*a simple title for a broad range of non-linear, complex and chaotic systems theories*" (2003, 238) – as an alternative to rationalist models, noting that the failure of rationalist and reductionist approaches in social science led to a questioning of linear models, for instance from Weber, Habermas or the post-modernist movement (2003, 242).

It was not only that the linear model was technically failing to do what it claimed (*i.e.*, predict, control and explain), it was also that the bases of this way of looking at the world were being questioned. Yet in public policy we still seem to yearn for impossible dreams of mastery of the policy process and its outcomes, for instance in a recurring but largely pointless emphasis upon evidence-based policy making, that uninspiring adjunct of the rational model (see Hallsworth *et al.* 2011). Parsons' (2002, 58) critique of evidence-based policy making further exemplifies the argument against the linear foundational understandings of knowledge and policy making as "*fundamentally a managerialist rather than a democratic or political project* and one where *the mantra of 'what works', points less towards a renewal of social science or politics or democracy, than a trip back to the future to revive an intellectually muddled form of positivistic and mechanistic managerialism.*"

It is not our intention, in discarding rational models, foundational approaches and modernist assumptions, to merely inhabit a fruitless contemplative world, devoid of practical relevance. On the contrary, we suggest that received approaches based on dominant policy models are the ones that have deserted the real world of practice. The approach we advocate is intended to inform both theory and the practical world of sense-making and policy initiatives. Some of the ways it might do this are:

- *An emphasis upon active learning*: going beyond the platitudes of the *learning organisation* to develop ways in which public policy organisations can gain from the learning, knowledge and creativity of their members. This includes cross-cultural and international learning but not the crude notion of simple policy transfer. It also involves recognition of learning as a shared process.

- *Sense-making*: basing practical policy solutions on the ways in which actors have themselves developed effective responses and found new solutions, whether in the policy organisation or in wider civil and political society (see Bang, 2010).

- *Using practical actors' perspectives*: exploring the creative solutions and ways of working of public sector employees in an environment where traditional bureaucratic structures have given way to innovative ways of working. This may involve seizing the opportunity to influence policy in a manner consistent with the *windows of opportunity* (Zahariadis 2008) where policy outcomes are determined on neither wholly rational nor purely institutional bases.

- *A narrative approach*: based upon tacit knowledge and actors' own stories.

- *A recognition of different solutions for different times and places*: sometimes there is nothing wrong with "muddling through" (Lindblom 1959). Sometimes it's all there is. Yet we may still reach a positive outcome.

- *An emphasis upon values*: upon the normative foundation of public policy activity and of the values of those active within it; a rediscovery of a genuine public service ethic, particularly in a greater role for community, voluntary and *Third Sector* organisations.

- *An approach based on agency*: on the activism of practical actors, not on determinist foundational models of theory and practice. This activism is based consciously in uncertainty, within which we perceive the prospect of creative sense-making and practical action rather than the existence of a problem to be eliminated.

CONCLUSION

The managerial target setting of NPM may have represented the last stand of modernism. It is the opposite of the actor-driven approach proposed here. Global economic crisis has exposed the vacuity of modernist thinking. 'Pulling the levers' or 'tending the machine' are the macho metaphors of modernism that never quite convinced, and which now seem absurd.

Bevir and Rhodes's (1999) response to foundationalism in the study of British government was through notions of traditions, narratives, decentering and dilemmas. We locate possible innovation in the story-based narratives of the actors concerned. Yet a concern with innovation alone may be the wrong focus for making sense of public policy in a fragmented world. Looking at innovation may tend to default to a concern with what governments are doing in policy terms, especially if such policies display novelty, but this may just lead to a *cul de sac* (as in 'modernisation' or NPM). Such an approach to innovation tells us little about imaginative solutions or the voice of actors.

Further, when public innovation is led by the State itself, or by powerful institutional actors or interests, it may produce negative outcomes. Innovation is not necessarily good. The innovative financial products of the banks were the principal contributor to the continuing international economic crisis.

Alongside innovation we would advance the argument for focussing upon the prior condition, creativity. Creativity is the necessary basis for meaningful innovation. Simply to look at innovation without creativity is to focus upon a process which may remain managerial and centrally-imposed. In short, we advocate a focus upon the axiology of innovation which allows an analysis of its component parts, its creative core, and its underlying value (also see Bessant and Tidd 2007; Davila *et al.* 2005; Rae 2007). If this is not done, any new management fad, without substance, may masquerade as innovation.

An approach based upon individuals' collective sense-making, learning, diversity and values can be placed at the heart of a perspective on creativity and innovation that discards modernism and foundationalism. The NPM phase has gone. The old dualisms that preceded NPM – Right and Left versions of steady progress toward the sunlit uplands of a good society – have for the most part passed into the history of modernism. Thus we (as policy actors) are left with the challenging but empowering task of constructing theoretical and practical sense from what we have. The specific roles occupied by policy actors, including public employees, may vary. For instance, Peters (2010) notes that while bureaucracy has retreated as a paradigm for the public sector, it has not been replaced by any coherent alternative. Both scholars and practitioners therefore have to cope with uncertainty and with *ad hoc* solutions, one of the themes of the present chapter. The specific role of public employees becomes ever less clear in these changing conditions. Peters offers an empirical typology of choices available to practitioners, including the options of *bureaucrat*, *manager*, practical everyday *policy maker*, *negotiator* in a mixed economy of providers and partnerships, and *democrat*, aware of competing political pressures. These roles, we suggest, imply an underlying creativity based on learning. This in turn underlies practical innovation.

Linking Street Level and High-Level Policy

In the United Kingdom, the election defeat of the Labour Party in 2010 was the point at which the received discourse of modernisation – a concept and practice which was, at once, optimistic, progressive, managerial, centralist, and modernist – came to an end, accompanied by unprecedented economic uncertainty. The British state had already been *hollowed out* (Rhodes *et al*, 2003) from above, below and sideways. The *differentiated polity* (Bache and Flinders, 2004), characterised by, amongst other things, heterarchy, central government steering, multiple lines of accountability, a fragmented civil service, multi-level bargaining and shared sovereignty should have alerted us to the impossibility of centrally prescribed processes of macro-reform, notwithstanding the significant role of the centre in retaining control of resources compared to other actors in the system (Bache, 2003).

Parsons' discussion (2010) of the work of key thinkers including Lindblom, Wildavsky and Rittel continues to provide us with a powerful historical context for understanding this dominant paradigm of modernism - and its ultimate deficiencies. An essential concern with problems and policy has propelled academic enquiry toward a model based on rationality and predictability. Following the return to modernism of the managerialist responses of the late 1990s and the early twenty-first century – something Parsons sees as a *remix* of old solutions presented as new and fresh – he now discerns a new criticality in challenging policy conventions in a world which has transcended the old wisdoms and critiques of Left and Right

To return to the recurring issue of *how* we allow the realisation of values, innovation by sense-makers, the legitimate governing of the policy world by elected representatives, and reconciling the demands put on them by the public we need to address the governing systems, processes and structures that generate top-down, foundational responses. This is no easy task and may indeed prove impossible or fruitless. *Umbrella* policies may be one answer – allowing for locally generated responses to local context under the banner of a broader high level policy initiative. Such *high level* policies will of course require top-down monitoring but this may be predicated on local circumstance rather than centrally set targets. Such a change may require an unravelling and then reconstitution of funding and reporting mechanisms rather than say whole structural change. As for the public: we may be required to think differently about blame, risk and responsibility. After all the public are major actors who may need to engage with governance in a more proactive rather than reactive way, recognising that actors are active at different levels. If we require values to be refocused then with that comes responsibility. The governance system may be required to facilitate a rebalancing of responsibility and accountability norms between parties in any new system.

Such changes are fundamental to our understandings of government, governance, power and control and may seem extreme in terms of moving away from comfortable norms, but in an uncertain and chaotic world something has to be given. A more comfortable solution may be afforded through a recasting of public service values. It is possible that the values that are held as the heart of public service provision may be achieved equally well through radical rethinking of `how` they are achieved. For example, are the values of equity and equality only achievable through strict process-driven administration or can a more individualistic interpretation around outcomes allow for more freedom in provision? Whichever way societies develop, there are some uncomfortable discussions to be done and choices to be made and with no guarantee that innovation based on anti-foundational bottom-up principles will ultimately result in positive change. We may all need to learn to operate in more uncertain domains where facts are contestable and givens are replaced by *best bets*.

Otherwise change, innovation and, indeed, policy-making may fall by default into unwelcome hands.

In sum, we would suggest:

Learning does not necessarily generate innovation, for several reasons: international constraints (including the EU, IMF and ECB) prescribe and proscribe the available policy choices. Indeed, international inter-State collaboration may stifle innovation, not enhance it. Learning may fail to challenge past practice, thus reverting to old foundationalist solutions.

Innovation is not necessarily positive in its effects: it can open-up old problems, undo previous fixes, and, especially, generate *unintended consequences* – the great weak link within rational policy models. Policy innovations can take us backwards (and produce the opposite of what was intended), for instance in English Higher Education where the introduction of tuition fees has greatly increased rather than decreased the level of public spending, or the current management of the Euro which has served to increase fragmentation rather than integration. We argue that bottom-up creativity and innovation gives more scope for positive outcomes than top-down.

Innovation without creativity may be process rather than substance, focussing on novelty alone without engaging the policy actors involved - such as the managerial *modernisation* of local government in the UK and elsewhere in Europe from the 1990s onward.

We cannot necessarily determine where either learning or innovation will take us: in fact it lies within the very definitions of learning and innovation that we cannot predict the course of events to follow. It is the fatal conceit of modernist and rationalist views of policy making that we can somehow define the destination as we begin the journey – we cannot, because the predictive claims of modernist thinking are based on false assumptions.

Ultimately, innovation based upon individual learning and creativity, rather than the policy prescriptions of government, can unlock the potential for solutions based on actors' own expertise and lived experience.

ACKNOWLEDGEMENTS

Declared none.

CONFLICT OF INTEREST

The authors confirm that this chapter contents have no conflict of interest.

REFERENCES

Bache, I. (2003). *Europeanization: A Governance Approach*, paper presented to the EUSA 8th International Biennial Conference, Nashville, USA, March 27-29.

Bache, I. & Flinders, M. (2004). Multi-level governance and the study of British politics. In I. Bache and M. Flinders (eds.) *Multi-Level Governance*, Oxford: University Press.

Bang, H. (2010). Everyday Makers and Expert Citizens: Active Participants in the Search for a New Governance. In J. Fenwick & J. McMillan (eds.) *Public Management in the Postmodern Era.* Cheltenham: Edward Elgar, (pp 163-191).

Bessant, J. & Tidd, J. (2007). *Innovation and Entrepreneurship*, London: Wiley.

Bevir, M. & Rhodes, R.A.W. (1999). Studying British government: reconstructing the research agenda. *In British Journal of Politics and International Relations*, 1:2, June, 215-239.

Bevir, M.; Rhodes, R.A.W. & Weller, P. (2003). Traditions of Governance: Interpreting the Changing Role of the Public Sector. In *Public Administration*, 81:1, 1-17.

Davila, T. Epstein, M. & Shelton, R. (2005). *Making Innovation Work: How to Manage It, Measure It and Profit from It*, New Jersey: Wharton.

Fenwick, J. & McMillan, J. (2005). Organisational Learning and Public Sector Management: An Alternative View. In *Public Policy and Administration,* 20:3, 42-55.

Fenwick, J. & McMillan, J. (2008). *Understanding Governance in an Era of Fragmentation and Uncertainty,* paper to the ASPA-EGPA 4th Transatlantic Dialogue, Milan, Italy.

Fenwick, J. & McMillan, J. (2010). Public Policy and Management in Postmodern Times. In J. Fenwick and J. McMillan (eds.) *Public Management in the Postmodern Era.* (pp 192-211). Cheltenham: Edward Elgar.

Geyer, R. (2003). Beyond the Third way: the Science of Complexity and the Politics of Choice. In *British Journal of Politics and International Relations,* 5:2, 237-257.

Gray, P. & Hart, P. (eds.) (1998). *Public Policy Disasters in Western Europe*, London: Routledge.

Gregory, R. (2007). New public management and the ghost of Max Weber: Exorcized or still haunting? In T. Christensen & P. Laegreid (eds.) *Transcending New Public Management: The Transformation of Public Sector Reforms*. Aldershot: Ashgate (pp 221-243).

Guarneros-Meza, V., Downe, J., Entwistle, T. & Martin, S. (2014) Putting the citizen at the centre? Assembling local government policy. In *Wales Local Government Studies*, 40:1, 65-82.

Hallsworth, M.; Parker S. & Rutter J. (2011). *Policy Making in the Real World: Evidence and Analysis.* London: Institute for Government.

Jacobs, C. (2009). *Management Rewired.* New York: Penguin Group.

Lindblom, C. E. (1959). The Science of Muddling Through. In *Public Administration Review*, 9:Spring, 79-88.

Lipsky, M. (2010). *Street-Level Bureaucracy: Dilemmas of the Individual in Public Services.* Second Revised Edition. New York: Russell Sage Foundation.

Massey, A. & Pyper, R. (2005). *Public Management and Modernisation in Britain.* London: Palgrave Macmillan.

Nonaka, I. & Takeuchi, H. (1995). *The Knowledge Creating Company.* New York: Oxford.

Osborne, S. P. & Brown, L. (2013). Introduction: Innovation in public services. In Osborne, S P & Brown, L (eds). *Handbook of Innovation in Public Services.* (pp. 1-11). Cheltenham: Edward Elgar.

Parsons, D. W. (2002). From muddling through to muddling up – Evidence based policy making and the modernisation of British government. In *Public Policy and Administration,* 17:3, (pp 43-60).

Parsons, D. W. (2010). Modernism redux: Po-Mo problems and Hi-Mo public policy. In J. Fenwick and J. McMillan (eds.) *Public Management in the Postmodern Era.* (pp. 12-38). Cheltenham: Edward Elgar.

Peters, G. (2010). Still the century of bureaucracy? The roles of public servants. In J. Fenwick & J. McMillan (eds). *Public Management in the 'Postmodern Era.* (pp 145-160). Cheltenham: Edward Elgar.

Piketty, T. (2014). *Capital in the Twenty-First Century,* Cambridge: Harvard University Press.

Rae, D. (2007). *Entrepreneurship: Innovation and Action.* London: Palgrave Macmillan.

Rhodes, R. A. W., Carmichael, P., McMillan, J. & Massey, A. (2003) *Decentralizing the Civil Service: From Unitary State to differentiated polity in the United Kingdom.* Buckingham: Open University Press.

Walliser, A. (2013). New Urban Activisms in Spain: Reclaiming Public Space in the Face of Crises. In *Policy and Politics*, 43:3, 329–350.

Zahariadis, N. (2008). Ambiguity and Choice in European Public Policy. In *Journal of European Public Policy*, 15:4, 514-530.

Subject Index

J

K

L

M

www.ingramcontent.com/pod-product-compliance
Lightning Source LLC
LaVergne TN
LVHW070947210926
848482LV00002B/124